INTRODUCTION TO

SOCIAL WORK
The People's Profession

Second Edition

INTRODUCTION TO

SOCIAL WORK

The People's Profession

Second Edition

Ira Colby
University of Houston

Sophia Dziegielewski
University of Central Florida

LYCEUM
BOOKS, INC.

5758 South Blackstone Avenue
Chicago, Illinois 60637

Published by

LYCEUM BOOKS, INC.
5758 S. Blackstone Ave.
Chicago, Illinois 60637
773+643-1903 (Fax)
773+643-1902 (Phone)
lyceum@lyceumbooks.com
http://www.lyceumbooks.com

Library of Congress Cataloging-in-Publication Data

Colby, Ira C. (Ira Christopher)
    Introduction to social work : the people's profession / Ira Colby,
Sophia Dziegielewski.—2nd ed.
        p. cm.
    Includes bibliographical references and index.
    ISBN 0-925065-48-X
        1. Social service—United States. 2. Social workers—United States.
I. Dziegielewski, Sophia F. II. Title.
HV91.C597 2004
361.3'2'0973—dc22   2003025466

Preface

Your career should be personally rewarding. Feeling a sense of accomplishment when you make a difference in someone else's life provides a natural high that is both uplifting and fulfilling. Social work is a profession that provides ample opportunities to make positive differences in others' lives and to help make our communities better and safer for all people.

In the pages that follow, you will be introduced to the social work profession—its obvious strengths as well as its limitations. You will see how social work started and how the field has grown from those humble beginnings working with poor and underserved populations to the worldwide profession of today. Each chapter introduces the beginning professional to what social work involves and the roles social workers perform. Although social work is an old profession, rich in tradition, it remains dynamic, flexible, and open to change. Indeed, with the field's focus on the "person-in-situation," the need to address continuous and repeated change is ongoing. To facilitate this process, in addition to examining the field of social work in its present form, we make suggestions for future exploration and expansion. Taking into account the past, the present, and the future provides fertile ground for social workers to develop new services, allowing the best possible care for the client.

By presenting the many different facets of social work, we attempt to provide a realistic and varied presentation that will help you develop a more authentic understanding and appreciation of the profession. At a minimum you will be exposed to what social workers do and the importance of considering the environmental context that surrounds all decisions. Social workers believe strongly in allowing ethical principles and a respect for cultural diversity to guide all practice decisions. Differences in individuals are acknowledged, and concepts such as dignity, worth, and respect, along with a nonjudgmental attitude, provide the cornerstone on which all intervention is built. In part, it is our hope that the success of this book will be measured by whether it can help the beginning social work professional answer the following question: Is social work really the profession for me? If so, let the book introduce you to the field and what rewards and challenges lie ahead. If not, may you gain an understanding of and respect for the field, an awareness of the needs and struggles that people face, and the knowledge that most of these problems and issues are not self-perpetuated.

Part 1 provides abroad overview of the profession, in which we introduce professional terminology and acronyms. This is followed by a discussion of social workers' typical employment settings, responsibilities, and salaries. After that we explore, albeit briefly, the rich traditions within the field of social work, highlighting how the past clearly relates to the present, making predictions about what the future has in store.

In part 2, the reader is introduced to the practice of social work at the micro, mezzo, and macro levels. We discuss concepts such as the client system and the notion that this system almost always involves more than one person. Although it is possible to view clients as individuals, they are most often addressed in terms of context or systems. This can involve individuals, families, groups, communities, or policies that either directly or indirectly affect client system well-being.

In the chapters in part 3, several examples of the various practice settings where social workers are employed are presented, along with suggestions for expanding current activities and exploring further development of new areas.

This book is unique in that it will challenge you to synthesize information about successes and events in the field. Activities are included to give the beginning professional a sense of hands-on learning. These activities will help you develop a more in-depth understanding of the profession. There is also an emphasis on the use of the Internet, a tool that is now part of all of our lives. Case examples are used throughout to help you see the interface between what is written in the text and actual practice.

On a personal note, we would like to say that putting together this second edition, selecting and updating the topics most germane to the social work field, was not an easy task—nor should it have been. This book represents more than forty-seven years of combined direct practice and teaching experience. We are both committed to using our passion for the profession to introduce others to this exciting and challenging field. As practitioners, we believe that much can be learned from the clients we serve. In fact, many of the examples we present have been drawn from our own practical, administrative, or academic experience. Using our actual experiences in direct practice and as educators helped us to decide how best to present information in a practical and informative way, one that is sensitive to students' interests and concerns while taking into account the expectations that social work programs have been for a beginning social work course.

This book would not be complete if we did not acknowledge the individuals in our own support systems who have made this effort possible. Ira Colby thanks his wife and best friend, Deborah, who for thirty years has honestly critiqued his teaching, writing, and thinking. Sophia Dziegielewski thanks her husband, family, friends, and colleagues, who respect and support her passion for the field and tolerate her workaholic ways.

Foremost, however, we would like to thank all the social workers who graciously allowed us to use their biographical sketches. We are also grateful for the editorial assistance of Hope Steele, Amber Neff, and Jenni Fry, all of whom take such great pride in the quality of their work. We continue to appreciate and admire the work of our photographer, Mary Whalen. We would also like to thank all those who kindly took time to review our work: Steve Anderson, Julie Richards, Thomas Broffman, Milo Jennings, Sandra Fogel, Margaret Jane Allen, Vijayan Pillai, Gaston Cummings, and Denise Chaisson-Breaux. Special thanks go to those who helped us find the unique individuals we feature in the book's biographies: Linda Haggerty, Julie Richards, Anne Sommers, John McNutt, Steve Anderson, Mary Whelan, and Shirley McDonald. Thanks go last to our publisher, David Follmer, who agreed with us and supported us fully in making this the most accurate and updated depiction of the social work profession possible.

Now, with all of that said, we invite you to begin this adventure in learning about one of the oldest helping professions ever developed. May this book and its description of the social work profession ignite a fire in you, as our careers in social work have done for us.

About the Authors

Ira Colby is Dean of the Graduate School of Social Work at the University of Houston; prior to this position he developed and directed the baccalaureate social work program at Ferrum College, taught at the University of Texas at Arlington, and directed a new school of social work at the University of Central Florida. He received his MSW from Virginia Commonwealth University and his PhD from the University of Pennsylvania. He is widely published and has presented papers at state, national, and international meetings and forums. His passions are golf and family, not necessarily in that order.

Sophia F. Dziegielewski is professor in the School of Social Work at the University of Central Florida. Previously, she taught in the School of Social Work at the University of Alabama, the Departments of Family and Preventive Medicine and Psychiatry at Meharry Medical College, the School of Social Work at the University of Tennessee, and in the U.S. Army Military College at Fort Benning, GA. She received her MSW and her PhD from Florida State University. In 2003 Professor Dziegielewski was noted in *Social Worker Today* for her work in the field of social work. She has over 70 publications and lectures widely across the United States.

Table of Contents

List of Boxes and Tables

Part **I**

The Context of Social Work

Chapter 1

Social Work: The Profession

"CALL ME A SOCIAL WORKER" IS HOW HERMAN MELVILLE, SITTING at his desk in his summer home, in Pittsfield, Massachusetts, might begin a novel detailing his social work experience. As the central character, he describes his work as rewarding and exciting with no two days alike. His cases, he says, run the gamut from simple to complex; while many are successfully resolved, some do not reach a happy ending. Throughout the novel, Herman would clearly set forth the many challenges facing new and rising social workers.

Herman Melville's novel might not make it to the *New York Times* best seller list, but it would be an honest attempt to portray the life and commitment necessary for today's social worker. The profession of social work is an old one whose story begins in the mid-1880s, when professional helping and assistance, often referred to as "social work practice," was first introduced. At this time, social workers were active with all types of people regardless of age, color, or creed, and this helping activity involved individuals, families, groups, and communities, in both public and private social service settings.

These initial efforts at helping have come a long way. As we enter the twenty-first century, the United States has, by government estimates, over half a million professional social workers. More than 150,000 of these workers are members of the **National Association of Social Workers** (NASW), the world's largest professional membership organization for social workers. Its membership comprises professional social workers in all walks of life, from those who work with the elderly to those who work with infants. For the professional training of all these social workers, there are slightly more than 700 social work education programs, ranging from the baccalaureate to the doctorate level. And that's just in the United States!

Social work professionals are employed in every nation of the world. Schools of social work can be found on every continent. This worldwide activity is represented by the **International Federation of Social Workers (IFSW)**, considered the principal international social work membership association. It held membership meetings in Hong Kong in 1996, Israel in 1998, Montreal in 2000, France in 2002, Australia in 2004.

THE PROFESSIONAL SOCIAL WORKER

Considering the enduring popularity of the social work profession, you may ask how and why this interest began and why it continues to grow in scope within

Name: Carl Hinrichs

Place of residence: San Francisco, CA

College/university degrees: New Mexico State University, BSW

Present position: Social Worker, St. Anthony Foundation

Previous work/volunteer experience: As a BSW student, I conducted my practicum placements at two agencies in southern New Mexico: a transitional living shelter for women and children, and a center for HIV services. I've also worked as a residential advocate at a domestic violence shelter, and have volunteered with both Habitat for Humanity and the San Francisco AIDS Foundation.

Why did you choose social work as a career? I wanted to pursue a career that was practical, meaningful, and in high demand. I enjoy helping others explore their potential, and I am forever fascinated by the human capacity to grow and adapt to change. Few careers offer the flexibility and diversity that social work allows. At St. Anthony Foundation, I work with homeless and low-income individuals in a variety of services including crises intervention, counseling and case management, rental assistance, and payee services. Many of our clients are dually and triply diagnosed and represent a vast array of ethnic, cultural, and personal backgrounds. Their histories and stressors include struggles with poverty, domestic violence, mental illness, substance abuse, HIV/AIDS, racism, and homophobia, just to name a few. I am continually amazed by their abilities to overcome such obstacles, and I feel privileged for the opportunity to walk with them through some of their struggles and triumphs.

What would be the one thing you would change in our community if you had the power to do so? One of the biggest problems that affects the population I work with is the lack of affordable housing in San Francisco. It is not uncommon for clients to be on waiting lists for public housing for five or more years. Individuals receiving Social Security and other public benefits often cannot afford decent housing, forcing them to live in crowded, substandard conditions. In a city of great wealth, there is a huge disparity between the rich and the poor. If more money was spent on subsidized housing, our community would see a great decline in homelessness.

the global community. The answer is simple: people across the world and in our own neighborhoods face similar problems and need the assistance that social workers provide. When these problems are individual in nature they are referred to as **microsystem** problems. Responsibility for finding solutions to microsystem problems often rests squarely on the shoulders of the individual client or family.

For example, when a single, elderly person falls at home and breaks an arm, he may need to be admitted to a local hospital for treatment. Often after admission, the emergency room physician refers the case to the **hospital social worker**, who is tasked with assessing the client's situation. Suppose that during the **assessment** process, the worker learns that the client has no immediate family and lives alone. Taking into account the needs of the client, the worker must help to develop a plan with the elderly client that ensures provision of the support and services needed. In many cases, this includes arranging home health care so that the client can receive medical services in the home. It can also include ensuring that the client has access to nutritious meals by arranging contact with a **Meals on Wheels** program. To increase socialization and provide mealtime activity, referral to a local neighborhood center's senior citizen's program can be made. Further, individual or group supportive counseling can be provided directly or by referral within the community. The role of the social worker through the microperspective is essential because this role stresses the individual client's personal and social needs in the assessment and **intervention** processes.

Did You Know...The member countries of the United Nations maintain missions in cities throughout the United States. You can learn from them about particular customs and cultural nuances that may affect your work with clients. Also, many international laws that affect practice pertain to individual visitors. If you're not sure about a particular situation, contact the relevant UN mission. Finally, a UN mission can provide you with a great deal of information about its home country's welfare system.

A second system often addressed in social work is the **mezzosystem**. Through the mezzoperspective, social workers highlight the needs of the client by focusing primarily on the environmental systems that can assist the individual. The client is linked directly to support systems that enhance and maximize individual functioning. From a mezzoperspective, family and friends are paramount. This perspective also incorporates those social workers who work in administration. These social workers run many of the programs that a client will need and can either initiate or oversee service delivery. When a client's problems are found to be by-products of a larger social system, such as the family or a group, this mezzosystem is usually the primary target of intervention.

Unfortunately, however, many problems have much wider roots in broader community or social institutions. To address these problems a social worker would use what is called a **macrosystem** approach. From the macroperspective, solutions to the problems that clients face must be tied directly to larger systems.

For example, providing decent and safe places to sleep for people who are homeless may require advocacy with local and state government. The social worker may need to initiate and organize a citywide movement to open a shelter. Indeed, macrointervention for this population is not as simple to accomplish as an inexperienced observer may think. At a minimum, in order to initiate macrochange the social worker needs to understand housing policy as it affects the homeless. She must also be knowledgeable about housing options and shelter alternatives used elsewhere. In addition to this basic knowledge, the social worker must also be aware of and anticipate resistance from the community that she is trying to serve. It is important to work with the larger community to get everyone to understand why a homeless shelter is really needed and to mobilize agreement. When working within the macrosystem, however, caution should always be exercised; providing a homeless shelter is much more complicated than simply securing the site and the funds to construct a building. In implementing this type of change, the social worker must be sensitive to current community concerns and political issues that can enhance or impede service assistance and progression.

This list of some of the most serious macrosystem social problems—homelessness, HIV/AIDS, physical and emotional abuse, mental health, substance abuse, and community development—touches on only some of the areas that make up the domain of social work practice. As highlighted by Specht and Courtney (1994), the ultimate goal of the profession is to seek *perfectibility* of the community, whereby all people are given the opportunity to live their lives to the fullest and to achieve their own potential. On first sight, the concept of perfectibility of the community may be alarming, since it appears to represent a utopian goal that is unattainable. Evaluated more closely, however, the aim of perfectability is not that unusual. Helping clients to improve their life situations and their capacity to achieve their full potential has been one of the central forces driving the profession since its modest mid-nineteenth-century beginnings.

TOWARD A DEFINITION OF SOCIAL WORK

What exactly is social work? Interestingly, although it is a well-established profession, any ten people will probably give you ten different answers. One weekend morning at a donut shop in Orlando, Florida, we asked ten people to describe what social workers do. We received the following responses:

- Social workers give out food stamps and money to freeloaders.
- I dunno.
- Don't they work at the welfare office?
- They help abused kids.
- My mom had one while she was in the hospital. She really liked that young gal!
- They work in mental hospitals.
- One helped my wife and I when we adopted our baby. He helped prepare us for parenting and has stayed in touch ever since. Now, some four years later, he still stays in touch.
- It is helping poor individuals to get services.
- Social workers are liberal thinkers that support programs for the poor.
- Help private and public agencies to help individuals in need.

Activity...Select ten people either at a local mall or at any other shopping area and ask them, "what is social work?" Write down their answers. Also, take notes on their nonverbal reactions to the question.

The variety of responses illustrates two major points. First, the profession is a diverse one, and this diversity means that the roles and tasks that social workers perform are varied and often poorly defined. Second, members of the general public are often confused about the profession. Many people simply do not understand exactly what the mission of this diverse profession really is. This confusion is deepened when social work professionals themselves define what they do on the basis of their scope of practice, using job-specific descriptions such as health care social worker, community organizer, adoptions worker, or mental health counselor. Today, the profession of social work remains flexible as it reflects a society where expectations are influenced by a market-driven, business-oriented service delivery system (Franklin, 2001). The diversity and broad purview of social work practice makes it difficult to reach a simple, all-inclusive definition of exactly what social work is.

Social work is not the only profession that is difficult to define; however, professions whose tasks are easier to outline are generally received more positively by the community. For example, most people are able to describe accurately what a dentist, a nurse, or a physician does, or they can quickly describe the role of a stockbroker or a lawyer. Defining exactly what a social worker can do, and is expected to do, is a lot more complicated.

Recently, a woman at a holiday party asked her niece what her college major was. The niece proudly announced, "social work." A disquieting hush spread over the room, and the party seemed to grind to a halt. Some of her relatives looked shocked and glanced around at other family members in astonishment. When her father noted the reaction, he simply shrugged his shoulders and said, "that's nice," secretly hoping this career choice was "just a youthful phase" and that she would change her major before year's end. Today, although she has become a successful university professor of social work, her father and other relatives still refer to her as "a psychologist"! When asked why they keep making this mistake, they reply that they can usually define to others what a psychologist does, but defining social work takes a lot more time and effort. "Besides," her father still asks, "is there really that much of a difference?" This question, although at first it may seem alarming, is one that those in the profession must face daily. What complicated this distinction further is the fact that many of these professions do perform many of the same functions, making it difficult to formulate an exact role for social workers, particularly those in what is generally referred to as "direct practice" (Franklin, 2001; Dziegielewski, 2004).

Many social workers, old and new, have at least one or two stories about how their families reacted when they announced that they had selected social work as a career, and many of the stories will be similar to the one above. The confusion surrounding what social workers do, as well as their "image" of working primarily with the poor and disenfranchised in our society, complicates efforts to define what social work is. Or, indeed, what people perceive it to be. Now, keeping in mind the difficulties of making a simple definition—just what is social work?

Let us start by considering some of social work's key attributes. First, the profession involves people helping people. Second, the practice of social work

A mother with her children and stepchildren is outside of a Boys & Girls Club. The club offers after-school, weekend, and summer programs and opportunities for children from first grade through high school.

generally involves addressing the needs of **at-risk populations** in a community. Third, in our society there is a belief that people need to be helped and that the community **sanctions** this helping activity. Fourth, most of the activity performed and services provided have been **agency based**, where social workers must now provide client services but also possess business acumen capable of understanding diverse administrative and profit-driven human service systems (Franklin, 2001). Fifth, social work is a profession and therefore requires some type of professional education and training as well as standards for **ethics** and conduct. Becoming aware of and understanding these ethical standards, which are embodied in a professional code of ethics, is crucial to approaching professional practice regardless of the employment setting (Freud & Krug, 2002a). Now, let's explore these ideas more fully to develop an understanding of the breadth and depth of the profession.

Thinking about *helping* people focuses our attention on what social workers actually do. Through programs and intervention services, social workers help people—individuals, families, groups, communities, and organizations—in their day-to-day life situations (see figure 1). A hallmark of social work helping is its focus on the interaction between person and social environment. While a psychologist, for example, would consider primarily an individual's psychological state in trying to help, social workers go beyond this to include the interplay between the individual's life situation and social environment.

In the provision of social work services, *at-risk populations* comprise those people who, for any number of reasons, are vulnerable to societal threats. Children and the elderly are often viewed as at-risk populations. Other people considered at risk are those who may be victimized by a person or group through a series of life events that leaves these people susceptible to unwarranted pain and resulting problems.

Sanction refers to the community's "blessing" or recognition of the need for a service or program. Professional sanctioning of services comes in many forms; state licensing and professional certification requirements are two common types. Community funding agents, such as the United Way, can also sanction an activity by supporting it financially. When a funding entity such as the United Way supports a social service agency, it is indicating its belief that the services provided are important to the community good. This type of support is often called having "the good stamp of approval." Having the legitimacy that comes from such support is essential in gaining community approval. Formalized public (or community) sanctioning of the provision of social services can also protect the public by distinguishing between authorized and unauthorized service delivery.

Agency-based practice consists of social work services generally conducted by or delivered under the auspices of social welfare agencies. Agencies can be public, funded by federal, state, or local tax dollars; or agencies can be private, funded by donations or foundations. Most practicing social workers are agency based; however, a small percentage do engage in independent professional social work. Independent practitioners are generally educated at the master's degree level or beyond. A fairly new trend in the field is for professionally trained social workers to become private practitioners in mental health and other health-related settings. Most professionals working in this area agree, however, that the old notion of long-term therapy has been replaced with brief interventions that clearly focus the social worker–client relationship that results in a clear emphasis on outcomes that are obtained in the fastest most efficient means possible (Dziegielewski, 2004; Franklin, 2001).

Professional education involves the preparation of individuals in social work practice. It takes place in baccalaureate and graduate-level degree programs at colleges and universities. *Professional training* builds on professional education. Generally, professional training begins in the classroom setting. Later, this educational foundation is expanded and strengthened by experience through the internship process. In their internships, students visit and work in field agencies. At these agencies they can practice the skills they have been taught in school. To further advance their professional training most social workers begin working in the field under the direct supervision of a trained and experienced professional social worker.

The last area among the key components of social work practice has to do with *ethics* and expected conduct. Each profession is established and coordinated under a professional set of standards, often referred to as a "code of conduct," that is designed to govern the moral behavior of those in the field. In social work, NASW through the National Delegate Assembly is tasked with maintaining and updating this document for the profession. It has been said that the social work Code of Ethics is one of the most comprehensive ever written. It is often used as a model for comparison by related professions. A copy of social work's Code of Ethics is included in appendix A of this book, and because it is critical to understanding professional conduct, it will be discussed further in subsequent chapters (NASW, 2000). In general, when defining social work practice, ethical and moral issues should always be evaluated (Reamer, 1998). Social workers use the guidelines for professional practice given in the Code of Ethics to understand their moral and legal obligations in assisting their clients. Social workers entering the field must not only be aware of this document; they must also agree to adhere to the standards it sets forth. Any questions about moral and ethical practice should be addressed by using the guidelines it provides. Therefore, the centrality of the Code of Ethics to all practice decisions is crucial to formulating a moral vision within our field that will help to determine both peripheral and procedural practices within the professional helping activities (Freud & Krug, 2002b).

Did You Know...In August 1996, NASW delegate assembly met in Washington, D.C., and updated social work's previous Code of Ethics. This was the first major revision since 1979. This updated and revised Code of Ethics went into effect January 1, 1997. The present Code of Ethics most individuals use as a reference point was published by NASW in 2000.

SOCIAL WORK DEFINED

A definition of social work is not easy to formulate or apply. Most would agree, however, that the field of social work involves working actively to change the social, cultural, psychological, and larger societal conditions that most individuals, families, groups, and communities face. The helping process emphasizes the use of **advocacy** to create societal conditions that lead to a stronger sense of **person-in-situation** or person-in-environment; this promotes the community good, which benefits all individuals. According to this perspective, social work is directed to two ends: first, to help resolve the micro- and mezzoissues that **clients** face, and, second, to create societal macrochanges that prevent or ameliorate such problems for all individuals, families, groups, or communities.

To initiate the helping process, a social worker may begin by working with an individual or family on an issue. This microlevel work will continue until the issue is resolved; however, the task of the social worker does not end here (see figure 2). This is especially true when the social worker recognizes that the causes of the client's problems are not unique to that client. Many seemingly individual problems have deep roots in the policies and procedures of larger institutions. When

A respite house client writing a note to a social worker who is leaving for a new job. The respite house offers services and weekend-away-from-the-family programs for persons with physical and emotional disabilities. These programs give caregivers and parents a break from their caregiving duties.

these problems have the potential to affect others in the community the social work practitioner must take a macroperspective. If current policies or programs may harm others unless certain changes take place, the social worker is called to action. The worker begins macrointervention and moves to promote changes in the larger system.

For example, Ellen, a social worker employed in a family agency, learned that her client had been evicted from his apartment. After helping the client to find a new apartment, Ellen discovered that the first landlord had not followed eviction procedures as outlined in the city's ordinances. Ellen must decide what to do next. For most social workers the task of helping the client would not be considered complete even though the client now has a safe place to stay. The social worker may feel the need to continue helping this client and future potential clients who may also fall victim to this failed system enforcement. In this case, Ellen could begin working on macroissues by contacting city officials to ensure that local ordinances are enforced and to make them aware of the problems that can occur when ordinances are not enforced. Her advocacy efforts could prevent other people in circumstances similar to her client's from becoming homeless.

In sum, a social worker's immediate focus is usually on a particular client population, providing service to individuals, couples, or families. These immediate efforts take a micro- or mezzoperspective; however, the macroperspective should never be ignored. Service provision in the field of social work cannot be defined simply, because in order to be successful it often must go beyond the identified client and include the larger system. Social work is both science and art. A skilled social worker must be knowledgeable about all aspects and perspectives of client helping and flexible in their application. The best-prepared social workers are those who recognize the importance of helping as a multifaceted process and who can easily move between micro-, mezzo-, and macrosystems with and on behalf of the client populations they serve.

BECOMING A SOCIAL WORKER

People sometimes call themselves social workers even when they do not possess the professional qualification needed to be a social worker. Many times newspaper articles, television news broadcasts, and talk radio hosts refer to "a social worker" whose mishandling of a case led to very negative consequences for an individual or family. The two following case examples are typical.

In the first case, a child abuse report is made to the state child protective services agency, but the child is not removed from the home. A few days later the child dies after a severe beating by the caretaker. The media reports that the social worker responsible for the case did not follow through with a proper investigation and ignored a variety of information and signals. The community is given the impression that if the social worker had just done his job, the child would still be alive. Unfortunately, there is no simple formula for handling such situations or for avoiding them in the first place—even though we want there to be one. The glaring fact is that a child has died and no one was able to help. This is disturbing to everyone, and it is difficult to look beyond the initial fact. However, if the event is not examined more deeply, other children could be placed in harm's way. It is also important to look beyond the media's simplified portrayal of the situation: Due to cutbacks and limited funding, or for other reasons, the person responsible for the investigation may not be a social work professional at all. In fact, this person's college degree and professional training may not be in the area of social work. For example, his education and training might be in the liberal arts, and he may have no formal training in the problem assessment and intervention methods essential to social work practice. Similarly, he may not be familiar with establishing the micro-, mezzo-, and macroperspectives needed to address client situations and problems.

The second case, which involves a young mother reported for child neglect, comes from the authors' firsthand experience. The mother has been sending her children to school without their coats, and the weather is too cold for such attire. A state social service worker visits the house and agrees that the mother seems unfit to handle the needs of her children. The state worker reports that the mother's responses to questions are very basic and brief and that she does not appear to understand the seriousness of what she is allowing the children to do. The worker recommends that all the children be removed from the home before any harm comes to them.

Later the case comes to the attention of one of the authors, who is facilitating the discharge of a client from the hospital. This social worker learns that the client is asking to be released from the hospital against medical advice. When she goes to see the client to discuss the situation, he explains that he recently suffered a small stroke and was immediately taken from his home and admitted to the hospital. He fears that his wife cannot care for their children properly, and he has to go home immediately. His wife is moderately retarded, and he has always handled most of the childcare. After the social worker talks with the client and places several phone calls to help him secure childcare coverage, he agrees to stay in the hospital for the remainder of his treatment. He agrees to stay because the social worker was able to make arrangements with some members of his church who will watch the children until his return home. Later that day, the client becomes very upset when a family friend tells him that his children are about to be removed from home. After receiving permission from the client to release information about the situation, the social worker contacts the state worker and tells him about the plan to care for the children. The removal decision is reevaluated, and because support is in place the children are not removed from home or the care of their mother.

In discussing the case, the social service worker obviously is frustrated. His caseload did not give him time to explore disposition options. He was also concerned that a child had died several weeks before in a case very similar to this one. Because of the attention paid to that case, he felt it was best not to take a chance on this one. He also did not realize that the mother was mentally retarded; he thought she might be on drugs or merely resistant to intervention. In trying to understand why he made such a limited assessment, the social service worker reports that he just did not realize the significance of the client's behavior. The worker reports that he has limited on-the-job training and that he often uses opportunities for inservice provision to catch up on his paperwork. Moreover, although this state requires that all social service workers have at least a four-year professional degree, his degree is in physical education.

Cases like these are all too common. For whatever reason—be it a desire to cut costs or a lack of recognition for professional intervention—there is a widespread but false impression that anyone can be a social worker and that anyone can handle the tasks and responsibilities expected of a social worker. Some people even believe they can be their own social workers.

For example, a plumber working for one of the authors asked her what she did for a living. When he heard she was a social worker, he smiled and said, "Oh, never needed one of them before; always do my own social work." When asked what he meant, he said, "Don't need somebody else to solve my problems. I can solve them for my family and myself. I had a lot of training on how to deal with people in school, and that helped." Such comments are very disturbing because they show that many people just don't know what social workers do. Furthermore, it was very tempting for the social worker to reply with "Yes, I know—I used to do my own plumbing too, but your expertise is why you are here now." When people assume that social work is simply everyday problem solving, they conclude that anyone can do it and that becoming a social worker is open to all. The irony in this statement is as pronounced as believing that everyone can do their own plumbing. Yet, because social work is such a diverse field and not as specific as plumbing, generalizations like this can be all too common.

Confusion also exists among helping and counseling professionals about who can be a qualified social worker. For example, at a public hearing held by the Florida Board of Mental Health Counselors, Marriage and Family Therapists, and Clinical Social Workers, a board member opposed the licensing of BSW and MSW social workers who do not do clinical social work. A marriage and family therapist added, "Anyone can do social work. There is such a thing as social work with a small 's' and 'w'."

On the surface this statement seems to make sense, and it warrants serious discussion. Certainly, all helping individuals must have "good" hearts and be compassionate as well as willing to help others. But can these qualities alone make someone a *professional* social worker?

Let's make a comparison. Suppose you have a sore throat, feel somewhat congested, and have hot and cold sweats. Your roommate says, "You may be coming down with the flu. Why don't you take brand X over-the-counter cold pills, use some brand Y throat lozenges, and stay home and rest." This could be very good, helpful advice, but does this mean your roommate is a medical doctor, albeit with a small "m" and "d"? Of course not—it seems crazy to even suggest that. Everyone knows that to be a medical doctor you need a formal education and supervised experience in a medical setting. You can't hang out a shingle that says "MD" just because you think you can diagnose some physical ailments.

So what are the requirements for becoming a social worker? Certainly there are personal attributes that a social worker must have. First, a social worker must like working with people. A social worker is involved with people from all walks of life. These people, who come from widely varying backgrounds, can have ideas and expectations very different from the social worker's own. Being aware of and sensitive to the beliefs of others is not always a simple task to accept and achieve. In dealing with different people a social worker must really want to understand the troubles that others face. So first of all, a good social worker must genuinely like working with diverse individuals.

Second, a social worker must want to help people. A professional social worker encounters all sorts of client problems, ranging from abuse and neglect to homelessness, from mental health issues to community-based substance abuse problems. A good social worker wants to help his clients in their efforts to figure out what is going on and how best to resolve their problems.

Third, a social worker wants the community to be a better place for all people. Through her professional activities, a social worker helps a specific client while at the same time she tries to better the community for all people. For example, ideally social workers want to end poverty and its debilitating effects on people and communities. Social workers envision communities where all people have access to decent housing and health care. They also strive to end unfair treatment of individuals, the "isms" that face millions of people today—racism, sexism, and ageism. The personal traits that foster the desire to work with and to help individuals, families, and communities are critical ingredients in creating a social worker. To finish the mix, however, these personal traits must be complemented by professional edu-

Name: Nicole Todd

Place of residence: Brooklyn, New York

College/university degrees: Western Michigan University, BSW, University of Chicago, School of Social Service Administration, AM

Present position: I currently work as a Counselor/Social Worker at the Hetrick-Martin Institute, home of the Harvey Milk High School. The Hetrick-Martin Institute is a non-profit organization that provides comprehensive youths services for gay, lesbian, bisexual, transgender, and questioning youth between the ages of twelve to twenty one.

Previous work/volunteer experience: Some of my other experiences include working in mental health, working with the Boys and Girls Clubs, being a community organizer, volunteering as a big sister, working as a human rights activist, and being a childcare worker.

Why did you choose social work as a career? I have always been drawn to working with people, particularly youth. I chose social work because it is one of the few disciplines that focuses on empowering groups and individuals within the context of their environment.

What is your favorite social work story? One of the benefits to working in this field is the opportunity to work in a variety of settings with various individuals. While living in Chicago, I had the opportunity to work at a Boys and Girls Club in the Robert Taylor Homes. This area is notorious for gangs, drugs, and violence. Many of the youth with whom I worked were frequently stereotyped as gang members. Working with these kids and their families, I had the chance to see first-hand the inaccuracy of this stereotype. Most of the kids I encountered were just like the young people I worked with in other settings: they have families who loved and cared for them, they strive to be successful, they desire love and affection, and they like to laugh and have fun. People need to realize that most individuals living in poor areas are not violent; rather, they are hard working, loving family members attempting to survive in a society that often criminalizes poverty.

What would be the one thing you would change in our community if you had the power to do so? I would like to change the way our community approaches social problems. I think it is crucial that all people within our society take responsibility and recognize that everyone's lives are affected when social injustices exist. I believe that if all individuals approached social problems with the perspective that it is the community's responsibility to address the problem, regardless of whether they feel personally impacted, our society would be more effective in creating social change.

cation and training. In the United States, professional social work education takes place in baccalaureate or graduate-level degree programs at specific colleges and universities.

Did You Know...The Council on Social Work Education (CSWE) is the only national standard-setting and accrediting body for social work education. It was organized in 1952 through the merger of two associations that coordinated baccalaureate and graduate programs, respectively.

For a U.S. social work program to provide professional education it must meet the **accreditation** standards of the **Council on Social Work Education (CSWE)**. CSWE is the national board that sets and oversees educational standards for social work programs across the United States. Other countries have their own accrediting bodies for social work education. For example, the Canadian Association for Social Work Education is responsible for accrediting programs in Canada, the Joint University Council for Social and Public Administration oversees social work educational programs in the United Kingdom, Finnish programs of social work are associated with the Scandinavian Committee of Schools of Social Work, Brazilian schools of social work are members of the National Association of Schools of Social Work, and Indian social work educational programs are members of the Association of Schools of Social Work. Overall, international accreditation associations can be found in nineteen different nations, in addition to five regional associations (Kendall, 1984). Although there are numerous accrediting associations throughout the world, the International Association of Schools of Social Work, in 2000, implemented a joint initiative with the International Federation of Social Workers to create global standards (http://www.iassw.soton.ac.uk/en/GlobalQualifyingStandards/Globalstandardsaugust2002.pdf). The standards are an attempt to develop consistency among social work educational programs around the world.

Regardless of where a professional social work program is located, it must withstand the rigorous scrutiny of an accreditation process, which entails the validation of explicit standards of practice (Barker, 2003). Curriculum format and delivery, which is the heart of the educational experience, must be coherent, built on a series of objectives, and offer specific educational content, including a supervised field placement or internship experience; through an internship the social work professional learns to apply in the field environment what has been taught in the classroom. Standards require that the faculty members who teach students possess certain types of degrees and in addition have professional work experience that can facilitate the education process. Accreditation standards also specify that a variety of institutional (e.g., college or university) resources be available. Finally, an accredited program must identify specific behavioral outcomes that all graduates are expected to demonstrate at the end of their course of study.

Activity...Ask to review your social work program's latest "self-study" for accreditation. Compare the self-study to the CSWE's Commission on Accreditation Handbook *and the* CSWE Educational Policy Accreditation Standards *found in appendix C. In order to be accredited, your program must conform to these standards. Being part of an accredited program is important for your future development.*

Attending and graduating from an accredited social work program is crucial for the future social work professional. Remember that only a graduate of an accredited social work program is recognized as a professional social worker. Because CSWE accreditation standards apply nationally, the public recognizes that a graduate of a BSW program in California has completed the same minimum educational requirements as a graduate of a BSW program in New Hampshire or Georgia. Uniformity of content through the country means that social workers can be hired in any state and meet specific educational requirements for employment and subsequent licensing in the field. This is particularly important for employers and supervisors of social work professionals because they can then assume that a particular educational background implies familiarity with certain content. Many employers report that this standardization of course content across social work programs makes social workers predictable employees in regard to what they have and have not been trained to do. In fact, an article in Consumer Reports states that one reason why social workers seemed to fare better than other helping and counseling professions in managed care was that they were more consistent in training and approach (Mental Health, 1995).

Did You Know…The initials BSW stand for Baccalaureate Social Worker and MSW for Master Social Worker. BSSW and MSSW also signify degrees in social work, Bachelor of Science in Social Work and Master of Science in Social Work. The most advanced degrees in social work are the DSW and the PhD. In most circles the MSW or the MSSW is considered the highest level needed to practice in the field.

BSW education prepares individuals for entry- or beginning-level social work practice. Baccalaureate studies occur in the junior and senior years of study. **MSW** education prepares individuals for advance practice, also called specialization or concentration practice. (We will explore advanced practice in more detail in chapters 5 and 6.) An MSW program requires two years of full-time study; a person with a BSW degree may be eligible for advanced standing in a graduate program, however, thus bypassing the first year of graduate work through mastery of beginning or foundation knowledge and skills.

A number of schools of social work offer academic programs leading to a doctoral degree, either a **PhD** or a **DSW**; such programs are not accredited by the CSWE, however. As a result, doctoral education varies greatly from school to school, with a program's focus set by its faculty's values and beliefs. Individuals pursuing doctoral degrees in social work will for the most part be employed in academic settings, though some will work in agency settings, primarily in administrative, supervisory, or research-related positions.

Social work education is a very large enterprise in the United States. According to CSWE statistics, there are close to 600 accredited baccalaureate and graduate programs, and programs are found in all fifty states and an additional 51 programs in candidacy status—that is, working toward initial accreditation (Lennon, 2002). In 2000, more than 22,000 junior and senior social work students were

working toward BSWs, 33,700 toward MSWs, and approximately 2,000 toward doc-
torates. More than 6,500 full-time faculty members were involved in social work
education (Lennon 2002).

MEMBERSHIP ASSOCIATIONS FOR SOCIAL WORKERS

All professionals have the opportunity to belong to membership organizations
or associations that represent their interests. An association provides professional
self-identity and an opportunity to meet colleagues in order to discuss ideas and
share innovations in practice. Some of the most familiar professional associations
are the American Medical Association (physicians), the American Bar Association
(lawyers), and the National Educational Association (teachers).

*Activity...Gather information about your local unit of NASW. Ask one of your instruc-
tors or a social worker in the community when your local unit of NASW will be meeting.
Try to attend the next meeting. Also, find out when the state board of directors of NASW
next meets. These meetings occur several times each year and are held somewhere in the
state. Try to attend one of these meetings to see the process firsthand.*

The *National Association of Social Workers* is the largest membership organization for social workers. In 2003, NASW membership totaled more than
150,000 persons. One important point to recognize is that membership is voluntary. Indeed, the federal government's Department of Labor estimates that there
are about 468,000 professional social work positions in the United States, which
means that many fewer than one-third of all social work professionals are members of NASW.

NASW was first organized in 1955, when five special-interest organizations
joined together. These five interest groups were the American Association of Group
Workers, the American Association of Medical Social Workers, the American Association of Psychiatric Social Workers, the American Association of Social Workers,
and the National Association of School Social Workers. In addition, two study
groups also joined: the Association for the Study of Community Organization and
the Social Work Research Group. The ideas of all these groups were merged: to
unify the profession (Alexander, 1995). Today, the national offices of NASW are
located in Washington, D.C., only a few blocks from the U.S. Capitol.

NASW regards itself as a bottom-up members' organization. What this means
is that governance and direction are established from below and responsibility lies
with the units and chapters in each state. Each state has its own chapter of NASW,
and each chapter is further subdivided into units. Each local unit covers a geographical area small enough to allow members to attend meetings and programs
together.

After joining NASW, each member is assigned to a state chapter and then to a
local unit that reflects where the person lives. Most local units conduct quarterly

or monthly meetings. These gatherings run the gamut of formality, from the very formal meeting with an invited speaker to the informal after-work get-together. Unit meetings offer social workers from the same geographical area an opportunity to meet on a regular basis and strengthen their professional networks.

The state chapter coordinates activities between the local units and offers ongoing educational opportunities, known as **continuing education**, around the state. It also brings to the attention of its membership issues in the state legislature that could affect the profession or clients being served. Most state chapters provide their members with a monthly newsletter as well as professional and social activities such as an annual or biannual convention. The state chapter is staffed by a paid employee, generally a social worker, and is governed by a board of directors elected by the membership of the state and serving for a prescribed term.

Did You Know… NASW News, *the monthly newspaper of NASW, is the primary source of news about opportunities for social workers across the United States. Each issue includes a classified section that lists, by state, job vacancies.*

The national office of NASW comprises divisions ranging from membership services to political advocacy to publications. The national office is responsible for carrying out the policy of the national board of directors, which is made up of elected social work members from across the country. The national office also publishes a monthly newspaper that provides an exhaustive overview of social work around the country. Other member benefits include opportunities to purchase life and malpractice insurance and reduced registration fees to national meetings (see box 1).

Box 1: Benefits of NASW Membership
✓ Subscription to Journal of Social Work
✓ Subscription to NASW News
✓ State chapter and local unit memberships
✓ Credit and loan programs
✓ Hospital indemnity option
✓ Toll-free telephone to the NASW Information Center
✓ Representation on Capitol Hill in Washington, D.C., and in state legislatures
✓ Discounts for NASW-sponsored continuing education programs
✓ Subscription discounts for specialty journals
✓ Car rental discounts
✓ Credit card option
✓ Term life insurance options
✓ Malpractice insurance
✓ Job link

Through local units, state chapters, and the national office of NASW, individual social workers have numerous opportunities to affect the profession. By holding leadership positions, serving on various committees, and attending local, state, and national meetings, individual social workers mold the profession and give direction to future activities.

Social workers belong to such groups in order to support specific interests. According to Tourse (1995), special interest associations provide professional identity and professional cohesiveness, monitor specialized practice, broaden the sphere of professional influence, and encourage development of specialized theory and practice. In addition to NASW, there are about 54 other national membership or professional social work associations in the United States. These various groups are based on a variety of attributes ranging from race and ethnicity to practice interests (see box 2 for examples of professional associations). In 2002, the National

---

Box 2: Other Social Work Membership Organizations

American Association of Industrial Social Workers: Social workers employed in employee assistance programs

Association for Community Organization and Administration: Community organizers and agency administrators and individuals interested in macroissues

North American Association of Christians in Social Work: Interdenominational association to assist members to develop Christian faith in social work practice

National Association of Black Social Workers: Association to influence practice and policy that impact all black ethnic groups

National Association of Oncology Social Workers: Individuals working with cancer patients

National Association of Puerto Rican/Hispanic Social Workers: Association concerned with advocacy and human services issues that impact the Latino community

National Federation of Societies of Clinical Social Work: State and regional societies that focus on issues relating to clinical social work practice

National Indian Social Workers Association: Association that works to develop understanding of native Americans and Alaska natives in tribal and nontribal organizations

Rural Social Work Caucus: Individuals working in and concerned about rural and small community human services

Society for Social Work Administrators in Health Care: Individuals seeking to promote effective social work health care administration

---

Association of Social Workers convened a meeting, known as the "Social Work Summit II," of the presidents and chairs of these various associations. The group agreed to hold periodic meetings in an attempt to coordinate on various common matters and to create formal lines of communication bewteen and among the various associations.

Most special interest groups sponsor an annual meeting, and some publish a journal or newsletter. These organizations' membership rolls are much smaller than NASW's, they often do not have state or local unit groups, and they generally do not have paid staff to run the organization.

SUMMARY

Social work is a diverse profession. It is not easily defined and, as a result, is often misunderstood by the general public and the greater community. One thing remains prominent: social work is a profession of people helping people. Despite possible confusion about the daily activities of social workers, there is growing recognition that social work plays an important role in today's society. Children, seniors, families, communities, the rich, the poor, and the middle class are all represented among the many clients who benefit directly from social work. Social work clients are found in all quarters of the country. Social work is a global profession, similar to other professions, with many of its efforts designed to assist and stimulate development rich in methods that incorporate strategy provided at the grass roots level (Engardio, 2002).

Today thousands of people studying in colleges and universities are striving to become professional social workers. The role of these new social work professionals is an essential one because it is these individuals who will steer the profession and support the mission of micro-, mezzo-, and macrointervention well into the twenty-first century.

Questions to Think About

1. What do you say to a friend who, after learning that you want to be a social worker, states, "You won't make any money doing that"?

2. What do you think a meeting of professional social workers, such as a local NASW unit meeting, would be like?

3. Do you know any professional social workers? What personal qualities do they have that you think might be useful for a social worker?

4. Do you think there should be one professional membership association, such as NASW, or a number of membership organizations as discussed in this chapter?

5. Why do you think there is a general misunderstanding of social work?

6. What are some ways social workers could help to educate family and friends about what it is they do?

References

Alexander, C. (1995). Distinctive dates in social welfare history. In R. Edwards et al. (Eds.), *Encyclopedia of social work* (19th ed., pp. 2631–2647). Washington, DC: NASW Press.

Barker, R. (2003). *The social work dictionary* (4th ed.). Washington, DC: NASW Press.

Dziegielewski, S.F. (2004). *The changing face of health care practice: Professional practice in the era of managed behavioral health care.* New York: Springer.

Engardio, P. (2002, October 14). Global poverty. *Business Week*, 3803, 108–116.

Franklin, C. (2001). Coming to terms with the business of direct practice social work. *Research on Social Work Practice.* 11, 2, 235–244.

Freud, S., & Krug, S. (2002a). Beyond the code of ethics, part 1: Complexities of ethical decision making in social work practice. *Families in Society*, Sept–Dec, 474–482.

Freud, S., & Krug, S. (2002b). Beyond the code of ethics, part 2: Dual relationships revisited. *Families in Society*, Sept–Dec, 483–493.

Kendall, K. (1984). *World guide to social work education.* New York: CSWE.

Lennon, T. M. (2001). Council on Social Work Education. Statistics on social work education in the U.S., 1999. Alexandria, VA: Council on Social Work Education.

Mental health: Does therapy work? (1995, November). *Consumer Reports*, pp. 734–739.

National Association of Social Workers (NASW). (2000). *Code of ethics for the national association of social workers.* Washington, DC: NASW Press.

Reamer, F. G. (1998). *Ethical standards in social work.* Washington, DC: NASW Press.

Specht, H., & Courtney, M. (1994). *Unfaithful angels.* New York: Free Press.

Tourse, R. W. C. (1995). Special-interest professional associations. In R. Edwards et al. (Eds.), *Encyclopedia of social work* (19th ed., pp. 2314–2319). Washington, DC: NASW Press.

Chapter 2

Social Welfare: A System's Response to Personal Issues and Public Problems

WHEN YOU HEAR THE WORDS "SOCIAL WELFARE" WHAT COMES TO mind? Many people think of food stamps, child abuse, and low-income housing. Before we begin to explain social welfare, test your knowledge of the subject by taking the following quiz. We expect that as a beginning professional interested in this field, some of your answers will be correct and others will be wrong; just give it your best guess.

Welfare Quiz

1. What is the most costly welfare program?
a) Food stamps   b) Medicaid
c) Low-income housing   d) Social security

2. Who makes up the majority (more than 50 percent) of people receiving public assistance?
a) Mothers and their children   b) Unemployed adults
c) Senior citizens   d) Single females

3. In the United States there are more black individuals than white individuals living in poverty?
a) True   b) False

4. Many individuals who receive welfare benefits have children just to get more money from the government.
a) True   b) False

5. When we talk about the unemployment rate we are referring to those people who are not working at the present time.
a) True   b) False

Name: Barbara W. White

Place of residence: Austin, Texas

College/university degrees: Florida A &M, BS, Florida State University, BS, MSW, PhD

Present position: Centennial Professorship in Leadership and Dean, School of Social Work, University of Texas at Austin

Previous work/volunteer experience: Associate Dean at the School of Social Work at The Florida State University, President of the National Association of Social Workers (NASW), a member of the Board of Directors of the International Association of Schools of Social Work, President of the Council on Social Work Education, (CSWE) Fulbright scholar on Women's Issues in India, member African American Women's Hall of Fame, 1999 recipient of the International Rhoda G. Sarnat Award for significant international or national contributions to advance the public image of professional social work

What do you do in your spare time? Read, travel, and attend theater.

Why did you choose social work as a career? I chose social work as a way to help fight social injustice and man's inhumanity to man.

What is your favorite social work story? During the Christmas holiday season, members of my faculty and staff visit a local nursing home with our own Santa. We bring musicals and become carolers and gift bearers. The responses from the residents provide a reminder of how much there is to do in our society to help improve life's quality for so many of our citizens.

What would be the one thing you would change in our community if you had the power to do so? I would address the issues that face one of our most vulnerable populations, our youth. I would eliminate homelessness and hopelessness among our youth.

6. The amount given to the poor in a "welfare" check is the same in all states.
a) True   b) True, but prorated for family size   c) False

7. More than half the people who receive welfare could be working but choose not to.
a) True   b) False

8. Which of the following groups are not considered to be welfare recipients by the U.S. government (circle all that apply)?
a) Schoolchildren   b) Seniors receiving social security
c) Armed forces veterans   d) Food stamp recipients
e) College students receiving Pell grants   f) Medicare recipients

9. **Aid to Families with Dependent Children** is the name of the *only* federal program that provides cash assistance to poor families.

a) True   b) False

10. In your own words define "social welfare."

Now turn to the back of this chapter to find the correct answers and see how you did. You'll find no answer to question 10. After reading this chapter come back and answer question 10 again. Be sure to compare your two responses to see if your first response is different from your second.

Are you surprised by some of the answers? Think about which questions you got wrong and what you learned from this brief quiz. Clearly, social welfare is a very complicated system that is often misunderstood.

In this chapter we discuss the dimensions of social welfare—in particular, what is meant by the term. We also direct attention to the role of the social work profession as well as that of each individual social worker within our current social welfare system.

TOWARD A DEFINITION OF SOCIAL WELFARE

To begin our discussion of the current social welfare system, we would like you to try this exercise. To prepare, take a piece of paper and a pencil and get ready to write down some of your ideas. First, think of your hometown or where you were raised. Second, imagine that you have the ability to make it into what you consider the "ideal" place to live. What kinds of services are needed to improve this neighborhood or community, bringing it to the perfectability that Specht and Courtney (1994) suggest is the profession's goal?

Social Services for Respect and Dignity

Use the following list of questions to suggest possible ideas and guide your thinking on this topic.

Housing and Employment

Would everyone have safe and affordable housing?

Would everyone be able to find employment?

Would employment pay well and include social and health benefits

Education and Services

Would the education of the young be given top priority?

Would the community help all schools to get the services and supplies they need (e.g., fully equipped classrooms and state-of-the-art technology)—public and private alike?

Would a safe learning environment be provided?

Community Safety and Security

Would senior citizens be protected from abuse and neglect?

Would senior citizens have access to the services they need to complete their activities of daily living?

Would children be protected from exploitation and abuse?

Would domestic violence be tolerated, and what options would be available to those who are victimized?

Would discrimination based on race, color, age, sexual orientation, and the like be tolerated?

Would food services be provided to those who cannot afford to buy their own?

Your own list probably includes many more considerations that you feel are essential to address. Nevertheless, we believe that if you compared your list with someone else's you'd be surprised at how similar the two lists are. Most people agree that in an ideal place, all people are treated with respect and dignity (see figure 1). Further, most people agree that for a community to be responsive, it needs to be a place where members are valued for who they are and what they can offer to their community.

Seems too simple, doesn't it? And, it's true, some issues are much more difficult to address. Most people cannot agree on what services are needed in a community, who deserves these services, and how many services need to be provided. To complicate things further, communities are not static entities. A community needs to shift and change in response to the social, political, and economic conditions that exist at the time. Changing times can create and worsen social problems. For example, in September 2003, the U.S. Bureau of the Census reported that 34.6 million people were in poverty (http://www.census.gov/Press-Release/www/2003/cb03-153.html), and of those living in poverty many are women, children, and the elderly. These people are also at particular risk of abuse and neglect, both physical and emotional.

Social and Economic Justice

The United States is among the wealthiest countries in the world. It has abundant natural resources and technology, yet many American citizens battle daily with poverty as well as emotional and psychological difficulties that can impede their ability to function at home and in their communities. In 2000, about one in six or 11.6 million children under age 18 lived in poverty (http://www.childrens defense.org/fs_chpov.php). In 2001, former Secretary of Health and Human Services Donna Shalala challenged our nation to assume a position that ensures the health and well-being of the nation's children (Shalala, 2001). Diverse people, including those of color and alternative sexual orientation, continue to suffer from

Figure 1: Students in a self-contained public school classroom for persons with emotional disabilities. Biweekly sessions with the social worker help the students to discuss their feelings.

discrimination and prejudice. Every day millions of children are ill fed, live in unsafe environments, and have no access to high-quality health care services. Furthermore, it comes as no surprise that in 2000, the former Surgeon General David Satcher reported that one of the greatest challenges for the United States health care system is to respond to both the physical and the mental health of our children (Satcher, 2000). These are only some of the overwhelming problems that American communities face. Determining who should get service priority is a daunting task. Different people have different impressions about what is needed. With each member of a community asked for input, the list of suggestions will grow.

For social workers, where the primary mission is to help individuals in need, it is clear that challenging **social injustice** is critical. The role of the social worker is crucial in challenging systems that do not treat all individuals fairly. If social justice equates to "fairness" in terms of human relationships within the society, then conditions such as unemployment, poverty, starvation, and inadequate health care and education are only a few of the problems that will need to be addressed. Furthermore, what remains central is that often the conditions that exist are beyond the control of the individual. From a social work perspective, the existing conditions should not be perceived as the fault of the individual. Often these circumstances develop because of coercion by others due to outside political and economic influences and to the social order of systems.

Addressing social justice and encouraging social change is so important to the field of social work that the preamble to the National Association of Social Workers Code of Ethics (1997) clearly states that "Social workers are sensitive to cultural and ethnic diversity and strive to end discrimination, oppression, poverty, and other forms of social injustice" (p. 1). Therefore, our purpose in this chapter is not merely to develop a laundry list of society's ills and social injustices; rather it is to identify how individuals within a community can begin to address these issues.

When a society strives for community betterment by developing methods and programs to promote social justice and address social needs, this effort is often referred to as **social welfare**. Our perceptions of social welfare vary. The term can bring to mind a myriad of pictures, ranging from the homeless person walking to the shelter to the tornado victim receiving assistance from the Red Cross. From the varied perceptions of social welfare, two common but opposed threads emerge.

On one hand, many people believe social welfare recipients are those who cannot make it on their own and need society's help and intervention. Some people also believe that most recipients are responsible for the misfortunes they are experiencing and, in some cases, have created their own problems. This misperception contributes to the view that welfare recipients are "not worthy" or lack the motivation to help themselves. It is important to note, however, that not everyone feels this way. Many people, on the other hand, believe that some of the problems facing welfare recipients are not of their own making. They think that these problems should be regarded as similar to unexpected crises or traumas. In times of crisis, almost everyone expects victims to seek government assistance; such help is considered a right of citizenship.

The varying opinions that people can hold about government assistance and the wide range of social welfare services that can be provided make an accurate definition of social welfare essential. If the concept is defined too narrowly, people may focus on a few programs that account for only a small portion of welfare spending and decide that welfare policy is too specialized. If social welfare is defined too broadly, people may decide that entitlements are being given too freely and that society's limited resources cannot sustain this policy.

SOCIAL WELFARE DEFINED

Let's approach the concept of social welfare by examining several existing definitions. Later we will formulate a definition of our own (see figure 2).

Social Welfare Is . . .

◆ The assignment of claims from one set of people who are said to produce or earn the national product to another set of people who may merit compassion and charity but not economic rewards for productive service (Titmus, 1965).

- ◆ "Collective interventions to meet certain needs of the individual and/or to serve the wider interests of society"(Titmus, 1959, p. 42).
- ◆ A system of social services and institutions, designed to aid individuals and groups to attain satisfying standards of life and health, and personal social relationships which permit them to develop their full capacities and promote their well-being in harmony with the needs of their families and community (Friedlander, 1955, p. 140).
- ◆ A subset of social policy, which may be defined as the formal and consistent ordering of affairs (Karger & Stoesz, 1994, p. 4).
- ◆ A nation's system of programs, benefits, and services that help people meet those social, economic, educational, and health needs that are fundamental to the maintenance of society (Barker, 2003, p. 221).
- ◆ An encompassing and imprecise term but most often it is defined in terms of "organizational activities," "interventions," or some other element that suggests policy and programs to respond to recognized social problems or to improve the well-being of those at risk (Reid, 1995, p. 2206).
- ◆ A concept that encompasses people's health, economic condition, happiness, and quality of life (Segal & Brzuzy, 1998, p. 8).
- ◆ Society's organized way to provide for the persistent needs of all people-for health, education, socioeconomic support, personal rights, and political freedom (Bloom, 1990, p. 6).

Figure 2: Students with emotional disabilities posing in front of a mural they created during their study of insects.

Close examination of these definitions shows that, while the phrasing differs, the content and focus are similar. Let's identify the common themes in these various statements as we develop a comprehensive definition of social welfare. First, social welfare includes a variety of programs and services that yield some type of benefit to their consumers. People participating in any type of welfare-based program benefit because they receive some form of assistance. Many times the assistance, or social provision, is given in cash. At other times social provision is given **in-kind**, for example, as clothes or counseling that the consumer did not have beforehand.

Second, social welfare, as a system of programs and services, is designed to meet the needs of people. The needs to be addressed can be all-encompassing, including economic and social well-being, health, education, and overall quality of life.

Third, the end result of social welfare is to improve the well-being of individuals, groups, and communities. Helping those systems in time of need will later benefit society at large.

RESIDUAL AND INSTITUTIONAL SOCIAL WELFARE

In their classic work *Industrial Society and Social Welfare*, Harold Wilensky and Charles Lebeaux (1965) attempt to answer a basic question: Is social welfare a matter of giving assistance only in emergencies, or is it a frontline service that society must provide? As part of their discussion, Wilensky and Lebeaux developed two important concepts that continue to frame and influence our understanding and discussions of social welfare: **residual social welfare** and **institutional social welfare** (see box 1 for examples). Wilensky and Lebeaux (1958) defined the terms as follows:

Residual: Social welfare institutions come into play only when the normal structures of supply, the family and the market, break down.

Institutional: Welfare services are normal, frontline functions of modern industrial society.

Box 1: Examples of Residual and Institutional Program

Residual	**Institutional**
Food stamps	Social security
Medicaid	Medicare
Head Start	Libraries
Temporary Assistance for Needy Families (TANF)	Health departments
Homeless shelters	Veteran's benefits

Residual Social Welfare

The residual conception of social welfare rests on the "individualistic" notion that people should take care of themselves and rely on government support only in times of crisis or emergency. People are not considered eligible for help until all of their own private resources, which may include assistance from the church, family wealth and inheritance, friends, employers, and so on—have been exhausted. Only then do public welfare efforts at assistance come into play. Therefore, in order to access residual social welfare services, people must first prove their inability to provide for themselves and their families. As a result the help received often carries the stigma of failure.

Qualifying for this type of service is often referred to as **selective eligibility**. When eligibility is selective, social services are delivered only to people who meet certain defined criteria. When a person needs cash assistance as a service, the eligibility determination procedure is commonly called **means testing**. To access means-tested programs, people must demonstrate that they do not have the financial ability to meet their specific needs. When a residual type of program provides cash assistance, clients must recertify their eligibility every few months. The recertification process is designed primarily to ensure that clients are still unable to meet their needs through private or personal sources.

People who receive residual services are generally viewed as being different from people who receive other kinds of services. They are often regarded as failures because they do not show the rugged individualism that is a cornerstone ideal of our society. Many times beneficiaries of residual programs are labeled as lazy, lacking in morals, and dishonest. They are often accused of making bad decisions and of needing constant monitoring because of their untrustworthiness. In short, people in residual programs carry a **stigma**.

Imagine for a moment that you are standing in the checkout line of your local grocery store. The person in front of you is paying for some items with food stamps. Noting this, you feel compelled to look more closely at what is being purchased. In the grocery cart are potato chips, soda, some candy, and beer, as well as other food items. You have similar items in your own cart. On a piece of paper, write down your first thoughts about this. Be honest, and allow yourself to express any thoughts you might have. One response to this kind of situation is shown in box 2.

Box 2: Food Stamps and the Video Game

Dallas Morning News. Letters to the Editor. January 1, 1983.

Last week I was passing through the checking line at a supermarket. In front of me was a young woman with two children about 5 and 6. She paid for her groceries with food stamps. On their way out they stopped by the store's video game machines. All three played the game, once each. In other words, the woman squandered 75 cents while letting taxpayers pay for the groceries. That money would have bought a dozen eggs for that "poor" family. I wonder if their color TV and stereo are working? I never have objected to my tax dollars being spent to help the truly poor, but I protest vehemently the idea of helping them pay for their entertainment or luxuries.

(Name Withheld)

Dallas, Texas

Name: Dianne Harrison

Place of residence: Tallahassee, Florida

College/university degrees: University of Alabama, BA, MSW, Washington University, PhD

Present position: Associate Vice President for Academic Affairs, School of Social Work, Florida State University

Previous work/volunteer experience: Former Dean of the School of Social Work, Florida State University; social worker in mental health settings; social work researcher and academician; certified sex educator; designed HIV prevention interventions; member of numerous community agency boards (telephone crisis hotline, women's prison, teen pregnancy program, local high school)

What do you do in your spare time? Aside from watching both of my kids play soccer, I read, watch movies, play tennis, and cook.

Why did you choose social work as a career? I did not really know much about social work but I knew I wanted to work with people. I went into a graduate program in social work basically because they offered me a scholarship. Once I experienced the courses and my first internship (in a mental hospital), I knew I had found a career that would be incredibly interesting and rewarding.

What is your favorite social work story? As a dean, I spent a lot of my time talking with social work alumni about their education and careers. On occasion, I would talk with both men and women who received their social work degrees but who never practiced social work. To a person, they each claimed that their social work education was a key to their success in their chosen career (whether it was law, banking, real estate, or parenting). Why? Because as social work students, they had all learned good communication, problem-solving, and people skills.

What would be the one thing you would change in our community if you had the power to do so? I would eliminate prejudices that are based on race, gender, physical ability, or socioeconomic differences. These kinds of biases and subsequent discrimination are a waste of our human energy.

The response illustrated in box 2 is not unusual. In fact, it is characteristic of the way many people view and react to beneficiaries of residual programs, and it raises some interesting questions. Do people receiving assistance have a right to entertainment? Or when they accept public assistance do they give up their right to the luxuries available to others not dependent on this social welfare service? As we will see in chapter 3, the history of social welfare is marred by a reluctance to help others in need. Residual programs and services are stigmatized, and those who need these types of services are constantly scrutinized. Many people believe that such services, although necessary as temporary forms of assistance or as last-resort charity, reinforce negative behaviors rather than promoting rugged individualism and a strong work ethic.

In summary, residual programs highlight narrow views of helping. Assistance is minimal and temporary and designed only to help people survive immediate problems or crises. These types of programs provide support only when no other support options are available. In other words, a residual program is a program of last resort. In the 1980s, American public welfare programs were categorized as essentially residual in nature. Collectively referred to as "the safety net," these programs could be accessed only after all other avenues of assistance had been exhausted.

There are three important points to keep in mind regarding residual programs. First, these programs are all means tested. To be eligible for benefits people must document their inability to care financially for themselves and their families. In a typical residual program, clients are routinely means tested or recertified for continued eligibility every few months.

Second, residual programs can create barriers for those who seek assistance. Numerous eligibility criteria, which often force clients to produce a variety of supporting documents and evidence, can be disheartening. Continual recertification processes can thus encourage clients to give up, forgoing assistance even when their needs persist.

Third, residual programs carry a stigma, and recipients are not proud to receive services. The **Food Stamp Program** is a typical residual program (see box 1). Food stamp recipients must qualify to receive program services, they must be recertified every few months by the state, and they are not viewed positively in the greater community.

Recall the food stamp recipient in our hypothetical grocery checkout line. How often do we look at what the person ahead of us is buying? Do we spend more time scrutinizing the purchases of those who pay with food stamps? If another person had been purchasing exactly the same items and paying with cash would our reactions have been the same? Probably not. Why? Since both individuals would have similar buying habits, why is there a difference in how these two people would be viewed? The sad reality is that the food stamp recipient carries a stigma. Some people believe that beneficiaries of residual programs such as food stamps cannot be trusted, are morally weak, and do not make good decisions. Food stamp clients are often thought to be different from people who do not receive public aid.

Institutional Social Welfare

The second conception of social welfare described by Wilensky and Lebeaux (1965) is institutional social welfare. This definition of social welfare gives it much broader scope and function than the residual definition does. In the institutional conception, the community is expected to assist individual members because problems are viewed not as failures, but instead as part of life in modern society. This broader community responsibility allows members in need to be provided services that go beyond immediate responses to emergencies. Help is often provided before people exhaust all of their own resources, and preventive and rehabilitative services are stressed.

Therefore, an institutional program, as opposed to a residual program, is designed to meet the needs of all people. Eligibility is **universal**. Institutional programs have no stigma attached and are viewed as regular frontline programs in society. In fact, institutional programs are so widely accepted in society that many are not viewed as social welfare programs at all (see examples in box 1). Institutional programs are often called "**entitlement programs**," meaning that services and benefits are available because of a person's earned status.

In concluding our discussion of residual and institutional provision of social welfare as outlined by Wilensky and Lebeaux, we must note the primary weakness of this framework: not all programs and services are easily classified as one or the other; some programs have both institutional and residual attributes. The **Head Start** program, for example, is institutional in nature but is means tested and restricted to a particular segment of the population. One solution is to expand the traditional dichotomy and classify social programs on a residual-institutional continuum. A program's position on the continuum reflects whether it is more residual or more institutional in design and to what degree. Some questions to help guide the classification process include:

1. Is the program short term or long term?
2. Is the program open to all people or a selected group of people?
3. Do program participants carry a stigma?
4. Does the public embrace the program?
5. Is the program controversial?
6. How would you feel if you were a program participant?

> *Activity…Ask fifteen to twenty people to define the term "social welfare." Then ask them to list five social welfare programs of which they are aware. Review these responses in light of the work of Wilensky and Lebeaux. Do you notice any patterns in the responses? How many of the responses would you identify as residual, institutional, or a mix of both types? In analyzing these responses do you find that people have a narrow or a broad view of social welfare? How do you feel about the responses you have received? Do you think your respondents' views are accurate?*

Although there are ways to classify social programs, ensuring that social justice is addressed through recognizing social stigma, misperception, and its influence on clients cannot be underestimated. The public does appear openly to support some forms of social welfare, but these feelings and expectations seem to vary based on individual perception and the service that is being received.

IS EVERYONE REALLY ON WELFARE?

Richard Titmus (1965), a famed British social scientist, argued that social welfare was much more than aid to the poor and in fact represented a broad system of support to the middle and upper classes. In his model, social welfare has three branches:

Fiscal welfare: Tax benefits and supports for the middle and upper classes

Corporate welfare: Tax benefits and supports for businesses

Public welfare: Assistance to the poor

Abramowitz (1983) applied the Titmus model to American social welfare. She identified a "shadow welfare state" for the wealthy that parallels the social service system available to the poor. She concluded that poor and nonpoor alike benefit from government programs and tax laws that raise their disposable income. In other words, were it not for direct government support—whether through food stamps or through a childcare tax exemption—people would have fewer dollars to spend and to support themselves and their families.

So, is everyone really on welfare? To address this question, let's focus first on college students. Did you know that college students are probably one of the largest groups of welfare recipients in the United States today? The vast majority of college students first attended public school, which was provided at no cost to them. Why? Because our government subsidizes the public school system. It is important for all children to have nutritious meals, and the daily school lunch is relatively inexpensive to purchase for all school students. In fact, try to buy the same meal in a restaurant and compare costs—the school lunch is much cheaper. Why? Because the government subsidies given to public schools lower the cost of these meals for all students. Okay, that's what happens in public school. Now consider the role of government in a public college. Compare tuition fees at a private college or university with those at a state- or community-supported institution. Why are tuition costs at the public college so much lower? Once again, the answer is simple: because of government subsidies. The government is very involved in subsidizing the educational needs of students at both the elementary and secondary and the college levels. Students are very much in need and dependent on these subsidies in order to complete their educations.

With all the support provided and the need for continuing support, doesn't it sound like welfare? Why then is there no stigma attached to this form of social provision? Some people may say, "I paid for my 'welfare' through taxes on my earnings, which makes me different from those people who did not." There is no easy response to this statement, and such attitudes continue to disturb social work professionals who do not agree with the distinction between the worthy and the unworthy that is often applied to social services. Is there really a difference in the welfare service provided? Could most individuals and families afford to pay the full tuition for college or the costs associated with operating a good-quality public school, including lunch? Government subsidies are important to the maintenance of society and are used by all people.

PUBLIC SOCIAL WELFARE

Social welfare is found in both public and private settings. "Public" refers to programs within the purview of state, federal, or local (city or county) government; "private" refers to services provided for profit and voluntary services.

Federal Welfare

The federal government classifies social welfare into seven areas: social insurance, education, public aid, health and medical programs, veterans' programs, housing, and other social welfare (see box 3). The 2004 United States budget totaled $2.23 trillion, of which $539 billion is allocated to the federal department of Health and Human Services Department.

Box 3: Federal Social Welfare Programs

Social insurance: Old-age retirement, workers' compensation, disability, unemployment assistance, railroad retirement, public employee retirement

Education: Elementary, secondary, and higher education; vocational education

Public aid: Cash payments under TANF, WIC, general assistance, emergency assistance

Veterans' programs: Assistance to veterans and their families, burial, health and medical programs, education, life insurance

Housing: Public housing

Health and medical programs: Hospital and medical care, maternal and child health programs, medical research, school health, other public health,, medical facilities construction.

Other social welfare: Vocational rehabilitation, institutional care, child nutrition, child welfare, OEO and ACTION programs, social welfare not classified elsewhere, food stamps

---

Social insurance has been and continues to be the most costly area of federal welfare, followed by education. In fact, these two areas account for more than 72 percent of *total* federal welfare expenses, whereas public aid accounts for only 13.8 percent of the federal welfare budget. It is interesting to note, however, that when "cutting welfare" is discussed, the emphasis is on public aid. But what would happen, for example, if the federal appropriation for food stamps were cut? In 2002 approximately $1.5 billion per month was spent on food stamps (note, there were 19.1 million people in 8.2 million households receiving food stamps)—certainly a lot of money by anyone's standards. Yet food stamps made up only 8 percent of *all* federal expenditures, that is, of the $2.2 trillion in 2002 expenditures, about $18 billion was spent for food stamps. In other words, cutting food stamps by, say, 50 percent would reduce the federal budget by less than 0.4 percent.

State Welfare

State welfare programs differ across the country. Each state is able to develop its own set of social programs to augment the federal government's initiatives. Typically a state establishes rules and provides funds for statewide social agencies. State social welfare agencies include protective services for children and juvenile justice. Funding for state services comes from two sources: **block grants** from the federal government and state tax revenues. A *block grant* is a lump sum of funds given to a state, which then has the authority to determine how best to spend the dollars. The federal government imposes few rules on block grants, allowing each state to determine how programs will be structured. A state can also supplement block grant funding in order to expand services.

Local Welfare

City and county welfare programs depend on local taxes for funding. Such funds are primarily used for community protection and support, such as police, fire, and other basic local services. Funding and provision of most of these types of local social services are considered mandatory. By contrast, many government officials and community leaders see social welfare provision as a minimal, "fill the gap" measure. Those in power are usually reluctant to develop and sponsor "costly" local services. As with state government programs, the types and levels of local welfare programs vary by municipality. Because of their "gap filling" status, local programs are generally residual in nature. Typical local programs include emergency food relief and housing and clothing vouchers.

PRIVATE SOCIAL WELFARE

Private social welfare consists of for-profit and not-for-profit agencies, also called *voluntary agencies* or *nonprofits*. Examples of nonprofits include the United Way, Red Cross, Salvation Army, Boys and Girls Clubs, Girl Scouts, YMCA, YWCA, Jewish Community Centers, Catholic Charities, and Family Services.

According to Karger and Stoesz (2001), private social welfare is not well understood; they characterized it as the "forgotten sector." For the most part, American social welfare has rested within the public domain since the 1930s when the government implemented a series of welfare programs to combat the effects of the

> *Activity…Go to your local (county or city) welfare office. Look around and try to get a feel for the setting. What messages does the physical structure send to the clients? Does this environment seem like a typical business setting? Do the setting and staff suggest an interest in serving the clients, and are the clients made to feel important? How does this facility differ from a physician's office? What sorts of informational brochures are available to read? How long do clients wait before a worker sees them?*
>
> *After you've visited a public agency, visit a private social service agency. What differences, if any, do you see between the two agencies? If differences do exist, what are they and why do you think they exist? Should there be any physical differences between public and private agencies?*

Great Depression. As the government took on greater welfare responsibility, the voluntary sector's activities lessened (Karger & Stoesz, 2001). With financial cuts in federal welfare funding taken hold in the early 1980s and holding well into the twenty-first century, private welfare has taken on new importance. This forgotten sector is now recognized as a crucial player in the delivery of social services.

The nonprofit sector relies on donations from public foundations and, to a much lesser extent, federal, state, and local governments. In order for nonprofits to provide services, their fundraising efforts must be successful. The success of fundraising depends on three factors: 1) the agency's ability to provide a high-quality program, 2) the agency's ability to communicate its successes, and 3) the community's financial ability to support the program. Karger and Stoesz (2001) noted, "As voluntary agencies become more dependent on the communities in which they are located, their success is tied to the affluence of those communities. Compared with those of wealthier communities, agencies in poor communities are unlikely to fare well" (p. 205). Therefore, in most instances, the level of private social welfare programming available depends directly on the financial well-being of the surrounding community. This dependence on private funding is particularly problematic during periods of economic turmoil, such as recession and rising unemployment. During these periods people have less money and time to donate to private charities, which in turn forces these organizations to make critical choices about which programs to close or cut.

According to the Social Security Administration, the role of the private sector in financing social welfare continues to grow, and this growth is needed to complement public social welfare expenditures and programs. Hoeffer and Colby (1998) referred to the private sector as the "mirror welfare state," a system of services that reflect public programs but are more supportive of the middle and upper classes than the poor.

Private welfare can be categorized into four areas: health, income maintenance (retirement), education, and welfare services. The data on private welfare are old with no recent reports published by the Social Security Administration. The old data do, however, offer some insight into the private welfare arena and allow us to consider its size and complexity today. In 1992 private welfare expenditures totaled $824.9 billion, a 75 percent increase over the 1985 level.

As with federal welfare spending, it's illuminating to examine where private sector funds are going. In particular, it is not the case that most of the spending, or even most of the increase in spending, is going to millions of poor people to gain the services they need. Of 1992 private welfare expenditures, $462.9 billion was spent on private health care; $164.7 billion was spent on income maintenance services, that is, retirement support programs. Thus health and income maintenance together accounted for 78.6 percent of all private welfare expenditures. By contrast, $75.8 billion, 9.2 percent, was spent on private welfare services. So although overall private expenditures have increased, the majority of these funds have gone to assist not the poor but rather the middle and upper classes. You might find it somewhat odd that we are relying on data from the early 1990s, but by 2003 the federal government had not updated their report on private welfare. We do know, however, that current spending proportionately remains the same. The focus of private welfare is directed to retirement and its supports, including health care and income maintenance, while private funding for programs targeting the poor remains consistently lower in the private sector.

SOCIAL WORK IN THE SOCIAL WELFARE SYSTEM

Social workers make up the primary professional group in the social welfare system. But social work is not the sole social welfare profession. Given the broad definition of social welfare used here and in the social work literature, many other professional groups are welfare providers as well. Although it is possible to lump the various professionals together and classify them all as welfare workers, it is more accurate to recognize that some professions are more concerned than others with people's social, health, wellness, and economic welfare needs. A useful way to differentiate among professions is to classify their level of involvement as either primary or secondary.

The primary category consists of professions whose principal efforts are in the provision of social, health, or economic services. The principal activities of professions in the secondary category are not directed toward welfare, but their work does at times involve social, health, or economic service provision (see box 4).

Box 4: Examples of Social Welfare Professionals by Primary or Secondary Classification

Primary	Secondary
Social workers	Police officers
Mental health counselors	Librarians
Schoolteachers	Recreational specialists
Marriage and family therapists	Road crews
Psychologists	Government officials
Psychiatrists	Military personnel
Nurses	
Sanitation workers	

Look at the professionals listed in box 4. What is your opinion of who is included and where they have been placed? Do you think the professionals listed would agree with where we have classified them? For example, how would an elementary schoolteacher react to being described as a welfare worker? We believe that many of the professionals listed above would openly disagree that they are welfare providers. It's possible that the stigma attached to programs and services offered under the rubric of "welfare" might influence their reactions. To explore this possibility, how do you think these professionals would reply to the following question?

> Do you as a professional provide a program, benefit, or service that helps people meet those social, economic, educational, health, and wellness needs that are fundamental to the maintenance of society?

We believe that as this question is framed—without addressing the concept of social welfare provision openly—the vast majority of the professionals listed in box 4, whether classified as primary or as secondary service providers, would answer yes. The simple truth is that although few professionals think of their activities in this way, providing welfare services is an integral part of their jobs.

Our broad definition of social welfare also suggests some rethinking of rigid ideas about social work. The social work profession has its roots in efforts to help the poor and disenfranchised (Hepworth & Larsen, 1993), neither of which is considered a desirable client population according to a narrow definition of social welfare. These efforts historically meant promoting and enhancing individual client well-being albeit in a societal or environmental context.

Over time, however, the traditional role of the social work professional has expanded. According to social work's revised Code of Ethics:

> The primary mission of the social work profession is to enhance human well-being and help meet the basic human needs of all people, with particular attention to the needs and empowerment of people who are vulnerable, oppressed, and living in poverty. A historic and defining feature of social work is the profession's focus on individual well-being in a social context and the well-being of society. Fundamental to social work is the attention to the environmental forces that create, contribute to, and address problems in living.

> . . . These activities may be in the form of direct practice, community organizing, supervision, consultation, administration, advocacy, social and political action, policy development and implementation, education, and research and evaluation. (NASW, 1996, p. 1)

For the social work professional, social welfare methods and programs now address diverse populations, which can include those who are homeless, suicidal, homicidal, divorced, unemployed, mentally ill, medically ill, drug abusing, and delinquent, just to mention a few. Moreover, the term "client" is now used inclusively and can mean individuals, groups, families, organizations, and communities. Adopting, in essence, the institutional perspective, the social worker must strive to restore and enhance client wellness and to provide preventive as well as basic, brief services. Strategies to assist clients must address all of these areas because often the factors involved are intertwined and interdependent (Dziegielewski, 2004; Skidmore, Thackeray, & Farley, 1997).

Activity...Now for a moment, pretend to be a United States Senator or a member of the United States House of Representatives. Your assignment is simple: balance the federal budget and eliminate the projected 2004 $307 billion deficit, which does not include the cost of the Iraq War. Go the following web site—http://www.budgetsim.org/nbs/shortbud-get04.html—and follow the directions. You will be asked to increase, decrease, or maintain expenditures for the federal government. Items you will consider include maintaining the 2001 and 2003 tax cuts, how you want to deal with the Iraq war, and the administration of justice.

The Fading "Public" versus "Private" Distinction

Changes in the social welfare environment have blurred once-clear distinctions in social work—for example, whether an agency that employs a social worker is public or private. For simplicity, "public" agencies are understood to be primarily, if not totally, funded through tax-supported dollars. It is the public agency that is regarded as most representative of social welfare services and programs. Most people believe that these agencies have primary responsibility for residual or means-tested social welfare programs. "Private" agencies, on the other hand, are believed to be voluntarily supported and to rarely have tax-supported dollars as part of their basic budgets. If public and private agencies were distinctly different, these straightforward definitions would suffice. However, in today's social service environment nothing could be further from the truth. There is no longer any clear distinction between public and private agencies because their funding and the services they deliver so often overlap. Many private agencies now actively seek public or tax-supported funds, and many public agencies now contract with private agencies and individual providers to provide services to their clients. Because private agencies can specialize in a way that public agencies, with their broad responsibilities, cannot, such contracts allow public agencies to secure services that they do not have the budget or the skilled personnel to offer on their own.

In addition to this blurring between public and private agencies a dispersion of social workers across both the public and private sectors has placed social work practitioners in new roles. Traditionally, social workers served in the public sector because these agencies and programs assumed primary responsibility for the poor and the underserved. Today, however, social workers practice in many different agencies that have many different goals and allegiances.

Cost Containment versus Quality

For all social workers the current state of social work practice mirrors the turbulence in the general social welfare environment. There is little consistency in the delivery of social welfare services as primary emphasis is placed on cost containment. Social welfare program administrators, forced to justify each dollar billed for services, may reduce the provision of what some see as "expendable services" designed to promote the mental health and well-being of clients. They may be tempted to regard the role of social workers as adjunct to the delivery of care and to cut back on professional staff or replace them with nonprofessionals simply to lower costs. These substitute professionals have neither the depth nor the breadth of training that social work professionals do. The result can be substandard professional services.

The employment of these kinds of paraprofessionals, though cost effective, is not quality driven. When social services are rushed or minimized, issues such as the individual client's sense of well-being, ability to self-care, and family and environmental support may not be considered. The involvement of social work professionals is thus essential to ensuring that personal, social, and environmental issues are addressed and clients are not put at risk of harm.

For social workers, a client who is discharged home to a family that does not want him is at risk of abuse and neglect. A client who has a negative view of herself and a hopeless and hapless view of her condition is more likely to attempt suicide or come to some other harm. Many paraprofessionals and members of other professional disciplines differ from social work professionals in that they do not recognize the paramount importance of culture and environmental factors to efficient and effective practice. Their outlook may enable the delivery of "cheap" service, but the care provided is substandard.

As social service administrators strive to cut costs by eliminating professional social work services the overall philosophy of wellness can be sacrificed. It is important to note, however, that staff reorganizations and reductions in social welfare services are rarely personal attacks on social work professionals. The changes and cutbacks in services and those who provide them are responses to an immediate need-cost reduction. Fluctuating employment and downsizing of social work professionals, as with allied health professionals, simply reflects the fluctuating demands of the current market (Dziegielewski, 2004; Falck, 1990).

SUMMARY

So what is social welfare? The residual view suggests that welfare support should be temporary, only for the poor, and as minimal as possible. If we look at actual public welfare spending, however, it seems that social welfare as practiced is much broader. In fact, everyone in society is a welfare recipient of one type or another.

Similarly, the role of the social work professional is broader than many people expect. Originally, social workers served the poor and disenfranchised; however, over the years the role of the social worker has expanded tremendously. Many social work professionals now provide services outside of the traditional social welfare realm. This diversity of style, task, and approach makes defining exactly what social workers do difficult. Clarity of definition has been further complicated by changes in scope of practice, roles served, and expectations within the client-professional relationship.

In the turbulent social welfare environment social work professionals face a constant battle of "quality of care issues" versus "cost containment measures" for clients (Dziegielewski, 1996; 2004). In addition, they must strive to maintain a secure place as professional providers in the delivery of social welfare services.

Quiz Answers

1. d) Social security. According to the federal government nearly 50 percent of all welfare expenditures go to social security retirement payments. Less than 1 percent of the welfare budget is spent on food stamps.

2. a) Mothers and their children. Approximately 60 percent of all welfare recipients, according to the U.S. Bureau of the Census, are mothers and their children.

3. b) False. The majority of people in poverty are white.

4. b) False. Under federal welfare rules a family on welfare that has another baby will not receive any additional benefits.

5. b) False. The unemployment rate identifies only those people not working who actively looked for a job within the past thirty days.

6. c) False. Each state determines the amount a family receives on public assistance. As a result, a person in Florida receives a different amount from someone in Alabama.

7. b) False. According to reports by the U.S. Bureau of Labor Statistics, more than 70 percent of public assistance recipients are women with children, children, and senior citizens.

8. All the groups listed are participants in programs the federal government defines as "social welfare." As a result, all of the groups are welfare recipients.

9. b) False. AFDC was replaced by TANF—Temporary Assistance to Needy Families in 1996.

10. Revise your answer to this question using the information presented in this chapter.

References

Abramowitz, M. (1983). Everyone is on welfare: "The role of redistribution in social policy" revisited. *Social Work*, 28(6), 440–445.

Barker, R. L. (2003). *The social work dictionary* (4th ed.). Washington, DC: NASW Press.

Bloom, M. (1990). *Introduction to the social work drama*. Itasca, IL: Peacock.

Dziegielewski, S. F. (1996). Managed care principles: The need for social work in the health care environment. *Crisis Intervention and Time Limited Treatment, 3*(2), 97–110.

Dziegielewski, S. F. (2004). *The changing face of social work: Professional practice in the era of managed care*. (2nd ed.). NY: Springer.

Falck, H. S. (1990). Maintaining social work standards in for-profit hospitals: Reasons for doubt. *Health & Social Work, 15*, 76–77.

Friedlander, W. (1955). *Introduction to social welfare*. Englewood Cliffs, NJ: Prentice-Hall.

Hepworth, D. H., & Larsen, J. (1993). *Direct social work practice: Theory and skills* (4th ed.). Pacific Grove, CA: Brooks/Cole.

Hoeffer, R., & Colby, I. (1998). Private social welfare expenditures in R. Edwards et al. (Eds.), *Encyclopedia of social work update*. Washington, DC: NASW Press.

Karger, H., & Stoesz, D. (1995). *American social welfare policy: A pluralist approach* (2nd ed.). New York: Longman.

NASW (National Association of Social Workers). (1996, August). *Code of Ethics* (adopted by the NASW National Delegate Assembly, August 1996). Washington, DC: NASW Press.

NASW (National Association of Social Workers). (1997). Code of ethics. Washington, DC: NASW Press.

Reid, P. N. (1995). Social welfare history. In R. Edwards et al. (Eds.), *Encyclopedia of social work* (19th ed.). Washington, DC: NASW Press.

Satcher, D. (2000). Foreword. In *U.S. Public Health Service, Report of the Surgeon General's Conference on Children's Mental Health: A National Action Agenda* (pp. 1–2). Washington, DC: U.S. Department of Health and Human Services.

Segal, W., & Brzuzy, S. (1998). *Social welfare policy, programs, and practice*. Itasca, IL: Peacock.

Shalala, D. E. (2001). Message from Donna E. Shalala, Secretary of Health and Human Services. In *U.S. Department of Health and Human Services, Youth Violence: A Report of the Surgeon General: Executive Summary*. Rockville, MD: U.S. Department of Health and Human Services, Centers for Disease Control and Prevention, National Center for Injury Prevention and Control; Substance Abuse and Mental Health Services Administration, Center for Mental Health services; and National Institutes of Health, National Institute of Mental Health.

Skidmore, R. A., Thackeray, M. G., & Farley, O. W. (1997). *Introduction to social work* (7th ed.). Boston: Allyn and Bacon.

Specht, H., & Courtney, M. (1994). *Unfaithful angels*. New York: Free Press.

Titmus, R. (1959). *Essays on the welfare state*. New Haven, CT: Yale University Press.

Titmus, R. (1965). The role of redistribution in social policy. *Social Security Bulletin, 28*(6), 34–55.

Wilensky, H. & Lebeaux, C. (1958). *Industrial society and social welfare*. New York: Russell Sage Foundation.

Wilensky, H. & Lebeaux, C. (1965). *Industrial society and social welfare*. New York: Free Press.

Chapter 3

How Did We Get Here from There?

TIME FOR A BRIEF HISTORY QUIZ:

    1. Why is the year 1492 important in American history?

    2. The New Deal was the name given to what set of programs?

    3. What did the Emancipation Proclamation address?

    4. What important event took place in Seneca Falls, New York, in 1848?

    5. Where was an immigrant arriving at Ellis Island most likely to be from?

    6. What is Salem, Massachusetts, perhaps best known for?

    7. The United States acquired California, Nevada, Utah, and parts of Texas, Colorado, New Mexico, and Wyoming as part of what act or event?

    8. What document preceded the U.S. Constitution?

    9. What does the term "Seward's Folly" refer to?

    10. What was at issue in the Dred Scott Case?

So, how did you do? (The answers are at the end of the chapter.) For most people taking this quiz the results are mixed. A few of the questions seem easy while others are complete mysteries. Yet each of these questions addresses a meaningful part of our American history. The importance of being familiar with such events is twofold: 1) it is important to know what has happened simply to be an educated citizen and 2) knowledge of the past can help us to understand both present and future societal developments.

In the field of social work, as in other disciplines, knowing the history of the profession is essential to understanding its past, present, and future. Unfortunately, however, studying history sometimes doesn't seem as exciting as learning about direct social work practice, policy, or social action. When history is discussed in the classroom or in less formal situations, it is almost always received with an air of indifference and reluctance. As one student remarked, "It's over and done with, so why should I be concerned about it? I want to learn how to help people. What happened two hundred years ago won't help me today."

Is this statement really valid? It's true that in social work practice, regardless of the model or technique employed, the emphasis is on the here and now. Nevertheless, most social workers recognize the importance of history in their practice. For example, when first meeting a client, the social worker asks probing,

Name: Jorge Munoz Bustamante

Place of residence: Miami, Florida

College/university degrees: Barry University, MSW

Present position: Clinical Social Worker

What do you do in your spare time? What spare time? I am very involved in the lives of my three children and my wife. My daughter is a freshman at Florida International. I have a sixteen-year-old son who is a junior in high school and is very involved in track and field. My thirteen-year-old son is completing middle school. Their activities keep me quite occupied. Additionally, I am involved in the Catholic Physician's Guild, and I offer a presentation called heart-centered-parenting to the community at large. I enjoy sailing and camping whenever I can.

Why did you choose social work as a career? In 1959 my family had to flee Cuba after my father's paint store was confiscated. A West Virginia family that vacationed on the island made possible our entry into the United States by sponsoring us. This family encouraged and supported us even though they had no obligation to do so. From them I learned the deep satisfaction that comes from serving others. In my senior year of college, a friend said to me, "Jorge, have you ever thought about a career in service?" Everything clicked and I signed up for VISTA a few months later. I haven't looked back since.

What is your favorite social work story? After I completed my undergraduate degree in 1973, I helped set up a daycare for migrant children. We would take my old station wagon into the fields and pick up as many preschoolers as we could cram in. We would then take them to the daycare and attend to their needs. As the children began to thrive it was the first time that I fully experienced the power of relieving the misery of others. It was also the first time that I became aware of the tremendous need and lack of resources.

What would be the one thing you would change in our community if you had the power to do so? Meanness and cynicism. In my community I perceive a great deal of fear, hardness, and lack of love and tolerance that act like an acid. People need to be more connected to their healthy and positive selves.

thoughtful questions about the client's past. This systematic accumulation of information is referred to as gathering a social history or a **psychosocial history**. A social work practitioner would never consider the social history that he completes on each client useless information. In particular, the social history is important to understanding and exploring the client's growth and development process as well as to identifying possible effects of events and relations with others in the client's past.

Activity...Contact your state NASW office and ask for names of local "Gold Card" members. These are people over age 60 who have been members of NASW for at least twenty-five years. Try to meet them to talk about social work twenty to thirty years ago. What do they see today that is different from when they started out in the profession? How do they think technology is influencing social work and social welfare?

The past offers valuable clues to interpreting the present and anticipating the future. History is essential to helping all of us better understand who we are and how we got here. It also influences our future decisions. Indeed, some people take the extreme position that we are so profoundly influenced by the past that it actually determines the future. This theory is called "determinism."

Whatever degree of importance we place on history, it is obvious that people— sometimes intentionally, sometimes unintentionally—use past experiences as a frame of reference for current and future experiences. For example, a baby only has to burn her hand once not to put it on a hot stove; in adulthood people rarely try this again because they know they can be painfully hurt. Although the causes and effects may not be clearly linked, a similar process can govern the relations we develop throughout our lives. Therefore, the importance of history should not be underestimated. We hope we have sparked your interest in history as a way to understand the roots of social welfare and general aspects of social work practice. In many cases considering the experiences of the past can teach us valuable lessons worth remembering.

Did You Know...Harry Hopkins, a social worker, was one of President Franklin D. Roosevelt's closest friends and was the administrator of a Great Depression program called the Federal Emergency Relief Administration.

This chapter will make a brief foray into social welfare history. In the past, comprehensive examinations of social welfare history have been undertaken by others (Chambers, 1967; Lubove, 1969; Trattner, 1989; Axinn & Levin, 1982; Katz, 1986; Jansson, 1988), and this area is well worth the effort of further investigation. We will briefly examine significant events and trends that influenced the emergence of our current American social welfare system.

THE ELIZABETHAN POOR LAW OF 1601

Most social work historians would agree that the watershed year for social welfare was 1601, when English poor laws were "codified" or brought together under one law. This codification is commonly called the *Elizabethan Poor Law of 1601*. Colonial America adopted the central tenets of this law, and many of its principles continue to underpin the design and implementation of our current social services.

An important note of caution: Let's not fall into a simple trap and believe that welfare began with the Elizabethan Poor Law of 1601. Karger and Stoesz (1994) tracked the development of the English poor laws back through a series of events to the mid-fourteenth century. Gilbert and Specht (1981, p. 17) noted that modern-day social welfare has roots in the Reformation period and the Middle Ages. And Trattner (1989), in his classic work *From Poor Law to Welfare State,* traced the roots of American welfare efforts to the ancient Greeks and Romans! In advanced social policy courses, you'll learn more about the rise of social welfare as a system, but for our purposes, we will begin with the Elizabethan poor laws.

Before 1601 in Europe welfare attempts to assist people in need were generally viewed as the province of the church. With the advent of the industrial era, great changes occurred in society. Many new and better paying jobs were created, and men and women of all ages were encouraged to apply. Rural communities began to decrease in population as people left the limited and shrinking opportunities of farm life for what the industrialized cities offered. Unfortunately, the promise of more jobs and a better way of life was not fulfilled for everyone, and many became unemployed and homeless. The newly destitute turned to the churches, the traditional providers of assistance to the poor. With the ranks of the poor growing to unprecedented levels, however, these urban churches did not have the resources or the expertise to cope with the swelling numbers of rural migrants and their assorted needs.

Faced with a growing population of urban poor, the English government implemented a series of sweeping reforms in an attempt to gain control of this problem. The result, the 1601 poor laws, radically changed the form, function, and scope of welfare assistance. First, the poor laws redefined welfare as no longer a private affair but a public responsibility. Second, the 1601 laws identified local government as the public entity responsible for the poor. Last, the poor laws denied relief if family resources were available (Katz, 1986, pp. 13–14).

In addition to setting the parameters for public aid, the 1601 poor laws divided potential recipients into two groups, the **worthy poor** and the **unworthy poor**. The worthy poor included the ill, the disabled, orphans, and elders. These people were viewed as having no control over their life circumstances. A second group of the worthy poor consisted of people who were involuntarily unemployed. Although they were seen as bearing some responsibility for their own situations due consideration was given to the fact that their misfortunes were beyond their control. The unworthy poor, on the other hand, included the vagrant or able-bodied who, while able to work, did not seek employment (Cole, 1973, p. 5).

Overall, when services were provided, assistance was first given to the worthy poor who were considered helpless to control their situations. Some assistance was provided to those who were involuntarily unemployed. No assistance was given to the unworthy poor, who were treated with public disdain.

COLONIAL AMERICA

The provision of public assistance in colonial America was tenuous at best. Influenced by strong Puritan and Calvinist views, most citizens regarded both the worthy and the unworthy poor as morally flawed. They believed that the poverty-stricken had somehow caused their own distress. This belief released society from any obligation to lend assistance and implied that it was the impoverished individual who was responsible for finding and providing a remedy. Aid or **charity assistance**, in any form, was thought to lead to an "erosion of independence and self-respect; the spread of idleness and the loss of the will to work; the promotion of immorality in all its ugly forms; and the increase in public costs through the growth of poorhouses and jails" (Katz, 1986, p. 40). Benjamin Franklin, for example, strongly opposed public aid: "[The] 'natural state' of working persons was one of sloth, wastefulness, and dissipation. The Common people do not work for pleasure, but for necessity" (Williams, 1944, p. 83). Relief, Franklin felt, simply provided an opportunity for people to return to their natural state of laziness at the expense of others.

Did You Know…In 1931, Jane Addams, social worker and founder of Hull House, was the first American woman to win the Nobel Peace Prize.

Based on a weak commitment to a public welfare system, American colonists developed a dual system of relief that was modeled on the English poor laws of 1601. The resulting programs provided aid to the worthy poor, who in this case comprised the ill, seniors, orphans, widows, and veteran soldiers. The unworthy or able-bodied poor, who included the involuntarily unemployed, were provided little if any assistance.

Assistance to the worthy poor was grudgingly given, primarily in the form of **outdoor relief**, which provided minimal assistance to individuals and families in their homes. The unworthy poor were not provided aid in their homes and often were encouraged to move on to another county. If assistance was required, the unworthy poor were required to return to their counties of origin to receive it. The unworthy poor were eligible, however, for **indoor relief**—the poorhouse.

Funds to support the worthy and unworthy poor were collected by local taxes assessed by the local **overseer of the poor**. In many ways this overseer was a colonial version of a social worker. The overseer was responsible for identifying who constituted the poor, what their needs were, and what the community should do to address their needs (see figure 1).

In general, the availability and accessibility of colonial public services reflected Franklin's negative view of relief. These programs were often designed with a punitive intent, in an effort to shame people out of their poverty. Typical of this approach was the auctioning of the poor into apprenticeships and indentured service to the lowest bidder—that is, the person who would charge the community least for taking a pauper off its hands. Another example of this reluctant attitude toward helping the poor is the treatment of a widow in Hadley, Massachusetts. In 1687, this woman, who had no resources of her own, was forced to live for two-week periods with those families who were "able to receive her" (Trattner, 1989, p. 18). Further, in Pennsylvania those receiving aid were required to wear a scarlet

Selected Dates in American Social Welfare History

1601	Elizabethan Poor Law enacted by the English parliament.
1642	Plymouth Colony enacts first poor law in the colonies.
1657	Scots Charitable Society, first nonprofit organization focused on the provision of welfare, founded in Boston.
1773	First public mental asylum opens in Williamsburg, Virginia.
1790	First public orphanage opens in Charleston, South Carolina.
1798	U.S. Public Health Department established.
1817	Gallaudet School, a school for the deaf, founded in Hartford, Connecticut.
1822	Kentucky opens first public asylum for deaf people.
1829	First asylum for the blind opens in Massachusetts.
1841	Dorthea Dix begins investigations into mental institutions in the United States.
1853	The Reverend Charles Loring Brace organizes Children's Aid Society.
1854	President Pierce vetoes federal legislation designed to use federal land for state asylums.
1865	Freedmen's Bureau is organized.

Check the *Encyclopedia of Social Work* under Distinctive Dates in Social Welfare History (Alexander, 1997) for other dates and events. What events in social welfare history impress or surprise you? What do you think is the most important social welfare event on the list? Why?

letter "P" sewn on their right sleeves "with the first letter of the county, city, or place of his or her residence underneath" (Heffner, 1913, p. 11). Even more extreme was a 1754 North Carolina law that allowed vagrants to be whipped in the public square simply because of their impoverished state (Rothman, 1971, p. 25).

Did You Know…Jeannette Rankin, a social worker, was the first woman elected to the U.S. Congress, representing Montana, in 1916.

Not all potential recipients of social welfare services were viewed negatively in colonial America. For example, veteran soldiers who had fought for the colonies were given a more honored status because, when poor, they were generally considered to be among the worthy poor (Axinn & Levin, 1982, p. 31). As early as 1624, veterans could expect to receive social welfare benefits as a right earned by the service they had provided. It was believed that since veteran soldiers had shown their willingness to risk life and limb in defense of their nation they deserved public aid if they needed it. Providing relief to veterans was not considered the responsibility of the town; rather it was the obligation of the colony. In addition, veterans did not have to satisfy residency requirements in order to receive aid (Axinn & Levin, 1982, p. 31). In summary, two of the primary components of colonial poor relief legisla-

Figure 1: A United Charities of Chicago caseworker or visiting housekeeper calling on a family about 1909. Formed when the Relief and Aid Society merged with the Bureau of Charities, United Charities of Chicago was the city's oldest private welfare organization. It was the best known of the family service agencies and worked on prevention, easing desperate social situations, and creating better living environments.

tion—local responsibility and residency—did not apply to veterans because they enjoyed the status of the worthy poor.

NINETEENTH-CENTURY REFORM EFFORTS

Throughout American history, immorality and pauperism have been tightly linked by the idea that poverty is a direct result of an individual's flawed character. Nineteenth-century programs intended to help the poor sought to do so by changing their behavior and making them overcome their personal failings. At the same time public opinion turned hostile toward all those living in poverty. As Benjamin Disraeli lamented following passage of the punitive 1834 British poor law reform, it was "a crime to be poor" (Trattner, 1989, p. 49).

Despite the strong resistance to helping the poor, poverty was widespread enough that some form of relief was necessary. Welfare organizations became more formalized and commonplace, particularly in large urban areas. The most prominent agencies for the delivery of social welfare services and programs for the poor were almshouses and asylums, charity organization societies, and settlement houses.

Almshouses and Asylums

The roots of service provision for the poor and disabled can be traced back as far as the 1700s to the first **almshouses**. Almshouses, also called "poorhouses," were intended to be places of refuge for the poor, medically ill, and mentally ill of all ages. In colonial times, however, caring for the family and its members was considered a private matter, and people who had any kind of family support were kept at home. Therefore, the almshouse was an "option of last resort," providing shelter and relief for society's outcasts—those who were poor, incapacitated, or suffered from contagious disease. Severely underfunded, almshouses were dirty and disease filled, and the workers who staffed them, who can be regarded among the earliest practical social workers and health care providers, often became ill (Dziegielewski, 2004).

Did You Know…In 1713 William Penn founded the first almshouse, in Philadelphia. In 1736 a second almshouse was founded at Bellevue Hospital in New York. The almshouse in Bellevue usually housed the mentally ill and later became one of the most famous mental health hospitals in the country.

At one point, almshouses housed all of the poor. However, eventually children were removed from almshouses by the efforts of the Children's Aid Society and later placed in orphanages. In 1851 the mentally ill were also removed and sent to improved facilities and asylums primarily through the crusading efforts of Dorthea Lynde Dix. Basically, the almshouse as "holding tank" was replaced with more segregated forms of institutionalized care such as orphanages and other residential facilities, referred to as "asylums."

Asylums, the most common human service organizations in the 1800s, became the homes for the blind, deaf and dumb, and insane and developed regimented programs formed by a guiding trinity of work, religion, and education. Tightly regulating an inmate's life with scheduled activities throughout each day, according to Rothman (1971, p. 145), reflected belief in the "therapeutic value of a rigid schedule." For example, in the Pennsylvania Hospital, patients were awakened at 5:00 a.m., "received their medicines at six, and breakfast at 6:30; at eight o'clock, they went for a physical examination, and then to work or to some other form of exercise. At 12:30 they ate their main meal and then resumed work or other activities until six, when everyone joined for tea" (Rothman, 1971, p. 145).

As can been seen from this cumbersome schedule, labor was a central component of asylum life. Inmates, as they were being taught jobs, learned the "value" and "importance" of work. This training, coupled with the regimented schedule, in theory imparted "habits. . . necessary for patients' recovery" (Rothman, 1971, p. 146). A poem allegedly written by a young woman in the Texas Asylum for the Blind reveals the negative side of work as the cornerstone of welfare programming:

> *Work, work, work*
> *till the brain begins to swim;*
> *work, work, work*
> *till the eyes are heavy and dim;*
> *seam, gusset, and bond,*
> *bond, gusset, and seam*
> *till over the buttons I fall asleep*
> *and sew them on in dream.*

Did You Know...The first American charity organization society was established in Buffalo, New York, in 1877.

Charity Organization Societies

A second innovative approach to combating poverty was the **Charity Organization Society (COS),** founded in London, England, in the mid-1800s. Besides its significance as a social welfare development, the COS is important to the history of social work because some social work historians view its founding as the profession's birth event. The first American COS, modeled after the British program, was founded in Buffalo, New York, in 1877 by the Reverend Humphrey Gurteen.

In the mid-1800s, charitable efforts proliferated in American cities, resulting in many duplicated and uncoordinated programs. COSs sought to organize the various charities within a city in order to reduce program duplication. A second objective was for COSs to certify the needs and claims of clients in a systematic, investigative fashion. Thus only those in need could receive services from the various charities. Finally, COSs sought to change the lives of the poor through home visits by volunteers.

COSs subscribed to the philosophy that poverty was a consequence of moral decay and the eradication of the slum depended on the poor recognizing and correcting their personal deficiencies (Boyer, 1978, p. 144). The **friendly visitor**, a key volunteer in the COS movement, was to establish a personal relation with each client through "home visits" and by serving as a role model, to help the poor change their behavior. The 1889 Buffalo Charity Organization Society Handbook declared that the friendly visitor soon would be a power in the home.

> In a very short time the houses would be clean and kept clean for her reception. Her advice would be sought. . . . In a word, all avoidable pauperism would soon be a thing of the past when the poor would regard the rich as their natural friends (Gurteen, 1882, p. 117).

Women volunteers, particularly those from middle and upper class families, were preferred for the role of friendly visitor. These women would be able to demonstrate and foster the values of the successful family to less fortunate individuals and families. In essence, by psychological and social osmosis, poverty and its companion evils would be uprooted through the kind works of middle class ladies. Specifically, Gurteen wrote,

> [All that is] needed to make our work a grand success . . . is hundreds of women from the educated and well-to-do classes, especially women of our city, who as mothers and daughters, coming from bright and happy homes—homes adorned by virtue and radiant with love, can impart to the cheerless tenement or the wretched hovel, a little of their own happiness. (1882, p. 116)

The COS movement also relied on female volunteers to staff the various organizations. As COSs became more accepted and formalized, the role of women changed. For example, COS women, by the end of the nineteenth century, were paid for their work, and COSs became a primary employment arena for women. It is interesting to note, however, that the first COS administrators were men and the first female administrator, Mary Richmond, was not appointed until late 1891.

Did You Know...Frances Perkins, a social worker, was the first woman appointed to the U.S. cabinet when in 1933 she was named secretary of labor.

In summary, the COSs were an important development in the history of social work because they provided the basis for the modern social service agencies of today. The workers they employed were some of the first to deliver social services in the home setting to poor and disenfranchised people. COSs provided an opportunity for systematic investigation of those in poverty and need. Home visitation, which today remains a highly valued social work intervention technique, allowed volunteers to learn more about individuals and their environments.

Did You Know...The first social work educational program started in 1898 as a summer training course at the New York Charity Organization Society. It later became Columbia University School of Social Work.

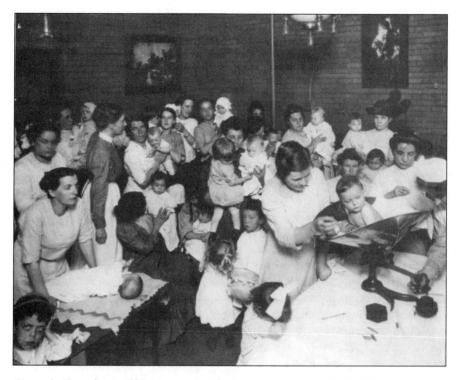

Figure 2: The Infant Welfare Society was founded in 1911 when the Milk Commission and the Children's Hospital Society joined forces. It trained nurses to staff milk distribution stations where they weighed babies, promoted proper nutrition, and provided mental and emotional guidance for women, children, and families.

Settlement House Movement

Another major British innovation also crossed the Atlantic during the mid-1800s and made a significant impact in the American social service arena. Known as the Settlement House Movement, its philosophy was remarkably different from that of the COSs. The Settlement House Movement sought the causes of poverty in macro- rather than microsystems. For example, poor education, lack of health care, and inadequate housing were considered the primary reasons for poverty. The settlement house was an actual house in a neighborhood where the workers lived year-round coordinating and providing programs, activities, and services directed to the needs of their neighbors.

The most famous nineteenth-century settlement house was Hull House, founded by Jane Addams and Ellen Gates Starr in 1889. Located in a poor west side Chicago neighborhood, Hull House forged a strong bond between neighborhood immigrants and social workers with its efforts to bridge the gulf between rich and poor. By the beginning of the twentieth century there were more than one hundred settlement houses located in the United States.

Name: Janina Henson-Dinio

Place of residence: Kitsap County, Washington

College/university degrees: St. Theresa's College, BA in Journalism, University of Washington, MSW

Present position: Therapist, Case Manager, Consultant/Minority Mental Health Specialist

Previous work/volunteer experience: Public Relations, Advertising and Training Manager, International Corporate Bank; teacher of Spanish and journalism; writer for local newspaper

Why did you choose social work as a career? I had always been sensitive to the need to help and provide human services. As an activist in my country of origin—the Philippines—I was part of a group that sought to address social inequity. When I migrated to the United States, I saw that the need to serve minority communities is just as great here. Even today, many services available to mainstream communities are not accessed by minority communities owing to lack of information and to language and cultural barriers. I see my role in the community as being a conduit of information from minority communities to professional and volunteer service providers and vice versa.

What is your favorite social work story? On many occasions, I have thought of going back to journalism due to the pressures of changing state and federal contract requirements and the unrelenting pace of change. At these times, I hesitated from taking that crucial step when people stopped me on the street and thanked me for the support and assistance I had provided them in a time of need. This "psychic income" compensates for a lot of the aggravation associated with clinical social work in the community mental health setting.

What would be the one thing you would change in our community if you had the power to do so? I have been in the helping profession for less than a decade. For social workers to survive stress and burnout, I would implement true outcome-based practice and decrease regulations. If bureaucrats are truly to manage by outcomes, social workers must be given the leeway to develop the objectives and programs necessary to achieve desired outcomes, guided by quality and service norms rather than regulations.

The Settlement House Movement initiated the macromodel for social work practice, more commonly referred to as "community organization" and "group work practice." Problems were seen as resting not with the individual but at the larger organizational or community level. Poverty was the result not of an individual's lack of morality but of a system that kept wages low, did not enforce housing or health codes, and maintained a marginalized working class. Through client empowerment, problems could be confronted and social resources redistributed.

Did You Know...The Scots Charitable Society, organized in Boston in 1657, was the first voluntary society in the colonies to focus on welfare needs.

THE TWENTIETH CENTURY

At the dawn of the twentieth century, the United States was poised to become a world economic leader. By the 1920s, economic prosperity seemed to come within reach of a growing number of Americans. Yet for blacks and immigrants economic gains were elusive. Blacks continued to suffer racism and discrimination under nineteenth-century Jim Crow laws. As immigration increased, laws inspired by xenophobia (fear of foreigners) framed social policy initiatives.

The prosperity of the first quarter-century quickly unraveled in the worldwide depression of the 1930s. By 1929, 1.6 million people were unemployed, and by the mid-1930s, nearly one in four Americans were unemployed.

Everyone knew someone—a brother, sister, father, mother, aunt, uncle, grand-parent, or friend—who was out of work. Poverty was no longer a distant concept reserved for blacks, immigrants, and other minorities. Very quickly, the philosophy that the poor were morally depraved and had no work ethic became unacceptable because now more people had become poor who were never poor before. The new poor were everyone's friends and family and didn't fit the image of the lazy, immoral poor.

With the presidential election of Franklin Roosevelt, relief measures were immediately put in place, followed by the ambitious **New Deal** programs. These programs were funded and coordinated at the federal level and dramatically changed government's ambivalent role in social welfare.

The most important New Deal initiative was the Economic Security Act of 1935, which established the social security system to provide cash assistance to retired workers. This act—which also established the precursors of AFDC and unemployment insurance—became the organizing framework for the federal social service system. By the end of the twentieth century, it has been amended on numerous occasions to include cash assistance, health benefits, and services for the disabled, the blind, families, children, and seniors.

The New Deal included initiatives directed toward a variety of people. The Federal Emergency Relief Act, the Civilian Conservation Corps, and the Works Progress Administration formed the backbone of the New Deal. All of these programs were unprecedented in that they were developed and coordinated by the

Activity...Go to a library and read, generally on microfilm, newspapers from the 1930s. Try to get a feel for life during the depression. Then visit a local nursing home or senior center to meet people who lived during the depression. Ask them how the depression affected their families and neighbors and how did it influence the rest of their lives.

federal government, but like local relief efforts of the nineteenth century they made work a condition of relief.

The New Deal essentially affirmed the federal government's role in social welfare. The national effort was unparalled in American history, until the massive social movement of the 1960s.

Social Reform in the 1960s

By 1960, slightly more than one in five Americans lived in poverty. In 1962, Michael Harrington's classic work *The Other America: Poverty in the United States* helped the nation to rediscover this poverty in its backyard. The short book had a profound impact within the halls of Congress and reawakened nationwide debate on the role of government in combating poverty.

In the early part of his administration, President Lyndon Johnson declared a "war on poverty" that would make full use of the nation's resources. The resulting initiative—later referred to as the "Great Society" programs—brought a new federal presence into local communities far different from previous welfare program efforts. Guided by the phrase "maximum feasible participation" of the poor, welfare programs involved the poor in local decision making in their neighborhoods and communities.

The coordinating agency for the Great Society was the Office of Economic Opportunity (OEO). Typical new welfare strategies include assistance to newborn babies and their mothers (Women, Infants, and Children—WIC), preschool education (Head Start), health care for seniors (**Medicare**) and the poor (**Medicaid**), employment programs for young adults (Job Corps), community action programs that encouraged neighbors to marshal resources, legal services for the poor, food stamps, and model city projects that were designed to provide assistance to the poorest neighborhoods.

The Great Society was spurred by a newfound belief that the nation could fight and win any battle it chose, and the War on Poverty had no borders. The Peace Corps, developed in 1965, sent volunteers to nations around the world to work in poor communities. Volunteers in Service to America (VISTA) was a domestic version of the Peace Corps with volunteers working in low-income American neighborhoods.

By the end of the 1960s, the Great Society was under growing attack for being too costly with too few benefits to the larger society. During the presidential administration of Richard Nixon, the influence of the OEO was minimized, and numerous programs were scraped. In their place Nixon proposed an innovative guaranteed annual income for the poor—a "negative income tax." Known as the Family Assistance Program (FAP), Nixon's plan would have subsidized a poor family by $2,400 a year. FAP required work or job training with the states eventually having full responsibility for program operation. This controversial proposal was ultimately rejected by Congress, but it was nevertheless a dramatic attempt to establish a minimum income based on work requirements.

The 1980s and Beyond: A Return to the Work Ethic

With the election of Ronald Reagan to the presidency and a more conservative Congress, public service relief programs became targets of a massive attack. Numerous federal public assistance programs were eliminated while others had their funding cut and their eligibility requirements tightened to weed out the unworthy poor. The results of this realignment were dramatic. Palmer and Sawhill (184, pp. 363–379) found that 500,000 families were removed from AFDC and an additional 300,000 families received reduced benefits. One million people were eliminated from food stamp rolls. In 1985, the National Anti-Hunger Coalition charged that the federal government was not spending allocated funds for the WIC nutrition program, depriving thousands of pregnant women and newborn infants of health and nutrition services.

Children, women, seniors, and minorities were the primary victims of the Reagan welfare reforms. The message of the 1980s was clear: First, public assistance was contributing to the national debt. Second, only the truly needy, the poorest of the poor, would be helped with a "safety net" to ensure survival. Third, welfare was a state and a local, not a federal, concern.

The safety net approach places responsibility for helping the poor and disadvantaged at the doorstep of local government and private sources; the federal government becomes a resource of last resort. To achieve this purpose the Reagan administration adopted three overriding goals with regard to income security programs: 1) reduce short-term spending by implementing changes in entitlement programs; 2) turn over welfare responsibility to the states; and 3) promote reliance on individual resources rather than create and maintain dependence on governmental benefits (Storey, 1982). The result was

> a patchwork of programs at the federal, state, and local level that results in gross inadequacies in education. . . . We have developed too few resources to prevention and maintenance, and too many to picking up pieces after the damage is done. On the other hand, the United States has established a broad welfare system for the non-poor while the middle and upper classes and corporate America are able to take advantage of many benefits and, to a large extent, have become dependent on government support. (American Assembly, 1989, p. 34)

Welfare reform continued in the 1990s with the 1992 presidential election of Bill Clinton, who promised to "end welfare as we know it." His ambition came within reach with later developments in Congress. The midterm congressional election in 1994 brought a Republican sweep, and in their "Contract with America" conservative congressional Republicans made welfare reform a top priority.

In 1996 Congress essentially ended federal relief programs with the passage of the Personal Responsibility and Work Opportunity Reconciliation Act. The new law abolished specific categorical programs and provided federal block grants to the states. Today, the federal government is no longer responsible for operating public welfare programs. No longer does the country have a national welfare program.

Rather each state operates its own set of public welfare services, each with its own set of eligibility criteria, program rules, and benefits. Another way of looking at public welfare is to recognize that the nation has fifty different welfare programs, each operating under a different set of rules. Commonalities come from conditions placed on federal block grants: a lifetime limit of five years of relief, a work requirement, and participation in job-training programs.

According to the Federal Welfare Reform Act of 1996, all adult welfare recipients are required to work, be registered for work, or be participating in a job-training or educational programs. The food stamp program—now run by the states—has similar eligibility criteria; failure to follow these work guidelines results in program disqualification. This welfare reform act also ended the AFDC program, in place since the New Deal. It was replaced by Temporary Assistance for Needy Families (TANF), a short-term program that incorporates lifetime limitations and work requirements.

The 1996 welfare reform is an example where knowledge of history can help us to understand what is happening today. The philosophy that undergrids today's welfare provision reflects some of Franklin's admonitions. The reluctance to acknowledge government responsibility continues. And with a lifetime limit on years of eligibility for welfare, so do deep concerns about dependence. Recipients are to be forced into a totally independent and self-reliant mode of existence.

SUMMARY

American social welfare history is marked by a deep mistrust of the poor. Persistent beliefs that the poor are immoral and lacking either the ability or the desire to work have inspired repeated attempts to condition relief on work and improved behavior—and, above all, to make relief as difficult to obtain as possible. Social welfare and ensuring social justice is much bigger than simply programs to support the poor and disadvantaged such as Section 8 housing and food stamps. The federal government provides support to a variety of groups: banks requiring bailouts, farmers needing subsidies, and cities requiring federal loans to make payrolls are just some of the many acceptable forms of welfare. In these circumstances, however, bankers, farmers, and mayors do not consider themselves "welfare recipients"; rather, federal supports are viewed as necessary subsidies that benefit the community.

Workfare, training programs, and stringent program eligibility requirements, coupled with ongoing recertification in order to continue receiving even minimal assistance, are the punitive features of today's federal and state welfare systems. When it comes to poverty Americans are inclined to blame the victim as much as ever. Rather than maintaining a dignified helping system accessible to the poor, American welfare policy is designed to exclude people and to discourage clients by constantly setting hurdles to eligibility.

Throughout its history, finding the appropriate balance between public and private responsibility has plagued American social welfare. There is a clear record of national ambivalence and resistance toward welfare services and the poor. The current debate on welfare is an extension of a discussion threaded through the nation's fabric since colonial times. The lack of national consensus on who is to receive what type of social provisions for what period of time and on how these services will be funded means that the debate will continue well into the twenty-first century. Therefore, social workers are challenged to promote social justice by working toward increased and improved services for all groups within the society. This challenge supports the notion that social justice is a human issue and much more than just a legal or moral issue (Monroe, 2003). Primary importance needs to be placed on: (1) understanding the current social, political, and economic environment; and (2) using this knowledge to educate and mobilize the community and other stakeholders to work together to identify and address social problems and to develop effective programs designed to address these needs.

Movies to See

Movies on social welfare history rarely win Academy Award consideration or excite producers. The following videos, while not specifically detailing social welfare history, help us to better understand people and their conditions in the past.

Across the Sea of Time: 1920s New York City through the eyes of Russian immigrants.

All Mine to Give: Orphaned children in nineteenth-century Wisconsin are put in different homes in order to survive.

America, America: In the 1890s, a Greek youth immigrates to New York City; emotional presentation of an immigrant's challenges.

April Morning: A solid portrayal of a teenager's life in the American colonies immediately before the American Revolution.

Attacks on Culture: A brief, forty-nine minute, examination of the U.S. government's legislative attacks on Native Americans.

Autobiography of Miss Jane Pittman: An examination of life from the Civil War through the 1950s as remembered by a 110-year-old former slave.

Avalon: A Russian Jewish immigrant family moves to New York City.

Black West: An examination of African American cowboys, the unsung heroes of the West.

Grapes of Wrath: Classic John Steinbeck story of family's search for a better life than in 1930s depression Oklahoma.

The Molly Maguires: Interesting film set in the 1870s Pennsylvania coal country, as the Irish try to organize a union.

Roll of Thunder Hear My Cry: Black teen copes with depression, poverty, and racism in 1930s Mississippi.

Separate but Equal: An examination of Thurgood Marshall as the NAACP attorney whose U.S. Supreme Court case led to the end of segregation.

Sounder: A sharecropper is forced to steal to feed his family; family deals with poverty and racism in the 1930s.

Wild Women of the Old West: The stereotype of the quiet housewife is broken with this analysis of women in the 1800s.

A Woman Called Moses: An examination of the life of Harriet Ross Tubman, a fugitive slave, founder of the underground railroad, and leader in the abolitionist movement.

Quiz Answers

1. In October 1492 Christopher Columbus reached the Bahamas, marking Europe's first documented contact with the Americas.

2. The New Deal was the name given to a set of social and economic programs established under the leadership of President Franklin D. Roosevelt in the 1930s to combat the depression.

3. The Emancipation Proclamation freed slaves in areas (rebellion states) no longer loyal to the union.

4. In Seneca Falls, New York, in 1848 women rights advocate Elizabeth Cady Stanton organized a convention that generated a declaration of women's rights.

5. Earlier immigrants arrived from northern and western Europe. By 1900, there was a significant rise in people from eastern and southern Europe.

6. In the late seventeenth century nineteen people were executed for witchcraft in Salem, Massachusetts.

7. In 1845 the United States annexed most of what is now Texas. Mexico ceded the remaining land in 1848 following the Mexican-American War.

8. The Articles of Confederation, adopted in 1777, united the colonies; it created a one-house congress.

9. In 1867, William Seward negotiated the purchase of land, now Alaska, from Russia for $7.2 million. It was called "Seward's Folly" because, until the discovery of gold, people saw little value in the far away purchase.

10. Dred Scott, a Missouri slave, sued for his freedom in 1847. The 1857 Supreme Court decision held that slaves were property and had no claim to the rights of citizenship.

References

Alexander, C. A. (1997). Distinctive dates in social welfare history. In R. Edwards et al. (Eds.), *Encyclopedia of social work, 1997 supplement* (19th ed.). Washington, DC: NASW Press.

American Assembly. (1989, November). *The future of social welfare in America.* New York: Columbia University, Barnard College.

Axinn, J., & Levin, H. (1982). *Social welfare: A history of the American response to need* (2nd ed.). New York: Harper and Row.

Boyer, P. (1978). *Urban classes and moral order in America, 1820–1990.* Cambridge, MA: Harvard University Press.

Chambers, C. A. (1967). *Seedtime of reform: American social service and social action, 1918–1933.* Ann Arbor: University of Michigan Press.

Cole, B. (1973). *Perspectives in public welfare: A history* (3rd printing). Washington, DC: Government Printing Office.

Dziegielewski, S. F. (2004). *The changing face of health care: Professional practice in the era of managed care* (2nd ed.). New York: Springer.

Gilbert, N. & Specht, H. (1981). *The emergence of social welfare and social work* (2nd ed.). Itasca, IL: Peacock.

Gurteen, H. (1882). *A handbook of charity organization.* Buffalo, NY: Charity Organization Society.

Harrington, M. (1962). *The other America: Poverty in the United States.* New York: Macmillan.

Heffner, W. (1913). *History of poor relief legislation in Pennsylvania, 1682–1913.* Cleona, PA: Holzapfel.

Jansson, B. (1988). *The reluctant welfare state: A history of American social welfare policies.* Belmont, CA: Wadsworth.

Karger, H. & Stoesz, D. (1994). *American social welfare policy: A pluralist approach* (2nd ed.). White Plains, NY: Longman.

Katz, M. B. (1986). *In the shadow of the poorhouse: A social history of welfare in America.* New York: Basic Books.

Lubove, R. (1969). *The professional altruist: The emergence of social work as a career, 1880–1930.* New York: Atheneum.

Monroe, I. (2003). Becoming what we ought to be: We cannot separate our efforts to heal the world from the difficult work of healing ourselves. *The Other Side, 39,* 1, 43–45.

Palmer, J., & Sawhill, I. (1984). *The Reagan record.* Cambridge, MA: Ballinger.

Report of the Trustees and Superintendent of the Texas Institute for the Blind. (1886). Austin, TX: Tripplet and Hastings.

Rothman, D. (1971). *The discovery of the asylum social order and disorder in the new republic.* Boston: Little, Brown.

Storey, J. R. (1982). Income security. In J. Palmer & I. Sawhill (Eds.), *The Reagan experiment* (Vol. 5, pp. 361–392). Washington, DC: Urban Institute Press.

Trattner, W. (1989). *From poor law to welfare state: A history of social welfare in America* (4th ed.). New York: Free Press.

Williams, H. (1944). Benjamin Franklin and the poor laws. *Social Service Review, 18,* 77–79.

Chapter 4

So You Want to Be a Social Worker!

THERE ARE NUMEROUS JOBS FOR SOCIAL WORKERS THROUGHOUT the country in cities, suburbs, and rural communities. According to the U.S. Department of Labor (DOL), through 2010 employment opportunities for social workers will be "faster than average" (http://www.bls.gov/oco/ocos060.htm). The growth in positions will be in both public and private agencies, large and small alike. Gerontology, long-term care services, health areas, substance abuse, school social work and private practice are cited in the DOL's *Occupational Handbook, 2002–2003* as having the greatest opportunities for social workers. On any given day social work job opportunities across the country are listed in NASW News. Here is a small sample of job openings as listed by NASW on their web page in October 2003 (http://joblink.socialworkers.org/search.cfm)

> Bilingual Social Worker, work with HIV infected/affected adults and adolescents in an outpatient setting. Minimum Requirements: MSW/CSW licensing, Bilingual Spanish/English. Sensitivity to ethnic and sexual minorities. Location: Rego Park, Queens Salary: $40K.

> If you're looking for a new job, you're faced with a whole lot of choices. Choices that affect your lifestyle, your career, and, ultimately, your family. You may already know us as a world-renowned heart center or as Napa County's regional trauma center, but we're also a great place to work. If you're looking to make a change, look no further. Here, you'll find warm smiles, familiar faces and the caring hands of your friends and neighbors. Values of Dignity, Service, Excellence and Justice are an essential part of life here. As a place for your next job, put your trust in the hands of the Queen. Requirements: We are currently seeking a full-time Social Worker. This position requires a MSW, one year social work in a health care setting, excellent communication skills and knowledge of community resources.
> Bilingual/Spanish a must. We offer an exciting team environment, a fabulous location in the heart of the wine country in Napa County, outstanding benefits and competitive pay.

> A WDC therapeutic aftercare program for children and teens affected by HIV/AIDS is in search of a Children's Therapist to provide direct services for individual clients. This therapist supports and assists clients as they anticipate and cope with major life changes including separation from and/or

Name: Claire Massey

Place of residence: Longwood, Florida

College/university degrees: Rhodes College, BA, Tulane University School of Social Work, MSW

Present position: School Social Worker

Previous work/volunteer experience: Community mental health worker at state and local levels

What do you do in your spare time? I like to spend time with friends and read.

Why did you choose social work as a career? I was drawn to the field partly because I am a "people person" by nature. I was also influenced by my mother's work as a school social worker for about 7 years and her stories about the job.

What is your favorite social work story? I was once working with a young man diagnosed with paranoid schizophrenia. During an interview, he started telling me about a book he had read called The Three Christs of Ypsilanti. The book was about a psychiatrist who brought together three patients, all of whom believed they were Jesus Christ. The book told what the psychiatrist did to try to help these clients see how unrealistic their beliefs were. It became clear to me as my patient talked that he did not get the contradiction of having three Christs. Instead, the book served to support his own belief that he himself was in the process of becoming Christ. I learned that when helping clients even the best intentions may not always work, and individualized assessment and plans to assist clients are always needed.

What would be the one thing you would change in our community if you had the power to do so? I would rid the community of poverty, inadequate housing, and insufficient medical care, especially for children.

death of loved ones and the secondary losses involving transitions between caregivers, homes, schools and communities. Grief counseling is a central responsibility. When appropriate, issues around medical illness, substance abuse and HIV/AIDS are explored in depth. Emphasis is placed on building communication, anger and stress management, and social skills. Play, verbal and art therapy techniques are employed as indicated by the client's strengths and preferences. This therapist is a member of a multidisciplinary interagency team that provides comprehensive life planning services to families living with HIV/AIDS. Responsibilities include initial intake and psychosocial evaluation, detailed documentation, and heavy phone contacts with family members and other service providers and collaborators. Attendance at monthly meetings is required. S/he also provides clinical supervision for a part time group art therapist on site. Requirements: Masters degree in counseling, social work or art therapy with a minimum of three years clinical experience, preferably in the fields of medical art therapy, and/or grief counseling. Art Therapy skills preferred. Experience with children, diverse communities, WDC agencies, and persons living with HIV/AIDS strongly advised. Spanish speaking a plus.

Become a member of a multidisciplinary team and provide quality Social Work services to patients and their families. Arkansas Children's Hospital is one of the largest pediatric hospitals in the nation and serves patients and families from diverse backgrounds throughout the region. Clinician must function independently but collaboratively. Setting is fast paced, with an emphasis on outcomes driven intervention. Clinician must have knowledge of family systems, effective communication, be flexible and assertive. Major job responsibilities include clinical assessment and intervention, developing treatment plans, psychiatric evaluations, abuse work-ups, bereavement, crisis intervention and referral to community resources.

Your skills and expertise can help others live life to the fullest. We are looking for Social Workers to provide social work services and bereavement support to patients and families as part of an interdiscplinary hospice team. Full time Positions in Chiefland and Lake City. Part-time Position in Jacksonville. PRN position in Gainesville. Requirements: Requires a Master's in Social Work, current license, and 1–2 years of experience with a proven understanding of the social and emotional factors effecting patients and family during a terminal illness. Experience working with an interdisciplinary team and current Florida driver's license/insurance required.

Outpatient Partial Hospitalization Program and Mental Health Clinic seeks two MSW's to work in community based program in Williamsburg, Brooklyn. 5 minutes from Manhattan, Small setting, congenial environment and competitive benefits. Salary $43,000. Requirements: MSW and fluent in Spanish required.

Do these prospective jobs sound interesting to you? You can read advertisements of this type in every issue of NASW News, the monthly newspaper of NASW. There is an array of employment opportunities for BSW, MSW, and DSW or PhD practitioners in every state. What is probably most exciting to the job seeker is that social work positions offer a variety of challenges working with individuals, groups, families, organizations, and communities.

This chapter explores the nature of employment opportunities in the field of social work. We first discuss the educational requirements to become a social worker and the role that accreditation standards play. Then we take an overview of prospects for social workers today, presenting salary and employment projections into the twenty-first century. We conclude with tips on finding that first social work job.

THE EDUCATION OF A SOCIAL WORKER

What educational criteria are need to make a person a social worker? The answer is simple: a baccalaureate or master's degree—that is, a BSW, BSSW, or BA or BS in social work or an MSW, MSSW, or MA or MS in social work—from a program accredited by the Council of Social Work Education. When students graduate from either of these kinds of degree programs in social work, they are considered to have practice degrees. A degree in sociology, psychology, anthropology, or any other "ology" does not make a person a social worker. The major difference between a degree in social work and these degrees is that sociology, psychology, and anthropology are science-based. People who major in these fields may specialize in practice or complete practice-based courses, but they are not based in practice as social work graduates are. It is also important to note that working in a social agency for ten years, even under the tutelage of a degreed social worker, does not alone make a person a qualified social worker. Further, a doctoral degree in social work, a PhD or a DSW is not recognized as a practice degree. These programs are not regulated by CSWE, and their graduates are considered researchers, administrators, educators, or scientific practitioners. As a result, entry into the social work profession is limited, and those interested in becoming social workers must pass through at least one of the two doors.

Having said this, maybe it's not quite that simple. Not to muddy the waters, but in some states, it is possible to be licensed to practice social work without having a degree in social work. For example, some states may choose to "grandfather in"— or make exceptions for—certain individuals to practice or sit for a qualifying exam. Generally, each state sets its own criteria and deadlines for this type of exception so it is best to contact the state licensing board directly to find out if and how these exemptions are made. For example, in Alabama certain client protection workers for the state have been grandfathered in and are therefore eligible to be licensed as baccalaureate-level social workers; these individuals do not have BSWs, a standard requirement in most states. West Virginia has also used a similar practice. Caution should be exercised, however, because people who use this nontraditional door into the field of social work may be disappointed if they move from the granting state. Other states may not honor their designated status, and no appeal based on reciprocity is possible. Remember, the best way to ensure entry into the field of social work is the traditional way: earning a baccalaureate or master's degree in social work from a program accredited by CSWE. Since grandfathered exceptions are so rare and policies vary from state to state, based on state need and requirements, we'll operate on the premise that a bachelor's or master's degree is the only way to enter the profession.

The difference between someone who simply wants to help and someone who is trained in the professional skills to give help is pronounced. Nevertheless, some professionals from other disciplines feel the strong requirements that must be satisfied to qualify as a social worker are unfair. That most states require a professional social worker to have either a bachelor's or a graduate college degree in social work strikes them as elitist. In fact, they might say, a lot of good people carry out important activities on behalf of individuals in need, and these helping workers should also be considered social workers. Most professional social workers would disagree because they believe that social work is indeed a profession and, as such, must have clear rules and requirements for entry. Social workers believe that within the field professionals are expected to confront the full range of human problems and do so in multiple practice settings (Burger & Youkeles, 2004); this requires professional education as a generalist.

To support this position, let's look at some professions and see what they require for entry:

Law: Completion of a baccalaureate degree in any discipline; graduation from a law program, accredited by the American Bar Association; passage of a state bar examination. At one time, a person was able to "sit" for the bar exam without graduating from a law program. In such cases, the individual was required to have worked in a law office, under the mentorship of a board-certified lawyer, that is, one who had passed the bar exam, for a number of years. This practice is no longer allowed.

Medicine: Completion of a baccalaureate degree, preferably in the hard sciences; graduation from a medical school, accredited by the American Medical Association; passage of a state medical examination. As with law school, medical school was in the past not a requirement for practice, but that too is no longer the case.

Nursing: Education in the scientific basis of nursing under defined standards of education and concern with the diagnosis and treatment of human responses to actual or potential health problems (PDR: Medical Dictionary, 1995). Most nurses have completed their education in accredited programs and can practice at the level appropriate to their educational qualifications. For example, a licensed practical nurse has graduated from an accredited school of practical (vocational) nursing (one year of training), passed the state exam for licensure, and is licensed to practice by the state authority. Similar requirements with varying education exist for the other levels of nursing at the associate, bachelor's, and graduate levels. An individual without a degree in nursing may assist a nurse in daily routines; often this individual is called a "nurse's aide." Regardless of education nurse's aides are not nurses and cannot perform the traditional duties of nurses licensed at different levels of skill acquisition.

Physical Therapy: Completion of a baccalaureate degree, with emphasis on biology, chemistry, physics, and social sciences, or graduation from a graduate physical therapy program, accredited by the Commission on Accreditation in Physical Therapy Education; in 1998, a doctorate in physical therapy was offered by eight programs. Baccalaureate, master's, and doctoral-level practitioners must pass a state exam before they are considered qualified to practice in the area of physical therapy.

Lawyers, physicians, nurses, and physical therapists are only a few of the professions that require professional education regulated by a professional accrediting body and, usually, passage of a state examination to practice. Examples of specific requirements for entry into particular professions abound.

Up to the nineteenth century, people were not required to complete any formal education in order to enter particular professions. Rather, someone hoping to enter a profession studied and worked as an apprentice under a practicing member of that profession who was recognized as experienced. This mentoring model was acceptable for three main reasons. First, at that time the relatively small number of colleges and universities were geographically inaccessible to many. Second, since there were fewer schools, the number who could participate in higher education was limited by the availability of educators and seats. Third, few families could afford the costs of a college education. Higher education was reserved for the elite and, for the most part, white males. With these limits on access to formal education most aspiring professionals found it productive to learn under the watchful eye and guidance of a successful practitioner.

With the spread of the public state college system and the democratization of all higher education the historical barriers were slowly chipped away. As formal education became more accessible many professionals moved their courses of study from the practical to the academic setting. Social work was no exception.

Did You Know…In 2003, New York had more accredited BSW programs (28) than any other state. Counting programs in candidacy as well, New York led the nation with 30 total BSW programs. California led the nation in accredited MSW programs, with 16 for the same time period. New York (42), Texas (38), and Pennsylvania (38) led the nation in total BSW and MSW programs, while Oregon and Guam (1 each) and Wyoming, Delaware, and Montana (2 each) have the fewest BSW and MSW programs (www.CSWE.org).

The first documented educational training program in social work was a six-week-long summer institute offered in 1898. Sponsored by the New York Charity Organization Society, this program is credited with helping to found the Columbia University School of Social Work. Before this summer institute was held almost all social work training took place within agencies and was provided by agency staff. In the years that followed social work education became a fixture of higher education. By 2003 there were 710 BSW, MSW, and DSW/PhD social work programs in American colleges and universities (table 1). There were also hundreds of social work education programs in other countries around the world.

Table 1: Number of Accredited BSW, MSW, and PhD Programs

Year	BSW	MSW	PhD	BSW and MSW in Candidacy	Total
2003	437	159	78	36	710
2000	420	139	67	51	677
1998	410	126	62	53	651
1996	388	117	56	52	613
1994	382	112	55	45	594
1992	374	106	53	41	574

Source: Lennon (2002) and www.cswe.org.

The twentieth century was critical for the developing field of social work. During this time social work was transformed from a volunteer activity into an established profession requiring a clearly designed education. When apprenticeship occurs now it is intertwined with or follows a competency-based education provided within the rigorous setting of baccalaureate or graduate study.

ACCREDITATION AND WHY IT MATTERS

As an aspiring social work professional you should be aware of the accreditation standards your social work program must meet. By meeting these standards your program assures you, and others, that when you complete its requirements you will be well prepared for your future career. Because of the importance of this information we present an overview of accreditation and explain how it relates directly to your development as a professional in the field of social work.

Council on Social Work Education

The Council of Social Work Education is the primary national organization that oversees and provides guidelines for social work education in the United States. The council was organized in 1952 with the merger of the National Association of Schools of Social Administration (NASSA), which had coordinated baccalaureate education, and the American Association of Schools of Social Work (AASSW), the membership body for graduate programs (Beless, 1995). In 2003, the number of CSWE member schools included 437 baccalaureate and 159 master's accredited programs (see table 1). In addition, 67 programs were in **candidacy**, or preaccreditation status. While not regulated by CSWE, there were 36 social work doctoral programs. And approximately 69,000 fulltime and part-time students were enrolled in either BSW or MSW programs (see table 2).

Although the council was formed by the merger of two organizations that concentrated on baccalaureate and graduate education respectively, undergraduate education appeared to take a back seat to graduate studies (Leighninger, 1987). It

Table 2: Number of BSW, MSW, and PhD/DSW Students and Graduates of Accredited Programs

Year	2000	1998	1997	1996	1995	1994
BSW students	35,255	42,443	48,050	56,038	42,974	45,604
BSW degrees awarded	11,773	11,435	12,356	10,305	10,511	10,288
MSW students	33,815	31,759	35,559	35,468	32,283	33,212
MSW degrees awarded	15,016	13,660	15,058	14,484	12,976	12,856
MSW applications made, first year	30,262	34,533	40,075	44,968	43,024	46,247
PhD/DSW programs	67	62	58	56	56	55
PhD/DSW students	1,953	2,102	2,436	2,087	1,949	2,097
PhD/DSW degrees awarded	229	266	286	258	279	294

Source: Lennon (2002).

Activity...Visit the CSWE web page at www.cswe.org and look for the listing of schools, colleges, departments, and programs of social work. Compare and contrast programs from around the country; compare urban and rural programs, large and small colleges/universities. What difference, if any, do you find? What kinds of electives do programs offer? How do BSW and MSW programs differ? What patterns of interesting educational activities do you find?

wasn't until 1974 that CSWE implemented accreditation standards for baccalaureate programs. As Gardellia (1997) noted, BSW and MSW educational programs were never fully integrated—that is, they have never viewed each other as equal partners—which has created tension between the groups. Moreover, the CSWE board of directors initially included ten seats for BSW educators and twenty seats for MSW educators (Gardellia, 1997, p. 39). Today, BSW and MSW educators hold equal numbers of seats on the board of directors, but tension remains between graduate and undergraduate educators, albeit at a lower level than in the early 1970s.

For social work students knowing how CSWE business is conducted can be helpful in understanding why their educational program is organized in a particular manner. CSWE is governed by twelve commissions: Accreditation, Education Policy, Field Education, Gay Men/Lesbian Women, Minority Group Concerns,

Figure 1: Middle school students meeting with a social worker to discuss various school and family issues.

National Legislation and Administrative Policy, Women, Social Work Practice, Program Research, and Publications and Media (Beless, 1995, p. 634).

Commission on Accreditation. The primary function of CSWE is the accreditation of baccalaureate and master's degree programs. Accreditation is coordinated by the **Commission on Accreditation**, a twenty-five-member committee that includes social work educators representing both BSW and MSW faculties, BSW and MSW students, and social work practitioners. These commissioners are volunteers who are appointed by the president of CSWE for three-year terms; a commissioner may serve no more than two consecutive terms, or a total of six years. A professionally paid staff supports the commission. The commission influences the direction of social work education through such activities as maintaining and updating accreditation standards; conducting commissioner **site visits** to programs in candidacy; voting on candidacy status, initial accreditation, and **reaffirmation**; and ensuring the quality of social work education and of the commission's functions.

Educational Policy and Accreditation Standards. The **Educational Policy and Accreditation Standards (EPAS)**, written by the Commission on Educational Policy, is a critical document to social work educators and program developers. The EPAS describes in broad terms the essence of social work education at the undergraduate and graduate levels. The document is so important to education that accreditation standards require social work students to be familiar with it. As a social work student you need to be aware of this policy statement, and if your program is being reaccredited, you might be asked to tell the site visit team what you believe it says.

The EPAS pronounces on a number of different subjects, including the curricular content and educational context to prepare students for professional social work practice. According to the EPAS, the BSW is the entry-level degree, and a BSW practitioner's interventions are developed within a **generalist practice** framework. The MSW is the advanced practice degree, and an MSW practitioner's interventions are developed within a **specialist practice** framework.

Generalist and specialist social workers can be characterized as follows:

Generalist: A social work practitioner whose knowledge and skills encompass a broad spectrum and who assesses problems and their solutions comprehensively. The generalist often coordinates the efforts of specialists by facilitating communication between them, thereby fostering continuity of care.

Specialist: A social work practitioner whose orientation and knowledge are focused on a specific problem or goal or whose technical expertise and skill in specific activities are highly developed and refined. (Barker, 2003)

Accreditation Standards for Social Work Programs

Educational Content for Baccalaureate and Master's Programs. The EPAS requires all social work educational programs include a liberal arts perspective and professional foundation content. The liberal arts perspective, according to the Commission on Accreditation, enriches understanding of the person-environment context of professional social work practice and is integrally related to the mastery of social work content. . . . It provides an understanding of one's cultural heritage in the context of other cultures; the methods and limitations of systems of inquiry; and the knowledge, attitudes, ways of thinking, and means of communication that are characteristic of a broadly educated person. (CSWE, 1994, pp. 99–100, 138)

That is why before you were allowed to enroll in your social work classes you were required to complete several courses in certain liberal arts. The completion of these courses satisfies part of the social work program's liberal arts educational requirement. Content areas completed most often are English, additional electives in the arts and humanities, science, history, political science, sociology, anthropology, and psychology. A point to remember: accreditation standards do not specify liberal arts courses that must be completed; rather it is your program faculty who have identified courses they feel will prepare you for the social work program's course of study.

According to the EPAS, the specific content of the professional foundation "is essential to the practice of any social worker, . . ." The professional foundation is the same for all accredited educational programs (see box 1). A BSW student in New

---

Box 1: Professional Foundation of Social Work Ethics

Social work values and ethics: Specific social work values and ethics and their implications for social work practice.

Diversity: Value and richness of human diversity and the impact on the social work process.

Promotion of social and economic justice: Dynamics and results of economic and social injustice, including all forms of social oppression and discrimination.

Populations at risk: People of color, women, and gay and lesbian persons; other at-risk populations related to the program's mission.

Human behavior and the social environment: Theories and knowledge focusing on the human bio-psycho-social development; those systems in which individuals live; and those systems that impact the system development.

Social welfare policy and services: History, mission, and purpose of the social work profession; methods of policy analysis and the development of social policy, including political and organizational systems.

Social work practice: Generalist social work practice with individuals, families, groups, communities, and organizations.

Research: Scientific approach to the evaluation of social work practice.

Field practicum: Work in a social services agency during which time the student engages in supervised social work practice to apply classroom learning.

York studies the same foundation content as a BSW student in Austin, Texas. As a result, the professional foundation is common ground for all social workers whatever their individual agency settings, client populations, practice functions, or practice methods. This common educational content is a real asset. In particular, the professional foundation helps supervisors and coworkers to know what new social workers have been taught and what has been stressed in their formal education. No such uniformity in educational content exists for some related disciplines such as the various counseling specialties.

Baccalaureate in Social Work (Educational Model). The typical baccalaureate social work program begins in the sophomore year of college and requires four to five semesters of study. Accreditation standards demand some form of admission process. Limited access programs require a formal application and review process for admission. Admission may depend on such criteria as cumulative grade point average (GPA), successful completion of the liberal arts requirements, reference letters, and a narrative statement. In programs that are not limited access, admission depends on successful completion of the liberal arts requirements. Whether access to a program is limited or not depends on school policy.

> *Activity...Meet with a social work advisor to discuss your program's admission process. Is the program a limited access program? What is the application process? Are all applicants accepted into the program? What are some of the reasons people are denied admission to the program? Explore with the advisor the program's liberal arts requirements. Why are these specific courses required? Are you surprised by some of the required courses?*

Accreditation standards require that students receive at least 400 hours of field education, though a particular program may demand more than this minimum. Programs currently use a number of models to address the **field placement** requirement. One option is "block placement," in which the student is assigned to an agency full time, forty hours a week, for an entire semester. A second approach, "concurrent placement," assigns the student to an agency one to three days a week while the student takes courses, usually for two semesters. A third approach combines concurrent and block placements: concurrent placement is made in the student's junior year of study and block placement in the senior year. This approach allows the student to be assigned to different agencies. What's more important to remember is that whatever field model your program uses, you must complete at least 400 hours in the field practicum. Because this requirement is set forth in the accreditation standards your program is very unlikely to allow modifications or exceptions.

Master of Social Work (Educational Model). Professional education at the master's level requires the equivalent of two academic years of full-time study and combines two components, foundation and specialization, in the program of study.

The professional foundation content is the same as for baccalaureate programs and is most often studied in the first year. Specialization takes place during the equivalent of the second year of full-time study and builds on the foundation education. According to the social work educational model, specialization must be firmly rooted in the foundation content. A specialization can be designed around different areas of social work practice (see box 2); second-year courses and field education should reflect this specialization area. Accreditation standards demand that MSW students complete at least 900 field hours. Students complete two placements, one in the foundation year and another in the specialization year, and these must total to a minimum of 900 hours.

Box 2: Specialization Models

Methodology: Specialization by intervention, such as critical social work, community organization, or group work

Setting: Specialization by agency setting or type, such as child welfare, mental health, criminal justice, rural practice, or gerontology

Population group: Specialization by a specific client population, such as children, families, women, and seniors

Problem area: Specialization by a focused problem, such as alcohol, tobacco, and other substances, mental illness, family violence, and poverty

Combination: Combination of specialization, such as methodology and population growth, for example, clinical social work with children.

A common complaint among newly enrolled first-year graduate students is that their field placements are not in their intended areas of specialization. Students need to remember, however, that first-year field placements are intended to be generalist in nature and to allow students to apply foundation knowledge, theories, and skills studied in the classroom. Specialization knowledge, theories, and skills are developed in the equivalent of the second year of study; it is at this point that specialization placements occur.

Students choosing a graduate program should know that not all programs offer a choice of specialization; some provide only one track of advanced study. A colleague has remarked that when reviewing admission folders for her graduate program, she feels that students know little about the program they are applying to. One student, for example, wanted to study administration, but the school only offers a clinical specialization. The student had a GPA of 3.8 and a Graduate Record Exam (GRE) score of 1,175. The admission committee, nevertheless, rejected the student's application because the student's career interests did not match the school's mission and curriculum. The applicant was very angry and complained about his rejection. Even when the committee's rationale was explained to him, he did not accept the decision, saying "What I want to do professionally has nothing to do with the type of program I want to apply to." The moral of this story: Make sure that your career goals match the school's mission and educational program.

Name: Maryann Petri

Place of residence: Palm Bay, Florida

College/university degrees: University of Central Florida, BSW, MSW

Present position: Counselor/Educator

Previous work/volunteer experience: Alzheimer's Association, Case Management and Guardianship Services

What do you do in your spare time? I enjoy playing water sports, bowling, and karaoke.

Why did you choose social work as a career? I chose social work because I enjoy engaging in social change activities and advocating for better conditions for the aged. Many times elderly individuals may be left to feel helpless and useless and I enjoy helping them and their families to prepare for the future and adapt to existing social conditions.

What is your favorite social work story? My favorite social work story is one that involved a homeless man suffering from pneumonia. The man was admitted to a nursing home for short-term care while he recovered. Although he did not need long-term care, he remained at the facility for approximately three years because he had no one able to support his return to the community. He had a married daughter who lived out of state with her new husband. Her husband felt that the responsibility of caring for his elderly father-in-law was overwhelming and awarded power of attorney and limited guardianship to the agency where he resided. I worked for many months to reunite my client with his family. I advocated for his veteran benefits and helped the family work through the issues that were preventing reunification. He was later reunited with his daughter and son-in-law.

What would be the one thing you would change in our community if you had the power to do so? I would acquire a state-mandated allotment of funds to provide parenting classes to all pregnant mothers- and fathers-to-be.

Advanced Standing (Educational Program). Some graduate programs offer "advanced standing." Advanced standing, which is limited to graduates of CSWE baccalaureate programs, allows these students to have certain courses waived because they learned the content in their baccalaureate studies. Advanced standing reflects the EPAS stipulation that a graduate program not require course work to be repeated once it has been mastered.

Social work is the only profession that offers an advanced standing option in its educational model. Even within social work advanced standing is very controversial in both theory and practice. The profession's ambivalence toward advanced standing is seen in its inconsistent application. Some programs waive the entire foundation year of study while others limit the exemption to one or two courses, some require successful completion of content-specific examinations, and some programs do not offer an advanced standing option at all. Some programs require BSW practitioners to enroll in the graduate program within a specific time period, ranging from four to seven years, following their baccalaureate graduation; otherwise, they are not eligible for advanced standing and are required to complete the regular two-year curriculum.

PhD/DSW (Educational Program). CSWE does not regulate doctoral study. As a result, doctoral programs differ in required courses, program structure, and specialization. Generally, a doctorate is required for people who teach in BSW or MSW programs. While not required for agency practice, there is a small, but growing trend in agencies to hire upper level administrators who hold doctoral degrees.

Two types of doctoral degrees are associated with social work, the PhD and the DSW. The PhD is the familiar Doctorate of Philosophy; DSW designates a Doctorate in Social Work. Basically, the two degree are more similar than different. When doctoral programs first originated in the field of social work, the DSW was awarded. As time passed and social workers were hired as educators, schools changed the doctorate to a PhD, and today that is the more common designation in academia. Both degrees require approximately the equivalent of two years of full-time study, passage of a comprehensive qualifying examination, and successful completion of a written dissertation. It is important to remember, however, that because doctoral-level programs, unlike master's and bachelor's programs, are not accredited by CSWE, careful exploration to find the right match between student and program is essential.

SOCIAL WORKERS TODAY

According to U.S. Department of Labor (2003) employment projections through the year 2010, social work is projected to be among the fastest growthing professions with lower unemployment and steady pay. A 1998 *U.S. News and World Report* special issue on careers identified social work as one of the "20 hot job trends" with growing opportunities.

The Department of Labor identified 468,000 social work jobs in 2000; 33 percent of these jobs are in state, county, or local government, but as the government contracts for more and more services from the private sector, many jobs will shift to private agencies (http://www.bls.gov/oco/ocos060.htm). According to Gibelman and Schervish (1997, p. 5), the number of people employed in social work and holding social work degrees will range from 645,000 to a high of 693,000.

Activity…Contact your state's department of labor. The agency is usually located in the state capital and may have an 800 number. Find out the department's employment projections for social workers in your state. Do the data match national trends?

No single information source provides a detailed overview of social work employment. One starting point is Gibelman and Schervish's (1997) analysis of the NASW membership. Their study, though based on a self-reporting survey of NASW members and thus not representative of all degreed social workers, nevertheless gives useful insight into the profession.

What Are Social Workers Paid?

Probably of most interest to people considering social work as a career is salary: how much can I make? Well, you won't be poor, and you'll be able to live a comfortable life. Current information on salaries are not available, but we can see that in the recent past the average income, while modest, was comfortable. Table 3 reports NASW's recommended minimum salary scale for employers, which is meant to be modified to reflect regional differences. These NASW data are somewhat old, reflecting 1990 salaries, but they give a starting point. In 2000 as part of Social Work Month, the annual celebration of the profession held every March, NASW noted that median salaries (50% above and 50% below) were $35,000 for an MSW and $25,000 for a BSW (www.nasdc.org/NASW/SWMonth2000/salaries.htm). Median social work salaries by setting were hospitals ($35,000), federal government ($46,900), child welfare ($32,000), and colleges and universities ($50,000). For more accurate salary information you may check with your local college or university career services office or with the state NASW chapter.

Table 3: Social Work Annual Income: NASW members: Social Work Employment/ Self Employment

	Under 30,000	30,000–39,000	40,000–49,999	50,000–59,999	60,000–79,999	80,000 or more	
*2001	22%	20%	18%	16%	14%	9%	Median Annual Income: $44,400.00
1999	24%	22%	17%	13%	14%	6%	Median Annual Income: $41,290.00

Information from: Social Work Income: NASW: Practice Research Network, 2:1, 2003.
*2001 salaries obtained from 2002 survey information.

The median salary for social workers in the mid-1990s was $34,215. Average salary by practice area ranged from a high of $40,472 (occupational social work) to a low of $33,158 (aging). Other practice areas included mental health ($39,626), school social work ($38,871), criminal justice ($36,963), medical health ($36,340), and children/families ($34,865).

As might be expected salary increased with education. Forty-six percent of BSWs earned between $20,000 and $30,000 while 67 percent of PhD/DSW holders earned more than $40,000. The largest proportion of MSWs, 38 percent, earned between $30,000 and $40,000.

Agency administrators' average salary was $44,147, followed by educators ($40,780), researchers ($40,347), policymakers ($38,445), trainers ($48,076), clinical practitioners ($35,355), and community organizers ($34,620).

Helpful Tips for Applying to Graduate School

There are more applicants to graduate programs than there are seats available. As a result, people are rejected. So, how do you strengthen your chances for admission?

1. Determine what you wish to do as a professional. You need to have a good idea of the type of work you wish to pursue—the more specific you are, the easier your application choices will be. Do you want to work with children or seniors, or doesn't it matter? Do you want to develop knowledge in clinical social work or community practice? Are you interested in developing expertise in mental health, criminal justice, or some other setting?

2. Identify the graduate programs that match your career interests. Begin with the CSWE web site, www.CSWE.org, and look at the various graduate programs. Contact those programs that interest you and ask for an "MSW application packet" and "graduate bulletin."

3. Be sure to follow the application process as outlined. Don't deviate from the school's application procedure, deadlines, or requirements; if you do, you are virtually guaranteeing your rejection.

4. Keep copies of all application materials. On average, each graduate program receives 385 applications. A university's graduate office probably processes thousands of applications. In short, it is easy for papers to be lost given the large number of applicants.

5. Don't pester the school by calling to ask what is happening with your application. What did the application packet and graduate bulletin say about letting you know? Call only after an excessive amount of time has passed from the stated notification date.

6. Your GPA is one of the most important pieces of information schools use in the admission process. While a high GPA doesn't guarantee admission, a low GPA doesn't help.

7. Recognize that reference letters are important, but most applicants generally receive strong letters. Admission committee members generally look at what letters do not say rather than what they say.

8. Most programs require the applicant to submit a written statement or responses to certain questions. Without a doubt this is one of the most critical items in the application packet. The written statement gives the admission committee the only direct vehicle to your soul. Be sure to answer all questions, and most important, make sure your statement is grammatically correct. Yes, spelling counts! A sloppy, poorly written paper tells the committee a great deal about how you approach your work. Treat the statement as the most important document you have ever written. Spend time with it. Have friends read it with a critical eye; take their comments seriously.

9. No matter how high your GPA and GRE score might be, you are not entitled to be accepted into any graduate program. No one is guaranteed acceptance into a limited access program. Assume that you will be rejected and that you need to work to minimize your liabilities and maximize your strengths.

As with any profession, gender discrimination exists. In 1995 men earned on average $37,503 compared to $34,135 for women in the mid-1990s. Gibelman and Schervish (1997, p. 135) found that the women's salary was below the median salary. Salary discrimination based on ethnicity was minimal, according to Gibelman and Schervish (1997, p. 136), and not statistically significant.

You can also get a feel for salaries by reading your local newspaper's classified advertisements (FYI-Sunday classifieds are your best bet for finding the most advertisements in the classified section). Also check with your college or university's Career Service Office and see what information they might available.

Activity...Check out the New Social Worker Online *web page (www.socialworker.com). You'll find a number of discussion boards and chat rooms dealing with a variety of topics, including careers, ethics, student forums, general items, announcements, and resource recommendations. Questions about jobs and salaries are hot topics on this web site.*

Where Do Social Workers Work?

To better understand where job opportunities might be, let's look at social work practice from four interrelated perspectives: job function, auspices, setting, and practice area:

Function: What Do I Do?

Direct service	Supervision
Management/administration	Policy development/analysis
Consultant	Research
Planning	Education/training

Auspices: Where Do I Work?

Public, local	Private nonprofit, sectarian
Public, state	Private nonprofit, nonsectarian
Public, federal	Private for profit, proprietary
Public, military	

Setting: What Type of Agency Do I Work In?

Social service agency	Nursing home
Private practice, self-employed	Criminal justice system
Private practice, partnership	College/university
Membership organization	Elementary/secondary schools
Hospital	Non–social service organization
Outpatient facility	Group home

Practice Area: What Is My Practice Area?

Children and youth	School social work
Community organization/planning	Services to the aged

Family services   Alcohol and other substance abuse
Criminal justice   Developmental disabilities
Group services   Occupational
Mental health   Public assistance

Any set of choices, one from each list, defines a social work position. For example, you can be a supervisor (function) in a private nonprofit, sectarian (auspices) nursing home (setting), providing services to the aged (practice area). Or you might provide direct service (function) in a public, local (auspices) outpatient facility (setting) as an alcohol and substance abuse counselor (practice area). The thousands of potential combinations demonstrate the versatility of social work employment opportunities.

Another way to discover the breadth of the social work profession is to examine CSWE studies of social work education programs. Each year the Council collects these data in order to track the state of the profession and to detect possible trends in education. In its 2002 study the Council identified fourteen different practice area concentrations in most social work schools (see table 4). The data in table 4 reinforces the impression of diversity in social work, although mental health, child welfare, and family services stand out as the three most popular concentrations among students.

**Table 4: Fields of Practice among 32,214 Graduate Students in 2000
in Social Work Education**

Field	Percentage of Students	
	1996	2000
Aging	2.7%	1.7
Alcohol or substance abuse	1.5%	.7
Child welfare	7.8%	7.4
Community planning	1.0%	1.5
Corrections	1.0%	.6
Family services	7.4%	6.8
Group services	.4%	.4
Health	5.1%	4.3
Mental health	11.0%	9.7
Mental retardation	.3%	.2
Occupational social work	.8%	.5
Public welfare	.2%	.1
Rehabilitation	.2%	.2
School social work	3.5%	3.1
Other	3.7%	7.1
Combinations	2.6%	2.4
Not determined	21.6%	17.9
None (methods only)	29.2%	35.3

Source: Lennon (2002).

GETTING A SOCIAL WORK JOB AFTER GRADUATION

There's no secret to finding a job, whether in social work, law, nursing, or any other profession: it takes a great deal of hard work and a lot of patience on the part of the job seeker. While jobs in general are available, it takes time to find the one that is right for you. A rule of thumb is that it takes three to four months to find a job from the time you begin your search in earnest. So if you want to have a job by June, you'll need to have your resume prepared and your search strategy developed and implemented no later than the preceding February.

A note of caution: Be prepared not to get the one job you've always wanted. Even for the most experienced social worker a job rejection letter hurts. Great jobs are waiting for competent social workers—they key is finding a position in which you can make full use of your knowledge, skills, and potential.

Did You Know…In 2003, of all social workers
90% of NASW members hold MSW degrees

40% of NASW members are employed in mental health

the average social worker is employed for 16 years and, on average, earns $45,000 annually

93% of NASW members are licensed or regulated by their state

40% of the American Red Cross volunteers are social workers

there are more clinically educated social workers than psychiatrists, psychologists and psychiatric nurses combined

over 170 social workers hold local, state, or federal elected office

there are 21,000 NASW members in the New York State and New York City chapters of NASW

Source: https://www.socialworkers.org/nasw/default.asp

Prepare Your Resume Carefully

Be sure your resume is up to date. You can get an easy-to-use resume software program at the college bookstore or computer store. There are also any number of books on resume writing that you can review. Ask your academic advisor or some other social worker for tips and ideas about what to highlight. Consider taking advantage of your school's job placement office by attending a resume-writing workshop. But recognize that most helpers in the resume-writing process are not well versed in social work; their work is geared to a general audience and does not reflect the nuances of social work. The key is to ask social workers in the field what they did and what they listed on their resumes.

Be sure your resume is clean and as error free as possible—no spelling errors, no photocopies with wrinkled edges, and so on. Your resume is your introduction to a potential employer, and you want to make the best impression possible. Consider writing an initial goal or objective for the type of work you want to do in the field. Be sure to link the contents of this statement with the job you are applying for. You may not have much paid clinical or administrative experience, so be sure to highlight volunteer experiences and start with your most recent field placement. For other tips and suggestions present a draft of your resume to a favorite social work instructor or a social worker in the field. Listen to their suggestions carefully because they have been through the employment process; hearing their "words of wisdom" *first* might save you a great deal of time and effort later.

Attend Local NASW Meetings or Meetings of Other Professional Groups

To facilitate your job search, attend local NASW meetings as often as you can. You can begin to network by attending meetings and becoming active with this group as soon as you declare your major. Dues for a student are a real bargain! Simply contact your state NASW office for information about your local unit and for the name of a contact person. You should be able to get an NASW membership application from your school's social work office or through the state NASW office.

While attending local NASW unit meetings you'll make new friends, begin to develop a professional network, and keep abreast of issues within your new social work community. Moreover, the monthly or bimonthly meetings often include time for members to announce job opportunities. Most people would be surprised at how much information about job openings and availability is spread by word of mouth and through these types of informal networks. For example, you may even get firsthand information on a position that has just become available from the contact person within the agency.

> *Activity…Attend a local NASW meeting. Talk to members about finding jobs and see what hints they can give you.*
>
> *Get on the World Wide Web and see what kind of jobs you can find in at least five different states. Try looking in large cities as well as small towns.*
>
> *Read a number of job announcements and look for qualifications that are minimum requirements versus those that are preferences.*
>
> *Visit your school's job placement office. See what the staff recommend about putting together a job search packet. Remember, it's never too early to begin collecting material for your resume.*
>
> *Put together a draft resume and pass it around asking for suggestions on how to make it better.*

Use Your Field Placement Experience

Each student must complete a field placement. Don't be surprised if your field agency offers you a position following graduation. The field site has the luxury of assessing your work; if you do an excellent job the agency may ask you to consider moving into a regular position. An agency benefits from hiring a field placement student who has already worked in the agency, because this "new" employee can be moved into a regular position more quickly and with less orientation time. Furthermore, there is little need for an initial skill and knowledge assessment period because the agency, through the internship experience, is well aware of the student's practice abilities and thus the level of supervision needed. Employment in a field placement agency also has advantages for the student accepting the job. The student already knows the agency and how she will fit into the overall organization. Based on direct experience the student knows that it is the setting in which she wants to start a social work career.

Read Local and National Newspaper Advertisements

Local newspapers, *NASW News*, and your state NASW chapter newsletter publish countless employment announcements. Familiarize yourself with the range of jobs that are available as well as the jobs that interest you the most. Read each advertisement carefully, and when you apply for a job be sure to follow the instructions; if it asks for a resume and the names of three references, provide just that— no more and no less.

Look closely at the words used in the announcement. Words such as "must have" or "minimum" or "required" signal baseline qualifications that the successful candidate must possess. For example, if the announcement requires an MSW degree and five years of post-MSW experience, don't apply if you are a newly graduated BSW or an MSW with three years of experience. On the other hand, words such as "should have" or "preferred" signal not minimum criteria but preferences. These words introduce the agency's wish list for the desired candidate, and employers understand that they often don't get everything on their wish lists. Let's say you find an interesting job for which you meet the minimum requirements but not the preferences, go ahead and apply.

Use the Internet

If you'd like a job outside of your local area, the World Wide Web and the Internet can be your best friends. Through the Web you can locate newspapers, state NASW offices, and employment services across the country. Use the Web's search engines to identify employment opportunities.

Get to Know Your Social Work Faculty Advisors and Instructors

One of your best sources of employment information and strategies is your program faculty. They are very interested in your success, they have years of experience, and they know people in the field in the surrounding community who can help you. Your social work teachers have probably had contact with most local agencies, and a good word, phone call, or reference letter from a faculty member can be one of your greatest aids in getting your first job.

Don't forget that many programs use adjunct or part-time faculty to supplement their full-time faculty. Adjunct faculty members who are employed full time in the community can help you in your job search because they are tied into the local informal social work network.

Did You Know...All states have some form of licensing or regulation of social work practice, but in many states such regulation is limited to MSW or advanced practice and does not apply to BSW practice. Be sure to check with your academic advisor to learn more about your state's particular licensing requirements.

NASW also regulates MSW and advanced social work practice through the Academy of Certified Social Workers (ACSW). A practitioner with an ACSW certification meets the following criteria: 1) NASW membership; 2) MSW degree; 3) two years or 3,000 hours of post-MSW experience; and 4) passage of a multiple choice examination, given after the experience requirement is satisfied. A social worker does not need to have the ACSW, but state law may require a practitioner to be licensed.

Explore Your Social Work Student Association or Club

Your program's social work student association or club can help in your job search. The association can invite area agency directors to provide workshops or panels on finding a job. The club can also sponsor a job fair on campus at which area agencies set up booths, distribute agency information, and recruit potential employees. The fair can be coordinated with the program's field office and the local NASW unit. Probably the best time to hold a job fair is in the spring, when most potential graduates are looking for jobs.

A job fair is a win-win-win situation. Students win because they have immediate access to potential employers. Agencies win because the fair is a cost-effective recruiting mechanism that reaches a large pool of potential job applicants. The social work program and university win because the job fair is a positive public relations tool that strengthens ties between the university and the community.

Last Thoughts about Your Job Search

We often get caught up in salary and look for the best-paying jobs. Yes, salary is important, but consider other aspects of the job as well. Who works at the agency? What kind of colleagues will you have, and can you learn from them? Your first job will be a major source of knowledge and experience. Will the job be exciting and offer you a variety of learning opportunities? What kinds of benefits are in place? These can range from health care and vacation time to pets—one organization allows staff members to bring their pets to work each Friday. (Now what does that say about the organization?)

A few years ago, a student came into the office very excited about a job offer she had received in New York City as a childcare worker. She said, "I'm getting a great salary. They're going to pay me $30,000!"

But what does $30,000 mean to a new, twenty-one-year-old social worker? Sounds like a great deal, but not really. Use the Web to find salaries for comparison purposes; the easiest way is to search for "salary converters." For example, as you can see in table 5, $30,000 in one city means something quite different somewhere else.

Table 5: A Salary of $30,000 in Houston, Texas, in 2003, Is the Same As . . .

City	Salary
Hartford, CT	$30,852
New York City (Manhattan)	84,823
Orlando, FL	30,339
Chicago, IL	54,218
Los Angeles, CA	43,692
Santa Fe, NM	36,092
Portland, OR	35,892

Source: http://www.homefair.com/homefair/calc/salcalc.html.

Remember that you need to be happy with what you find. Make sure the setting offers you an opportunity for continued professional growth and self-fulfillment. Don't focus only on the salary—there is much more to a job than money!

SUMMARY

Students entering social work will find the field rich in opportunities. The profession's future is bright.

In embarking on a professional career in social work the selection of an educational program is important. A social work career should begin with either a baccalaureate or a master's degree, and this degree must come from a CSWE-accredited program. Request admission information directly from the programs you are interested in attending. Programs are located in every state in the United States and throughout the world. (See appendix D for U.S. programs.) Be sure to gather information early so you have plenty of time to prepare what is required. Some baccalaureate programs have open admission, while others use a formal admission process. Admission to graduate programs, on the other hand, is usually competitive, and about 40 percent of applicants are turned down.

Employment possibilities for social workers can be found in both public and private settings. They involve a wide range of activities and tasks and a variety of practice areas. Simply stated, practice opportunities for social work professionals are open and diverse.

The key to a successful work experience in social work is planning your education carefully—whether BSW or MSW—and making the most of it. Take advantage of your educational opportunities to develop new knowledge, theories, and skills that will make you more competent. Remember, before you can help the individuals, groups, families, and communities that you will serve, you must first help yourself to be the best equipped professional, with the best foundation of education and training possible.

References

Barker, R. L. (2003). *The social work dictionary* (4th ed.). Washington, DC: NASW Press.

Beless, D. W. (1995). Council on social work education. In R. Edwards et al. (Eds.), *Encyclopedia of social work* (19th ed., pp. 632–636). Washington, DC: NASW Press.

Burger, W. R. & Youkeles, M. (2004). *Human services in contemporary America*. Belmont, CA: Brooks Cole.

U.S. Department of Labor, Bureau of Labor of Statistics. (2003). *Occupational handbook*, 2002–2003 edition. Washington, DC: U.S. Government Printing Office.

CSWE Council on Social Work Education. (2003). www.cswe.org.

CSWE Council on Social Work Education. (1994). *Handbook of accreditation standards and procedures*. Alexandria, VA: Author.

Gardellia, L. G. (1997). Baccalaureate social work. In R. Edwards et al. (Eds.), *Encyclopedia of social work, 1997 supplement* (19th ed., pp. 37–46). Washington, DC: NASW Press.

Gibelman, M., and Schervish, P. H. (1997). *Who we are, a second look*. Washington, DC: NASW Press.

Leighninger, L. (1987). *Social work: Search for identity*. Westport, CT: Greenwood.

Lennon, T. (2002). *Statistics in social work education in the United States, 2000*. Alexandria, VA: CSWE.

PDR: Medical Dictionary. (1995). *PDR medical dictionary* (1st ed.). Montvale, NJ: Medical Economics.

U.S. News and World Reports: 1998 career guide. (1997, October 27).

Part **II**

The Practice of Social Work

Chapter 5

Social Work Practice

STEVE, AN UNDERGRADUATE SOCIAL WORK STUDENT, STOPPED BY to see one of the authors in his office. Steve was enjoying his introduction to social work class, he had not missed a session, and he believed his final grade would be high. Steve often had questions to ask and really enjoyed taking part in class discussion, so it was no surprise when he asked a question: "So, how do you do it?" Not quite sure what he meant by "it" the instructor asked Steve to clarify what "it" was. Very seriously he said, "You know, social work. How do you 'do' social work?"

Today, some twenty years after this visit, Steve, who now has an MSW along with his BSW degree and is employed in a public mental health facility, laughs about that question. "I guess I was looking for that magical pill you give a client, the one thing we do to help a person in pain. I just believed that social workers had a bag of tricks that 'poof' solved the person's problems. How wrong I was."

Pondering how exactly to "do" social work is where most professionals start, and even for seasoned practitioners, the quest never ends. Steve, like so many beginning social workers, was unsure of what to do in social work practice and was hoping for a simple answer. Wouldn't it be wonderful if the unique and ambiguous challenges of human life could be easily addressed by giving a pat answer, taking a simple pill, or using a standard procedure. It's tempting, but wholly unrealistic. If social work practice required nothing more than simple prescriptions, then there would be limited need for formal education beyond the basics, for supervision, or for continuing education.

In fact, the practice of social work stems directly from the mission of the profession, which is not simple or standardized. If you look at the definition of social work set forth in chapter 1, you'll be looking in the right direction for practice guidance. Social workers seek to enhance social function, promote social justice, and help people to obtain resources.

Did You Know... The number of social work jobs doubled in the 1930s, from 40,000 to 80,000, as public sector income maintenance, health, and welfare programs were created in response to the depression (NASW, 1993).

Changes in the detailed definition of social work have occurred over time, yet the basis for social work practice has not changed:

Name: Rey C. Martinez

Place of residence: Las Vegas, New Mexico

College/university degrees: University of Hawaii, BA, Boston University, MSW, Florida State University, PhD

Present position: Associate Professor and Research Chair

Previous work/volunteer experience: Assistant Professor: University of Texas, El Paso, Program Evaluator for the Viet Nam Veteran Families Project, Adjunct Faculty at Florida State University, Assistant Director for a Campus Alcohol and Drug Resource Center

Why did you choose social work as a career? My dad taught high school Spanish and was a wrestling coach. His personal commitment to helping each student/athlete had a tremendous impact. Similarly, my mom was employed by DHHS. As a strong client advocate, she often assisted non-English speaking persons in court.

What is your favorite social work story? A student once confided "Soy horrible en matematicas y temeroso de numeros" (I am terrible at math and afraid of numbers). Señora Beltran not only overcame her fear of statistics, but one evening was so engrossed in her work that she lost track of time and neglected to inform her adult children of where she was. Fearing the worst, the family called the police and began checking local hospitals. We had a good laugh at the graduation party but at the time it was not funny.

What would be the one thing you would change in our community if you had the power to do so? Northern New Mexico suffers from tremendous drug problems, particularly with black tar heroin. More treatment services are needed, especially those that can work with the entire family system. Drug abuse does not occur in a vacuum. Parents, spouses, siblings, and other family members need support and guidance to break from the vicious cycle.

Today's definition: Social work is the professional activity of helping individuals, groups, or communities to enhance or to restore their capacity for social functioning and to create societal conditions favorable to their goals (NASW, 1993). Barker (2003) goes on to say that "social work is the applied science of helping people achieve an effective level of psychosocial functioning and effecting societal changes to enhance the well-being of all people" (p. 408).

Traditional definition: "Social work seeks to enhance the social functioning of individuals, singly and in groups, by activities focused on their social relationships which constitute the interaction between man [individuals] and his [or her] environment. These activities can be grouped into three functions: restoration of impaired capacity, provision of individual and social resources, and prevention of social dysfunction" (Boehm, 1959, p. 54).

The tasks that social workers undertake, the agencies in which they work, and the social policies they support are aimed toward three overarching goals: to enhance client social functioning, to remedy client dysfunction, and to promote social justice (Hepworth & Larsen, 1986, p. 13–15). BSW and MSW educational programs, through course work and field practicum experiences, develop the necessary value-driven knowledge and skills to support social work practice.

UNDERSTANDING DIVERSITY

Although today's definition of social work may seem simple, recognizing the diversity, uniqueness, and complexity in what constitutes individuals, groups, or communities needs further exploration. As a professor of social work and a practicing clinician, one of the authors was asked by a student "how come in class you rarely give case examples of what might be considered the traditional family?" The response was clear: "If you mean the traditional family as constituting the biological parents with 2.4 children, who have never been divorced, etc., I rarely get them on my caseload." At first, this statement may seem shocking, but these changes remain reflective of our current social times. In fact, today's traditional family may be better characterized as yesterday's nontraditional family. Diversity of family includes those units headed by a single parent, by gay or lesbian partners, and by a grandparent or other relative, and inter-racial units.

Today, in practice, it has become evident that the basics of what has traditionally constituted social structure and expectations within individuals, family groups, and communities has changed.

When seeking to understand individuals and families, the uniqueness, worth, and dignity of each individual and family system must be recognized. Social workers are expected to recognize these differences through a nonjudgmental lens or perspective that embraces diversity rather than discourages it. This requires that social workers become familiar with what is considered ethical practice as well as implement all practice strategy in the most nonjudgmental way possible. From this perspective individual dignity and worth stand at the forefront of all helping activities. Social workers will actively be engaging with many individuals of different social classes, genders, races, ethnicities, gender and social orientations as well as differing belief systems and spiritual views. Furthermore, the awareness of this type of diversity will be coupled with varying personal and social problems, including individual health and mental health problems, family issues, racism, sexism, and violence, just to name a few. Therefore, for practice to be effective with individuals, it must be transactional. In transactional practice each event is viewed in multiple dimensions, and case-specific factors, practice models, ethical principles, and issues of power must all be considered (Mattaini, 2001). Furthermore, each event is shaped by contextual factors such as agency practices, natural networks, and social institutions. Social workers must not only be aware of these changes but also must be aware of how to utilize knowledge of these changes to help individuals, families, groups, and communities enhance or restore their capability for social functioning.

So often, under the guise of "diversity," we lump or group an entire population and from there make broad sweeping assumptions. For example, consider the term "Hispanic": what comes to mind when you hear someone refer to a person or family as "Hispanic"? From a U.S. Census perspective, "Hispanic" includes all people of Latin or Mexican decent or origin. As a result, people from Cuba, Mexico, Argentina, Brazil, and Spain, for example, are all "Hispanic." Yet would you say the culture, its traditions, mores, and folkways are the same for each these nations, or do you think a person from Cuba is different from an Argentine? Of course, Cubans are very different from people from Argentina as well as from Mexico, Brazil, and Spain.

The consideration of human diversity for social work practice requires that we reflect on and consider how such diversity impacts our worker-client relationship and ensuing problem-solving process.

Although there are numerous potential examples that highlight the need for recognition of diversity and expanding beyond the traditional definition of the family, the African American child provides one case in point. For example, all children use their cultural experiences to interpret their immediate surroundings, the interaction of others, and the interpersonal patterns of society. Similarly, culture and family are the first two powerful influences that determine how children of any culture understand, internalize, and act on what is expected of them by their family, community and the larger society (Dziegielewski, Leon & Green, 1998). Yet, in the case of African American children, frequent discriminatory experiences provide these children with additional information and feelings to decipher and understand. During times of emotional or psychological turmoil, human nature requires that African American children strive for meaning in their lives, using their "cultural lens"—their values, beliefs, and experiences. In social work practice, these children present a rich and complex biopsychosocial picture that requires examination of the biological, psychological, and social factors within a historical and cultural framework (McAdoo, 1997). In order to address issues of individual diversity and to carry out this task efficiently, culturally sensitive social workers must be aware of their own values, the African American child's values, and how both relate and integrate with the larger society in which all must co-exist. Ridley (1995, p. 10) noted that even the most sincere, caring and ethical practitioner can be guilty of "unintentional racism." Therefore, all helping professionals who provide services to African American children need to be sensitive to the culture of these children.

To address diversity, develop cultural sensitivity, and provide effective services, social work practitioners need to recognize, understand, and appreciate geographic and regional differences among children of color (Gonzalez-Ramos, 1990).

Although the primary experience of the African–American child today may reflect the influence of American society, the impact of the family's place of origin should not be minimized. The African–American family today may have values and traditions from northern states, southern states, or Caribbean areas. Similarly, family values may reflect differences in urban versus rural expectations and traditions (Congress, 1997). Congress (1997) recommends that social workers identify appropriate tools to conduct culturally sensitive assessments. One such tool is the culturagram that takes into account different aspects of the culture and empowers families to perceive their specific culture as important within the larger society. Families are also empowered to examine their problems as stemming from cultural clashes between the family's culture and that of the mainstream society.

THE BASICS OF PRACTICE

It is important to recognize, however, that you will be introduced to practice in only general terms in parts 2 and 3 of this book. You will not be qualified to do social work after reading these chapters. Remember, your career in social work is just beginning and numerous courses and field experiences are in front of you. It is these that when put together will provide you with the foundation for social work practice. This chapter will review the basic concepts related to the delivery of social work services and examine the helping process and its application to the practice of social work.

Before we begin to explore the "doing" of social work, however, we need to remind ourselves that the practice of social work is intended to achieve the profession's purpose of helping clients. A question that must be explored is: Why have you decided that this is the profession for you? Be honest with yourself as you explore the areas of social work practice and decide which holds your interest the most. The initial motivation for many helping professionals comes from wanting to learn more about themselves and their families. This is not unusual, nor is it particularly problematic. However, when this is part of your motivation for choosing the field you must be ultra-aware that the helping services you provide are not designed to help you—they are for the client. Other typical reasons for choosing a helping profession include the need to be needed, the desire to give something back to society and humankind, the need to care for others, and the desire for prestige and professional status. As you embark on a helping career it is essential first to examine what motivated you and why. Later, ask for feedback from other professionals who know you, particularly your social work teachers and professionals experienced in the field. Remember, choosing a career path is not simple or quick. Nor is staying in the field automatic. For many of us, the pressures created by the kind of work we do require constant self-examination throughout our educational and professional careers. Some students may decide relatively early that this is not the work for them. After all, a helping career is not the best choice for everyone, and it is a good idea to establish this before putting a great deal of time, effort, and expense into pursuing it.

*Activity...*Is Social Work Practice Really For Me? *On a piece of paper write the following questions and answer them individually. For this exercise you may at first feel more comfortable answering them by yourself. Later you may choose to discuss your answers with your instructor or academic advisor. Feel free to add questions to this list. You might also want to save your answers and revisit them later in your professional career.*

What first attracted you to the profession of social work?

What needs of your own are likely to be met by serving as a social worker?

Who in your life has been instrumental in helping you choose this career?

Have you ever received help from a social worker? What did you like most about this person? What did you like least?

What do you believe you can contribute to the field of social work?

In what ways do you believe this profession can help to make you feel like a better person?

CONCEPTS ESSENTIAL TO SOCIAL WORK PRACTICE

We have described social work practice as both art and science. The art of social work involves the sensitive coordination of complex activities to help clients. The science entails selecting, merging, and understanding potentially voluminous amounts of information and applying the conclusions to a specific case situation. While many are successful in learning the science of the profession, the art is difficult to acquire. The interplay of art and science means that effective social work practice grows from the relation between knowledge, skills, and values and ethics (see box 1). Social work practice requires unique skills, either specialized or gener-

Box 1: Dynamic Interplay of Knowledge, Values and Ethics, and Skills

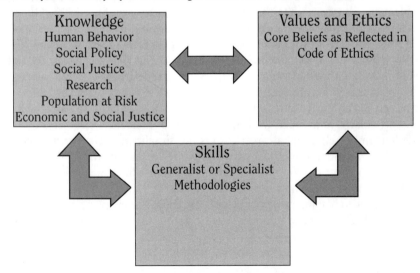

Knowledge
Human Behavior
Social Policy
Social Justice
Research
Population at Risk
Economic and Social Justice

Values and Ethics
Core Beliefs as Reflected in
Code of Ethics

Skills
Generalist or Specialist
Methodologies

alist in nature, that are derived from specific knowledge areas and guided by a clear, fundamental set of values and ethics.

Skills

That we speak of "doing" social work implies that a social worker has a set of specific skills that she uses in practice. These skills, which are inseparable from the helping process, include the ability to perform critical tasks in working with clients: basic communication, exploration, assessment and planning, implementation, goal attainment, termination, and evaluation of the services rendered (Hepworth, Rooney, & Larsen, 2002).

Skill building and acquisition are the bridge between values and knowledge and all subsequent social service activities (Vass, 1996). Unless knowledge and values underlie skills the practice of social work is undefined and vague. Social workers must have basic competencies in the following skill areas:

- *Cognitive skills*, including analytic skills and the capacity to evaluate and understand research
- *Administrative skills*, including record keeping and report writing
- *Interpersonal skills*, including verbal and nonverbal skills, understanding, self-awareness, use of authority, working with diversity, working in partnership, and the ability to make and sustain positive working relationships
- *Decision-making skills*, including authority and responsibility
- *Use and management of resources* (Vass, 1996, p. 63)

A social worker must be able to balance many critical aspects of the practice relationship with each client. For example, the worker must first establish and then maintain a worker-client environment of trust. In this environment the client can feel safe when revealing emotions and thoughts that might disturb an untrained practitioner, because for the skilled worker the ethical values of client worth, dignity, and self-determination are paramount. The worker also must know how and

---

Did You Know...Often you will hear social workers discuss "an empathetic relationship" or read in the social work literature about the importance of "empathy" in the social work process. What is the difference between empathy and sympathy? It was once described as follows:

Sympathy *is what you feel when you begin actually to feel the pain of the client. In a sympathetic relationship the helping professional cannot be objective or render the nonjudgmental intervention required. Say, for example, you wear a size 8 shoe and your client wears a size 7. If you actually put the client's shoes on your own feet, your feet will be so squeezed that you cannot concentrate on the issues the client is facing.*

Empathy, *on the other hand, is what you feel when you remain in your own shoes while imagining what it is like for the client in his or her situation. The client's situation is assessed based on direct observation and information provided by the client or people from the client's environment. In an empathetic relationship the helping professional uses objective and subjective information and professional helping skills to truly understand the client's situation and the pain that the client is experiencing.*

when to approach those of the client's problems that need further explanation and exploration. The skilled social worker is well versed in empathetic communication and helps the client to clarify and confront what may be difficult issues to address. In short, the skilled professional social worker is an expert at establishing a positive worker-client relationship in which problem identification, helping, addressing, and subsequent healing can take place.

Knowledge Base

The practice of social work is based on a specific body of scientifically tested knowledge. Practice evolves from the knowledge base as social work skills first developed in the academic curriculum later mature through field experiences and continuing education. Without the appropriate knowledge base and awareness of the theoretical constructs that undergird professional practice, skills would be nothing more than a series of unrelated actions that cannot address total person-in-situation who is at the heart of professional social work practice. Conversely, knowledge evolves from current practice through practice-based research and evaluation of social work interventions. Without such research and evaluation, social work knowledge would quickly become static, outdated, and unfounded.

In many ways, knowledge drives all of a professional's daily actions with and on behalf of clients. Knowledge supports practice in its efforts to be client centered and directed to the unique situation of each client. The knowledge base of professional practice premises, skills, and techniques allows social workers to choose the specific set of skills clearly embedded in a theoretical framework that best apply to a particular client situation. In other words, to achieve client-centered practice, the professional knowledge base must come first.

To create a consistent and comprehensive knowledge base of professional practice all social work educational programs require mastery of foundation content in nine areas: social work practice, human behavior and the social environment, social welfare policy and services, social policy, field practicum, research, diversity, social work values and ethics, populations at risk, and promotion of social and economic justice (see box 1 in chapter 4).

Knowledge needs to be directed toward three areas for the development of integrated, competency-based social work practice:

♦ *Knowledge that informs the social worker about the client*: Psychology, sociology, social problems, social policy, and antidiscrimination.
♦ *Knowledge that helps the worker plan appropriate intervention*: Social work practice theory and models of intervention, methods of social work intervention, and processes involved in social work intervention.
♦ *Knowledge that clarifies the worker's understanding of the legal, policy, procedural, and organizational context in which his practice occurs*: Federal, state, and local public legislation; social welfare policy and procedures; and organizational contexts (Vass, 1996).

Values and Ethics

Values and ethics are the third critical component of social work practice. At the start of your social work education, perhaps during the application procedure itself, you were probably introduced to our professional Code of Ethics. This document can be called an "ought to" guide: it specifies how social workers ought to conduct themselves and their helping activities in the professional setting. We cannot emphasize too much of the importance of becoming familiar with this code from the very start of your career and learning how it will apply to your practice activities.

Activity...As a class or by yourself look at the NASW Code of Ethics, in appendix A, and think about how it will shape your practice experiences. Which parts of the code do you find comforting and compatible with your beliefs? Which parts are more difficult for you to understand or support?

All professionals embrace specific values. Although social work values are spelled out in a number of documents, the primary reference for the profession's value base is the NASW Code of Ethics (reproduced in appendix A). The code establishes a set of clear beliefs that define ethical social work practice and thus act as a unifying force among all social workers (Reamer, 2001). The way we work with and on behalf of others, how we view social issues, and the remedies we consider for individual, group, or community ills are all firmly rooted in our value base. Reamer (1995, p. 894) identified the following core values for the social work profession:

- Individual worth and dignity of people
- Respect for people
- People's capacity for change
- Client's right to self-determination
- Client's right to confidentiality and privacy
- People's right to opportunities to realize their own potential
- Social change
- People's right to adequate resources and services to meet basic needs
- Client empowerment
- Equal opportunity
- Antidiscrimination
- Diversity
- Willingness to transmit professional knowledge and skills to others

As you read the code and consider Reamer's points, several common themes begin to emerge, but let's look at three in particular.

First, all people, no matter who they are or what their circumstances, should be treated with respect and civility. Respect and civility are cornerstones of a just society. We show respect in any number of ways: being on time for appointments, and apologizing to clients when we're late; calling people Mr. or Ms. until they ask us to do otherwise; listening to others without interruption, and without looking at our watches during interviews.

Second, when given the opportunity, people have the ability to participate in solving their own problems. We understand that not all people can participate fully in such processes, but we also recognize that everyone should be encouraged to participate as much as possible. We support client participation when we help them to figure out ways to identify and deal with their problems; we do not say, "If I were you, I would . . ." Clients have strengths, and we must help them to discover and use these strengths as energy sources for change.

Third, although it's not stated explicitly in the code or among Reamer's points, we can infer the basic principle that we do no harm to people. Our work is to help not harm. We cannot hold back any effort if we believe it will help our clients.

As you become more familiar with the Code of Ethics, compare it with other value statements, such as that of the International Federation of Social Workers (appendix B). What similarities do you find? The words and phrases may be different, but the respect for the human condition and the goal of social change are the same.

As professionals, social workers must pursue the art of helping within a context shaped by values and ethics. Practice that is not guided by values or ethics has no meaning because such practice will fail to recognize the unique circumstances of our clients, their individual needs, and appropriate change strategies. Unless we operate within an ethical framework our clients might as well be telling their problems to a computer!

DIFFERENTIATING BETWEEN GENERALIST AND SPECIALIST SOCIAL WORK PRACTICE

Social work practice is organized around two principal conceptual models, the generalist and the specialist. Generalist social work is more broadly defined and targeted toward a wider variety of clients and problem areas. Specialist social work is more narrowly defined with a sharper focus on specific issues or a particular client population.

Generalist Practice

Landon (1995) has asserted that regardless of how hard the profession has tried, there still is no completely agreed upon definition of generalist practice—although he did believe consensus existed on key elements of the definition. First, most professional social workers agree that generalist social work practice is primarily reserved for BSW social workers, although a few graduate programs now offer a specialization reflective of additional course work in the area of advanced generalist practice. Second, generalist social workers are prepared for entry-level social work practice. Last, in generalist practice social workers most often apply

some type of "systems approach" to professional practice and subsequent intervention. According to the *Social Work Dictionary* a social work generalist is a practitioner "whose knowledge and skill encompasses a broad spectrum and who assesses problems and their solutions comprehensively" (Barker, 2003 p.176).

The broad-based generalist approach to social work practice integrates the client's needs with those of the environment. In accepting the importance of the person-in-situation social workers are leaders in understanding and interpreting the interaction between behavioral, psychological, and social factors in the client's condition with environmental factors that the client faces daily.

Generalist social work follows a multilevel integrated process for addressing the interplay between personal and collective issues applying it to a variety of human systems, such as societies, communities, neighborhoods, complex organizations, and formal groups, as well as individuals and families (Miley, O'Melia, & Dubois, 1998). According to Miley, O'Melia, and Dubois (1998), generalist practice depends on four major principles. First, generalist practice recognizes the importance of human behavior and the connection between this behavior and the social and physical environments that surround each human being. Second, generalist practice understands that changes in the client's environment must include changes in systems interactions to better the environment for all affected. Third, generalist practice works at every level of a system to assist in bringing about needed changes. Last, generalist practice assists in macropractice while also conducting research on the efficacy and effectiveness of the approaches that are used.

Specialist Practice

The specialist social worker provides a more focused, higher level of intervention. A specialist always possesses an MSW degree and is prepared for advanced social work practice. According to the *Social Work Dictionary* a specialization is "a profession's focus of knowledge and skill on a specific type of problem, target population, or objective" (Barker, 2003, p. 415). Social work specializations have developed in a number of ways over the years. One comprehensive scheme categorizes the various social work specializations into eight different types:

Models
- *Methods*: casework, group work, community organization
- *Fields of practice*: school, health care, occupational social work
- *Population groups*: children, adolescents, and elderly people
- *Problem areas*: mental health, alcohol and drug abuse, corrections, mental retardation

Specific Factors
- *Geographic areas*: urban, rural, neighborhoods
- *Sizes of target*: individual (micro), family group (mezzo), and community (macro)

Name: Sandra F. Brown

Place of residence: Cape Elizabeth, Maine

College/university degrees: Colorado College, BA, Simmons College School of Social Work, MSW

Present position: Clinical social worker for Scarborough Schools, and private practice in Portland, ME.

Previous work/volunteer experience: Clinical social worker, outpatient department, Jackson Brook Institute; licensed clinical social worker, Child Abuse Treatment Team, Somerville Mental Health Clinic; licensed clinical social worker, Italian Home for Children. Fund-raising for Center for Grieving Children, Hurricane Island Outward Bound School, Kids First Center.

What do you do in your spare time? Run, play tennis, ski, hike, kayak, and garden.

Why did you choose social work as a career? I was certified to teach in undergraduate school, but found that I was more interested in the student's lives, struggles, and families, and how I might help on that level.

What is your favorite social work story? I worked with a family who had two children who were placed in residential treatment for several years. This father had never been considered as a viable parent for these children, and when given the opportunity, worked hard and became a consistent, loving parent to his children. This father worked hard to learn parenting skills and how to manage on a day-to-day basis with his boys, in spite of his own challenges. Both children were able to leave residential treatment and live with their father.

What would be the one thing you would change in our community if you had the power to do so? I would increase the mental health services for both children and adults and get rid of the stigma that is often attached to those seeking mental health services.

♦ *Specific treatment modalities*: behavior modification, ego psychology, Gestalt therapy, cognitive therapy
♦ *Advanced generalist* (Hopps & Collins, 1995, p. 273)

After an extended period of MSW practice, the specialist worker is eligible for independent practice. Through state licensing laws for practice (see chapter 15 for a fuller discussion of licensing and regulation of social work practice) and professional practice certifications the MSW practitioner can move into private practice or practice independently within the agency context.

Social work is one of the most diverse fields of practice imaginable. Specialist social workers are found in numerous settings: public and private agencies, public and private hospitals, clinics, schools, extended care facilities, private practice, private business, police departments, courts, and countless other workplaces, too numerous to name. But the multiplicity of practice specializations has created a major weakness, a professional Achilles' heel if you may. Meyer (1976) said it best when she wrote, "[Whereas] other professional specialists become expert by narrowing their parameters, social workers have had to increase theirs." This diversity in practice and settings makes it difficult for the broader community to understand what social workers do. And given the wide range of our specializations, any attempt to reduce or narrow our efforts will, as Hopps and Collins (1995) suggested, create tension, conflict, and fragmentation within the profession.

In summary, generalist and specialist social workers have different focuses. Specialization of social work practice usually occurs at the master's level. Specialist social workers are all first trained in the generalist approach to practice and later embark on more specialized career tracks by choosing more concentrated areas in which to apply their skills. It is also in specialization that many professional educators believe "real" training as counseling professionals and therapists occurs. MSW social workers with supervised experience (and certification or licensure) are usually free to engage in full non–clinically supervised counseling activities. In the field of social work, the master's degree is generally considered the terminal practice degree. For those studying at the doctorate (DSW or PhD) level the focus is on research or science rather than clinical practice.

THE EMERGENCE OF EVIDENCE-BASED SOCIAL WORK PRACTICE

It is safe to say that the public expects high-quality service and "state of the art" care (Shortell & Kaluzny, 1994). Whether we pay for services directly through out-of-pocket costs or indirectly with our tax dollars, we want to receive the best services possible. These expectations extend to social workers, and indeed, the profession itself expects all services and activities performed on behalf of clients to be of the highest quality. Yet how do we demonstrate to the public that our activities are effective?

Social workers have historically been accused of avoiding the use of empirical techniques to establish practice efficiency and effectiveness. As we move into an era of professional accountability and client rights, however, all this has changed. Challenges made to the profession to prove service effectiveness and ensure that interventions are germane to client issues are being embraced.

The challenge to tie evidence-based research and evaluation to practice is not new. For example, in 1978 Fischer wrote the following:

> It seems to be difficult to avoid the conclusion that unless major changes are made in the practice methods—and hence, the effectiveness—of casework, our field, if not the entire profession of social work, cannot long survive. Indeed, unless such changes are made, it is not clear that as a field, we deserve to survive. On one hand, we have the option of choosing—and building—a new revitalized future for social casework, one rooted in the superordinate principle that our primary if not our sole allegiance is to serve our clients with demonstrable effectiveness. On the other hand, we can

continue our outmoded practices, denigrate and resist new approaches to practice, and bury our collective heads in the sand when confronted with the vaguest hint of a threat that we may not be doing all in our power to provide effective services. (p. 310)

The new revitalized casework that Fischer envisaged is today called **evidence-based social work practice**. All social workers, generalist and specialist alike, are expected to apply its principles to their activities. The Social Work Dictionary defines empirically–based social work practice as "a type of intervention in which the professional social worker uses research as a practice and problem-solving tool; collects data systematically to monitor the intervention; specifies problems, techniques, and outcomes in measurable terms; and systematically evaluates the effectiveness of the intervention used" (Barker, 2003, p. 141).

For the beginning social work professional, it is important to understand that in evidence-based social work practice, the application of clear-cut research and evaluation models is guided by four broad ideas. First, research findings must be relevant to practice by assessing the change in a client's level of effectiveness after a specific intervention directed at a specific problem. Second, applications, practice and evaluation models, and findings are to be drawn from research reports. Third, research findings are to be disseminated so that the results are known in the practice community. Finally, other social work professionals should be able to interpret, understand, and apply what they read to what they do. Evidence-based practice mandates that in developing a practice intervention with a client, the practitioner must include systematic research activities that will provide feedback on the intervention's effectiveness, controlling for bias, while being potentially replicable (Thyer, 2001). In addition, the practice intervention may give additional information on how the client's ability to resolve the problem can be strengthened.

THE STEPS IN PROFESSIONAL HELPING

Work with clients in social work practice has five steps. These are illustrated in box 2. Note that evaluation is not a distinct step but rather takes place throughout all steps of the social work process.

Step 1: Problem Identification

The first step involves problem identification. The social worker helps the client to identify and concretely define the problem(s) to be addressed by the intervention process.

The role of the worker is clear: to apply logical thinking to identify the beginning, the end, and the dynamics of the problem (Ragg, 2001). The client's problems are discussed thoroughly, and the client is made aware that the social worker is serious and dedicated in his efforts to help. It is in this initial step of the helping process that the social worker establishes the rapport that will characterize the remainder of the practice experience. A working alliance is developed that allows

---

Box 2: Social Work Process

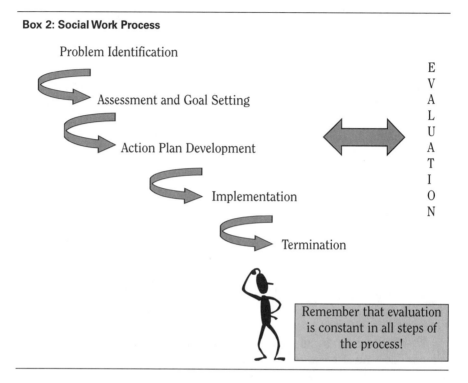

Problem Identification

Assessment and Goal Setting

Action Plan Development

Implementation

Termination

E
V
A
L
U
A
T
I
O
N

Remember that evaluation
is constant in all steps of
the process!

---

the client to begin to feel comfortable yet eager to embark on changes. The practitioner avoids simply giving advice to the client.

The social worker is a professional who at all times remains objective in educating, advocating, facilitating, and intervening on behalf of the client. Moreover, as ironic as it may sound, the social worker always begins to plan for termination of the practice encounter early. In fact, as will be explained in chapter 6, termination should be discussed and decided in the first session. The client is thus well aware of what is coming and what needs to be accomplished by the end of the therapeutic term.

At the end of each session or meeting the technique of "summarization" is used. The client is asked to state what was covered in the session and what progress was made in regard to the identified goals and objectives. Never summarize the session content for the client: it should always be done in the client's own words. Letting the client state what he or she got from the session helps the social worker to determine what really was accomplished and whether both client and social worker are aiming toward the same intervention outcomes.

It is also during this initial step that the social worker decides how accountability or practice effectiveness will be evaluated after the intervention is completed. Exactly what will be measured, and how, varies from case to case. No "magic pill" ensures evidence-based practice. We hope, however, that knowing its importance piques your interest in the research course you have yet to take.

Step 2: Assessment and Goal Setting

The second step involves helping the client to set goals and objectives that can be accomplished (Dziegielewski, 2002). Worker and client assess the client's need for assistance and how specifically the problem can be addressed. The "goal" is the overall end that the client wants to accomplish and the "objectives" are the concrete steps that the client will take to get there and that allow measurement of the outcome (Dziegielewski, 2002). Setting goals and objectives, when done adequately, has the following valuable consequences:

♦ Ensures that worker and client agree on intervention focus and purpose
♦ Provides to the client how to address the problem, while providing a basis for continuity of session content across the intervention process
♦ Provides a basis for selecting appropriate treatment strategies
♦ Assists the social worker to structure session content and monitor progress of the intervention
♦ Gives outcome criteria (the objectives) for measurement of intervention effectiveness

When setting goals and objectives the following always apply. First, the goal and objectives must relate to what the client wants to achieve at the end of the intervention. Second, the goals and objectives must be defined in explicit terms so that the client knows what is expected of him or her. Third, the objectives must be feasible. Clients must believe they can succeed in the process, otherwise they may become disheartened and drop out of the intervention process. Fourth, the goals and objectives must be consistent with the skills and abilities of the helping professional. Social workers should never try to address medical problems that they know little about. For example, if the social worker does become unsure of her abilities, supervision, consultation, and continuing education options should be explored before the social worker goes any further in the intervention process. Ensuring quality of services in this way is important for the client and the social worker.

Fifth, whenever possible, goals and objectives should be stated in positive rather than negative terms. Sixth, all goals should be mutually negotiated with the client; however, if you have reservations about a goal or objective you must say so. Clients need your input in their decision making. Be sure, though, that your hesitation reflects concern for the client's good and not your own personal bias.

Step 3: Action Plan Development

Once goals and objectives have been clearly identified, the social worker helps the client to develop a plan of action. The role of the social worker is paramount in identifying strategies for action and change. The worker may be able to provide the direct supervision or consultation necessary to implement the plan. Often, however, the social worker does not have the required expertise—he may be a generalist when a specialist is needed—and will contract with another provider or use work strategies to assist the client in meeting the objectives.

The action plan may include one task or a series of tasks. Each task is specific and clear and supported by a time frame to be monitored by both worker and client. Each task builds on previous efforts, and together they lead to the goals and objectives identified. As with goal setting, each task must be understood by both client and worker and, most important, must be within the client's ability to achieve.

Every action plan must have clearly established contingency plans. These plans specify what the rewards will be for completion of the practice strategy agreement and what the consequences will be for noncompliance. Clients must participate in this part of the change process because they will be the ones who must accept the consequences of their action or inaction.

Step 4: Implementation

Implementation takes place when the client is ready to put the plan into action. During implementation, the worker and client together monitor the client's progress; this activity is part of the evaluation that is the empirical side of our practice. Therefore, practice evaluation is basically a determination as to whether there has been useful improvement with the problem situation (Corcoran, Gingerich & Briggs, 2001). Through monitoring, worker and client are able to assess progress toward the goal, judge the effectiveness of the intervention and/or tasks, examine the client's reactions to the progress or lack thereof, and enhance motivation (Hepworth, Rooney & Larsen, 2002). Ongoing monitoring also allows worker and client to identify barriers as well as strengths in the process. New strategies can be built to overcome or cope with the barriers. And most important, monitoring provides the client with feedback on positive experiences that in turn reinforce the change efforts.

Implementing an action plan can be intimidating for a beginning social worker. Social work practice knowledge is essential because the social worker will be expected to use multiple practice strategies to assist the client. These can involve the application of planned skills such as modeling, behavioral rehearsal, role playing or simply the use of paper-and-pencil exercises in which the client writes down feelings experienced as well as steps to be completed in the action plan. Referrals for additional help and assistance should also be considered and discussed at this time—for example, additional individual therapy, group therapy, couples therapy, or family therapy.

Step 5: Termination

The last step in the social work process involves termination. Client and social worker end their working relationship and describe how any change strategy that has been developed will be continued. Many clients realize at termination that they want additional help. If this happens, the social worker informs the client of options for continued intervention and emotional growth by giving appropriate referrals. Referrals for group therapy, individual growth-directed therapy, couples therapy, and family therapy can be considered.

Evaluation and Follow-Up

Successful practice intervention achieves significant changes in a client's levels of functioning and coping. Measures that can substantiate these changes are essential to evidence-based practice. Measuring intervention effectiveness can be as simple as making a follow-up phone call to discuss how things are going, or as structured as scoring the client's behavior on a standardized scale at the beginning of treatment and at the end and then comparing the two. Scales that measure depression, trauma, and so forth, are readily available. If more advanced methods of measuring practice effectiveness are expected, more advanced training and planning are warranted.

Planned practice evaluation and follow-up at the termination of intervention is essential, but these are steps that have historically been forgotten. As a matter of fact, when you consider the five steps in the social work process, research and evaluation seem to be missing. And if these are missing, how does the process we've outlined lead to empirically based social work practice? In fact, they're not missing—it's simply that they're not a separate step: research and evaluation should be included at each step of the helping process.

PRACTICE APPLICATION: THE ROLE OF THE MEDICAL SOCIAL WORKER

Ms. Martha Edda had been living with her family for approximately a year. Before then she had lived independently in her own apartment. Ms. Edda had to leave her apartment after a neighbor found her unconscious. The apartment was unsafe, with rotted food, urine, and feces throughout. Upon discovery, Ms. Edda was immediately admitted to the hospital. Originally, she was believed to have had a stroke; later she was formally diagnosed with a neurological condition called "vascular dementia." Doctors believed that she was in the moderate to advanced stage of this condition because Ms. Edda, at age 62, had pronounced movement and memory difficulties.

After discussion with the hospital social worker, it became obvious that Ms. Edda needed a supervised living arrangement. Joan, Ms. Edda's daughter, admitted how guilty she felt about what had happened to her mother, but she did not feel she could handle her mother at home. The social worker reminded Joan that the family would be able to benefit from Ms. Edda's receiving services from a home health care agency and that a community daycare program could be explored. After convincing her family to give it a try, Joan took her mother home.

Once in Joan's home, Ms. Edda did receive home health care services. However, much to her daughter's surprise all services stopped after just two months because

Figure 1: An elderly man leaves a rural West Virginia home after a visit from a home healthcare worker. In many such rural areas there is a shortage of physicians and medical facilities.

Ms. Edda's physical therapy was discontinued. Joan relied heavily on these services, particularly the nurse's aide who helped to give Ms. Edda a bath. Ms. Edda weighed 170 pounds and could not help in getting herself into or out of the tub. Joan recruited the help of her husband, who reluctantly agreed. Unfortunately, Ms. Edda could not get into the adult daycare center in the area because no spaces were available. She was placed on a waiting list. Ms. Edda required help with all of her activities of daily living, and her daughter was afraid to leave her at home alone during the day. So Joan quit her job to help care for her.

On the morning of January 12, Joan found her mother lying face down in her bed. She had become incontinent of bowel and bladder, she was unable to speak, and the features appeared distorted on the left side of her face. When Joan could not rouse her mother she panicked and called an ambulance. Ms. Edda was immediately transported to the emergency room.

In the emergency room, the staff began to run numerous tests to see if Ms. Edda had suffered a stroke. Plans were made to admit her to the hospital, but no beds were available. Because Ms. Edda needed supervised monitoring and a hospital bed might become available in the morning, an agreement was made to keep her in the emergency room overnight. In the morning she was admitted to the inpatient hospital. While in the hospital Ms. Edda remained incontinent and refused to eat. She was so confused that the nurses feared she would get out of bed and hurt herself, so she was placed in restraints for periods throughout the day.

After two days most of the medical tests had been run and were determined to be negative, and Ms. Edda's vital signs remained stable. The physician felt that her admission to the hospital could no longer be justified, and the social worker was notified of the pending discharge. On placing the call to prepare Ms. Edda's family for her return home the social worker was told that the family would not accept her and that they wanted her placed in a nursing home. The social worker was concerned about this decision because she knew that Ms. Edda did not have private insurance to cover a nursing home stay and she was too young to be eligible for Medicare. This meant that an application for Medicaid would have to be made. This state-funded program had a lower reimbursement rate, and most privately run nursing homes drastically limited the number of Medicaid clients they would accept. After calling around the social worker was told that no beds were available.

When the social worker explained her discharge problem to the physician, he simply stated, "I am under pressure to get her out, and there is no medical reason for her to be here. Discharge her home today." Since it was after 4:00 p.m. and the administrative offices had closed for the day, the social worker planned to try to secure an out-of-area placement the following day.

When the physician returned at 6:00 p.m., he wanted to know why the client has not been discharged. The nurse on duty explained that a nursing home bed could not be found. The physician became angry and wrote an order for immediate discharge. The nurse called Ms. Edda's family at 6:30 p.m. and told them about the discharge. Ms. Edda's family was angry and asked why she was not being placed in a nursing home. The nurse explained to the family that discharge orders had been written and she was only trying to do her job. Ms. Edda's daughter insisted on speaking to the discharge physician prior to picking up her mother. A message was left for him, and at 8:00 p.m. her call was returned. The physician sounded frustrated when he told Joan that all medical emergencies had been addressed and Ms. Edda had to leave the hospital immediately. Ms. Edda's daughter became furious and yelled, "If she is still incontinent and in restraints, how do you expect me to handle her?" Hearing how upset Joan was, the physician softened his voice and said, "I will put the nurse on the phone to update you on her condition. In addition, the social worker will call you in the morning to arrange home health care services."

When Ms. Edda's daughter arrived at the hospital, her mother was hooked to an IV, wearing a diaper, and still in restraints. Pleased to see a member of Ms. Edda's family the nurse sent for a wheelchair, unhooked the intravenous tubing, removed the restraints, and helped place Ms. Edda in the wheelchair for transport to the family's car.

Discussion. Unfortunately, situations like this one continue to exist. This case example is a true depiction of events. The social worker was responsible for discharge planning, but many other issues needed to be addressed to best serve the client and her family. With perseverance, and the help of the hospital social worker Joan was eventually (several months later) able to place her mother in a nursing home. However, the strain on Joan was so great that she ended up asking to be placed on medication to combat depression. Joan also began to fight with her husband and children over numerous issues related to the time required for her mother's care and the loss of the second source of family income. As in most American families, her earnings were used not only to supplement basic needs (rent, food, etc.) but also to pay for family luxuries (movies, eating out, etc.). It is clear that in such situations the price of the "cost effective" managed care strategy far exceeded the dollar value placed on it: the client and her family became silent victims. The role of the social worker—officially labeled a "discharge planner"—is involved considerably more than just finding a place for the client to go. Referrals, counseling, and openness to service flexibility make the social work professional an invaluable member of any interdisciplinary team. (The case scenario is adopted from Dziegielewski, 2004).

SUMMARY

Social work practice evolved from mid-eighteenth- and nineteenth-century efforts to assist the poor. In those early years activities were carried out by volunteers, with few organizational supports and limited training if any. Today the profession has a well-established knowledge base, a clearly articulated value orientation, and diverse practice methodologies and interventions, all of which are transmitted to the new practitioner through formal educational processes.

The practice of social work is generally conducted in one of two major frameworks: the generalist and the specialist. That the profession has both members who can work with a wide range of clients and members who can focus more sharply on particular groups of clients is our greatest strength. This is the reason we find social workers in so many different types of social agencies and organizational settings.

Social work practice has never been static. It has evolved dramatically since its beginnings, and it will continue to change in the future. To grow and adapt, practice must be conducted within a systematic, well-thought-out process that allows both the use and the production of scientifically tested knowledge and skills and that is founded on a clear, coherent set of professional values.

References

Barker, R. L. (2003). *The social work dictionary* (5th ed.). Washington, DC: NASW Press.

Boehm W. (Ed.). (1959). *Social Work Curriculum Study* (Vol. 1). Washington, D.C.: Council on Social Work Education.

Congress, E. (1997). *Multicultural perspectives in working with families*. New York: Springer.

Corcoran, K., Gingerich, W. J., & Briggs, H. E. (2001). Practice evaluation: Setting goals and monitoring change. In Briggs & Corcoran (Eds.), *Social work practice: Treating common client problems* (pp. 66–85). Chicago: Lyceum.

Dziegielewski, S. F., Leon, A.., & Green, C. (1998). African American children: A model for culturally sensitive group practice. *Early Child Development and Care, 147* (44), 83–97.

Dziegielewski, S. F. (2004). *The changing face of health care practice: Professional practice in the era of managed care* (2nd ed.). New York: Springer.

Dziegielewski, S. F. (2002). *DSM-IV-TR* in action*. New York: Wiley and Sons.

Fischer, J. (1978). *Effective casework practice: An eclectic approach*. New York: McGraw-Hill.

Flowers, J. V., Miller, T. E., Smith, N., & Booraem, D. C. (1994, April). The repeatability of a single-session group to promote safe sex behavior in a male at-risk population. *Research on Social Work Practice, 4* (2), 240–247.

Gonsiorek, J. C. (1982). Results of psychological testing on homosexual populations. In W. Paul, J. D. Weinrich, J. C. Gonsiorek, & M. E. Hotvedt (Eds.), *Homosexuality: Social, psychological and biological issues*. Beverly Hills, CA: Sage.

Gonzalez-Ramos, G. (1990). Examining the myth of hispanic families' resistance to treatment: Using the school as a site for services. *Social Work in Education, 12*, (4), 261–274.

Hepworth, D. H., & Larsen, J. A. (1986). *Direct social work practice: Theory and skills* (2nd ed.). Chicago: Dorsey.

Hepworth, D. H., Rooney, R. H., & Larsen, J. (2002). *Direct social work practice: Theory and skills*. Pacific Grove, CA: Brooks/Cole.

Hopps, J. G., & Collins, P. M. (1995). Social work profession overview. In R. Edwards et al. (Eds.), *Encyclopedia of social work* (19th ed., pp. 2266–2282). Washington, DC: NASW Press.

Landon, P. S. (1995). Generalist and advanced social work practice. In R. Edwards et al. (Eds.), *Encyclopedia of social work* (19th ed., pp. 1101–1108). Washington, DC: NASW Press.

McAdoo, H. (1997). *Black families*. Thousand Oaks, CA: Sage.

Mattaini, M.A. (2001) The foundation of social work practice. In Briggs & Corcoran (Eds.), *Social work practice: Treating common client problems*. (pp.15–35). Chicago: Lyceum.

Meyer, C. (1976). *Social work practice* (2nd ed.). New York: Free Press.

Miley, K. K., O'Melia, M. & Dubois, B. L. (1998). *Generalist social work practice: An empowering approach*. Boston: Allyn and Bacon.

NASW (National Association of Social Workers). (1993). *Choices: Careers in social work*. Washington, DC: Author.

Proctor, C. D., & Groze, V. K. (1994, September). Risk factors for suicide among gay, lesbian and bisexual youths. *Social Work, 39* (5), 504–513.

Ragg, D. M. (2001). *Building effective helping skills: The foundation of generalist practice*. Needham Heights, MA: Allyn & Bacon.

Reamer, F. (1995). Ethics and values. In R. Edwards et al. (Eds.), *Encyclopedia of social work* (19th ed., pp. 893–902). Washington, DC: NASW Press.

Reamer, F. G. (2001). Ethics and values in clinical and community social work practice. In Briggs & Corcoran (Eds.) *Social work practice: Treating common client problems*. (p.85–106). Chicago: Lyceum.

Ridley, C. R. (1995). *Overcoming unintentional racism in counseling and therapy*. Thousand Oaks, CA: Sage.

Shortell, S. M., & Kaluzny, A. D. (1994) Foreword. In S. M. Shortell & A. D. Kaluzny (Eds.), *Health care management: Organizational behavior and design* (3rd ed., p. xi). Albany, NY: Delmar.

Thyer, B. (2001). Evidence-based approaches to community practice. In Briggs & Corcoran (Eds.) *Social work practice: treating common client problems*. (pp.54–65). Chicago: Lyceum.

Vass, A. (1996). *New directions in social work competencies, core knowledge, values, and skills*. Thousand Oaks, CA: Sage.

Chapter 6

Recognizing Diversity and Applying it to Generalist Practice

IN HIS FIRST FIELD PLACEMENT JUAN, A SOCIAL WORKER WORKING with older people, often found himself struggling. He joked that he was waiting for the single-problem client to come in so that he could carefully choose the very best method of helping. Although he sincerely wanted to help his clients to address their problems and he remembered what he had been taught in school, the thought of applying this knowledge was frightening. In school Juan had learned numerous intervention methods that supported his generalist approach to practice, but he was concerned that he would not interpret the client's problems correctly or would make the wrong decisions when he began helping activities. Ideas such as the "individual worth" and "dignity" of each client were strong in his memory. He knew that he should never compromise his professional values or show lack of respect for the client's culture, values, or beliefs. For Juan, as for many beginning social work professionals, discovering the best thing to do never seemed easy.

Furthermore, Juan was never sure exactly who his client was. Was it the person suffering from the problem? Was it that person's family? Was it the group or community in which the person lived? Or was the "client" even more extensive—was it the policy or legislation that led to the client's problem that required change? Or was it all of the above?

Juan's experience is quite normal for a beginning social worker. As we've commented, social work is not purely a science. Many aspects of helping have much more about them that is art than science. The skills required to practice this art take time and experience to develop and, in fact, also depend on continual updating of the science of social work.

Deciding how best to handle a client's situation is never easy, nor should it be. The best practice interventions require constant assessment, reassessment, and collaboration with other professionals. Furthermore, on any professional team, options will vary on how to interpret, best select, and apply strategies of helping. Remember, applying helping skills to problem situations is an art; situations vary and options are diverse. This diversity is one of the strengths of social work, and an important part of the helping process is identifying and supporting alternative and innovative strategies. The goal is not chaotic improvisation, however. The general

Name: June Martin Perry

Place of residence: Milwaukee, Wisconsin

College/university degrees: North Carolina Central University, BA in Sociology University of Wisconsin-Milwaukee, MSSW, University of Wisconsin-Milwaukee, PhD student in the Department of Urban Studies

Present position: CEO and co-founder of New Concept Self Development Center, Inc.

Previous work/volunteer experience: Employee in the Protective Service Unit, as a Family Counselor, and as a Purchase of Service Coordinator in the Milwaukee County Department of Public Welfare. More recently, a seat on the Board of Directors for many schools, nonprofit, and charitable organizations, Associate Steward at St. AME Church, Chair of the Mayor's Commission on Crime-Youth and Mental Health Committee, and Co-chair of the 2000 Census project for the city of Milwaukee.

Why did you choose social work as a career? I grew up in a community in South Carolina where those who had more reached out to their neighbors and shared what we had with the less fortunate. Volunteerism was a way of life that has led me to a very rewarding career.

What is your favorite social work story? Over the years, I've met many people who say to me, "You don't remember me but..." This is the best part because these are people who I served as a case worker who feel I have impacted their lives positively. I also am proud to be able to hire people who used to be New Concept clients!

What would be the one thing you would change in our community if you had the power to do so? Gun deaths are ravaging our community and creating a culture of violence that is beginning to be tolerated. I would remove access to fire arms.

---

practice consensus is that all interventions with a client should take place within a practice framework and have clear theoretical foundations.

In this chapter we explore the concept of diversity and introduce generalist social work practice. From this orientation all clients, individuals, families, and groups, are viewed through a culturally sensitive "lens"; this means that client strengths are recognized and supported at each step of the helping process. We also discuss the three most common approaches to social work practice: micropractice, mezzopractice, and macropractice. Social workers must be well versed in all three, though their efforts to assist clients may be concentrated at only one or two of the levels.

DIVERSITY AND SOCIAL WORK PRACTICE

A distinguishing hallmark of the social work profession is its insistence to view practice within a specific context, which is commonly referred to as "**contextual**

practice." As a client-centered approach, contextual practice suggests that all practice methods consider a variety of unique attributes or characteristics, which in turn, influence what we do with and on behalf of clients. One type of intervention may work for one person or group, but it may not necessarily be good for another. The characteristics that an individual, family, group, or community bring to the relationship are powerful influences that shape and mold the unique intervention.

Why? Because we are all different, we come from different backgrounds, experiences, ideas, philosophies, and traditions. A simple way to understand basic differences is to read John Gray's very popular book, *Men Are from Mars, Women Are from Venus* (1992), which details gender differences. Think back to your introductory sociology course: we learn from sociology that norms, mores, and folkways create our individual skeletal system from which our character and behaviors take shape.

The first step toward understanding differences is recognizing that the life experiences of each individual can be different. For example, a lesbian women, or a person with HIV/AIDS, or a person with a disability, might not experience a similar event in the same way. Furthermore, there will always be cultural differences between those who are designated "Hispanic" who are Mexican, Cuban, Puerto Rican, or Spanish, just as there are differences between Asian Americans who are Chinese, Filipino, Japanese, Korean, Vietnamese, or Samoan. Yet at times the unfortunate mistake is made that places all individuals in certain groupings together and they are assumed to be alike. It is critical always to remember that individual differences will always exist in all attempts at grouping.

This makes the second step in understanding and recognizing diversity factoring in individual differences and life experiences of each individual as part of the intervention strategy. In this way we can recognize the uniqueness of the individual and understand the influence and power of these unique dimensions on the human experience. Therefore, before we talk about the types of practice utilized in social work it is crucial to understand diversity, and how these perceived "differences" influence practice. And, once identified, we must understand how this information can be integrated into generalist practice strategy.

Understanding, recognizing, and integrating diversity into practice strategy is so important in the field that many social work programs, undergraduate and graduate alike, require students to complete one or more courses that cover this topic. Also, it is not surprising that in several chapters within a variety of contexts this topic will continually resurface. Space limits our discussion and focus; so although not all groups can be included in our discussion, we expect that by the end of this chapter you will understand two key points: first, cultural, racial, or ethnic dimensions are critical pieces to consider when working with clients. Second, not ALL people who constitute certain similar groups are the same.

MEASUREMENT OF DIVERSE PEOPLE—THE U.S. CENSUS

Since 1790, the United States census has been taken every ten years. The "count" gives the government direction in a variety of matters, such as the number of U.S. Representatives assigned to a state or the amount of funding a state receives from the federal government for certain programs. Census data are used by public and private agencies to chart population trends and shifting mobility patterns. These planners then interpret data and project need and response to "changing demographic patterns." For example, at the turn of the twentieth century, census data revealed significant migration streams of people from rural communities to the nation's urban areas, and within a few short years the majority of the nation's population lived in urban areas.

The "count" is completed by a national survey. For the 2000 census, the Census Bureau adopted two surveys, a long form and a short form (www.census.gov/dmd/www.infoquest.html), with individuals randomly selected to complete the forms. The short form was six pages long and the long form, asking for much more detailed information, was twelve pages long.

Activity...Visit the United States Census Bureau web page (www.census.gov) and download a copy of the short and long forms for the 2000 census. Which do you think provides information that gives a better picture of the United States? Why?

According to the 2000 census, the United States population is 281,421,906—but note, this number is already out of date! This is because the survey was conducted in 1999, and as we moved into the twenty-first century, the population continued to grow, and the growth that occurred after the numbers were recorded in 1999 is not reflected in the 2000 numbers. In addition, it is also difficult to count every person in the United States. For example, how would you count the homeless population, in particular those who do not live in shelters but stay on the street? How do you count the migrant worker population? And how do we know where every house, home, or shelter is in the United States where people stay? Dated census information and undercounting of the poor and underserved in the population are just two reasons why the numbers generated by the census data are not an absolute measure.

DIVERSITY BY RACE AND ETHNICITY IN THE UNITED STATES

The United States is a patchwork quilt of people with males, females, old, young, multi-race, single race, an array of ethnic groups, rural and urban—these being just a few ways to identify diversity. However, the most common denominator when thinking about diversity seems to be race.

Essentially one determines his/her race by self-identification, which may be sociopolitical in nature rather than anthropological by design (U.S. Profile of general demographic characteristics, 2000, census of population and housing (May, 2001). Washington, DC: U.S. Department of Commerce). In 1997, the federal government's Office of Management and Budget identified five racial categories that remained the key organizing groups to identify diversity in the 2000 census: American Indian and Alaska Native, Asian, Black or African American, Native Hawaiian and other Pacific Islander, and White. Within these groupings are subgroups. For example, Asian includes Asian Indian, Chinese, Filipino, Japanese, Korean, Vietnamese, Cambodian, Hmong, Laotian, Thai, and Other Asian. Within these subgroups are additional identifiers: Hmong, for example, includes people who categorize themselves as Hmong, Laohmong, or Mong.

Although looking at numbers can be confusing, table 1 provides important information. According to the 2000 census, the population is slightly more female than male, with 74 percent of the people over age 18, whites account for 75 percent of the population, and the African-American population slightly larger than the number of Hispanic/Latinos.

In looking at the application and understanding of diversity in regard to generalist practice it is crucial to remember that diversity is not limited to racial identity, but also includes a variety of other attributes. Knowledge and recognition about these "differences" is important and can help the social worker better understand and develop effective practice intervention plans.

Table 1: U.S. Population By Race, Ethnicity and Gender, 2000–2002

Race	July 1, 2002 Population	July 1, 2001 Population	July 1, 2000 Population	Census 2000 Population
TOTAL POPULATION	288,368,698	285,317,559	282,224,348	281,421,906
White	232,646,619	230,664,347	228,645,315	228,104,485
Black or African American	36,746,012	36,283,895	35,816,129	35,704,124
American Indian and Alaska Native	2,752,158	2,713,047	2,673,620	2,663,818
Asian	11,559,027	11,128,048	10,695,959	10,589,265
Native Hawaiian and Other Pacific Islander	484,314	474,652	464,972	462,534
MALE	141,660,978	140,075,610	138,469,654	138,053,563
White	114,939,130	113,863,214	112,767,750	112,476,314
Black or African American	17,485,319	17,256,399	17,026,280	16,971,124
American Indian and Alaska Native	1,377,944	1,357,962	1,337,890	1,332,929
Asian	5,559,556	5,367,954	5,175,426	5,127,744
Native Hawaiian and Other Pacific Islander	246,203	241,313	236,432	235,203
FEMALE	146,707,720	145,241,949	143,754,694	143,368,343
White	117,707,489	116,801,133	115,877,565	115,628,171
Black or African American	19,260,693	19,027,496	18,789,849	18,733,000
American Indian and Alaska Native	1,374,214	1,355,085	1,335,730	1,330,889
Asian	5,999,471	5,760,094	5,520,533	5,461,521
Native Hawaiian and Other Pacific Islander	238,111	233,339	228,540	227,331

Source: http://eire.census.gov/popest/data/national/tables/asro/NA-EST2002-ASRO-02.php

THE GENERALIST SOCIAL WORKER AND DIVERSITY

Generalist social workers are employed in a variety of agencies, both public and private, and must develop helping relationships with all kinds of clients. Generalist work therefore, as articulated in the CSWE Curriculum Policy Statement, requires a broad range of knowledge and skills that allow problems and their solutions to be assessed comprehensively (Barker, 2003). Moreover, generalist social workers often coordinate and help to expand on the work of other professionals. In such cases the generalist is an invaluable member of the helping team, not only facilitating communication but also fostering continuity of care (Barker, 2003; Dziegielewski, 2004).

Did You Know...In 1998 the field of social work in the United States celebrated a century of professional social work education and recognized more than 100 years of contributions to the well-being of individuals, groups, families, communities, and the natural environment. This was such an important event that Volume 43, Number 6, of the NASW journal Social Work *was dedicated to accomplishments in social work practice.*

Taking an Empowering Approach to Practice

In today's social work practice environment, the idea of "empowerment" should not be underestimated. It is the uniqueness of the individual, group, or community that we must accentuate in each step of the helping process, whatever method of practice we select. Almost all clients respond favorably when they are acknowledged for their strengths and challenged to achieve their full potential.

Empowerment, as a central theme of social work practice, reflects the profession's emphasis on strengths and suggests that the client has the ability to make decisions and pursue change. So often in looking at a problem we focus on the "pathology" rather than on the strengths that the client brings to the situation. For example, when addressing the needs of a disabled client, we can focus on his inability to participate fully at the workplace. This narrow view ignores valuable information, however. The client may be having trouble functioning and may have been unsuccessful in some ways, but what about the ways in which success has been achieved? The disabled often overcome barriers that the nondisabled may not even notice. Social workers must ask what strengths the client has and how the client has overcome obstacles in his life. The emphasis is placed on the client's strengths, resiliency, and coping style, with a clear focus on the client's ability to succeed. What makes more sense if you want to motivate and support someone: focusing on strengths and successes or on problems and failures?

Empowerment also requires that we work to provide access to the resources and knowledge necessary for a client to succeed. We cannot expect clients to succeed if they don't have the resources; at the same time, resources without knowledge yield limited positive results.

Did You Know...The Hollis-Taylor report, a study conducted in 1951, showed that the social work profession was becoming increasingly specialized and fragmented in the delivery of services. Many social workers were treating client problems on a case-by-case basis. The report emphasized a more generic orientation to social work practice, with greater concern for social issues and social action. Many objectives set in this report were accepted by the profession and now form the basis of what is taught in many schools of social work today (Barker, 2003).

Trust, respect, and treating the client with civility are all part and parcel of empowerment. Without these core ingredients, we cannot foster the client's sense of self-worth and ability to look realistically at and resolve a problem. People often say, "Social workers empower their clients"—as if social workers have a bag of magic dust that we sprinkle on clients. Poof, we empower the client! In reality, empowerment comes from within. Social workers help clients to find and sharpen the skills and tools they possess and to look for the resources they may need. Social workers facilitate the empowerment process, but it is clients themselves who make it happen. In addition, when assisting the client to become empowered, the cornerstone of all intervention efforts rests in the social worker's ability to understand his or her own values, while not imposing those values and beliefs on others (Hodge, 2003). From this perspective the social worker recognizes the importance of not encouraging the client to change his or her views to reflect that of the social worker.

The Systems Perspective

Social work's mission is to engage in helping activity that enhances opportunities for all people in an increasingly complex environment. Social work professionals deal with a variety of human systems—individuals, couples, families, groups, organizations, and communities. In its simplest form a "system" consists of parts that interact so that a change in one part can affect all the others and the relations among them.

In future social work classes and texts, you'll come across the term "client system." The addition of the word "system" to "client" indicates that an individual, her family, her group, and her community are all related; all are part of the individual's "galaxy" of relations, where each relation influences the others. In considering the client system we focus on the individual within her relations with other parts of her system and seek to understand the extent to which other parts of the system influence the client.

Activity...Look at yourself as a system. Identify the components of your "galaxy"— family, friends, associations, workplace, and other aspects of your life. Imagine arranging these items with "me" in the middle and drawing a circle around each one to indicate the portion of your environment that it makes up. Do any of the circles overlap? For example, do you work with any members of your family? Is one circle more influential than the others? Why? Do any of the circles influence the others?

Although a client may initially seek help alone, the social worker may determine after assessment that the client system needs to expand and include a spouse or a significant other to increase the chances of positive change. Consider the case described in box 1: the social worker was given a referral to see one client, Don; but after meeting and talking with him, the social worker realized the importance of including Don's wife and his dietitian. A basic assessment, intervention plan, and referral process initiated by the social worker helped to harness the strengths of the client system, thereby helping Don to promote his own physical health.

In addition to addressing Don's particular needs, the social worker believed that advocacy might be needed in order to help other clients like Don. The social worker talked with other professionals in the hospital to see whether anything similar had occurred before. It soon became apparent that what had happened to Don wasn't unusual. The discussions that the social worker initiated led to the issue being brought before the hospital's quality care management team. Later the hospital developed a new protocol that required all diabetic clients to be interviewed and information about their living situations to be assessed. This advocacy did not

---

Box 1: The Case of Don: The Systems Perspective

Don, a 54-year-old man who was not following his diabetic diet, was referred to a social worker for discharge planning. Don's medical condition was worsening and his physician had become very frustrated with Don's noncompliance with his assigned treatment. According to the physician, Don was well aware that he was causing himself harm and might actually lose his eyesight if he did not change his behavior. In the interview with the social worker, Don appeared resistant. He stated that he was trying but that he found it hard to stick to his diet. He was too busy and tired when he got home from work to worry about the food he ate.

During the interview the social worker explored Don's situation by asking questions about his lifestyle, his job, and whether he lived alone. Don stated that he had been married for 30 years and had no children. Don's wife was a homemaker who prepared most of the meals, which included packing him a sack lunch to take to work every day. In an attempt to find out more about Don's support system the social worker asked Don if his wife had participated in the dietetic counseling he was provided. Don seemed surprised and said no, she had not. When asked why his wife had not participated in any of the educational sessions about his condition, Don replied that she had not been invited.

With Don's permission, the social worker called his wife to talk about their both coming in. The social worker also asked Don if he would come back and bring his wife so that they could discuss his diabetic condition with the dietitian and his physician. At Don's request the social worker agreed to join them in these meetings, helping Don and his wife to explore what they needed to do to safeguard his health. The meetings were arranged, and the couple was counseled prior to discharge. After this intervention and at a six-week follow-up Don continued to follow his diet regime. He even joked that his wife was enjoying the cooking classes that she had attended and now he never knew what he was going to eat for lunch or supper.

benefit Don directly, but it did benefit others who could now be prevented from falling into a situation similar to the one Don experienced.

For the generalist social worker who uses a system's perspective, helping activity assumes four roles: education, advocacy, facilitation, and intervention. While performing these helping activities social workers often go beyond working with the originally identified client.

First, education of the client is essential. Education is intended to make clients aware of the services they need as well as to empower them to address problems that previously seemed insurmountable. The social worker's practice activities often involve helping clients to secure the information they need and fostering connections that link clients to services and resource systems that can contribute to resolving their problems.

Social workers can educate clients in many different areas. For example, in Don's case the social worker helped to provide education by meeting with Don, his wife, and the dietitian to discuss the medical need for Don to maintain the proposed diet and the consequences if he does not. The worker facilitated the dialogue between the dietitian and the family and helped to support both in asking questions and clarifying discussion. After the meeting, Don's wife understood what was needed from her, and Don's diet compliance improved dramatically. This case demonstrates how a social worker can assist by educating the entire client system—the client, his family, and other members of the delivery team.

Education is important in all practice settings. Child abuse, domestic violence and incest dynamics, parent-child relations, caregiving, homemaker services, and health care, just to name a few, are areas where education commonly takes place. Social workers understand the importance of going beyond the traditional bounds of counseling. They can assist in educating clients to better maintain the safety, security, and wellness not only of themselves but of their families.

Activity...Go to the library and find the journal Social Work, *Volume 43, Number 6. Think about what the articles in this special issue tell you about the following questions:*

1. What types of contributions did social workers make in micro-, mezzo-, and macropractice?

2. How do social workers feel about the Code of Ethics, and what does it mean to each area of social work practice discussed in this chapter?

3. What issues in the history of social work do you believe helped to make the profession what it is today?

4. What issues in the field of social work need the attention of today's workers?

Indeed, social workers are uniquely placed to participate in education, particularly in the areas of prevention and continued health and wellness: "As a go-between of services, the social worker is the linkage between the person and a system of support that maintains health, or that may be the means of detecting illness early, or of preventing deterioration of the problem" (Skidmore, Thackeray, & Farley, 1997).

Name: Diane DesPlantes

Place of residence: Plainfield, New Jersey

College/university degrees: Fordham University, BA, Hunter Graduate School of Social Work, MSW

Present position: Clinical Therapist

Previous work/volunteer experience: Counselor for sexually abused children, Director of E.D.F., Bilingual Counselor, Parenting Education Educator for N.J. Hispanics for Higher Education, and Plainfield Teen Parenting Program

What do you do in your spare time? I enjoy reading, body building, and gardening.

Why did you choose social work as a career? I was heavily influenced by my personal experiences with poverty, being a woman of color. I am aware of the struggle to have a voice within my culture and of the obstacles outside of my culture. It created a desire within me to help others in all communities who are lost and without a voice.

What is your favorite social work story? When I first arrived at the Juvenile Correctional Facility, the administration, guards, and other personnel treated me in an offhand way, as though as a social worker I was nothing more than an ineffective bleeding heart. After a few months of hard work I was glad to see this impression change. The administration and staff marveled at the positive effect my sessions had on the clients. Clients' written assessments displayed the positive changes that had occurred through therapeutic interventions. Now, the climate has changed and I am greeted with respect and approval.

What would be the one thing you would change in our community if you had the power to do so? Many professionals are focused on their own achievements and lose sight of the fact that college teaches theory and not the practical life experiences needed for patient-centered treatment. We need to come out of our comfortable worlds and be more empathetic with those cultures, beliefs, and economic situations that are different from our own.

Second, advocacy helps clients to identify their own strengths and use individual and community resources to support their efforts to change. Advocacy does not always mean doing something for the client; it often means helping or teaching the client how to do things for herself. Issues of individual worth and dignity must always be considered. Therefore, every social worker must know how to maintain cultural integrity while fostering change, allowing diversity to flourish.

Third, facilitation consists of making connections among different resource systems that enhance their responsiveness and usefulness. The social worker may contact agencies that can support the client as well as mobilize the client and others in the client system. It is here that we find direct intervention, whereby the social worker actually makes the connections that are needed to help the client—for example, transportation to a medical appointment, or registration with such programs as Meals on Wheels. Direct intervention occurs when the client is unable to intervene on his own behalf or simply needs assistance to do so successfully.

PERSON-IN-SITUATION: GUIDING THE PRACTICE FRAMEWORK

Generalist practice is more than simply combining methods of practice such as casework, group work, and community organizing. It requires a theoretical practice framework involving structured ideas and beliefs that provide a foundation for helping. Within this framework we apply knowledge and theory that is consistent with social work values and ethics from a person-in-situation context. This person-in-situation or person-in-environment context, is what differentiates social work from other helping professions. In addition, most professional social workers feel strongly that practice must be guided by theory. Therefore engaging in practice that recognizes no theory is deficient and decreases the helping efforts while depriving the client system of needed professional helping activities.

The systems perspective is part of the conceptual framework that social workers use to understand and assess human relations in context. It reflects the person-in-situation or person-in-environment stance that has always underpinned social work practice, focusing attention on an individual, a collective, a policy, a program, a practice, or any concrete or abstract unit in dynamic interaction with an environment.

A practice framework must also always address issues of human diversity. As we have stated throughout this book social workers always recognize and respect human diversity when forming and maintaining professional relations. Furthermore, social workers are committed to promoting social justice and professional ethical conduct. Social work has historically been concerned with oppressed and disadvantaged populations. The profession's focus on human diversity and social justice reinforces its ethically driven commitment to serving people who do not receive an equitable share of social resources. This commitment and adherence to a professional code of conduct is essential for any type of professional practice, be it generalist or specialist.

> *Did You Know...Lee Frankel (1867–1931) was an early social work educator and developer of family casework theories and practice. He established the Training School for Jewish Social Work in New York and became a national leader in early health and welfare organizations (Barker, 2003).*

For beginning social work professionals, deciding where to begin and how best to engage the client can be difficult because this choice must be linked to the theoretical principles that underlie certain types of helping activity. To accomplish this goal, the social worker reviews the client's situation and based on the client's needs decides what theoretical perspective to use. In other words, the client, not the worker's comfort with or allegiance to a particular practice theory, drives the choice of perspective. The theoretical practice approach and helping strategy employed are firmly based in the reality of the client's environment.

At times making this link may seem too difficult or time-consuming, but acknowledging the relation between environment and practice method is critical. For example, one of the authors worked with an elderly male client with a history of alcohol abuse who received treatment only to be discharged back into an environment that encouraged him to resume drinking. The return to his previous environment negated much of the influence of the intervention and started a pattern of repeated rehabilitation attempts with numerous admissions to treatment centers. He always seemed to respond well while in the program but on discharge quickly relapsed into alcohol abuse. After numerous interventions had failed with this client he was referred to a social worker. The social worker assessed his situation thoroughly and examined the type of home environment to which he was returning. The social worker discovered that because of his instability and troubles with alcohol the client was unable to maintain a bank account. Therefore, when it came time for him to cash his social security check he used the local bar as his bank: His check would arrive each month, he would pick it up, and there was only one place to cash it—that local bar. To complicate matters, the bar would cash checks only if a purchase was made. It's clear what the consequences were. Assessing the client's discharge environment was a critical component in applying the helping strategy. To assist the client the social worker initiated a supervised living arrangement and helped the client to get a bank account of his own, where his social security check was directly deposited.

In formulating a helping strategy the method chosen must be congruent with the needs and desires of the client system being served as well as reflective of the values and ethics of the social work profession. Beginning social workers often feel trapped within a system driven by social, political, cultural, and economic factors so powerful that they influence the practice techniques and skills that are utilized. In addressing the needs of the poor, the disadvantaged, and those who are culturally different from the majority culture, it is the diversity of problems and of people who experience them that makes social work practice an art. How can social workers constantly evaluate what is happening to the client and whether societal factors—race, sexual orientation, and so forth—affect the way a problem is viewed? How can the beginning professional take into account all system variables that affect the helping relationship? How does a social worker maintain the dignity and worth of each client served and ensure that her own feelings and prejudices never enter the helping relationship? Furthermore, if a client has values or beliefs that could lead to hate crimes and actions, the social worker must be able to identify theses feelings and help the client address them before a potential hate crime erupts (see box 2).

Box 2: Hate Crimes a Consequence of Diversity

The social work profession celebrates all forms of diversity and recognizes that differences among people provide valuable opportunities and tools in the helping relationship. At the same time, there is another side to diversity that we must address – fear of others and their differences. Sociology refers to this as *xenophobia* a fear or hatred of foreigners or strangers. Hate crimes are a direct by-product of xenophobia and are directed at people who are "different"—differences are based on any characteristic(s) such as race, gender, sexual orientation, religious affiliation, or political views. Simply stated, there is no logic to a hate crime other than fear. Social workers recognize that clients are often victims, or at-risk of being victims, of hate crimes.

All to often, diversity is associated with "hate crimes"—any of various crimes . . . when motivated by hostility to the victim as a member of a group, as one based on color, creed, gender, or sexual orientation (http://www.infoplease.com/spot/hatecrimes.html).

The Southern Poverty Law Center (http://www.splcenter.org/) is a nationally recognized organization that tracks and combats hate crimes in the United States. According to the Center, there are in the United States 602 active hate groups and 158 "Patriot Groups," that is, organizations that define themselves as opposed to the "New World Order" or advocate or adhere to extreme antigovernment doctrines (http://www.splcenter.org/intelligence-project/ip-index.html; http://www.splcenter.org/intelligenceproject/ip-index.html). Examples of hate crimes and their location are listed below. Using intimidation through emotional, physical, or psychological means, hate crimes are a mechanism to oppress individuals and groups.

Examples of hate crimes in the United States, 2002–2003

JOHNSTON COUNTY, N.C.
After getting a tip about a plot to blow up the local sheriff's office, the county jail and the sheriff himself, federal and local law enforcements officers arrested xxxx, fiery leader of the Nation's Knights of the Ku Klux Klan, on July 19. After the arrest, a search of xxxx's home uncovered an Uzi and an AK-47, two homemade bombs and bomb-making materials. In January, xxxx pleaded guilty to weapons charges. While he awaited sentencing, his wife and three other local Klan members were charged with the murder of an unidentified man. The victim was allegedly killed because he knew about threats against law enforcement officers supposedly made by xxx, grand dragon (or state leader) of a Klan faction based in nearby Robeson County.

BOSTON, MASS.
Two members of a neo-Nazi terror cell, xxxx and xxxx, were convicted on July 26 in a conspiracy to bomb Jewish and African-American landmarks and leaders.

SEMINOLE, FLA.
When police answered a domestic dispute call on Aug. 22, they ended up searching the townhome of podiatrist xxxx, uncovering plans and ammunition for a series of attacks on Islamic targets in Florida. xxxx, who was reportedly seeking to retaliate for the Sept. 11 attacks and the Palestinian intifada, faces up to 30 years in prison. His wife, xxxi, charged in October with being his accomplice, agreed to cooperate with prosecutors in a plea bargain.

Box 2: Hate Crimes a Consequence of Diversity—(*Continued*)

LEWISTON, IDAHO

On Oct. 3, FBI agents seized pipe bombs, homemade land mines, 13 firearms and 13,000 rounds of ammunition from antigovernment activist xxxx, who was arrested on seven federal counts and held without bond. A member of the Idaho Mountain Boys militia group, xxx is also a co-conspirator in a plot to kill U.S. District Court Judge xxx.

PHOENIX, ARIZ.

When an Oct. 16 brawl spilled out of the River City Pockets pool hall, police say three white supremacists viciously attacked 20-year-old xxxx., who was standing nearby waiting for a taxi after applying for a job at the club. The three allegedly chased, tackled and stomped Bailey to death while yelling "white power."

LOS ANGELES, CALIF.

Jewish Defense League (JDL) National Director xxxx, charged with plotting to bomb a mosque and a congressman's office, was declared brain dead on Nov. 4 after slashing his throat and then plunging from a balcony in an apparent suicide in federal prison.

REDDING, CALIF.

xxxx, a devotee of the anti-Semitic Christian Identity religion who teamed with his little brother to firebomb three California synagogues and an abortion clinic, killed himself in Shasta County Jail on Nov. 17. His trial for murdering a gay couple—a crime he said was "God's will" in a confession to newspaper reporters—had been scheduled to start this January.

SANTA ANA AND LONG BEACH, CALIF.

Three of Southern California's most active neo-Nazis were arrested on Nov. 18. xxxx and boyfriend xxxx, members of Blood and Honor, were charged with possessing bomb-making materials. xxxx founded Women for Aryan Unity, a group closely affiliated with the neo-Nazi World Church of the Creator, and launched an "Aryan Baby Drive" to distribute food and clothing to poor white families. xxxx, head of the "Brandenburg Division" of the Aryan Nations, was arrested on weapons charges. During a search of his apartment, investigators said they found a letter advocating that the Aryan Nations partner with Islamic extremists.

There are no easy answers to these questions. To address each of these questions and give it the attention it deserves would take several books just to begin. Yet it is critical that each client system be treated individually, no matter how similar a case may be to one the social worker has already encountered.

SELECTING A PRACTICE METHOD

A multitude of factors must be considered in selecting the most appropriate practice method. Who makes up the client system? What is the target of change?

Box 2: Hate Crimes a Consequence of Diversity—(*Continued*)

CHEROKEE COUNTY, N.C.

Federal authorities searched more than a year before nabbing xxxx, a white-suprema-cist shortwave radio operator and former stalwart of the Kentucky State Militia, on Nov. 22. Anderson had fled into the woods in October 2001 after allegedly firing 25 shots with an automatic at a sheriff's deputy who had stopped him for a traffic violation.

OLYMPIA, WASH.

xxxx, a former member of the antigovernment Jural Society who had recently attended a meeting of the anti-Semitic Christian Identity movement, was arrested this Jan. 18 on firearms charges.

LEESBURG, VA.

On Jan. 23, armed FBI and Secret Service agents raided the home of xxxx, a former National Alliance staff member who owns the neo-Nazi Web site www.tightrope.com. Calvert, who was not arrested, sent an e-mail message to supporters saying the agents seized "10 shitloads" of stuff under the pretext of a copyright infringement for Nike/Nazi shirts he had made.

MACON, GA.

xxxx, founder and leader of the black supremacist hate group Nuwaubian Nation of Moors, pleaded guilty on Jan. 23 to 77 state charges of molesting 13 children of his cult members.

PHOENIX, ARIZ.

White supremacist xxxx was sentenced to death on Jan. 24 for murdering his two housemates in 2000. Prosecutors said xxxx killed one of the housemates, xxxx, because he believed her unborn baby had been fathered by a black man.

SANTA FE, N.M.

Former Minutemen Militia member xxxx was arrested on Feb. 14 in connection with two anti-environmental crimes: putting a pipe bomb in an environmental group's mailbox and setting a forest fire in June 1998 that scorched more than 5,100 acres of the Jemez Mountains and nearby Pueblo land. It took more than 800 firefighters and $3.5 million to contain the blaze.

Source: http://www.splcenter.org/intelligenceproject/ip-index.html

What resources are available to the client system? What is the probability of success given the many elements that can affect the situation? This already sounds complicated, and in fact, it is only a small part of what needs to be considered when choosing a practice method. You'll learn more about these factors, and others, in future social work practice classes.

Although it is beyond the scope of this book to explain the many theoretical and practice frameworks available to social workers and how to use them, we explain the most common practice methods: micro-, mezzo-, and macropractice:

Did You Know...The term "homophyly" acknowledges that people derive comfort and support from people who are like themselves. Culturally sensitive social work practice recognizes this phenomenon. It is one reason why social workers are always encouraged to use a client's own naturally occurring support network whenever possible. Clients are more likely to achieve needed changes when they can work within a system that is familiar to them.

Microlevel practice: More commonly called direct or clinical practice with target populations including individuals, families, and groups; primarily uses face-to-face interaction with client

Mezzolevel practice: Involves agency administration with minimal client contact; examines agency effectiveness and policy implementation

Macrolevel practice: Defines client more extensively to include the community or organizations; often deals with broader social problems that impact the community (Hepworth & Larsen, 1990)

In the broadest of terms, micropractice is undertaken with individuals, families, and groups; mezzopractice directs our attention to organizational administration; and macropractice involves change within larger systems, such as communities and organizations. You might be thinking that we're playing semantic games, that micro, mezzo, and macro are just new names for casework, group work, and community practice. This is not really true because all three perspectives—micro, mezzo, and macro—apply a systems perspective to analyzing the presenting problem. For example, there are not foci in micropractice; the individual's system is the focus—note the use of singular versus plural. Micropractice involves an individual client with a presenting problem, and our work includes assessment of the system's role in creating, sustaining, or solving the problem—in fact, the system may play all three roles.

As we discussed in a number of places in this book, social work has two significant professional goals. The first is to help people to achieve their potential and to adjust more effectively to the demands of their environment. The second is to make social resources more responsive to people's needs, particularly for poor and disadvantaged people, who often are avoided or neglected. Incorporating these goals into the helping process reinforces social work's dual focus on personal and social problems and emphasizes the importance of linking micro-, mezzo-, and macrochange efforts.

Micropractice

In box 3 we present the case of Maria, who became a client but not through her own choice. Following her rape, she became almost immobilized, unwilling to leave her apartment or see others. A victim's advocate social worker proved instrumental. She was a constant presence for Maria during the critical time following the rape. The advocate explored issues from Maria's childhood and identified unresolved feelings that had resurfaced with the rape. Rather than trying to provide in-

Box 3: The Case of Maria: Microgractice

Maria, at age 22, was a victim of rape at her workplace. At the outset of the criminal investigation she met a victim's advocate, who was a BSW social worker employed by the police department. The advocate brought Maria to the hospital and became a major support person for her in the following days. During one of their conversations, the advocate learned that Maria had been a victim of sexual abuse during her childhood. The rape, compounded with her childhood experiences, now had put Maria in a very vulnerable emotional and psychological state: she was unable to go to work or meet family or friends, saying that she would rather just stay at home. Maria was blaming herself for the rape, stating, "I deserved it. Look at my whole life. I deserve it all." The BSW advocate quickly recognized that Maria needed more in-depth help. She referred Maria to a family service agency, where Maria first took part in individual sessions with an MSW social worker.

After a month, the social worker asked Maria how she felt about joining a group of women who had been raped. At first Maria refused, but with gentle, persistent encouragement from the social worker she reluctantly joined the weekly group. Maria's group included seven other women aged 18 to 52. All of the participants reached out to Maria and welcomed her. The social worker, who facilitated the group, told Maria that she did not need to talk unless she wanted too. Discussion at Maria's first group meeting focused on a particular topic: "The Court Hearing." Women shared their fears about the hearings, and some who had been through the courts shared their experiences. Subsequent sessions looked at anger control, relationship building, and becoming a survivor. Maria became an active member of the group and after one year joined the police department as a volunteer victim's advocate.

depth clinical help to Maria, the advocate referred her to a more advanced, MSW social worker, who had expertise in violence against women. The skilled worker was able to help Maria by using a mezzointervention model that employed a variety of process, education, and therapeutic techniques. Group sessions helped to validate Maria's experiences and those of the other group members as well as to consistently examine the broader system's impact on each of their lives.

In micropractice, as in all social work methods, social worker and client work together to establish goals and objectives and to develop the steps that must be taken to reach these goals. A typical microapproach has social workers dealing with clients, family members and significant others, and at times other groups of people. Maria, for example, was first seen as an individual and later referred to the group setting to continue the intervention process. Had Maria's family lived in the same geographic area they too might have become directly involved in the healing process.

Mezzopractice

Mezzopractice involves minimal face-to-face client contact, focusing rather on administrative intervention within the agency organization. Typical administrative titles include supervisor, unit director, director, executive director, chief executive office, and president.

But don't leave this chapter with the impression that microworkers do not engage in mezzoactivities. In fact, any competent social worker will be knowledgeable and possess basic abilities in mezzotasks. Organizing your workload, preparing monthly reports, conducting policy analysis, supervising staff, and making public presentations to service groups are all mezzotasks that microworkers will find themselves undertaking.

Did You Know ...Hull House is the most famous of all settlement houses, founded in Chicago in 1889 by Jane Addams. Settlement houses were community centers where poor and disadvantaged residents of the area could go for help. These centers were major innovators in social reform.

Individuals in mezzoroles develop expertise in a number of areas but particularly the following:

◆ Policy formulation and implementation
◆ Program development
◆ Funding, budgeting, and resource allocation
◆ Management of internal structures
◆ Staff and professional supervision
◆ Organizational and professional representation with internal and external groups
◆ Community presentations
◆ Ongoing evaluation of agency effectiveness (Hepworth & Larsen, 1990)

Generally, you will find MSW workers assigned to mezzopositions in agencies, while BSW workers are limited to direct service lines. This may not be the case in rural and small communities, however, where with fewer MSW professionals available, the BSW worker is more likely to find an administrative assignment. Although their knowledge and skills may not be as broad and as deep of those of MSW practitioners, baccalaureate practitioners do possess beginning knowledge and skills in mezzowork.

Macropractice

Macropractice directs the worker's attention to change in the larger community, organizational, and policy arenas. Similar to "community organization," macrowork involves helping individuals, groups, and communities who have common interests to deal with "social problems and to enhance well-being through planned collective action" (Barker, 2003, p. 84). Typically, micro- or mezzopractice identifies problems, needs, concerns, or issues that need to be addressed through larger change strategies (Netting, Kettner, & McMurtry, 1993). Just as micropractitioners and mezzoworkers have specialized knowledge and skills, so too does the macroworker. The macroworker has expertise in the following areas:

- Communities, their composition and type—for example, geographic or professional
- Power structures within communities and influence within communities
- Policy-making procedures
- Human service organizations, their purposes, functions, and constituencies
- Dynamics and nuances of social problems
- Macro-specific tasks such as collaboration and capacity building, negotiation, task group dynamics, marketing, research and analysis, and teaching

Macropractice builds on private issues that become public matters. Substance abuse, for example, involves individuals. Yet the abuse quickly becomes a public matter when it leads to increased crime related to the selling of drugs, lack of workforce participation or missed work due to drug abuse, poor school grades and eventual dropout, and family dysfunction. In the example described in box 4, the macroapproach involved a not-so-subtle nonviolent confrontation with a local storeowner. The owner wasn't sure which would be worse: the wrath of the drug dealers or the lack of neighbors who would purchase items from his store. He decided the latter, and with help from the local police department, drug sales disappeared from the area. An interesting note: when the group's organizer was told that the dealers were only going to another neighborhood, he responded, "Then that's their problem and they will have to organize them out of the community like we did."

Box 4: The Case of a Drug-free Community: Macropractice

A drug-related shooting took place in the middle of the day in a poor area of town. A few people gathered that evening in a local church and decided that they had had enough, but they didn't know what to do. One of the participants was a social worker from the local neighborhood center. She suggested that the group in fact knew what it wanted—a drug-free community—but now needed to figure out where to begin in order to make this happen. The group expanded and created a neighborhood drug-free task force to act as a "conduit" for the community. Neighbors were invited to share their frustrations at meetings held in churches, school halls, and the neighborhood center. Local social service agencies and elected and appointed officials were asked to come and listen to the neighbor's concerns.

Out of these meetings came a plan for a march through the neighborhood, with the police leading the parade and marching with citizens. The group decided to include a social action activity by marching to the primary spot where drugs were sold, a mom-and-pop convenience store, one block from the public elementary school. Once at the store, the marchers, about two hundred people, formed a long single-file line, and each walked in without saying a word and left one dollar on the counter. The police stood in front of the store and within minutes there was a noticeable disappearance of the drug pushers! Over the following weeks, the storeowner worked with the local task force and police; the drug pushers stopped selling in the neighborhood and moved out of the community. The storeowner joined the task force when it took on other substance abuse issues in the community.

In this application of macropractice the social worker helped the group to develop a plan of action and supported the group as it organized itself. The worker facilitated the process, helped to mobilize significant agencies and local leaders, and provided background research—essentially providing the neighborhood group with the tools it needed to become successful. What began as an individual problem ended up as a community macroissue whose resolution brought about significant changes in the daily lives of individuals, families, and organizations in the neighborhood.

Did You Know...Mother Jones was Mary Harris Jones (1830–1930), a community organizer and labor union advocate who led many strikes against inhumane treatment of children and adults. She advocated better child labor laws and less dangerous working conditions in the mining and steel industries (Barker, 2003).

In Brief: Short-Term Intervention Approaches

Having looked at micro-, mezzo-, and macropractice, we would not be helpful if we didn't touch on one major issue facing social workers who practice at the microlevel.

Whether we like it or not, current social work practice is now dominated by brief, or short-term, practice models (see, for example, figures 1a, b). There are many reasons for this trend, but the major influence is money: getting the "biggest bang for the buck." Insurance companies, as third-party payers (those who pay a provider for services for another person, thus "third party"), and health care orga-

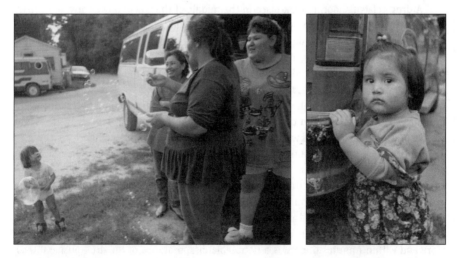

Figures 1a, b: Scenes in a migrant farm worker camp in Michigan. Workers come to Michigan in June to pick strawberries and leave in late fall after the apple harvest. The workers travel in vans and trucks as they move from one region of the country to another, following the harvest cycles.

nizations limit the time during which a client system may receive a service. Simply stated, third-party payers will not underwrite long-term intervention if a short-term model will help, even if the end is less desirable than what a longer term approach may yield. Social workers therefore employ time-limited approaches as a major practice model.

In other cases clients simply don't have the time, desire, or money for long-term social work microservices. People today are working more hours, sometimes two jobs, and have less time to devote to the "self." With less time available, they are unwilling to commit extra time and energy to go beyond simply addressing the cause of the problem. Practitioners can become frustrated when the presenting problem and the underlying issues clearly require a long-term model but the client system, for any number of reasons, is only willing or able to look at the surface issue.

So often, new social workers aren't all interested in social welfare policy. Students taking policy courses often complain, "Why do I need this course? It has nothing to do with social work!" The ongoing national debate about health insurance and resulting services shows one reason why we need to understand policy and how to influence its scope and design. Our practice grows out of policy: Change policy and you can change practice. Change the ways that third-party payers reimburse for service and you can change your practice. These days insurance rarely covers long-term encounters, and short-term, time-limited practice is the norm.

So what do we mean by short-term, or brief, practice? Short-term practice generally ranges from six to eight meetings (Wells & Phelps, 1990); however, as many as twenty have been noted (Fanger, 1995). For many social workers only seeing a client system once is becoming commonplace (Dziegielewski, 2004).

We must realize social work practice encounters are going to be brief. Planning for this short duration in implementing a helping strategy is critical; lack of planning can result in numerous unexpected endings for the client (Wells, 1994) and can also contribute to feelings of failure and decreased job satisfaction for the social work professional (Resnick & Dziegielewski, 1996; Holliman, Dziegielewski & Datta, 2001).

WE ALL MAKE MISTAKES!

A number of years ago a t-shirt often worn at social work gatherings had a Superman logo on the front; but rather than a big "S" the yellow and red lettering spelled out "Super Social Worker." The apparent exaggeration was ironic because at times the efforts of social workers really did seem Herculean. No one can dispute, however, that social workers are human beings and therefore, unlike Superman, are vulnerable and capable of making mistakes. However hard we try, everyone of us is subject to err. Social workers are only human!

Therefore, all social workers must try to minimize the number of mistakes they make and, of course, mitigate any potential harm to the clients served. Moreover, a mistake should be viewed as a "learning moment." A natural reaction may be to act defensively and try to blame someone else; however, professionals must take responsibility for what they do. When in supervision with a trained professional, the beginning social worker has the opportunity to explore a mistake and replay what happened, as if watching it on videotape. It is important to evaluate what actually happened and what might have happened had some other strategy been implemented. Social workers use professional supervision as a forum for these detailed discussions so that the same or similar mistakes can be avoided in the future. The most powerful resource that a social worker has is the ability to seek supervisory help or peer consultation about a problem.

CULTURALLY SENSITIVE PRACTICE

Social workers must help clients to maintain cultural integrity and must respect diversity. The term "ethnic identity" is generally defined as common heritage, customs, and values unique to a group of people (Casas, 1984; Queralt, 1996; Worden, 1999). Social science researchers often gather information on race and ethnicity, yet the difference between the two concepts is pronounced. Race is partially based on physical characteristics of genetic origin (Helms, 1990). Ethnicity embraces a much broader range of commonalities, such as religion, customs, geography, and history. These commonalities between individuals and within a community define and bond members, thereby giving an ethnic backdrop to everyday life. Ethnicity can thus influence thinking and feeling and can pattern behavior in both obvious and subtle ways (Leon & Dziegielewski, 1999). Generally, however, it is easy to overlook the deeper influence of ethnicity because it often appears to be natural and to consist simply of daily behavior—for example, what individuals eat or how they react.

> *Activity...Ethical, culturally sensitive social work practice emphasizes the concepts of "respect," "self-determination," and "remaining nonjudgmental." Together with a fellow student, and without using any references, outline briefly what you understand each of these ideas to mean. Then consult a social work resource such as the* Social Work Dictionary *or the* Encyclopedia of Social Work *and define them again. Compare your first set of definitions with the second. Were there any differences? If so, what were they?*

The development of ethnic identity occurs on a continuum determined by acceptance of one's ethnicity (Helms, 1990). Clients may either embrace or reject their ethnicity, depending on how it relates to personal identity or to identity ascribed by a particular reference group that dictates behavior and decision-making practices (Helms, 1990). Personal identity is how an individual sees himself, whereas ascribed identity is how society values or perceives him. Crucial to understanding the concept of ethnicity is realizing that although it is a potent factor in the professional helping relationship, it is not easy to identify and the degree to which it influences life decisions and behavior is not the same for every client.

When providing culturally sensitive practice social workers must avoid applying a narrow cultural "lens" that can interpret client system traditions and problem-solving processes as abnormal or dysfunctional. In mental health, for example, social workers must thoroughly understand, appreciate, and assess cultural differences in order to enable providers to develop culturally compatible services for the clients that they serve. For example, the social worker who works with an Asian client needs to be aware of Asian customs and expectations. In Asian cultures, there may be resistance to outside intervention as family matters are viewed as private. It is important for the social worker to be aware of and to respect this cultural tradition and to know how it can affect the helping relationship. Culturally sensitive services must extend beyond the general task of making services more accessible and include specifically relevant therapeutic interpretations to guide the framework being used (Leon & Dziegielewski, 1999).

One last issue in providing culturally sensitive practice from a systems perspective is that for the time being, the beliefs and values of social workers and other helping professionals generally reflect those of the greater society. These workers may view different client systems through their own cultural lens and consequently overlook the need to help the client and his system to maintain cultural and ethnic heritage as well as feelings of integrity throughout the intervention process. Professional helpers must be aware of their probable tendency to assess clients based on their own values, beliefs, biases, and stereotypes (Boyd-Franklin, 1989; Dupper, 1992; Dziegielewski, 2002). Lack of awareness of ethnicity and culture may distort perceptions of clients and of their family dynamics (Dziegielewski, Leon, & Green, 1998). The potential danger here is that the client's right to self-determination may be violated (Hepworth & Larsen, 1993). Providing ethnically sensitive practice requires social workers to assess clients and client systems very clearly in regard to the effects that culture, environment, and family can have on behaviors and responses. Being aware of ethnicity and culture and accepting diversity are essential in culturally sensitive practice.

Did You Know...Examinations such as those used to measure intelligence can be "culturally biased" and thereby inaccurately depict an individual's intelligence or aptitude. For example, a test may ask questions about American history that place immigrants at a disadvantage. Social workers need to be aware of this potential problem and must work with each individual client to ensure that he or she is represented fairly and accurately.

In closing, culturally sensitive practice requires that the social worker:
◆ Identify and discuss the impact of psychological problems than can result from adaptation to a new situation or environment
◆ Encourage the development of positive and supportive peer relations
◆ Encourage relations outside of the client system that can help to reduce feelings of isolation and facilitate transition

◆ Help the client to develop new coping skills with which to negotiate the new environment

SUMMARY

To understand the practice of social work within a culturally sensitive framework you must appreciate the broad range of activities and areas that practice involves. Choosing from among the varied roles and tasks that social workers perform, as well as identifying what constitutes the client system, is not easy within the dynamic social work practice environment. So it is not uncommon for beginning professionals to struggle with basic practice principles and how best to help the client they serve. Our advice is simple: Don't worry! This can happen even with the most experienced MSW practitioner. Deciding what helping approach to use and when to apply it requires a delicate balancing act among the needs of the client, the demands of the environment, the skills and helping knowledge available to the social worker, and the sanction of the social welfare agency.

Social workers help a variety of different type of people, groups, and communities whose issues, concerns, and needs more often than not are unique to their particular status. The information gleaned from diversity and difference strengthens the social worker's ability to be an effective practitioner and helps develop a specialized intervention that reflects the client system specific needs.

So where does the social worker begin with matters of diversity? From a social work perspective, diversity first must be recognized; second it must be understood; and third, this knowledge needs to be applied in providing ethnic-sensitive practice. Once we take hold of diversity from these three venues, we then integrate this information into practice strategy.

In closing, realize that recognition, understanding, and acceptance of another person, in this case a client, does not mean abandoning one's personal values and beliefs. In the professional helping relationship, our personal beliefs are set aside as we embrace those of the client system. The new and experienced professional social worker both struggle with difference and diversity: *"Why do they do that"*; *"That life-style repulses me"*; *"Their views are not mine."* Such reactions are human and natural. But in social work, the client is our primary concern, not the worker's individual value and belief system. At the same time, our personal values and beliefs may be in such conflict with those of a particular client that we are not able to help that client. At that time, we transfer the case to a worker who can effectively work with a client—this is in the client's best interests and reflects the professional's ability to determine his or her own level of effectiveness.

When confronted with a new culture or experience, it is of paramount importance that the social workers learn about the culture. Pieces of the human experience simply cannot be disregarded simply because the social worker is not familiar with it. Discovery comes through many venues—including talking with colleagues. Always allow clients to help you learn and develop sensitivity to those matters with which you are unfamiliar. Remember, helping is a two-way street and reciprocity is commonplace in a just society.

Helpful Resources

Profile of general demographic characteristics, 2000, census of population and housing (May, 2001). Washington, DC: U.S. Department of Commerce. http://www.census.gov/dmd/ www.infoquest.html

http://www.apa.org/pubinfo/answers.html#whatis

http://hab.hrsa.gov/tools/progressreport/

http://www.who.int/hiv/facts/en/plwha_m.jpg

http://eire.census.gov/popest/data/national/tables/asro/NA-EST2002-ASRO-02.php

The numbers from the Census Bureau provide important information regarding the breadth of diversity. The numbers, however, do not illustrate the latent issues such as racism, prejudice, and discrimination. Disproportionate levels of poverty, individual and family incomes, and high school and college graduation rates are just some of the indicators that demonstrate that diverse people can be "treated" differently than others.

Recognizing and understanding diversity can help the social worker understand how clients can develop anger, hostility, passivity, low self-esteem, poor self-worth, and a sense of hopelessness. The social work relationship considers these may be "some of the baggage" that a client outside the mainstream brings to a social work relationship.

Recognizing the strength in client system diversity can assist in the helping process. For example, strong family and, in particular the extended family, is a hallmark in the African-American community. Acknowledging this strength will allow the social worker working with an African-American client to consider the possible role of the family or extended family in the helping process. Recognizing and understanding diversity is the essence of "contextual practice"—seeing each client as an individual who is set within a specific culture, and whose decisions and actions result from his or her life experiences.

Today's society suffers from a multitude of complicated problems that need to be addressed, and social workers, like other helping professionals, are being pressured to assess and address them as quickly and as effectively as possible. Varied social work roles and fluctuating environmental influences reinforce the ongoing need for educational preparation and training in practice. Even after receiving a degree, every social worker needs to enhance his knowledge and skill bases while developing new areas for more effective practice. We must all continue learning and growing in order to anticipate the needs of our clients.

Social workers believe that competent ethical practice is more than simply helping clients by using what is known. It also involves knowing the client, respecting cultural diversity and the uniqueness of the individual, assessing the environmental situation, and recognizing the strengths and limitations of the intervention strategy employed as well as the resources available to the client. The social worker must decide what method of change to use and at what level—micro, mezzo, or macro—the client will best be served.

Microapproaches to social work practice help clients, whether individuals, families, or groups, to feel better about themselves and to address previous relationship experiences that are affecting new or current relationships. Mezzopractice strengthens an agency's ability to respond more congruently with worker practice needs and client issues. And macropractice confronts larger issues that affect individuals, families, groups, or communities.

In this chapter and in chapter 5 you have been exposed, albeit briefly, to social work practice. You've read a few case scenarios and seen how different social workers have tried to help their clients. These cases offer you a glimpse of the exciting, challenging, and often frustrating world of the practicing social work professional.

Social workers are needed in the practice arena to address the wide array of social problems. And yes, while social workers face numerous external pressures from funding groups, we cannot allow these to limit our practice strategies. Clients need and continue to want supportive services, and as the number of people suffering from anxiety and depressive disorders, self-destructive behavior, and life-threatening illnesses continues to grow, so does the need for social workers who engage in professional practice.

References

Barker, R. L. (2003). *The social work dictionary* (5th ed.). Washington, DC: NASW Press.

Boyd-Franklin, N. (1989). Black families in therapy. New York: Guilford.

Casas, J. M. (1984). Policy, training, and research in counseling psychology: The racial/ethnic minority perspective. In S. D. Brown & R. W. Lent (Eds.), *Handbook of counseling psychology* (pp. 785–831). New York: Wiley.

Dupper, D. (1992). Separate schools for black males. *Social Work in Education, 14* (12), 75–76.

Dziegielewski, S. F. (2004). *The changing face of health care social work: Professional practice in managed behavioral health care* (2nd ed.). New York: Springer.

Dziegielewski, S. F. (2002). *DSM-IV-TR™ in action*. New York: Wiley and Sons.

Dziegielewski, S. F., Leon, A.. & Green, C. (1998). African American children: A model for culturally sensitive group practice. *Early Child Development and Care, 14*, 7, 83–97.

Holliman, D., Dziegielewski, S. F., & Datta, P. (2001). Discharge planning and social work practice. *Social Work in Health Care, 32* (3), 1–19.

Fanger, M. T. (1995). Brief therapies. In R. Edwards et al. (Eds.), *Encyclopedia of social work* (19th ed., pp. 323–334). Washington, DC: NASW Press.

Gray, J. (1992). *Men are from mars, women are from Venus*. New York: Harper Collins.

Helms, J. E. (Ed) (1990). *Black and white racial identity: Theory, research, and practice*. Westport, CT: Praeger.

Hepworth, D. H., & Larsen, J. A. (1990). *Direct social work practice: Theory and skills* (3rd ed.). Belmont, CA: Wadsworth.

Hepworth, D. H., & Larsen, J. A. (1993). *Direct social work practice: Theory and skills* (4th ed.). Pacific Grove, CA: Brooks/Cole.

Hodge, D.H. (2003). Value differences between social workers and members of the working and middle class. *Social Work, 48* (1), 107–119.

Leon, A. M. & Dziegielewski, S. F. (1999). The psychological impact of migration: practice considerations in working with Hispanic women. *Journal of Social Work Practice. 13* (1), 69–82.

Netting, F. E., Kettner, P., & McMurtry, S. (1993). *Social work macro practice*. New York: Longman.

Queralt, M. (1996). *The social environment and human behavior: A diversity perspective*. Boston: Allyn and Bacon.

Resnick, C., & Dziegielewski, S. F. (1996). The relationship between therapeutic termination and job satisfaction among medical social workers. *Social Work in Health Care, 23* (3), 17–35.

Skidmore, R. A., Thackeray, M. G., & Farley, O. W. (1997). *Introduction to social work* (7th ed.). Boston: Allyn and Bacon.

U.S. Census Bureau, Population Division (2003). Census Data: Table NA-EST2002-ASRO-02—National Population Estimates—Characteristics. Release Date June 18, 2003.

Wells, R. A. (1994). *Planned short-term treatment* (2nd ed.). New York: Free Press.

Wells, R. A., & Phelps, P. A. (1990). The brief psychotherapies: A selective overview. In

R. A. Wells & V. J. Giannetti (Eds.), *Handbook of the brief psychotherapies* (pp. 3–26). New York: Plenum.

Worden, M. (1999). *Family therapy basics* (2nd ed.). Pacific Grove, CA: Brooks/Cole.

Part III

Settings for Social Work Practice

Chapter 7

Poverty and Income Maintenance

THROUGHOUT ITS HISTORY THE CORE FUNCTION OF THE SOCIAL work profession has been service on behalf of those who are economically, socially, or politically disadvantaged. From the earliest efforts of the COSs and settlement houses of the nineteenth century, social workers have always tried to help people to achieve their potential and participate in the development of their communities.

As we enter the new millennium, the United States has experienced unparalleled economic growth. There are more millionaires and billionaires than at any time in U.S. history. The stock market has boomed to new and unexpected heights. Unemployment and inflation have reached their lowest levels in decades, and new job opportunities abound. While institutes such as the Carter Center report that reducing poverty for all is a possibility (Carter, 2000). All of these developments are signs of a growing, prospering economy. Yet as Chelf has noted, even with all these gains the United States remains a society of sharp economic contrasts (1992, p. 21). While many Americans live in affluence, a large part of the population is unable to benefit from the nation's economic triumph.

Poverty is determined primarily by income because it is income that allows the purchase of necessary material resources (Coulton & Chow, 1995, p. 1874). Closely tied to poverty and income is the ability, or inability, to purchase or access high-quality health care, decent and safe housing, and an adequately nutritious diet. As Darby wrote, "Being poor hurts. By itself, poverty diminishes the quality of life" (1996, p. 3). Certainly, many heroic examples exist of people and families who have risen above the limitations of poverty by taking full advantage of public welfare programs and services. But such cases are rare. Living in poverty far more often is associated with negative life experiences that can leave deep scars. Crime, low educational attainment, inadequate health care, substandard housing, and minimum wage employment with little opportunity for promotion are among the many debilitating experiences faced by the poor. For the economically disadvantaged—that is, people who cannot financially support themselves and their families—life is not easy.

Imagine what it would be like not to have enough money to feed, clothe, or house yourself and your family. Now imagine what it would be like if, in addition to these troubles, you were viewed negatively and treated differently simply because your income is low.

Name: Panu Lucier

Place of residence: Anchorage, Alaska

College/university degrees: University of Alaska, Anchorage, BSW

Present position: Director, Rose Urban Rural Exchange

Previous work/volunteer experience: Teacher's Assistant, School counselor, Youth coordinator, Court Appointed Special Advocate

What do you do in your spare time? Outside of work, I have continued my role as a volunteer CASA. I enjoy spending time with my three grandchildren, walking my Siberian Husky, traveling, spending time outdoors, and listening to music.

Why did you choose social work as a career? Social work offered me a flexible and professional degree guided by a code of ethics, values, and theories that are very compatible with the values of Alaska Native cultures, specifically, our relationship with and respect for all living things.

What is your favorite social work story? I helped convince the court to return four little boys to their village after they were taken into state custody while visiting Anchorage with their mother. I escorted them home. From them I learned courage and never to give up hope.

What would be the one thing you would change in our community if you had the power to do so? I would break down the social and political barriers that contribute to the division of the "haves" and the "have-nots" so that all people have access to education, health, and social services, which are essential to the integrity of a healthy community.

Poor people are often regarded as contributing less than their share to society. Indeed, with our society's emphasis on rugged individualism, it's difficult not to view the poor in a negative light. Well-educated people who we believe should know better sometimes make statements like "Poor people are disadvantaged because they don't work or try hard enough to better themselves." Many people also believe that recipients of social welfare services are immoral because they often have live-in partners while maintaining single-parent families. These misconceptions about the poor are more than just a matter of perceptions—these false assumptions often determine how poor people are treated and what services they are given.

Think about it. Can you remember any discussions you've had with friends or family about people who are impoverished? How were these people characterized? How often have discussions of this type become emotionally charged? Did your friends or family members feel strongly about what they'd seen or believed to be the case? Now think about pronouncements you've heard politicians make in the heat of political campaigns. How did the politicians present the issue of poverty, and what kinds of plans were proposed to address it? Why do you think people who want to hold office seem constantly to attack poverty-related social programs? We believe the reason is that most of the time politicians wish to please their constituents, so they pander to widespread beliefs and attack these programs as costly and wasteful.

Regardless of your opinion about people who live in poverty, it is clear that the poor and disadvantaged inspire strong emotions. Views and expectations about those living in poverty are founded on myths and stereotypes that unfortunately are assumed to be fact. We actually know quite a lot about poverty, however, particularly that the state of poverty is persistent. Poverty affects all races and ages. Poverty affects both men and women. Poverty is found in urban, suburban, and rural communities. Those who live in poverty are often disadvantaged or disenfranchised by the greater society. Finally, poverty cannot be isolated within a particular segment of society. Through its effects on educational performance and crime, poverty affects everyone in society and the quality of life for all people (see figure 1).

Did You Know…In 1995, in the United States 36.4 million people, 13.8 percent of the population, were living in poverty.

In this chapter, we first try to cut through many of the myths that surround the poor and impart critical information to make you a more informed helper. We then look at several important social programs and assess their effectiveness within a framework of facts rather than mythology.

POVERTY DEFINED

According to the *Social Work Dictionary* **poverty** is *"the state of being poor or deficient in money or means of subsistence"* (Barker, 2003, p. 333). Other definitions similarly stress the link between resources and livelihood: Poverty is a *"condition of being without basic resources"* (Segal & Brzuzy, 1998, p. 78). According to Karger & Stoez (2001) and Coulton & Chow (1995) poverty is defined as deprivation.

Two ideas further refine the concept of poverty: **absolute poverty** and **relative poverty**. Absolute poverty is determined by comparison with a fixed numerical standard that is applied in all situations and usually reflects bare subsistence. Relative poverty is determined by comparison with some normative standard that may reflect a living standard far higher than subsistence. Absolute measures are usually income based. For example, if a person's annual income is below a certain figure, then the individual is regarded as poor. On the other hand, a relative measure—though still income based—would compare the individual with someone else. A single person with a $35,000 annual income is not absolutely poor but is poor relative to Bill Gates, one of the richest men in the world. A second kind of relative measure is based on the ability, or inability, to meet a standard set and approved by

Figure 1: The children in this photo are siblings. They live with their parents in this trailer and another the same size. The trailers are in a parking lot at the edge of a large city in Ireland.

the community. For example, if immunizations are expected but a family cannot afford them for its children, then that family is considered poor by this measure. Absolute measures make it easy to count people and minimize subjective variables. The key is identifying a threshold below which people are counted as poor. Relative measures are much more difficult to formulate or to reach consensus about. They are also difficult to use. For example, people sometimes say that poor people in the United States have it easy compared to poor people elsewhere. But this is like trying to compare apples with oranges. Different countries have different beliefs, values, and economic and social systems, all of which affect the standards by which people are judged to be poor.

Measuring Poverty

The U.S. government measures poverty using a standard called the **poverty threshold**. Mollie Orshansky, director of the Social Security Administration in 1963, conceptualized the poverty threshold as an absolute measure so that statistical processes could be used to simply count the number of poor. Orshansky's formula is based on the amount of money that a family must spend on food and on the portion of overall income that this expense constitutes. Orshansky assumed that a family spends one-third of its total income on food. After calculating the cost of a minimum, or economy, food plan as determined by the Department of Agriculture, she multiplied that amount by three to establish the poverty threshold. This value, which is essential in determining benefits, is updated annually and adjusted for inflation, family size, and age, and to reflect the increased cost of living in Hawaii and Alaska. Its application is simple: a person or family whose gross income falls below the poverty threshold is counted as being in poverty.

Did You Know…According to the National Center for Children in Poverty in 1998, 23.2 percent of the children under age 6 live in poverty in the United States.

Having explained the poverty threshold calculation, let's complicate matters a bit. The poverty threshold was the government's original attempt to establish a poverty measure, under the oversight of the Social Security Administration, and its purpose is to establish a basis for counting retrospectively the number of people who live in poverty. Each year, however, another branch of the federal government, the Department of Health and Human Services (HHS), is responsible for issuing poverty guidelines (see table 1). These prospective guidelines, which closely approximate the poverty threshold, are used in determining financial eligibility for certain federal programs (see table 2). The poverty guidelines are needed because the poverty threshold data for a given year are not generated until summer of the following year). Thus, poverty thresholds for 2002 were not published until 2003, and agencies using these data to determine program eligibility at the beginning of the year 2004 would then be using two-year-old information.

An important point to remember: the HHS poverty guidelines are used for determining eligibility for many federal programs but not for all of them. Examples of federal programs that use the HHS guidelines are Head Start, Low-Income Energy Assistance Program, food stamps, National School Lunch and School Breakfast programs, Legal Services for the Poor, Job Training Partnership Act,

Table 1: 2003 HHS Poverty Guidelines

Size of Family Unit	48 Contiguous States and D.C.	Alaska	Hawaii
1	$ 8,980	$11,210	$10,330
2	12,120	15,140	13,940
3	15,260	19,070	17,550
4	18,400	23,000	21,160
5	21,540	26,930	24,770
6	24,680	30,860	28,380
7	27,820	34,790	31,990
8	30,960	38,720	35,600
For each additional person, add	3,140	3,930	3,610

Source: Federal Register, Vol. 68, No. 26, February 7, 2003, pp. 6456–6458.

Table 2: Poverty Thresholds for 2002 by Size of Family and Number of Related Children under 18 Years (Dollars)

Size of family unit	Related children under 18 year								
	None	**One**	**Two**	**Three**	**Four**	**Five**	**Six**	**Seven**	**Eight or more**
One person (unrelated individual)									
Under 65 years	9,359								
65 years and over	8,62								
Two persons									
Householder under 65 years	12,047	12,400							
Householder 65 years and over	10,874	12,353							
Three persons	14,072	14,480	14,494						
Four persons	18,556	18,859	18,244	18,307					
Five persons	22,377	22,703	22,007	21,469	21,141				
Six persons	25,738	25,840	25,307	24,797	24,038	23,588			
Seven persons	29,615	29,799	29,162	28,718	27,890	26,924	25,865		
Eight persons	33,121	33,414	32,812	32,285	31,538	30,589	29,601	29,350	
Nine persons or more	39,843	40,036	39,504	39,057	38,323	37,313	36,399	36,173	34,780

Source: U.S. Census Bureau. http://www.census.gov/hhes/poverty/threshld/thresh02.html.

WIC, and Job Corps. Some of these programs use a percentage multiple of the guidelines, such as 125, 150, or 180 percent (Institute for Research on Poverty, 1998). For example, a program may use 125 percent of the HHS guidelines to determine eligibility. In 2003 this eligibility standard for a four-person family was a $18,400 x 125%, or $23,000—in other words, a family of four was eligible for the program if its income was below $23,000. The percentages of the HHS guidelines used by different programs are established by congressional committees and, predictably, can create a great deal of confusion between programs. Moreover, several well-known programs are not tied to the HHS guidelines: Supplemental Security Income, Social Services Block Grant, Section 8 housing, the Earned Income Credit, and Temporary Assistance for Needy Families.

Activity…Using the 2003 poverty guideline for a family of four, $18,400, imagine what life is like. You'll have $ $1,533.33 each month for expenses. Using Orshansky formula's assumption, one-third of your income, $511.11, goes for food, leaving you $1,022.22 for other expenses including housing, transportation, health care, clothing, recreation, and so on. Put together a monthly food menu—what type of meals, and so forth—with the $511.11. Find a place to live and set up other expenses with the remaining $1,022. The two children are ages 5 and 13, and the two adults are the biological parents.

Now, how realistic do poverty guidelines seem to be? What does this exercise tell you about the level at which poverty guidelines are set? If this were your family of four and these were the resources you had available, could you make ends meet?

Did You Know...A single parent with two children making the minimum wage and working forty hours a week will not make enough money to raise this family above the poverty threshold. This parent, in 2002, would need to make $8.67 per hour to be above the poverty threshold .

Other Considerations in Measuring Poverty

Setting poverty thresholds and thus establishing exactly who will be counted as poor is very controversial. Orshansky's definition, when examined closely, has all sorts of limitations. First, it doesn't consider geographical differences in cost of living, other than for Alaska and Hawaii—and this is an important consideration in the United States. Go back to table 5 in chapter 4 to see how far the same amount of money goes in different cities. Second, the threshold is based on food costs but does not adjust for the different nutritional needs among children, women, women of child-bearing age, and men. Last, assuming that one-third of a family's income is spent on food purchases is itself problematic. Over the years this has not proved to be a well-founded assumption.

Did You Know...In statistics the mean, median, and mode are indicators of how a set of numbers tends to focus around central values. Applied to income, the mean income is the average income of a population—50 percent of the population has income above median income and 50 percent below—and the mode income is the most frequently occurring income.

Beyond problems with the formula used to determine poverty is the question of what should or should not be counted as income. For example, should federal cash subsidies such as social security retirement payments be counted as income? Should income be established as the pretax or the posttax amount? Should the cash value of in-kind benefits from federal subsidy programs such as food stamps and Section 8 housing be counted as part of a family's income?

As exhibited in table 3, how income is defined affects actual poverty estimates. Moving down the table, income is adjusted in steps so that we can observe the effects on the poverty rate: first, government cash benefits are removed—then private non-wage income is added, federal tax payments are removed, the primary antipoverty tax credit is added, state tax payments are removed—and finally government benefits are added successively.. Critics of the federal government's income maintenance programs argue that the poor are receiving numerous supports and these should be "counted" as income, which in effect raises a number of individuals above the poverty threshold. For a moment, what do you think would happen to the number of people in poverty if you do a combined "count" that includes Earned Income Credit (EIC), means-tested cash transfers, food stamps, non-medical non-cash transfers, and rent subsidies? Will the number of people in poverty increase or decrease? If you think decrease, you are correct—but will this "net" number portray a realistic picture of the nation's poverty level?

Table 3: The Marginal Effect of Taxes and Transfers on Poverty Estimates, 2000 (Numbers in thousands. Based on a November 2001 correction.)

2000 Income measures	Number below poverty	Poverty rate
Official definition	31,054	11.3
Official less payroll taxes plus net capital gains	33,392	12.1
Official less federal and state income taxes plus net capital gains	31,400	11.4
Official less federal and state income taxes plus net capital gains and earned income credit (EIC)	27,454	9.9
Official less taxes plus net capital gains and EIC	29,914	10.8
Official less nonmeans-tested cash transfers	49,509	17.9
Official less means-tested cash transfers	33,113	12.0
Official plus means-tested non-medical noncash transfers	27,902	10.1
Official plus foodstamps	30,039	10.9
Official plus rent subsidies	29,899	10.8
Official plus regular-price school lunch	31,017	11.2
Official plus all non-medical noncash transfers	27,859	10.1
Official less taxes plus EIC and all noncash transfers	26,336	9.5

Source: U.S. Census Bureau, Current Population Survey, March 2001.

The data presented show that federal programs do improve income levels and thus remove individuals from poverty. The data also show, however, that people who rely on federal benefits for large parts of their income are extremely vulnerable to the slightest modifications in program eligibility conditions and benefit levels.

So, are we really doing a disservice to all poor people when we count such uncertain income? What rate do you believe most accurately reflects existing poverty the 11.3 percent determined by definition 1 or the 9.5 percent determined by definition 14, or one of the other rates? Does it really matter which definition is used? If the official poverty rate declined slightly because governmental subsidies were added to income calculations don't you think this information would be used to justify reductions in welfare programs? And, if welfare programs actually were reduced, wouldn't the poverty rate rise again?

Nevertheless, agency administrators and welfare advocates often argue that data produced by a standardized process applied consistently from year to year, even if the process is rife with potential measurement flaws, are essential. Such numerical measures allow a community to follow trends in poverty and to assess the effects of different attempts to reduce poverty among its citizens. In other words, even though the poverty rate itself may have little intrinsic meaning it is nonetheless important because its fluctuations over time serve as a barometer of economic well-being.

Number in Poverty versus Poverty Rate

Note that our discussion of measuring poverty started with counting the number of people in poverty but is now framed in terms of the poverty rate. The poverty rate is a more illuminating way to quantify poverty because it provides context by expressing the number of people in poverty as a percentage of the total population. This context is important for two reasons. First, the scale of poverty is difficult to judge if we know only the number of poor people: One thousand people in poverty is a far more serious problem if the total population is 2,000 than if it is 100,000. The poverty rates, 50 percent and 1 percent, show how different the two situations are. Second, trends in poverty cannot be judged by changes in the number of poor people alone. Suppose over a decade the number of people in poverty rises from 1,000 to 2,000. If the total population remains stable at 100,000, the poverty rate has doubled from 1 to 2 percent; if, however, the population grows from 100,000 to 200,000, the poverty rate is unchanged at 1 percent—the rate distinguishes between worsening poverty and population growth.

Did You Know...In 2002, the number of people living below the poverty threshold totaled 32.9 million, or 11.7 percent of the U.S. population. To think about how large this number actually is, consider that the total population of the Northeast—Maine, New Hampshire, Vermont, Massachusetts, Connecticut, Rhode Island, and New York—is slightly smaller. Or consider that the total population of the following states approximates the number of people in poverty: Idaho, Montana, North Dakota, South Dakota, Wyoming, Colorado, Utah, Nevada, Arizona, New Mexico, Nebraska, Oklahoma, Iowa, Louisiana, and Arkansas. That the United States is one of world's most technologically advanced societies and has one of the highest standards of living makes it difficult to comprehend the number of Americans who live in poverty.

Examine table 4, and remember that the U.S. population has grown every year since the nation's founding. You can now "read" different eras in the recent history of poverty. In the 1960s the number of people in poverty actually declined, a dramatic development, as evidenced by the sharp drop in the poverty rate from 22 to 12.1 percent. This decrease was achieved primarily through the federal government's activist War on Poverty. Over the following years the poverty rate fluctuated, peaking at 15.2 percent in 1983 and 11.3 percent in 2000, while the number in poverty trended steadily upward with the growing population. Indeed, although poverty rates in the mid-1990s were far below the 1959 level, the numbers in poverty were not far different.

WHO ACTUALLY CONSTITUTE THE POOR?

Poverty cuts across all races, ethnic groups, and ages and darkens the lives of both men and women. In this country there has always been a myth that the poor are almost all nonwhite. Yet this is far from true (see table 5). Numerically there are more whites in poverty than any other single race. However, poverty rates for blacks and those of Hispanic origin are much higher than that for whites. The data in table 5 also undermine the idea that most poor people should be supporting themselves. Children, those under age 18, account for almost 36 percent of all poor, and seniors, those age 65 and over, account for more than 10 percent.

Table 4: Poverty Status, 1959–2002

Year	Number in Poverty (in thousands)	Poverty Rate	Year	Number in Poverty (in thousands)	Poverty Rate
2002	34,570	12.3%	1979	26,072	11.7%
2001	32,907	11.7	1978	24,497	11.4
2000	31,054	11.3	1977	24,720	11.6
			1976	24,975	11.8
1999	32,258	11.8	1975	25,877	12.3
1998	34,476	12.7	1974	23,370	11.2
1997	35,574	13.3	1973	22,973	11.1
1996	36,529	13.7	1972	24,460	12.5
1995	36,425	13.8	1971	25,559	12.5
1994	38,059	14.5	1970	25,420	12.6
1993	39,265	15.1			
1992	38,014	14.8	1969	24,147	12.1
1991	35,708	14.2	1968	25,389	12.8
1990	33,585	13.5	1967	27,769	14.2
			1966	28,510	14.7
1989	31,528	12.8	1965	33,185	17.3
1987	31,745	13.0	1964	36,055	19.0
1986	32,221	13.4	1963	36,436	19.5
1985	32,370	13.6	1962	38,625	21.0
1984	33,700	14.4	1961	39,628	21.9
1983	35,303	15.2	1960	39,851	22.2
1982	34,398	15.0			
1981	31,822	14.0	1959	39,490	22.4
1980	29,272	13.0			

Source: Baugher and Lamison-White (1996).

Poverty and Location

For the most part, the poor live in metropolitan areas (77.3 percent), with 40.7 percent living in central cities. These statistics mirror what most people believe, namely, that poor people primarily live in urban areas and the inner city. Few Americans think of the poor as living in rural areas or small communities, which seem tranquil places not generally associated with poverty. Yet 22.7 percent of the poor live in such communities. And indeed poor people living in rural areas and small communities present a unique challenge to service providers because the services and resources they need are often too few or too difficult to access.

Did You Know...The term "Hispanic" is unique to the United States? No other nation uses this word. "Pertaining to the culture of Spanish- and Portuguese-speaking people...this term is often applied to people of Latin American ethnic background...Some people prefer the term 'Latino' " (Barker, 1995, p. 216). According to the U.S. Bureau of the Census, which first used the word in 1980, a person of Hispanic origin can be of any race. This means that people who describe themselves as Hispanic can have diverse backgrounds and very different mores and cultural expectations.

Table 5: Profile of Persons in Poverty, 2002

	Number in Poverty (in thousands)	Poverty Rate in Subpopulation
Total	34,570	12.1%
White	24,074	10.3
Black	8,894	23.9
Asian and Pacific Islander	1,243	10.0
Hispanic	8,555	21.8
Under 18 years	11,175	16.3
18 to 64 years	17,760	10.1
65 years and over	3,414	10.1
In families	23,215	9.9
Northeast	5,687	10.7
Midwest	5,966	9.4
South	13,515	13.5
West	7,739	12.1
Lives in metropolitan areas	25,446	11.1
Lives in Central Cities	13,394	16.5
Lives outside metropolitan	7,460	14.2

Source: http://www.census.gov/prod/2003pubs/p60-222.pdf.

Poverty and Race

As table 6 clearly shows, poverty rates for blacks and Hispanics have been about twice that for whites for years. Averages by decade show that over time the differences have lessened, but they remain extreme.

Minority groups are affected to very different extents by poverty. Poverty rates can vary greatly from one racial or ethnic group to another.

Poverty and Gender

Landrine and Klonoff (1997) began their exploration of discrimination against women by observing that numerous studies have documented continuing discrimination against women in a wide variety of arenas including employment, housing, health care, and social services. In particular, they stated, "thousands of studies" have shown that women are systematically paid less than men (Landrine & Klonoff, 1997). Even social workers, members of a profession that proudly advocates for social and economic justice, work in organizations and agencies that discriminate against women. Gibelman and Schervish (1997) found that in 1995 the median income for female social workers was $34,135, compared with $37,503 for their male counterparts! Schervish's findings are supported by a CSWE study that reported that female social work faculty members receive lower salaries at all academic ranks than their male colleagues (Lennon 1997).

During the twentieth century, American family structure underwent significant changes. Two-parent families declined while single-parent families increased; birthrates declined for the general population but rose dramatically among

Table 6: Poverty Rates by Race and Hispanic Origin; 1959–2002

Year	All Persons	White	Black	Hispanic
2002	12.1	10.2	24.1	21.8
2001	11.7	9.9	22.7	21.4
2000	11.3	9.5	22.5	21.5
1999	11.6	9.7	23.1	22.1
1998	12.7	10.5	26.5	27.1
1997	13.3	11.0	29.3	30.3
1996	13.7	11.2	28.4	29.4
1995	13.8	11.2	29.3[b]	30.3[a]
1994	14.5	11.7	30.6[b]	30.7[a]
1993	15.1	12.2	33.1[b]	30.6[a]
1992	14.8	11.9	33.4[b]	29.6[a]
1991	14.2	11.3	32.7[b]	28.7[a]
1990	13.5	10.7	31.9[b]	28.1[a]
1989	12.8	10.0	30.7[b]	26.2[a]
1988	13.0	10.1	31.3[b]	26.7[a]
1987	13.4	10.4	32.4[b]	28.0[a]
1986	13.6	11.0	31.1[b]	27.3[a]
1985	14.0	11.4	31.3[b]	29.0[a]
1984	14.4	11.5	33.8[b]	28.4[a]
1983	15.2	12.1	35.7[b]	28.0[a]
1982	15.0	12.0	35.6[b]	29.9[a]
1981	14.0	11.1	34.2[b]	26.5[a]
1980	13.0	10.2	32.5[b]	25.7[a]
1975	12.3	9.7	31.3[b]	26.9[a]
1970	12.6	9.9	33.5[b]	22.8[a]
1965	17.3	13.3	41.8[b]	
1959	22.4	18.1	55.1[b]	NA
1990–95	14.3	11.5	31.8[b]	29.7[b]
1980–89	13.8	11.0	32.9[b]	27.6[b]
1970–79	11.8	9.0	31.6[b]	23.1[c]
1960–69	17.5	13.7	37.11[d]	NA

Source: Baugher and Lamison-White (1996); http://www.censusbureau.gov/prod/2003pubs/p60-222.pdf.

[a]Data for 1972.
[b]Data for 1966.
[c]Data for 1972–79.
[d]Data for 1966–69.

teenagers; and women entered the workforce in great numbers. The United States now has many single-parent families that depend on the wages of a female head of household for their income.

Female-headed families are three times more likely to be in poverty than all families (table 7). Even more disturbing are the data for black and Hispanic female-

Table 7: Poverty Rates for Families by Race and Hispanic Origin; 1959–2002

Year	All Families	Families with Female Householder, No Husband Present			
		Total	White	Black	Hispanic
2002	10.4%	28.8%	24.1%	38.2%	36.4%
2001	9.9	28.6	24.3	37.4	37.8
2000	9.6	28.5	23.2	38.6	37.8
1999	10.2	30.4	24.7	41.0	40.7
1998	11.2	33.1	27.6	42.8	46.7
1997	11.6	35.1	30.7	42.8	50.9
1996	12.2	44.3	38.9	52.8	61.2
1995	12.3	36.5	29.7	48.2	52.8
1994	13.1	38.6	31.8	50.2	54.8
1993	13.6	38.7	31.0	53.0	53.2
1992	13.3	39.0	30.8	54.0[a]	51.5
1991	12.8	39.7	31.5	54.8[a]	52.7
1990	12.0	37.2	29.8	50.6[a]	53.0
1989	11.5	35.9	28.1	49.4[a]	50.6
1988	11.6	37.2	29.2	51.9[a]	55.0
1987	12.0	38.1	29.6	54.1[a]	55.6
1986	12.0	38.3	30.6	53.8[a]	52.9
1985	12.6	37.6	29.8	53.2[a]	55.7
1984	13.1	38.4	29.7	54.6[a]	56.2
1983	13.9	40.2	31.2	57.0[a]	55.1
1982	13.6	40.6	30.9	58.8[a]	60.1
1981	12.5	38.7	29.8	56.7[a]	55.9
1980	11.5	36.7	28.0	53.4[a]	54.5
1975	10.9	37.5	29.4	54.3[a]	57.2
1972	10.3	38.2	27.4	58.1[a]	53.5
1965	15.8	48.9	35.4	65.3[a]	NA
1959	20.8	49.4	40.2	70.6[a]	NA

Source: http://wwwcensus.gov/hhes/poverty/prevdetailtabs.html; Baugher and Lamison-White (1996).

[a]Data from 1966.

headed households. In 2002, 38.2 percent of black female-headed families and 36.4 percent of Hispanic female-headed families were in poverty—more than one in three families! Also, policies or work reform programs that purely address work as the sole purpose for reducing reliance on the state have been questioned (Walter, 2002).

This hierarchy of poverty faithfully reflects income inequalities. The nation's median income for all households in 2002 was $42,900. For two-parent families it was $56,747 compared with $13,143 for families with a female head of household. (DeNavas, 2003, p. 9). Again race and ethnicity make a difference. Ethnic and gender discrimination together generate extremely low salaries for minority women and "impair women's ability to support themselves and their children" (Landrine & Klonoff, 1997, p. 8):

> If a job paid White men $20,000, then White women received $15,000, Black women $12,200, and Latinas $11,000 for the same work.

> If a job paid White men $35,000, then White women received $26,250, Black women $21,350, and Latinas $19,250 for the same work.

> If a job paid White men $50,000, then White women received $37,500, Black women $30,500, and Latinas $27,500 for the same work. (p. 8)

The group with perhaps the greatest risk of poverty consists of teenage parents and their children. The Children's Defense Fund (1998, pp. 81–82), a national non-profit children's advocacy organization, has reported a reversal and slow decline in teenage pregnancy in the 1990s, but only 25 percent of teens giving birth were married. According to the Congressional Budget Office, within one year of giving birth to their first child, 50 percent of unwed teenage mothers go on welfare, and within five years, 77 percent are receiving welfare benefits (Besharov, 1996, p. 35).

Poverty and Age

The younger the person, the more likely he or she is to live in poverty. In 2002, 16.3 percent of children were in poverty and the age cohort with the next largest poverty rate was young adults, ages 18 to 24 (table 8). In the primary work years, ages 25 to 54, poverty rates decrease. Finally, for people in retirement and relying on fixed incomes, poverty rates increase.

Despite a rise in poverty rates with retirement the percentage of seniors in poverty is lower than the rate for the whole population—10.4 percent. This was not always the case. In 1959, 35.2 percent of seniors lived in poverty compared with 22.4 percent of all people—and between 1967 and 1970, the senior poverty rate ranged from 29.5 to 21.6 percent, compared with a range of 14.2 to 12.6 percent for the whole population. The sharp decline in the poverty rate for seniors was a result of specific federal legislation (Jansson, 1993, p. 306). The Older Americans Act of

---

Table 8: Poverty Rates by Age Group and Ethnicity, 2002

		Percentage below Poverty Threshold		
Group	Total	18 and under	18–64	65 and over
All	16.7	16.3	10.6	10.4
White	13.4	12.8	8.7	8.9
Black	32.3	32.1	19.9	23.8
Asian	11.7	11.4	9.7	8.4
Hispanic	28.6	28.2	18.1	21.4

Source: http://ferret.bls.census.gov/prod/2003pubs/p60-222.pdf.

1965, the Supplemental Security Act, and the indexing of social security retirement checks in the early 1970s all helped to raise seniors' fixed incomes above the poverty threshold. It's important to recognize that the reductions in senior poverty are primarily due to federal support that pushes income levels slightly above the poverty threshold. Karger and Stoesz (2001) reported that in addition to seniors in poverty, another 7 percent are "near poor," with incomes just above the poverty threshold.

Did You Know...Children have been getting poorer as our nation grows richer. American children are twice as likely as adults to be poor. Children in the United States are 1.6 times more likely to be poor than those in Canada, 2 times more likely than those in Britain, and 3 times more likely than those in France or Germany. What is most astonishing is that the United States is the wealthiest of these nations and has the lowest unemployment levels (Children's Defense Fund, 1998).

Of all the figures we have discussed so far those that probably disturb people the most are the ones that involve our nation's children. For the better part of twenty years, poverty rates for children hovered around 20 percent—that is one in five children being poor. But in the mid-1990s, these rates began to decline. By 2000, poverty among children declined to 16.2 percent. While trends were gloomy for the last quarter of the twenty-first century, the recent decline of children in poverty can be attributed to the nation's economic strength and growth. The Children's Defense Fund, a national advocacy organization for children, notes that while child poverty decreased in general rates, it did rise in working-class families. "The rise of child poverty in full-time working families presents a challenge," said Deborah Weinstein, CDF's Director of Family Income. "It means we need to rethink how we continue to fight child poverty in this country" (http://www.childrensdefense.org/fs_chpov.php).

We know that poverty has negative consequences for those who live in it, but what specific effects does it have on children? What exactly does it mean to be a child raised in an impoverished home? Some facts can help to answer these questions:

1. Poor children are twice as likely as nonpoor children to have stunted growth, iron deficiency, and severe asthma.

2. Low-income children are three times more likely to die during childhood.

3. According to the Centers for Disease Prevention and Control (CDC), poor children are more likely to die before their first birthdays than children whose mothers smoked during pregnancy.

4. Every year spent in poverty increases the chances that a child will fall behind grade level by age 18.

5. Three out of four poor children live in a working family (http://www.childrensdefense.org/fs_cpfaq_facts.php).

Table 9: Poverty Rates for Children, 1959–2002

Year	Under Age 18
2002	16.7%
2001	16.3
2000	16.2
1999	16.9
1998	18.9
1997	19.9
1996	20.5
1995	20.2
1994	21.2
1993	22.0
1992	21.9
1991	21.8
1990	20.6
1989	19.6
1988	19.5
1987	20.3
1986	20.5
1985	20.7
1984	21.5
1983	22.3
1982	21.9
1981	20.0
1980	18.3
1975	17.1
1970	15.1
1965	21.0
1959	27.3

Source: http://www.childrensdefense.org/fs_cptb_young18.php;
http://www.childrensdefense.org/fs_cptb_child00.php.

We've seen that race and ethnicity affect poverty rates for women and for the general population, so we shouldn't be surprised to learn that race and ethnicity also affect age-specific poverty rates. In 1995 poverty rates were 41.5 percent for black youths and 39.3 percent for Hispanic youths, compared with 16.2 percent for white youths. Poverty rates were 25.4 percent for black seniors and 23.5 percent for Hispanic seniors, compared with an overall senior poverty rate of about 10 percent (Baugher & Lamison-White, 1996, pp. C-5–C-7). These numbers represent long-standing inequalities.

WHY IS THERE POVERTY IN A WEALTHY NATION?

Entire university courses are devoted to studying how poverty can exist in the midst of great wealth. Countless books and articles also attempt to answer this

Figure 2: Subsidized housing in a small midwestern city. These units were built for low-income working-class families and are located on the edge of the city.

question. The breadth of this topic allows us only to review some theories put forth to explain why poverty continues to exist.

Karger and Stoesz (1994, pp. 146–152) identified four theories of poverty: the culture of poverty, the underclass, eugenics and poverty, and the radical school of poverty. Each differs markedly from the others, and depending on your philosophical and political views you may have strong reactions, positive or negative, to some or all of the theories:

Culture of poverty: Poverty and its traits are transmitted from one generation to the next. Behavior is learned and repeated. There is a sense of hopelessness, indifference, and dependence and a focus on the present rather than the future. Impulse control is lacking, and resignation and disintegration of the family if pervasive.

Underclass: A population is clustered around similar behaviors and beliefs and is outside the dominant or majority section of society. Its neighborhoods deteriorate, employment opportunities diminish, and marriage rates decline. The underclass is on the outside looking in and is not able to access society's opportunity structure.

Eugenics: Poverty is tied to genetics. Accumulation of wealth depends on ability, which is directly related to intelligence, which is inherited. The "most capable" citizen should receive the greatest benefits, which in turn will stimulate this group to take greater leadership in society.

Name: Dana Kaplan

Place of residence: Burlington, Vermont

College/university degrees: University of Vermont, BSW

Present position: Case Manager

What do you do in your spare time? In my spare time, I do what I am doing right now…I sit in a coffee shop and write, or read books, or the local newspaper. I am in an indie-pop band, so we spend a lot of time either practicing, or playing shows. If I am not with them, I'm usually listening to music or playing the guitar. I love spending time with my friends, cooking, being outside, and going for bike rides. I grew up in New York City, so I like to people watch. I also take photographs and love a good yard sale.

Why did you choose social work as a career? I happened upon the field of social work more than anything else. I didn't know what the term meant until I visited the University of Vermont and saw it was an option for a major. I thought it was fantastic because it was doing what I knew I already loved—working with people—but on a professional level. I've come to view it as less of a "career" choice, and more of just something I am involved in, something that's important to me to do as an active member of my community.

What is your favorite social work story? I was recently working with a client who was sleeping in his car with his two dogs. The client was reluctant to come in for regular case management sessions, but would drop by when the need arose. One of his dogs got an eye infection, and the client was without the money to pay for the care. This was case management outside the box. I was able to network with a local veterinary office that provided the medical care needed. That afternoon I found myself driving to a local pet store who graciously donated two dog sweaters to the client. Currently, they are living in a motel and both dogs are healthy and warm. I like this story because the situation was unique. Practicing social work can encompass such a broad range of services, depending on each individual's particular needs and desires. This time it was case management for a dog—who knows what it will be tomorrow.

What would be the one thing you would change in our community if you had the power to do so? I'd create more affordable housing, and a livable wage. I'd bridge the gaps that exist between different sub-groups of people: the university students, the locals, the mentally ill, the queer and the straight, the wealthy, and the economically challenged. If we could all listen to each other's stories a bit more, and be open to the differences that do exist between us, we might have a better understanding of one another, and I bet things would run more smoothly. Now where's the magic wand?

Radical school: Poverty is exploitation of one group of people by another. The purpose of poverty is to provide a source of cheap labor—the cheaper the labor, the greater the profits. A second purpose of poverty is to provide the middle class with a group to whom it can feel superior, which moderates tension between the middle and upper classes.

Each of these theories is much more elaborate than the brief summaries we give here. At the end of the chapter we list further reading on these four theories.

Setting forth another perspective Darby (1996, p. 20) listed five factors that have produced poverty:

Decline in low-wage jobs: Fewer jobs are available for the labor pool.

Immigration: New immigrants take low-paying jobs away from unemployed residents.

Decline in labor force participation and work effort: Work effort among men is down over the long term.

Breakdown of traditional family structures: The number of single-parent families has increased, particularly among blacks.

Drugs: Alcohol, tobacco, and other drugs (ATOD) continue to plague the most disadvantaged populations. ATOD use among inner city youth is increasing.

According to Darby, these five factors are intertwined. Therefore, efforts to address poverty that are limited, in that they are only aimed at one of these five areas, can be futile. Rather, efforts must be coordinated to target all of these areas.

Johnson and Schwartz (1988) divided the causes of poverty into three broad areas: economic, social, and political. Economic causes relate to unequal distribution of income across society, inadequate income supports in public assistance programs—TANF and food stamps, for example—and unemployment and underemployment rates. Social causes of poverty refer to negative views the public holds of the poor, the strong belief in self-reliance, and discrimination against people based on race, ethnicity, and gender. Political causes include lack of participation in the political process by the poor and unjust social policies. Poverty and welfare programs are not popular in political circles and seem to be more vulnerable to public scrutiny and cutbacks than other public programs.

PROGRAMS TO AID THE POOR

It is time to examine current programmatic responses to poverty in the United States and to consider how these programs are viewed and how their recipients are treated. This section presents a brief overview of major public assistance programs.

In chapter 3 we learned that the modern welfare system has its roots firmly planted in the Great Depression of the 1930s and the passage of the Economic

Security Act of 1935. A second major federal welfare initiative occurred in the 1960s with the advent of President Johnson's War on Poverty. Finally, a third, dramatic shift in federal social welfare programs for the poor took shape with the passage and implementation of the Personal Responsibility and Work Opportunity Reconciliation Act of 1996.

This act was a sweeping reform of the role of the federal government in welfare provision. This 1996 act dramatically restructured programs to aid the poor and ended the nation's six-decade-old guarantee of cash assistance to poor families.

Temporary Assistance for Needy Families

The 1996 act created a new federal program, Temporary Assistance for Needy Families (TANF), which replaced AFDC. TANF, which is commonly referred to as "welfare," is the monthly cash assistance program for poor families with children under age 18. In 2002, a family of three (mother and two children) may qualify for TANF if their gross income is below $784 a month and assets are worth less than $1,000. TANF differs from AFDC in several ways:

1. States no longer have to help all families judged by the federal government to be in poverty but can use their own definitions of poverty and eligibility.

2. Parents must work within two years of receiving their cash benefits, and the option to shorten this two-year period is given to each state.

3. States must impose a sixty-month (five year) lifetime limit on TANF aid, and although states can shorten this length of time, they are not allowed to expand it. Therefore, five years is the lifetime limit.

4. Funds are given to states in block grants, which allow each state significant discretion in how to use the funds (http://www.childrensdefense.org/fs_cpfaq_welf.php).

Implementation of state discretion and time limits. No longer is cash assistance to the poor an entitlement, it is now short term and variable (Ginsberg, 1998, pp. 188–189). Taking advantage of the flexibility allowed by the federal legislation some states modified TANF services by setting stricter time limits on how long someone in poverty could receive cash assistance. The U.S. House of Representatives, in its reauthorization of the Personal Responsibility, Work and Family Promotion Act of 2003 (H.R.4), called for increasing the number of hours a parent/caretaker must work in order to receive benefits; the House bill proposed a required 40 hours, up from 30 hours, per week. Of this time, a minimum of 24 hours must be in "core" activities, which may be paid or unpaid with the remaining hours spent in unspecified activities, such as education or training (http://www.childrensdefense.org/TANF_fact_sheets_2003/default.htm). H.R.4 is severely underfunded, with an a five-year appropriation of $1 billion compared with a Congressional Budget Office estimate of $8 to $11 billion needed just to cover child care costs! (http://www.childrensdefense.org/TANF_fact_sheets_2003/default.htm).

TANF provides states the flexibility to structure its programs within broad and flexible guidelines set by the U.S. Congress. As a result, states have different names for the programs, time limits, program requirements, and cash benefits. Essentially, a person living in Florida is treated differently than a person living in Wisconsin. Even with this flexibility, this variation takes place within an iron constraint. The lifetime limit of 60 months is a national limit. If a person receives TANF aid for 50 months in one state and then moves to a state with a lower time limit, such as Florida, then the second state's limit has already been exceeded and the person receives no further TANF aid there. Even if the person had moved to a state that had not lowered its time limit, only a further 10 months of TANF assistance would be available.

Work requirements. TANF requires adults to work, a significant departure from the AFDC program and the philosophy behind the War on Poverty of the 1960s. The law mandates that by 2002, a person must work a minimum of thirty hours each week, a rise from the twenty weekly hours required in 1997. A child's TANF benefits can be reduced or eliminated if the parent is not participating fully in the program.

A further example of the state centered approach of TANF is reflected in the various names for the state's programs. As shown in table 10, names for the programs vary across the country, which leads to confusion by the general public.

Few forms of preparatory education and job training meet the work requirement. For example, adults over age 20 attempting to earn GEDs and most people working toward college degrees are not eligible for TANF. Community service may be used in place of work, but this option is left to the discretion of individual states.

As with most TANF implementation issues, states can establish their own guidelines on how soon a person must be working to avoid elimination from TANF rolls. Virginia requires a person to be employed within ninety days; other states demand employment within twenty-four months.

Child care. An important component of TANF is the requirement that communities provide childcare to TANF participants. As adults, in unprecedented numbers, are now required to work, there will be large increases in demand for childcare program slots—children cannot be left at home, unattended and unprotected. Funding is required for childcare services to support low-paid employees passing through the TANF system. Unfortunately, according to the Children's Defense Fund (http://www.childrensdefense.org/TANF_fact_sheets_2003/default.htm), not enough funds have been appropriated to support childcare for all of the poor. Social work professionals will be needed to assist these parents in finding low-cost childcare so that they can maintain their jobs.

Did You Know…To qualify for TANF aid a parent that is a minor must live at home with parent(s) or in a home supervised by an adult. Also a teen mother must attend school or a training program once her baby is twelve weeks old.

Table 10: Names of State TANF Programs

State	Name
Alabama	FA (Family Assistance Program)
Alaska	ATAP (Alaska Temporary Assistance Program)
Arizona	EMPOWER (Employing and Moving People Off Welfare and Encouraging Responsibility)
Arkansas	TEA (Transitional Employment Assistance)
California	CALWORKS (California Work Opportunity and Responsibility to Kids)
Colorado	Colorado Works
Connecticut	JOBS FIRST
Delaware	ABC (A Better Chance)
Dist. of Col.	TANF
Florida	Welfare Transition Program
Georgia	TANF
Guam	TANF
Hawaii	TANF
Idaho	Temporary Assistance for Families in Idaho
Illinois	TANF
Indiana	TANF, cash assistance; IMPACT (Indiana Manpower Placement and Comprehensive Training), TANF work program
Iowa	FIP (Family Investment Program)
Kansas	Kansas Works
Kentucky	K-TAP (Kentucky Transitional Assistance Program)
Louisiana	FITAP (Family Independence Temporary Assistance Program), cash assistance; FIND Work (Family Independence Work Program), TANF work program
Maine	TANF, cash assistance; ASPIRE (Additional Support for People in Retraining and Employment), TANF work program
Maryland	FIP (Family Investment Program)
Massachusetts	TAFDC (Transitional Aid to Families with Dependent Children), cash assistance; ESP (Employment Services Program), TANF work program
Michigan	FIP (Family Independence Program)
Minnesota	MFIP (Minnesota Family Investment Program)
Mississippi	TANF

Food Programs

Food stamps. The federal Food Stamp Program was designed to fight hunger and malnutrition. Prior to the Great Depression, no national coordinated effort addressed these fundamental issues. The problem was largely left to the states and local communities to deal with. For the most part, antihunger programs distributed actual food items. This practice moved to the national level when, in 1933, the Federal Surplus Relief Corporation was created to distribute surplus food.

Table 10: Names of State TANF Programs—(*Continued*)

State	Name
Missouri	Beyond Welfare
Montana	FAIM (Families Achieving Independence in Montana)
Nebraska	Employment First
Nevada	TANF
New Hampshire	FAP (Family Assistance Program), financial aid for work-exempt families; NHEP (New Hampshire Employment Program), financial aid for work-mandated families
New Jersey	WFNJ (Work First New Jersey)
New Mexico	NM Works
New York	FA (Family Assistance Program)
North Carolina	Work First
North Dakota	TEEM (Training, Employment, Education Management)
Ohio	OWF (Ohio Works First)
Oklahoma	TANF
Oregon	JOBS (Job Opportunities and Basic Skills Program)
Pennsylvania	Pennsylvania TANF
Puerto Rico	TANF
Rhode Island	FIP (Family Independence Program)
South Carolina	Family Independence
South Dakota	TANF
Tennessee	Families First
Texas	Texas Works (Department of Human Services), cash assistance; Choices (Texas Workforce Commission), TANF work program
Utah	FEP (Family Employment Program)
Vermont	ANFC (Aid to Needy Families with Children), cash assistance; Reach Up, TANF work program
Virgin Islands	(FIP) Family Improvement Program
Virginia	VIEW (Virginia Initiative for Employment, Not Welfare)
Washington	WorkFirst
West Virginia	West Virginia Works
Wisconsin	W-2 (Wisconsin Works)
Wyoming	POWER (Personal Opportunities With Employment Responsibility)

Source: www.acf.hhs.gov/programs/ofa/tnfnames.htm As of 9/04/2002.

The first Food Stamp Program project, which ran from 1939 to 1943, used two types of stamps: blue and orange. Blue stamps could be used only for surplus commodities, while orange stamps allowed the purchase of any type of food.

Did You Know...In 1997 the average amount of food stamps per person per meal was less than $.80.

Some key points about TANF

Total TANF recipients (February 2000): 129,822 (99,817 children, 30,005 adults) Number of cases (families): 53,171

- TANF budget, FY 99: $184.8 million ($54.4 million state funds)
- From January 1997 to June 2000, the number of families receiving cash assistance decreased by 53.8 percent, or 61,994 families.
- TANF makes up 11 percent of DHR's budget, or 2 percent of the state's FY 2000 budget.
- Average number of families and individuals receiving cash assistance each month:

	1995	1996	1997	1998	1999
Families	139,253	132,627	114,154	84,513	65,198
People	383,177	360,035	302,473	220,417	153,060

Racial/ethnic breakdown:

White: 17 percent   Hispanic: 1.3 percent
Black: 80.9 percent   Asian: 0.3 percent

- Legal immigrants make up about 2.4 percent of those receiving cash assistance.
- About 82 percent of all families receiving TANF have three or fewer people in the family; 11 percent have four, and 7 percent have more than four.
- The average length of time families with an adult included in the grant have been receiving TANF is 18.3 months. As of September 1999, about 17 percent of all families with an adult had been receiving TANF continuously since January 1997.
- Average monthly cash benefit through February 2000: $223
- Average family size: 3 (mother, 2 children)
- Maximum monthly benefit for family of three: $280
- Poverty level for a family of three: $1,157/month
- Standard of need for family of three: $424/month
- Percentage of TANF families with a working member: 9 percent

In 1961, a demonstration Food Stamp Program was started. It led in 1964 to the passage of the Food Stamp Act. Under the auspices of the Department of Agriculture, clients received stamps that allowed them to purchase certain American-grown or -produced food at certain supermarkets. The current program structure was implemented in 1977 with the goal of alleviating hunger and malnutrition by permitting low-income households to obtain a more nutritious diet through normal channels of trade.

The 1996 welfare reform efforts included a $27 billion cutback in the Food Stamp Program over six years, to be achieved primarily by reducing, denying, or ending assistance to needy families.

Participation in the Food Stamp Program in April 2003 (the latest data available) increased by 220,683 persons from the previous month, to 21,239,873 persons.

In April 2003, 21.3 million people received food stamps; by that month, the number of food stamp participants had increased in 29 of the 33 preceding months (http://www.frac.org/html/news/fsp/03apr.html).

Eligibility for the Food Stamp Program is based on financial and nonfinancial factors. The application process includes completing and filing an application form, being interviewed, and verifying facts to determine eligibility. With certain exceptions, a household that meets the eligibility requirements is qualified to receive benefits. Most legal immigrants who were in the United States as of August 22, 1996, and who are children, elderly, or disabled are eligible for food stamps, while undocumented immigrants and many legal immigrants are ineligible for food stamp benefits. Some able-bodied, childless, unemployed adults have time limits on their receipt of food stamp benefits. Households, except those with elderly or disabled members, must have gross incomes below 130 percent of the poverty line. All households must have net incomes below 100 percent of poverty to be eligible. A household may have up to $2,000 in countable resources (e.g., checking/savings account, cash, stocks/bonds).

The maximum food stamp benefit for a family of three, in April 2003, was $366 per month—note, this is based on a family with $0 income! Households may have $2,000 in countable resources, such as a bank account. Households may have $3,000 if at least one person is age 60 or older, or is disabled. Certain resources are not counted, such as a home and lot and the resources of people who receive Supplemental Security Income (SSI) or benefits under the Temporary Assistance for Needy Families (TANF) program. In 2003, the maximum gross monthly income for a family of four is $1,994 or $23,928—note this is before taxes and other deductions. The maximum benefit for a family of four is $471—note, this means the family has little to no income to receive this monthly allotment. Another way to consider this monthly allotment is that a family of four will receive $15.48 per day for meals or slightly more than $5.00 per meal for four people.

School lunch and breakfast and other food programs. Other federal food programs we need to consider in addition to food stamps include the National School Lunch and Breakfast Program, WIC, and Meals on Wheels. Targeted toward the poor, these programs were developed as supplements for specific vulnerable population groups.

The National School Lunch Program (NSLP), which provides school children in the United States a lunch every school day, was created by Congress following World War II. At that time, the military draft showed a strong correlation between physical deficiencies and childhood malnutrition.

In 1998, Congress expanded the NSLP to include cash reimbursement for snacks served in certain afterschool educational and enrichment programs. During the 2001–02 school year more than 27.2 million children participated in the National School Lunch Program through more than 97,000 schools and residential child care institutions. On a typical school day, 15.6 million of these 27.2 million total participants were receiving free or reduced price lunches.

The National School Breakfast program was established by Congress as a pilot program in 1966 in areas where children had long bus rides to school and in areas where many mothers were in the workforce. The program was standardized as a permanent entitlement in 1975 to assist schools in providing nutritious morning meals to the nation's children. Research clearly shows that beginning each day with a nutritious breakfast results in better and stronger learning outcomes. Studies conclude that students who eat school breakfast increase their math and reading scores as well as improve their speed and memory in cognitive tests. Research also shows that children who eat breakfast at school, in particular closer to class and test-taking time, perform better on standardized tests than those who skip breakfast or eat breakfast at home.

On a typical day during the 2001–02 school year, 8.1 million children in more than 75,000 schools and institutions participated in the breakfast program. Of these children, 82 percent received free or reduced-price breakfasts. To receive free breakfast, household income must be at or below 130 percent of the federal poverty level; for reduced-price breakfast, income must be at or below 185 percent. Children from households with income above 185 percent of the federal poverty level pay most of the price for breakfast, although their meals are still partially subsidized. For the 2003–04 school year, 130 percent of the poverty level is $19,838 for a family of three; 185 percent is $28,231. Parents apply to their children's school for their children to receive free or reduced-price meals. The same application covers both lunch and breakfast. However, children from households that receive food stamps, Temporary Assistance for Needy Families (TANF), or the Food Distribution Program on Indian Reservations (FDPIR) are automatically eligible for free school meals.

The Special Supplemental Nutrition Program for Women, Infants, and Children (WIC) was enacted in 1972 to provide nutritional counseling and basic food supplements to prenatal and postpartum low-income women and their children. According to the Children's Defense Fund (1998, p. 43), every $1 spent on WIC saves $3.50 in future federal supports including health, education, and cash assistance. Women generally receive food vouchers that entitle them to certain items including milk, eggs, cheese, infant formula, cereals, and fruits and vegetables. The type and amount of food is specified, limiting the adult's selection. Income guidelines require that a family's income must fall below 185 percent of the U.S. poverty threshold, or $33,845 in 2002. About 47 percent of all babies are enrolled in the WIC program with a monthly average of 7.47 million participants. In WIC's first month of operation in 1974, 88,000 people participated.

Targeted to supplement and improve the nutritional needs of seniors in poverty, the Meals on Wheels program began in 1972. In some instances, meals are provided in the senior's home, while in other cases, meals are provided at a central location such as a senior center. An important and unintended benefit of the program is that seniors, many of whom are isolated, are provided daily contact with others. Volunteers who deliver meals to seniors are able to check on the elderly and ensure that all is fine with them.

Supplemental Security Income

Supplemental Security Income (SSI) was enacted in 1972 by combining three categorical programs that had been part of the Economic Security Act: Old Age

Assistance, Aid to the Blind, and Aid to the Totally and Permanently Disabled. Prior to 1972, these three programs had been run by the states. With the creation of SSI, operations were transferred to the federal government.

SSI is a means-tested public assistance program. Age is not an eligibility requirement. Potential clients include the mentally retarded, those over age 65 who have little or no income, those who are legally blind, those disabled because of physical or mental impairment, some people who are visually impaired but do not meet the requirements for blindness, addicts and alcoholics in treatment, and children under age 18 who have an impairment comparable to those that determine eligibility for adults.

In May 2003, SSI participants totaled 6.8 million who received an average monthly payment of $413.46 (Social Security Administration, 2003). To be eligible for SSI, an applicant's resources must be minimal. Assets were limited to $2,000 for an individual and $3,000 for a couple, excluding a home; the value of a car was limited to $4,500 Generally, a person who has unearned income of less than $572 a month will qualify for a federal SSI payment. A couple generally can qualify with unearned income of less than $849. Because a large portion of earned income is disregarded, a person who earns up to $1,189 a month ($1,743 for a couple) may receive a federal payment. (However, people who are applying for SSI disability benefits and earn more than $800 a month probably won't be eligible for benefits.)

Not all resources are counted in determining whether an applicant meets the resource limit. The following are excluded (that is, not considered) to be personal resources:

- *A home* regardless of its value.
- *Personal effects or household goods* with a total value of $2,000 or less are not counted. If the total value exceeds $2,000, the excess counts.
- Typically the value of *one car* does not count.
- *Life insurance policies* with a total face value of $1,500 or less per person are not counted.
- *Burial plots or spaces* for an individual and immediate family generally do not count.
- *Burial funds* for an individual and spouse do not count if they are specifically set aside for burial purposes and do not exceed $1,500 per person.
- *Resources* held under the Uniform Gifts to Minors Act or held in trusts that are administered by custodians or trustees may not be counted.
- *Property* essential to an individual's self-support is not counted. Such property may include nonbusiness income-producing property and property used to produce essential goods and services.
- *Resources* that a person who is blind or disabled needs to fulfill an approved plan for achieving self-support are not considered.
- *Disaster assistance* and certain Native corporation stocks held by natives of Alaska also are excluded.
- *Any retroactive SSI payments or retroactive Social Security benefits* paid to a recipient are not counted as resources for six months after they are received.

◆ *Crime victims' compensation payments* are not counted.
◆ *State and local government relocation assistance* is not counted as a resource for nine months after it is received (see www.ssa.gov/pubs/ 11015.html).

Legal Immigrants

One of the most radical changes introduced by the 1996 welfare reform act was the sweeping elimination of legal immigrants from all public programs. Legal immigrants become eligible for public assistance only when they become citizens or have worked for forty calendar quarters (ten years). A public outcry led to the amendment of the law to allow legal immigrants receiving SSI on or before August 26, 1996, to continue to receive payments. Yet this wasn't the case for all programs. As a result of the legislation approximately 300,000 legal immigrant children were removed from food stamp rolls (Children's Defense Fund, 1998, p. 7).

Ginsberg (1998, p. 192) identified the rationale behind this decisive move against immigrants: Legal immigrants should seek and obtain citizenship. Until then new immigrants are expected to support themselves or find assistance from private sources, including family or sponsors.

Earned Income Credit

The Earned Income Credit (EIC), also called the Earned Income Tax Credit (EITC), is a tax credit for working families with low incomes. One of the Clinton Administration's major welfare initiatives, it was developed to stimulate work among the poor. The EITC is a federal income tax credit for low-income workers who are eligible for and claim the credit. The credit reduces the amount of tax an individual owes, and may be returned in the form of a refund.

Eligible working families, either with or without children, pay less federal income tax or receive a larger tax refund. To claim the EITC, you must meet certain rules. These rules are summarized in table 11.

Income and family size determine the amount of the EITC. To qualify for the credit, both the earned income and the adjusted gross income for 2003 must be less than $29,666 for a taxpayer with one qualifying child ($30,666 for married filing jointly), $33,692 for a taxpayer with more than one qualifying child ($34,692 for married filing jointly), and $11,230 for a taxpayer with no qualifying children ($12,230 for married filing jointly).

In most cases, the EITC benefit does not affect other program benefits such as housing supplements, TANF, food stamps, Medicaid, and SSI.

SUMMARY

Poverty cuts across all races and ethnic groups, both genders, and all age groups. Indeed, more whites are poor than members of any other group. Nevertheless, poverty rates reveal that some groups are especially vulnerable (Carter, 2000).

Table 11: Earned Income Credit in a Nutshell

First, you must meet all the rules in this column.	Second, you must meet all the rules in one of these columns, whichever applies.		Third, you must meet both the rules in this column.	
Chapter 1. Rules for Everyone	Chapter 2. Rules If You Have a Qualifying Child	Chapter 3. Rules If You Do Not Have a Qualifying Child	Chapter 4. Figuring and Claiming the EIC	
1. You must have a valid social security number. 2. Your filing status cannot be Married filing separately. 3. You must be a U.S. citizen or resident alien all year. 4. You cannot file Form 2555 or Form 2555-EZ (relating to foreign earned income). 5. Your investment income must be $2,550 or less. 6. You must have earned income.	7. Your child must meet the relationship, age, and residency tests. 8. Your qualifying child cannot be used by more than one person to claim the EIC. 9. You cannot be a qualifying child of another person.	10. You must be at least age 25 but under age 65. 11. You cannot be the dependent of another person. 12. You cannot be a qualifying child of another person. 13. You must have lived in the United States more than half of the year.	14. Your adjusted gross income (AGI) must be less than: $33,178 ($34,178 for married filing jointly) if you have more than one qualifying child, ·$29,201 ($30,201 for married filing jointly) if you have one qualifying child, or $11,060 ($12,060 for married filing jointly) if you do not have a qualifying child.	15. Your earned income must be less than: ·$33,178 ($34,178 for married filing jointly) if you have more than one qualifying child, $29,201 ($30,201 for married filing jointly) if you have one qualifying child, or $11,060 ($12,060 for married filing jointly) if you do not have a qualifying child.

Source: Internal Revenue Service (2003)

Women, minorities, and children suffer disproportionately from poverty. One in six of all children are in poverty and one in four of children under age 6.

No consensus exists about causes of poverty, and theories to explain it are diverse and controversial (O'Gorman, 2000). The ideas proposed range from an individual's genetic makeup to deep, complicated structures of society. Also, considering the popularity of terms such as "family empowerment," it is time to do more than use these terms and to address the long-term effects of such concepts and how they can be measured (Bartle, Counchonal, Edward & Staker, 2002).

All social work professionals need to be aware that 1996 was a pivotal year in redirecting 61 years of entitlement programs and that as a result governmental antipoverty strategies have changed dramatically. Public programs are now time limited with greater state discretion in imposing limits. In most cases, once a family exhausts its TANF lifetime limit it is left to its own devices. TANF represents a new direction in welfare programming that stresses employment and penalizes clients who do not work or are unable to meet program requirements on a consistent basis.

As social work professionals, what does this mean for us? The social worker's role in public assistance programs is not as clear as it once was. A visit to your local food stamp or TANF office reveals that few, if any, of the workers are professional social workers. The public may believe that social workers run these programs, but the reality is that we do not. The need to assist the poor remains, however, and many people still believe that this is where social workers as professionals need to be.

McPhee and Bronstein (2003) outline four central implications for social workers in this area. First, social workers are encouraged to find ways to include the opinions and wishes of program recipients in future changes and continued implementation of the program. Second, the common myths about the poor and women on governmental and state subsidy in particular need to be identified and addressed based on evidence not opinion. Third, adequate resources need to be provided to front line workers to assist them to do their jobs. Fourth, if TANF is going to claim that it supports families, then the disproportionate concentration on work needs to be addressed, as in many ways this can be counter-productive to basic family reunification.

Poverty and its ravages can't be washed away by finding people jobs and wishing them well. Nor will it occur through providing minimum wage jobs for women and children living in poverty, because unfortunately no matter how hard you work raising a family out of poverty from these types of efforts will never work (O'Gorman, 2002). Clients need to be linked with appropriate resources—they need workers who understand the emotional and psychological toll that poverty takes and who can suggest how best to respond to this personal turmoil. Someone with a personal problem expects the best possible professional service from the social worker at the local mental health center. A patient in the hospital expects high-quality care from the hospital's social worker (Dziegielewski, 2003). Why should a poor person expect and receive a lower level of care?

A probably more important question concerns the sixty-month limit on welfare. What happens at the end of five years? Do we really believe that people forced without proper education into low-paying jobs will be self-sufficient within sixty months? And remember, a number of states have shorter time limits, some as short as twenty-four months. Where will these people go? Will they simply disappear? Of course not. They will remain in our communities—some more visible than others. Some people will say that they were given a chance and we shouldn't do anything else. But what will happen when the first child dies on the streets because a parent's TANF time expired? This question is extremely relevant because for TANF, positive effects depend on improved income, not just the ability to increase employment (O'Gorman, 2002). What will happen when our country experiences an economic recession and jobs are just not available?

The poor will always be part of our society, and we must have public policies in place that protect them rather than cause them harm. Social workers can and should take the lead in promoting just social policies that create opportunities for all people to achieve their full potential and gain economic independence.

References

Barker, R. (2003). *The social work dictionary* (5th ed.). Washington, DC: NASW Press.

Bartle, E.E., Couchonnal, G., Canda, E.R., & Staker, M.D. (2002). Empowerment as a dynamically developing concept for practice: Lessons learned from organizational ethnography. *Social Work 47* (1), 32–44.

Baugher, E., & Lamison-White, L. (1996). *Poverty in the United States, 1995 (Current Population Reports, Series pp. 60–194)*. Washington, DC: U.S. Department of Commerce, Bureau of the Census.

Besharov, D. J. (1996). Poverty, welfare dependency, and the underclass trends and explanations. In M. R. Darby (Ed.), *Reducing poverty in America: Views and approaches* (pp. 13–56). Thousand Oaks, CA: Sage.

Carter, J. (2000). Reducing poverty: It can be done. *New Perspectives Quarterly, 17* (1), 41–44.

Chelf, C. P. (1992). *Controversial issues in social welfare policy, government and the pursuit of happiness*. Newberry Park, CA: Sage.

Children's Defense Fund. (1998). *The state of America's children: Yearbook, 1997*. Washington, DC: Author.

Coulton, C., & Chow, J. (1995). Poverty. In R. Edwards et al. (Eds.), *Encyclopedia of social work* (19th ed., pp. 1867–1878). Washington, DC: NASW Press.

Darby, M. R. (1996). Facing and reducing poverty. In M. R. Darby (Ed.), *Reducing poverty in America: Views and approaches* (pp. 3–12). Thousand Oaks, CA: Sage.

DeNavas et al. (2003). U.S. Census Bureau Current Population Reports. *Income in the United States: 2002* (pp. 60–221). Washington, DC: U.S. Government Printing Office.

Dziegielewski, S.F. (2004). *The changing face of health care social work: professional practice in behaviorally based managed care* (2nd ed.). New York: Springer.

Gibelman, M., & Schervish, P. H. (1997). *Who are we: A second look*. Washington, DC: NASW Press.

Ginsberg, L. (1998). *Conservatives social welfare policy: A description and analysis*. Chicago: Nelson-Hall.

Institute for Research on Poverty. (1998). *Poverty thresholds and poverty guidelines*. Retrieved from http://www.ssc.wisc.edu/lrp/.

Internal Revenue Service (2003). Forms and Publications. Retrieved from: www.irs.gov/formspubs/page/0,,id%3D104425,00.html#T3.

Jansson, B. S. (1993). *The reluctant welfare state: A history of American social welfare policies* (2nd ed.). Pacific Grove, CA: Brooks/Cole.

Johnson, L. C., & Schwartz, C. L. (1988). *Social welfare: A response to human need*. Boston: Allyn and Bacon.

Karger, H., & Stoesz, D. (1994). *American social welfare policy: A pluralist approach*. New York: Longman.

Landrine, H., & Klonoff, E. A. (1997). *Discrimination against women: Prevalence, consequences, remedies*. Newberry Park, CA: Sage.

Lennon, T. (1997). *Statistics on social work education*, 1996. Alexandria, VA: CSWE.

McPhee, D.M., & Bronstein, L.R. (2003). The journey from welfare to work: Learning from women living in poverty. *Affilia, 18*, (1), 34–38.

O'Gorman, A. (2002). Playing by the rules and losing ground. *America, 187* (3), 12–16.

Segal, E., & Brzuzy, S. (1998). *Social welfare policy, programs, and practices*. Itasca, IL: Peacock.

Social Security Administration, Supplemental Security Record, (2003). Recipients (by type of payment), total payments, and average monthly payment, May 2002–May 2003. Retrieved on September 23, 2004 from www.ssa.gov/policy/docs/statcomps/ssi_monthly/2003-05/table1.html.

U.S. House Committee on Ways and Means. (1991). *Overview of entitlement programs*. Washington, DC: U.S. Government Printing Office.

Walter, M. (2002). Working their way out of poverty? Sole motherhood, work, welfare and material well-being. *Journal of Sociology, 38* (4), 361–382.

Further Reading on Theories about Poverty
Culture of Poverty

Banfield, E. C. & Lewis, O. (1966). *The unheavenly city*. Boston: Little, Brown.

Moynihan, D. P. (1965). *The negro family: The case for national action*. Washington, DC: Office of Policy Planning and Research.

Underclass

Auletta, K. (1982). *The underclass*. New York: Vintage.

Ricketts, E., & Sawhill, I. (1988). Defining and measuring the underclass. *Journal of Policy Analysis and Management, 7* (2), 316–325.

Wilson, W. J. (1987). *The truly disadvantaged*. Chicago: University of Chicago Press.

Eugenics

Jensen, A. R. (1969). How much can we boost IQ and scholastic achievement? *Harvard Educational Review, 39*, 1–23.

Shockley, W. (1976). Sterilization: A thinking exercise. In C. Bahema (Ed.), *Eugenics: Then and now*. Stroudsburg, PA: Doidon, Hutchinson and Ross.

Radical School

Gil, D. (1981). *Unraveling social policy*. Boston: Schenkman.

Piven, F., & Cloward, R. (1971). *Regulating the poor*. New York: Vintage.

Chapter 8

Child Welfare Services

IN 1995, OVER 70 MILLION CHILDREN UNDER AGE 18 MADE UP 26.8 percent of the U.S. population (Baugher & Lamison-White, 1996, p. C-5). In March of 2002 this number was raised to 72 million (U.S. Census Bureau, 2003). With the median income for American households being $46,300 for non-Hispanic White Americans (U.S. Census Bureau, 2002). Supporting and caring for these millions of children, taking into account the limited incomes most parents have, is the single most important investment we can make in the future of our society. In twenty years, people now in their mid-40s will rely heavily on the children of today to keep the United States prosperous.

We cannot overestimate the importance of today's children to tomorrow's society. Don't you want the best and brightest people leading our country? Don't you want competent and self-assured people in the labor force, supporting the retirement of workers of today? We need to start raising these bright and competent people early. Through current investment in support and intervention we can avoid a future in which millions of undereducated and at best minimally competent Americans continue to suffer from personal and social problems deeply rooted in their childhood.

The importance of nurturing children is not a new idea. Indeed, a complex child welfare system exists to give children the opportunity to grow and reach their full potential. Karger and Stoesz have asserted, however, that child welfare programs and services are controversial because "they sanction the intervention of human service professionals in family affairs that are ordinarily assumed to be private matters related to parental rights" (1994, p. 338). As long as some people believe that child welfare is based on intrusion in private matters it will "remain among the more controversial in American social welfare" (Karger & Stoesz, 1994, p. 339).

Most of us can remember being told that being a child should be "fun." Many adults long to return to a simpler time in their lives when cares and responsibilities were few and far between. For many, Norman Rockwell's images of small-town America capture the ideal childhood. Television too has actively promoted the idea of families as caring groups always having fun, even during hard times. *Father Knows Best, Good Times, The Brady Bunch*, and *The Cosby Show* illustrated life in suburbia and the city within a happy and caring family. When outside help was required, it often came from extended family members, friends, neighbors, religious organizations, and even membership associations.

Name: Sharonda V. Kelley

Place of residence: Alexander City, Alabama

College/university degrees: Miles College, BSW

Present position: Family and Children Service Unit Social Worker

Previous work/volunteer experience: Internship at Jefferson County DHR in Birmingham, AL.

What do you do in your spare time? Spare time is very precious and rare for me at the moment, but in my spare time I enjoy laughing at my two-year-old daughter Brooklyn and teaching her how to count and read. I'm twenty-four, and health and image is everything to me at the moment, so I work out at least three days out of the week. I also enjoy reading books by Catherine Palmer when I want to relax and try to have peace of mind, and most of all I love to dance and go out with my friends when I can!

Why did you choose social work as a career? Not knowing much about the profession of social work, I just simple tried it and it grew on me. I really enjoy linking, educating, and advocating for people.

What is your favorite social work story? One day I was transporting two foster kids back home from a visit with their mom and the sweetest thing happened. The toddler was crying like always because she didn't want her mom to go. So I gave her and her brother a lollypop each. Halfway down the road I looked in my rearview mirror to see that she was smiling and sucking away on that lollypop. The fact that it was all around her mouth made her even more precious. The moment was so captivating because she was happy, he was happy, and it made me happy.

What would be the one thing you would change in our community if you had the power to do so? The unemployment rate. The community that I live in was once run by a big athletic company, but now it is slowly fading with time, and it's affecting my community really badly. My heart hurts for the moms and dads that are being laid off, and most of all for the young adults who chose not to further their education. If I had a lot of money, I would bring in all types of businesses to Alexander City to keep its people from having to commute so far for work.

In this society we expect, and the media encourages us to expect, that *no* child will face the horrors of poverty, homelessness, abuse and neglect, and inadequate health care, or live in an environment where crime, alcohol, tobacco, and drug abuse are the norm. This is a worthy goal, but we sometimes satisfy these expectations simply by denying that such problems exist. After all, if the media did tell negative stories, ratings would probably plummet. Few sponsors, if any, would want to be the ones to tell America that all is not well with its children. But all is *not* well with America's children. For millions of children life is filled with turmoil. These children repeatedly face crises that may eventually lead to chaos and tragedy.

In this chapter, we look in depth at America's children. We examine what life is like for many of them and explore the laws, programs, and services geared toward helping them. In addition, we discuss how the public and voluntary child welfare systems work together.

CHILD WELFARE DEFINED

Let's begin by looking at how **child welfare** has been defined. The *Social Work Dictionary* defines child welfare as

> that part of human services and social welfare programs and ideologies ori-
> ented toward the protection, care, and healthy development of children.
> Child welfare measures are found in national, state, and local programs, and
> are usually designed to prevent conditions that interfere with the healthy
> and positive development of children. (Barker, 1991, p. 35)

Heffernan, Shuttlesworth, and Ambrosino, like Barker, offer a very broad view of child welfare that encompasses "programs and policies that address the needs of children, youth, and families as diverse as the type of needs experienced" (1988, p. 167). Linderman (1995) also stresses the formal organizational aspects of child welfare. His definition of child welfare characterizes it as both a public and a voluntary effort to coordinate seven interrelated objectives:

- ◆ Protect and promote the well-being of children
- ◆ Support families and seek to prevent problems that may result in neglect, abuse, and exploitation
- ◆ Promote family stability by assessing and building on family strengths while addressing needs
- ◆ Support the full array of out-of-home care services for children who require them
- ◆ Take responsibility for addressing social conditions that negatively affect children and families, such as inadequate housing, poverty, chemical dependence, and lack of access to health care
- ◆ Support the strengths of families whenever possible
- ◆ Intervene when necessary to ensure the safety and well-being of children

Dobelstein (1996), however, omits the voluntary sector from his discussion and concludes that child welfare involves a broad range of public activities undertaken on behalf of children. Mirroring Dobelstein's view, Chelf describes family and child welfare policies as "covering a broad spectrum of public efforts . . . [and] closely interwoven with several other policy sectors such as health, nutrition, education, and income maintenance, making them somewhat a confusing patchwork of policies and programs" (1992, p. 108).

The work of Kadushin and Martin is especially important in understanding social welfare because they view it from a social work perspective. For them, "child welfare is concerned with the general well being of all children. It encompasses any and all measures designed to protect and promote the bio-psycho-social development of children" (1988, p. 1). Gil gives another straightforward definition of child welfare: "In the simplest terms, as well as in a most profound sense, child welfare means conditions of living in which children can 'fare well," conditions in which their bodies, minds, and souls are free to develop spontaneously through all stages of maturation" (1985, p. 12).

All these definitions of child welfare have several points in common. First, the child welfare system is firmly established within the public sector. Second, child welfare policy is closely tied to and directly influenced by family policy. Third, the policies, services, and programs included in child welfare cover a broad area, but all aim to provide children the environment they need for positive growth and full development. Taking into account these commonalities, we define the child welfare system as the system of services and programs that protect, promote, and encourage the growth and development of all children in order that they can achieve their full potential and function at their optimal level in their communities.

AMERICA'S DIVERSE CHILDREN AND THEIR FAMILIES

Although there are more white children than any other racial or ethnic group, population increases for blacks and Hispanics have been far greater than for whites (see chapter 7, table 6, p. 154). The Hispanic population in the United States has grown quite dramatically, but it is important to note that these rates may be inflated. The term "Hispanic" is difficult to define. In the U.S. census Latinos can classify themselves as Hispanic, black, or white; in other cases, they might be listed as both Hispanic and black. Part of the growth in the Hispanic population may actually reflect resolution of this confusion as individuals switch affiliations.

Just as American children have become more diverse so too have their families. The family is a critical institution in shaping and transmitting from generation to generation the values and rich traditions of culturally and ethnically diverse Americans. The kaleidoscope of families includes those whose roots are Anglo-European, Native Indian, African, Latino, Asian, and Middle Eastern, to mention a few. American families, whatever their ethnic heritage, are expected to respond to the expectations and norms of this society, even though many have very different cultural traditions, values, beliefs, norms, folkways, and mores. Some families hold their distinctive beliefs so strongly that they refuse to change; instead, they pass the same set of rigid expectations from one generation to the next. The key challenge for families is to balance the rich traditions and customs of their cultural heritage with the values and beliefs of the dominant society.

Family structures are also becoming more diverse. No longer do families mirror the traditional stereotype of a two-parent household in which the father works and the mother maintains the home. Single-parent households, homosexual par-

---

Did You Know...In 1996, 68 percent of American children lived with two parents, down from 85 percent in 1970; about 24 percent lived only with their mothers, 4 percent with their fathers, and 4 percent with neither parent (Brunner, 1997, p. 365).

Child Fact Sheet

◆ 11.7 million American children younger than 18 lived below the poverty line.

◆ More than half the children born in the 1990s will spend some of their childhood in a single-parent family.

◆ Only one in four children in a single-parent family receive child support payments.

◆ The average monthly child support payment to a child in a single-parent family is $168 or $2,000 per year.

◆ Over 2.5 million households with children live in substandard housing.

◆ Children account for 40 percent of the nation's homeless.

◆ One out of every six American children (16.3 percent) was poor in 2001. By race and ethnicity, 30.2 percent of Black children, 28.0 percent of Hispanic children, 11.5 percent of Asian and Pacific Islander children, and 9.5 percent of Non-Hispanic White children were poor.

◆ Three out of four poor children live in a working family. 74 percent of children in poverty live in a family where someone works full or part time for at least part of the year. One out of three poor children (34 percent) lives with someone who worked full time year round.

◆ There are more poor White Non-Hispanic children (4.2 million) than poor Black children (3.5 million) or poor Hispanic children (3.6 million), even though the proportion of Black and Hispanic children who are poor is far higher. More poor children live in suburban and rural areas than in central cities.

◆ Poor families have only 2.2 children on average.

◆ Most child poverty is not temporary: 80 percent of children poor in one year are still poor the next year.

◆ Poor children are at least twice as likely as nonpoor children to suffer stunted growth or lead poisoning, or to be kept back in school.

◆ Poor children score significantly lower on reading, math and vocabulary tests when compared with otherwise-similar nonpoor children.

◆ A baby born to a poor mother is more likely to die before its first birthday than a baby born to an unwed mother, a high school dropout, or a mother who smoked during pregnancy, according to the Centers for Disease Control.

Source: www.childrensdefense.org/fs_cpfaq_facts.php

ents, and parents who both work are all becoming more common. For many, parents working outside the home, and in some cases having a second job, is not a choice but a necessity.

Divorce rates are increasing, and more children are seeing their parents split up than ever before. In the thirty-two years between 1960 and 1992, the number of divorces tripled from 400,000 to 1,200,000 annually, with nearly 50 percent of all marriages ending in divorce (Lindsey, 1994, p. 73). Although these numbers have been challenged, the rate appears to remain at 48–50 percent in 2003 (Americans for Divorce Reform, 2003).

Another significant force shaping family structure is the growth in the number of children born out of wedlock to single parents. Between 1950 and 1991, the number of such births increased almost ninefold from 140,000 to 1,200,000 annually (Lindsey, 1994, p. 74). Although the birthrate for adolescents—that is, the number of children born per 1,000 adolescents—declined in the early 1990s, 518,389 babies were born to teenage mothers in 1994 (Children's Defense Fund, 1998, pp. 81, 82). In that year, 36 percent of children lived with a single parent who had never married the birth partner (Brunner, 1997). Increased divorce rates and high out-of-wedlock birthrates have together fueled an increase in the number of single-parent households. This increased number of out-of-wedlock births, however, does not seem relevant to teenagers. For example, in 2002, the birth rate for teenagers was 5 percent lower than it was in 2001 and 10 percent lower than it was in 2000 (CDC, 2003). The exact reason for this decline is not known, but it is possible that these lower numbers may be related to a decrease in the overall number of births and to preventive education.

Have you ever wondered why so many people worry about the growing number of single-parent households? Why does it matter whether a family is single-parent or two-parent? The primary reason is that two-parent families usually have a greater income and therefore greater resources with which to carry out their parenting obligations and responsibilities. Simply stated, by pooling their income two parents have more money for the family to spend on goods and services. Lindsey (1994, p. 87) estimated that the difference between two- and one-parent families is so great that a single parent earns only 25 percent of what two parents can earn. Underlying this figure is the fact that most single parents are women, who have income levels much lower than average.

A two-parent family is also better able to supervise its children. With two adults available, whether taking turns or jointly, more nurturing parent-child time is available. A single parent often has no one to help ease the childcare burden. The single parent thus faces alone enormous challenges, having to manage a lower family income and singlehandedly maintain a safe and nourishing home environment (Lindsey, 1994, p. 87).

A third significant development changing family structure is the rise in "blended families." A blended family is one in which the primary caretakers did not give birth to one or more of the children who live in the household. Such families are most often the result of divorce and remarriage. With the high rate of American divorce and lifestyle adjustment, blended families are becoming more common.

These families often face a difficult task because supportive relations may need to be developed even before they can be nurtured. Becoming a blended family requires adjustment because members may enter and reenter the family at various times throughout their lives. These adjustments intensify the need to establish and maintain family unison and support. Although all family systems need constant negotiation to maintain equilibrium, blended families face the added struggle of keeping their balance as family members come and go.

The growing diversity and changing structure of American families is the focus of much attention. The kind of family situation regarded as "ideal" is often shaped by a **political lens**. Think about political candidates and their campaign rhetoric and advertisements. How often have you seen "the family" play a starring role in a local, state, or national election? The Republican Party's *Contract with America* (Gillespie & Schellhas, 1994) and the Christian Coalition's (1995) *Contract with the American Family* placed the family as the centerpiece of all political activities. Why have children and families become such hot political items? Three reasons come to mind immediately:

Every human being was once a child: Having been a child and had experiences that influenced the way you think and feel about things as you aged helps raise your consciousness in this area. Most of us identify with children's issues simply because of our own experiences. All of us had positive and negative childhood experiences. Most of us cherish the good times and wish we could have avoided the bad ones. Few, if any, adults believe it is in a child's best interest to suffer physical or emotional pain. Therefore, people support and encourage programs and services that prevent and alleviate children's suffering.

Children are vulnerable: Most adults agree that all children should be protected and have a safe environment in which to grow. Adults are responsible for ensuring that children are shielded from various risks.

Everyone has a family: Just as all of us were children once, we were all raised in some kind of family. Our families probably differed vastly. Some people had two parents; others come from single-parent homes. Some people were raised with siblings, others without. Some were raised in foster homes or were adopted; others had aunts, uncles, or other relatives as their primary caretakers; and for some, institutions played the family role. No matter what our family background, our experiences mean we have strong feelings about what families should be like.

THE RIGHTS OF CHILDREN

Children have fewer rights than adults (Wineman, 1995, p. 465). In this, two counterbalancing forces are at play. On one hand, we recognize that children generally are not able to make mature decisions. This is not a negative statement about young people but rather refers to their inexperience. For this reason, children's rights are limited, and critical decisions about and responsibility for their lives rests, not with them, but with their caregivers. On the other hand, we also recognize that children need protection—sometimes from their own caretakers. As a result, we have established a complex system of child protective services.

Figures 1a, b, c: These photographs were developed in an Arts Outreach project for teenage mothers. The program, "My Life, My Lens, My Child," was part of an effort to help the mothers to finish high school. The program, staffed by social workers and teachers, taught photography skills, provided enrichment, and offered a positive school experience. The mothers photographed their children in various settings and created collages.

The interesting history of children's rights thus for the most part reflects ambivalence. From a legal standpoint children are treated differently than adults. Children can face "status offenses"—that is, crimes based on status, in this case age. For example, a child can be arrested or detained for drinking alcohol, smoking cigarettes, being truant or being a runaway. An adult cannot be arrested merely for smoking or drinking (unless doing so causes a public disturbance) or for running away from home or being truant.

The overriding principle of **parens patriae**—under which children can become wards of the state—guided interpretations of children's rights. This principle supported creation of a broad range of juvenile services including parent-child relationships (Crosson-Tower, 1998, p. 270). Taking this basic position, child advocates were able to argue that children should be viewed in a different light from adults and offered rehabilitation rather than punishment.

In 1899, the first juvenile court was established in Chicago based on the principle of *parens patriae* and the belief that children could be rehabilitated, which required a legal system far different from the punishment-based adult system. By 1925, all but two states—Maine and Wyoming—had juvenile courts; by 1945 all states had such courts. Prosecution took a back seat to treatment as the primary

focus of the juvenile justice system. Hearings were closed to the public to protect the child's right to confidentiality, and all juvenile legal records were sealed once the child reached the legal age of maturity, generally age 18. The juvenile court operated very informally. Attorneys were rarely provided for child offenders, and trial by jury and the right to appeal a decision were not available options. In these courtrooms hearsay evidence was admitted. Remember, the court's purpose was twofold: 1) to identify the problem and 2) to develop and implement an appropriate treatment plan.

The juvenile court changed dramatically as a result of U.S. Supreme Court decisions in the 1960s. Juveniles were given many of the legal protections enjoyed by adults. Courts were required to allow attorneys to be present; witnesses could be cross-examined; defendants had the right to refuse to incriminate themselves; and guilty decisions (or, in some states, "not innocent" decisions) had to meet the legal standard of reasonable doubt.

In recent years, as violent juvenile crime has worsened, people have begun to ask whether children should also face some of the same penalties as adults. Horrific crimes committed by children in 1998 alone left many people in shock. Two young boys, ages 8 and 9, in Chicago, Illinois, murdered a young girl in order to ride her bicycle; two teenagers in Arkansas shot and killed schoolmates; another teenager walked into a school hallway and indiscriminately murdered his junior high school peers. The Chicago youth were released to their parents because state law forbade the incarceration of a child under age 10; these cases sparked a national debate over whether the teens should be tried in adult courts and, if found guilty, should serve their sentences in adult prisons or even be subjected to the death penalty. Is there an answer? At what age do we stop trying to rehabilitate young people? As you have probably guessed there are no clear-cut answers to these questions.

In a nutshell, historically children have had few rights, and there has been little agreement on what further rights, if any, they should be granted. In the past, the courts have primarily defined children's rights with regard to criminal proceedings against them. In addition, children have the right to financial support and education (Gustavsson & Segal, 1994, pp. 4, 6). Today, the United Nations continues to bring the rights of children to the forefront. The UN Convention on the Rights of the Child adopted in 1989 a declaration of children's rights. By 2003, 192 countries had formally ratified this Act, and the two remaining countries, the United States and Somalia, had announced agreement to do so (Convention on the Rights of the Child, 2003).This important declaration is very specific in identifying the issues facing children:

> Preamble . . . Childhood is entitled to special care and assistance. . . . The child . . . should grow up in a family environment, in an atmosphere of happiness, love, and understanding. . . . The child, by reason of his physical and mental immaturity, needs special safeguards and care, including appropriate legal protection.

> Article 3 (1). In all actions concerning children . . . the best interests of the child shall be a primary consideration.

Article 18 (1). . . . Both parents have common responsibilities for the upbringing and development of the child. Parents or, as the case may be, legal guardians, have the primary responsibility for the upbringing and development of the child.

Article 19 (1). State parties (government) shall take appropriate legislative, administrative, social and educational measures to protect the child from all forms of physical or mental violence, injury or abuse, neglect or negligent treatment, maltreatment or exploitation, including sexual abuse, while in the care of parent(s), legal guardian(s) or any other person who has the care of the child (United Nations, 1989).

THE DESIGN OF THE AMERICAN CHILD WELFARE SYSTEM

Formal child welfare programs and services are found in both public and private settings. Government programs—local, state, and federal—are augmented by both for-profit and nonprofit agencies. Together, these programs form a complex system that starts with prenatal care and ranges to opportunities for teenagers.

Programs are varied, but they can generally be categorized as child protective services, family preservation, out-of-home services, and other services.

Child Protective Services

Child protective services (CPS) is probably the best known as well as the most controversial children's program. The intent of CPS is to protect children from abusive situations in order that they can grow and develop.

We've all heard stories about abusive CPS workers responding to unfounded charges, taking children from their parents, breaking up families, and ruining the lives of countless people. In fact, the CPS worker investigates each allegation of abuse or neglect and determines whether the charges are founded or unfounded. A case is opened if the investigation demonstrates that abuse or neglect is indeed occurring. A child is only removed from the home if his life is in immediate danger. An open case may receive direct services from the agency or from other contract agencies, such as a family service agency. The case is reviewed by CPS staff and is closed once all goals are achieved.

All states provide some form of CPS. In 1962, a study of battered children in hospitals recommended that suspected cases be reported so that protective measures could be taken. By 1966 all states had passed legislation concerning abuse (Lindsey, 1994, p. 92).

As of 1996, there were 2,025,956 reports of alleged child abuse or neglect, involving some 3,000,000 children. Of those investigated, 28.3 percent were

---

Did You Know... Neglect *is maltreatment through the failure to provide needed, age-appropriate care. Physical abuse is physical injury resulting from punching, beating, kicking, biting, burning, or otherwise harming a child (National Resource Center on Child Abuse and Neglect).*

The Beginning of CPS: The Case of Mary Ellen

In 1873, Mrs. Etta Angell Wheeler, a church visitor in New York City, learned from people in a neighborhood about a 9-year-old girl, Mary Ellen Wilson, who had been whipped and left alone for hours on end. Neighbors in her apartment building heard the child's cries time and again. The New York City Department of Charities had placed Mary Ellen in this home when she was 18 months old. There had been no followup by the agency to assess the placement. Mrs. Wheeler sought help from a number of charitable organizations and the police to protect Mary Ellen, but no agency was willing to intervene and no CPS organization existed. She turned for help to Mr. Henry Bergh, president of the New York Society for the Prevention of Cruelty to Animals. The society intervened with court action and Mary Ellen was removed from the home.

The court found the home to be abusive. The foster mother, Mrs. Mary Connolly, was arrested and found guilty of assault. The court decided that Mary Ellen was to move to a group home, but Mrs. Wheeler asked that the child be placed in her care. Mary Ellen moved in with Mrs. Wheeler's mother and stayed with her until the mother's death.

Within a few months of the reported abuse, the New York Society for the Prevention of Cruelty to Children was founded, the first such organization in the world. (Watkins, 1990)

substantiated, 6.1 percent indicated abuse or neglect, and 57.7 percent were unfounded. According to statistics the most common form of maltreatment was neglect (57.7 percent), followed by physical abuse (22.2 percent), other types of maltreatment (10.5 percent), sexual abuse (12.3 percent), emotional maltreatment (5.9 percent), and other (14.5 percent; U.S. Department of Health and Human Services, 1998, pp. 2-1, 2-3, 2-7–2-8).

Slightly more than half of victims were under age 4, 53 percent were female, and 53 percent were white. About 77 percent of the perpetrators—that is, people who victimized children—were parents, and another 11 percent were other relatives (U.S. Department of Health and Human Service, 1998, pp. 2-8, 2-9, 2-10, 2-14).

According to the Children's Defense Fund the number of abuse and neglect cases continues to rise. It reports that between 1985 and 1995, the number of reports rose by 61 percent and the number of confirmed reports by 31 percent. The Children's Defense Fund also believes that these numbers undercount the true incidence of abuse and neglect, a claim it supports by citing a note that the number of abused and neglected children was actually triple the number reported by the U.S. Department of Health and Human Services (Children's Defense Fund, 1998, pp. 51, 53).

Today, according to the Child Maltreatment 2001 (Children's Bureau, 2003), approximately 903,000 children were found to be victims of child maltreatment. Maltreatment categories typically include neglect, medical neglect, physical abuse, sexual abuse, and psychological maltreatment.

Family Preservation Services

Family preservation services seek to stabilize troubled families in a short period of time (Linderman, 1995, p. 424). They require intensive, direct social services with the entire family. The goal of family preservation is to prevent child removal from the parental home when direct services may avoid the need for such out-of-home placement, to keep families together, and to strengthen family bonds (Tracy, 1995, p. 973). Gaining popularity in the 1970s and 1980s, these services received a boost in 1980 with the passage of the Adoption Assistance and Child Welfare Act (P.L. 96–272). The 1980 act called for reasonable efforts to be made to keep children within their families and to minimize family disorder.

The Convention on the Rights of the Child (2003) identifies important issues for children. Work in this area is intensive, requiring anywhere from six to ten hours of direct worker-family contact each week. The typical case requires four to twelve weeks of contact, and a worker's caseload should range between two and six families. In addition, the worker is on call twenty-four hours a day, providing a mix of services (Edna McConnell Clark Foundation, n.d.).

Research on family preservation has shown some positive outcomes. The first study examined Homebuilders, a program in Washington. The research findings revealed that out-of-home placement was avoided in 97 percent of cases (Lindsey, 1994, pp. 41–43). The Edna McConnell Clark Foundation reported that family preservation workers are extremely positive about this form of intervention. Clients too are strong supporters of family preservation programs: 99 percent are satisfied with services, 87 percent rated services as helpful, and 97 percent would recommend family preservation to other families in similar situations (Edna McConnell Clark Foundation, n.d.). Tracy (1995, p. 978) wrote, however, that not all reports reveal such high success rates, and in fact much more research is needed to establish the validity of family preservation.

Out-of-Home Services

Out-of-home services are programs for children no longer living with their biological or legal guardians, whose parental rights have been or may be terminated. Typical out-of-home programs are foster care, residential care, and adoption.

Foster Care. The *Social Work Dictionary* defines foster care as physical care for children "who are unable to live with their natural parents or legal guardians" (Barker, 2003). The goals of foster care include 1) maximum protection for the child, 2) permanency, and 3) family preservation. Foster care is generally organized through state or county social services. It may be provided within foster family homes, residential group homes, or institutions (Everett, 1995, p. 375).

A child is placed in a foster home temporarily. Placement may be made at the start of a CPS investigation if the worker assesses that the child's life is in immediate danger. The family is entitled to a court hearing, in most states within twenty-four to seventy-two hours of the time of removal, if the child was removed without

Myths and Facts about Out-of-Home Placements

Myth: Foster care is in the best interests of children who have known the hurt of abuse and neglect.

Fact: In some cases, when the child is at great risk, removal from the home is necessary, but it is not necessarily the solution. The devastating norm for foster children is multiple moves, extended stays, and no stable permanent family ties.

Myth: Foster care is principally a problem of poor and minority families.

Fact: Problems leading to abuse and neglect know no race or class boundaries. Of all children entering foster care and substitute care, almost 55 percent are white, 22 percent are black, and 10 percent are Latino.

Myth: Children placed in foster care are typically younger than 5 years of age.

Fact: Roughly half the children in out-of-home care are over age 10. However, the greatest growth in such placements is for infants under 1 year of age.

Myth: Most children in foster care are placed there because of physical or sexual abuse.

Fact: More than half of child removals are for neglect.

Myth: Child abuse is on the rise.

Fact: While the number of reports has increased, the evidence does not clearly substantiate that the actual incidence is on the rise. The growing number of reports may be a result of the public's growing awareness of child abuse and of resources to contact.

Myth: Parents whose children are removed from the home do not want their children, do not deserve their children, and cannot or will not change their behavior.

Fact: Experts working with troubled families find that their problems are more extreme versions of similar issues confronting any family. Troubled families often lack resources, knowledge, and skills that most take for granted. Most parents want their children and really want to be good parents. Proper help can help many families, but it must be timely.

Myth: Child protective service workers are well-trained professionals but have little authority to protect children.

Fact: The child protective service worker position is an entry-level job requiring minimal education. Most states do not require education in social work and allow a person to work in this position with a degree in music, math, and other non–human service disciplines. Caseloads are usually high, pay and morale low, and employee turnover high. Child protective service workers have a wide range of authority, including the power to remove a child from a home, in some instances without supervisor or court approval. (Edna McConnell Clark Foundation, n.d.)

a court order. In other cases, placement may occur after a court hearing, if a CPS investigation finds that this action is in the best interests of the child. Any placement must be in the least restrictive setting. For example, a foster home is less restrictive than a residential treatment center; placement with a relative is less restrictive than removal to a nonbiological foster home.

Children in foster care are provided with certain protections including the following:

- ◆ A detailed written plan that describes the appropriateness of the placement, the services to be provided to the child, and a plan for achieving permanence
- ◆ Periodic case review at least once every six months, though a jurisdiction may review a case more often
- ◆ A state inventory of children who have been in care for more than six months in order to track these children and the goals related to their placement
- ◆ Procedural safeguards that involve parental input in the development of case plans
- ◆ Reunification or permanency planning services, which programs include day care, homemaker services, counseling, parent education, adoption services, and followup (Everett, 1995, p. 381).

For example, in 1994, an estimated 41,161 children were in substitute care in the state of Illinois (Department of Children and Family Services, 2003). For the most part, all states are similar in that most children in foster care are placed in foster family homes; most are boys; about three-quarters have no known physical disabilities; and half are in care for more than two years (Everett, 1995). As of July 2003, the Department of Children and Families in the State of Illinois estimated 20,508 children in substitute care. This decreasing number has been credited to early intervention efforts and permanency services such as adoption.

How are foster parents selected? What is their motivation—money? What about reports that children in foster homes are often subjected to more abuse? (Mushlin, 1991, pp. 102–104). Kantrowitz and King (1991, p. 98) defended foster parents by stating that most have a calling, a sense of altruism, for the work. People choose to be foster parents because of their love for children. Their decisions to take children into their homes have to be for something more than the money because reimbursement rates are so low (Kantrowitz & King, 1991, p. 98). At the time daily reimbursement rates ranged from $5.00 to $12.00 (remember, this article was written in 1991, so reimbursement figures are higher today).

We need to keep in mind that children in foster care are coming from terrible home situations. Because permanency planning interventions are preferred, only those children in the most unbearable situations are removed. Most foster children are burdened by a unique set of complex problems that requires understanding and compassion. Being a foster parent is not easy, and it does require a special person.

Residential care. Residential group care, also called institutional care, takes place in physical settings apart from the natural parents or legal guardians.

Residential settings include residential treatment centers, state hospitals, detention centers, runaway shelters, and halfway houses. All have a common theme: caring for groups of special needs children, twenty-four hours a day (Whittaker, 1995, p. 451).

Did You Know... The first residential program for children was established in 1729 in New Orleans. The program was developed by Ursuline nuns to care for children orphaned as a result of a battle with Native Americans at Natchez.

A number of trends in residential care have been consistent over time:
- ◆ The number of residential facilities is increasing though the actual number of youth in care has declined.
- ◆ The two main types of new facilities are juvenile delinquent centers and mental health centers.
- ◆ The average number of children in facilities has declined to fewer than thirty per facility.

Did You Know... The terms runaway, throwaway, *and* push-out *describe youths (under age 18), who no longer live at home with their legal guardians. A* runaway *is a person running away from home. A* throwaway *is a person forced or thrown out of home by the caretaker. A* push-out *is a person who with the agreement of the caretaker decides it is in everyone's best interest that he or she leave home.*

Residential programs are also available for children who no longer live with their legal caretakers. Typically such programs are shelters that provide temporary housing and counseling. The purpose of the runaway shelter is to get youths off the streets, provide protection, and attempt to reunite children with their families. Social service providers recognize the importance of getting runaways off the streets and into services as quickly as possible. Colby (1990, p. 282) reported that after living on the streets for two weeks, 75 percent of runaways turn to theft, drugs, prostitution, or pornography for support.

Activity...Contact your local runaway shelter and ask about the rules of admission and length of stay. Ask what happens to youths who leave the shelter but do not return home.

State-established limits on the length of time that young people may reside in shelters generally restricts these settings to homeless youths. Some programs require parental consent for children to remain in shelters. What happens to the youth whose parents do not grant permission for her to remain in the program? And some programs do not allow disruptive youths or youths with mental health problems to enter shelters. What types of community programs, if any, are available for these youths?

Adoption. The *Social Work Dictionary* defines adoption as *"accepting and treating a child legally as though born into the family."* (Barker, 2003). Adoption creates a *"legal family for children when the birth family is unable or unwilling to parent"* (Barth, 1995, p. 48).

Massachusetts is credited with being the first state to enact an adoption law, in 1851 (Cole, 1985, p. 639), though some cite Mississippi, in 1846, and Texas, in 1850, as having earlier adoption statutes (Crosson-Tower, 1998, p. 356). Whichever state was first, there is consensus that the Massachusetts legislation served as the model for other states (Kadushin & Martin, 1988, p. 535; Crosson-Tower, 1998, p. 639). By 1929 all states had enacted some form of adoption law.

During the nineteenth and much of the twentieth centuries most children in need of homes lived in orphanages. Young people were placed in orphanages for any number of reasons, including having poor parents who couldn't afford to raise them, having been born to unwed mothers, or having no parents because of death or abandonment (Crosson-Tower, 1998, p. 357).

Charles Loring Brace, a minister and organizer of the Children's Aid Society in New York City, led one of the more compelling child welfare efforts of the nineteenth century. Brace developed what became known as the Orphan's Train, through which some 50,000 to 100,000 urban orphans were placed on midwestern and western farms (Quam, 1995, p. 2575). The children, picked up on the streets of New York City, were put on a wagon train heading west. In town after town, city after city, the train would stop and put the youths up for adoption. Brace believed that moving waifs off city streets, away from the temptations of urban life, to more rural, tranquil lives of work and family, would allow them to be prosperous and productive (Brace, 1872).

The Orphan's Train was a manifestation of the nation's prevailing belief, no less strong today, that children should live in wholesome environments where caretakers can provide for their needs. Remember the basic child welfare principle: in the best interests of the child? Brace's program and other child-saving programs, including orphanages, were built on this ideal.

Today, adoption takes place in many different ways. These include placing children through child placement agencies and through direct agreements between two parties sanctioned by the courts.

"Agency-based adoption" occurs in government, nonprofit, and for-profit family welfare settings. It entails a rigorous and time-consuming process, which generally includes the following steps:

Identification of suitable children ensures that all children in need of adoptive homes are identified.

Freeing for placement is the legal process by which custody of the child is removed from one set of parents in order that it can be assigned to the adoptive parents.

Preparation for adoption involves working with the child before adoption to prepare him for his new family. Potential adoptive parents are closely

Name: Lindsey Dula

Place of residence: Fort Worth, Texas

College/university degrees: Texas Christian University, BSW and BS in Psychology

Present position: Child Protective Service Specialist, Investigator

Previous work/volunteer experience: Rape Crisis and Victims Services through the Women's Haven of Fort Worth, Meals on Wheels, Juvenile Sex Offender Group Leader

Why did you choose social work as a career? Due to a combination of lifelong volunteerism and intense interest in human behavior, social work was the most direct route to client interaction.

What is your favorite social work story? That's my favorite thing about my career! Everyday is a different story, with a different family and new problems to tackle and solve. I think it would be impossible to choose a favorite.

What would be the one thing you would change in our community if you had the power to do so? Education. Our society often turns a blind eye to the ongoing problem of child abuse. The majority of the public is exposed to select cases only due to coverage by the media, at which time appropriate disgust, disbelief, and outrage are shared by the population. As the cameras turn to the next story and the articles cover tomorrow's events, child abuse again returns to the shadows. Public education will introduce child abuse as an unacceptable and intolerable act, affecting behavior, reaction, and legislation.

scrutinized by the agency to ensure they have the resources needed to raise a child in a loving, caring environment.

Selection of adoptive parents is conducted by the agency after close review of applications and supporting materials. The agency's goal is to match a child with the adoptive parent who can best meet her unique needs.

Placement with adoptive family is characterized by many social workers as one of the most exciting days for worker, family, and child. It is a time of joy as the new family begins its life together. Everyone involved often sheds tears!

Postplacement services include a variety of agency-based supports to the family as it makes the transition to a new system of relations. By placing a child with a specific family, the agency is affirming that the placement is in the best interests of the child. To increase the likelihood of success, the agency offers the family continuing supports ranging from individual and family counseling and support groups to social worker home visits. Again, the agency wants as few disruptions as possible with the adoption. Nevertheless, sometimes the child is removed from the adoptive parent's home. When this happens, the social worker does not blame anyone or refer to the original placement as a failure but instead looks again at what supports are needed for the child and what type of child is best suited for that particular family.

Legal finalization of the adoption takes place after a period of time following initial placement. There is a popular myth that adoption is final when the child is placed with the family. Not so for agency-based adoptions. The final legal assignment of custody is made after an extended period of time. The period varies among agencies; the norm seems to be six months to one year following placement. The court is the final authority in legally assigning custody of the child to the adoptive parent. The court's decision is reached after review of the agency's reports and recommendations.

Postadoption services provide children with any needed supports such as counseling, and parents with educational or ongoing counseling sessions. Agencies recognize that it may be in the best interests of the child for support services to be provided for extended periods beyond the legal adoption phase (Cole, 1985).

Have you seen advertisements in your college or local newspaper that read something like this?

Loving couple with a great deal to give looking to adopt a newborn. Will pay all fees, including prenatal, delivery, hospitalization, legal, and followup costs. Please call. . . .

Some families resort to private sources, also called "independent adoption," rather than use agency-based adoption services. Agreements are reached between the two families involved, and the courts, assisted by attorneys, finalize the legal arrangements. These adoptions can take place much faster and with less red tape than the agency-based process. The prospective adoptive parents usually provide financial support for the pregnant mother and her family, cover all related health costs, and often add a financial stipend—that is, a salary.

Independent adoption is costly, running to tens of thousands of dollars. For-profit adoptions are against the law. Recognize that with independent adoptions there is less scrutiny and follow-up than with agency-based services. Cole suggested that problems with independent adoptions could be reduced if the following steps are taken:

♦ Courts require a detailed statement of all monies that change hands relating to the adoption.

♦ Violators are vigorously prosecuted and subjected to severe sanctions.

♦ Communities provide enough financial support to adoption agencies that they can offer the same level of health and maintenance care that takes place with independent adoption (1985).

There are three potential pools for adoption: healthy infants, children with special needs, and children from foreign countries (Kadushin & Martin, 1988). Fewer healthy infants are available for adoption because of the increased availability of birth control and abortion (Crosson-Tower, 1998). Unfortunately, it is not uncommon for a couple to be told the waiting period for a healthy infant may be up to ten years!

A special needs child has unique characteristics that can include "race and ethnicity, medical problems, older age (over age 3), attachment to a sibling group, developmental disabilities, and emotional difficulties" (Crosson-Tower, 1998, p. 374). Such children are much harder to place because of their special needs and are more available than healthy infants for adoption.

In recent years, more and more people are looking to the international community for children to adopt. Children born in areas of civil strife or extreme poverty are the main subjects of such adoptions. Latin America, Vietnam, Korea, the Philippines, India, and other Asian countries have been the principal nations and regions sending children to the United States (Crosson-Tower, 1998).

CHILDREN WITH SPECIAL NEEDS

In 1998, 36,000 of the approximately 120,000 children adopted in the United States were adopted from the public foster care system. In 1999, the number of immigrant visas issued to orphans coming to the United States rose to 16,396 (National Adoption Information Clearinghouse, n.d.). These two groups consist of many children who have suffered abuse, abandonment, and/or neglect.

Due to a history of trauma, these children are considered "special needs" and require special parenting once adopted into permanent homes. The term *special needs* is often associated with children within the United States' welfare system. Each state's specific criteria may vary slightly, but in general, these children are identified as special needs because they meet one or more of the following criteria: 8 years of age or older, emotionally handicapped, physically handicapped, a member of a sibling group, minority heritage, mentally handicapped, history of physical abuse, sexual abuse or neglect (Groze, 1996; Florida Administrative Code, 2002). Due to their trauma histories, special needs children can be difficult to parent. Adoptive parents of these children do not start with a clean slate; they adopt not only the child of the present, but they also adopt the experiences of the child's past. The experiences imbedded in these children often make adoptive parenting a serious challenge and can "compromise the child's ability to join with and be accepted by a family" (Smith & Howard, 1999).

The social stigma of adoption has a long history in our society with disparaging community attitudes toward adoptive kinship, and for the most part Americans still consider adoption second best to having children by birth (Wegar, 2000). This prevailing mindset continues to leave adoptive parents to experience social stigmatization in their everyday lives (Miall, 2000). Adoptive mothers of special needs children in particular often go through their own grieving process and may experience feelings of shock, denial, anger, depression, and physical symptoms of distress and guilt. The adoptive mother's dream of the child she wished for or expected are soon replaced by the realities of her actual child. After a brief honeymoon period, the adoptive mother of a special needs child may experience a shocking realization that her new child is unhealthy, either physically or emotionally. Despite the information she was provided prior to the adoptive placement, many adoptive mothers cannot comprehend the full realm of the behaviors and difficulties of the child prior to placement. Consequently, the mothers may experience being in shock and having feelings of bewilderment and may start making excuses for the child's behavior. After living with a child who is unresponsive to the parents, anger and rage can often surface. The adoptive mother may discover feelings of guilt for not truly loving her adoptive child and for feeling ambivalent or angry toward her child (Acord, n.d.).

Many times the biases of society are as strong, if not stronger, within the nucleus of the immediate family and extended family. Adoption of a special needs child involves integrating their adopted children into the entire family social system. Therefore, Pavao (1998) stresses the importance of educating the extended family about adoption issues and feelings that may surface and including them as part of the preadoptive process for families. Rosenthal and Groze (1990) found that the approval of extended family members was directly correlated to the success of an adoptive placement. Conversely, Rosenthal wrote in a later paper that a key predictor of increased risk for adoption disruption is "low levels of support from relatives or friends" (Rosenthal, 1993, p. 81). Therefore, it is important to realize that a lack of support from the extended family can work to undermine the legitimacy of the adoptive placement for the adoptive mothers. This makes the need for post-adoption services a necessary part of practice for social workers.

In summary, a final but controversial point about adoption is that our discussion has been framed by the notion of placement in the best interests of the child. Yet one practice in adoption may run counter to this central tenet of child welfare: there is strong pressure to place children with adoptive families of the same race or ethnicity. The justification is that the cultural needs of a child far outweigh other placement considerations. For example, the National Association of Black Social Workers does not support the placement of African-American children in nonblack homes. Or consider the 1978 Indian Child Welfare Act, which places responsibility for adoption of Native American children within tribes rather than with traditional public child welfare agencies. The 1978 law requires Native American children to be placed with extended family members as a first option and then with other tribal families, regardless of the wishes of the parents.

Should adoption be constrained by race and ethnicity and other cultural factors? Does the compelling need for permanency override the cultural needs of a child? Can a child develop cultural competence and identity in a home of different racial or ethnic origin? What about religion? In Judaism, for example, the religion's law is that a child born to a Jewish mother is always Jewish. Should a Jewish child always be placed in a Jewish home? Should Catholic children always be placed with Catholic families? Is it best to keep a child in a temporary foster home if no culturally similar family can be found? There are no easy answers to these questions.

Other Services

A number of other child welfare services meet additional needs of children. It is impossible to discuss all of them, but we touch briefly on two important program areas.

Youth programs. Most of us at one time or another have participated in youth programs sponsored by such groups as the YMCA, YWCA, Boys Clubs, Girls Clubs, Blue Birds, Girls Scouts, Boys Scouts, Brownies, Little League baseball, and so on. Many agencies in our communities work with young people through an array of programs ranging from gym-and-swim to therapeutic prevention.

The YMCA, for example, offers parent-child programs called Y-Indian Guide and Y-Indian Princess. The parent and child meet with other parents and children one evening each week. Ostensibly providing recreational opportunities, these programs also ensure that the parent and child have at least one evening each week of quality interaction. In addition, the parent and child carry out tasks and activities in the home between group meetings. These activities strengthen relations when time is limited.

Youth programs have four important functions in our communities:

◆ Youths have positive peer experiences in a formal supervised atmosphere.
◆ Youths learn to interact with others in groups.
◆ Youths are able to develop their own extended networks outside of the family.
◆ Through the programs youths find a safe haven, particularly with after-school, weekend, or evening activities, which take place when caretakers may be at work and unable to supervise their children.

CHILD SEXUAL ABUSE AND TRAUMA

According to the U.S. Department of Health and Human Services, *sexual abuse* is a type of maltreatment involving a child in sexual activity that provides sexual gratification or financial benefit to the perpetrator. This includes involving children in contracts for sexual purposes, prostitution, pornography, exposure, or other sexually exploitative activities (Gil, 1996). Sexual abuse of children is a difficult area for most people to talk about because of the emotional reactions it causes.

For years, acknowledgment of sexual abuse was avoided and considered an issue not to be discussed (Karp & Butler, 1996). As society's awareness of children's issues grew, so did awareness about child sexual abuse. It is estimated that by the time children reach age 18, one out of every four females and one out of every six males has been confronted with sexual abuse (Deblinger & Heflin, 1996). This means that by the time many children reach adulthood their lives have been affected by some type of sexual abuse.

By being aware of the different signs of child sexual abuse the social worker can best select from the many techniques for assessing the presence of sexual abuse in children (Karp & Butler, 1996). Most social workers use techniques such as play therapy, and look for and document the physical indicators of sexual abuse (Dammeyer, 1998). Physical indicators include difficulty walking or sitting, torn or bloody underclothing, bruises or bleeding in the external genital or anal areas, and venereal disease and pregnancy (Miller, Veltkamp, & Raines, 1998). Behavioral symptoms can also help assess sexual abuse in children. They include: sleep disturbances; withdrawal, regressed behavior; age inappropriate, sophisticated or unusual sexual knowledge or behavior; extreme self-blame or fear; and poor interpersonal skills (Miller et al., 1998). With the apparent increase in cases of child sexual abuse, social workers need to be skilled at assessing children who are victims or suspected victims of child sexual abuse (Cohen-Liebman, 1999).

SUMMARY

Children are an essential part of our country's future development. What we do with and for them benefits all of us. Homer Folks, in 1940, wrote, "The safety of our democracy depends in large measure upon the welfare of our children" (White House Conference, 1942).

Our nation's history shows a sense of ambivalence toward children. While we want to protect them—even from themselves—we also want to ensure they are provided as many opportunities as possible.

How we care for our children tells us a great deal about our society's beliefs, hopes, and aspirations. We do a great deal to care for our nation's children, but we need to do more. We need to find ways to guarantee every child a healthy, caring home. A stimulating environment that encourages growth and development should be the norm for all children. We can accept nothing less.

Child welfare is an exciting field. It is in constant flux, though always under the watchful eyes of the public and of policymakers. Social workers have been, are, and will continue to be significant players in child welfare.

References

Acord, M. (n.d.). The nine stages of grief in parents with RAD kids. *KC Connections Newsletter*. Retrieved June 22, 2001 from http://www.syix.com/adsg/articles/9stages.htm.

Americans for Divorce Reform. (n.d.). Divorce statistics collection: Summary of findings so far. Retrieved November 13, 2003, from http://www.divorcereform.org/results.html.

Barker, R. L. (1991). *The social work dictionary* (2nd ed.). Washington, DC: NASW Press.

Barker, R. L. (2003). *The social work dictionary* (5th ed.). Washington, DC: NASW Press.

Barth, R. P. (1995). Adoption. In R. Edwards et al., (Eds.), *Encyclopedia of social work* (19th ed., pp. 48–59). Washington, DC: NASW Press.

Baugher, E., & Lamison-White, L. (1996). *Poverty in the United States, 1995 (Current Population Reports, Series pp. 60–194)*. Washington, DC: U.S. Department of Commerce, Bureau of the Census.

Brace, C. L. (1872). *The dangerous classes of New York and twenty years' work among them* New York: Wynkoop and Hallenbeck.

Brunner, B. (Ed.). (1997). *1998 Information please almanac*. Boston: Information Please.

Centers for Disease Control. (June 25, 2003). U.S. Department of Health and Rehabilitative Services. *National Vital Statistics Reports, 51* (11), 1–20.

Chelf C. P. (1992). *Controversial issues in social welfare policy: Government and the pursuit of happiness*. Newbury Park, CA: Sage.

Child Welfare League of America. (1989). *Standards for service to strengthen and preserve families with children*. Washington, DC: Author.

Children's Bureau. (2003). *Child maltreatment 2001*. U.S. Department of Health and Human Services. Washington, DC: U.S. Government Printing Office. Retrieved November 13, 2003, from http://www.acf.hhs.gov/programs/cb/publications/cm01/outcover.htm.

Children's Defense Fund. (1998). *The state of America's children yearbook, 1997*. Washington, DC: Author.

Christian Coaliltion. (1995). *Contract with the American family*. Nashville, TN: Moorings.

Colby, I. (1990). The throwaway teen. *Journal of Applied Social Sciences, 14* (2), 227–294.

Cole, E. S. (1985). Adoption: History, policy, and program. In J. Laird & A. Hartman (Eds.), *A handbook of child welfare: Context, knowledge, and practice* (pp. 638–666). New York: Free Press.

Cohen-Liebman, M. S. (1999). Draw and tell: Drawings within the context of child sexual abuse. *Arts in Psychotherapy, 26*, 185–194.

Convention on the Rights of the Child. (2003). Child maltreatment summary 2001: Key findings. United Nations Children's Fund UNICEF: Status of the Ratification. Retrieved November 13, 2003, from www.unicef.org.

Crosson-Tower, C. (1998). *Exploring child welfare: A practice perspective*. Boston: Allyn and Bacon.

Dammeyer, M. D. (1998). The assessment of child sexual abuse allegations: Using research to guide clinical decision-making. *Behavioral Sciences and the Law, 16*, 21–34.

Deblinger, E. & Heflin, A. (1996). *Treating sexually abused children and their non-offending parents: A cognitive-behavioral approach*. Thousand Oaks, CA: Sage Publications.

Department of Children and Family Services. (2003). DCFS Foster Care, Illinois Department of Children and Family Services. Retrieved November 13, 2003, from http://www.state.il.us.dcfs/fc_foster.shtml.

Dobelstein, A. W. (1996). *Social welfare: Policy and analysis* (2nd ed.). Chicago: Nelson-Hall.

Edna McConnell Clark Foundation. (n.d.). *Keeping families together: Facts on family preservation services*. New York: Author.

Everett, J. E. (1995). Child foster care. In R. Edwards et al. (Eds.), *Encyclopedia of social work* (19th ed., pp. 375–389). Washington, DC: NASW Press.

Florida Administrative Code, 409.166 Special needs children; subsidized adoption program (2002).

Gil, D. (1985). The ideological context of child welfare. In J. Laird & A. Hartman (Eds.), *A handbook of child welfare: Context, knowledge, and practice* (pp. 11–33). New York: Free Press.

Gillespie, E., & Schellhas, B. (Eds.). (1994). *Contract with America*. New York: Times.

Gustavsson, N. S., & Segal, E. A. (1994). *Critical issues in child welfare* Thousand Oaks, CA: Sage.

Gil, E. (1996). *Treating Abused Adolescents*. New York: Guildford Press.

Karp, C. & Butler, T. (1996). *Treatment strategies for abused children: From victim to survivor*. Thousand Oaks, CA: Sage.

Groze, V. (1996). A 1 and 2 year follow-up study of adoptive families and special needs children. *Children and Youth Services Review, 18* (1/2), 57–82.

Heffernan, J., Shuttlesworth, G., & Ambrosino, R. (1988). *Social work and social welfare: An introduction* St. Paul, MN: West.

Kadushin, A., & Martin, J. A. (1988). *Child welfare services* (4th ed.). New York: Macmillan.

Kantrowitz, B., & King, P. (1991). Foster care can protect children from abuse. In C. Wekesser (Ed.), *America's children: Opposing viewpoints* (pp. 96–99). San Diego, CA: Greenhaven.

Karger, H. J., & Stoesz, D. (1994). *American social welfare policy: A pluralist approach* (2nd ed.). White Plains, NY: Longman.

Linderman, D. S. (1995). Child welfare overview. In R. Edwards et al. (Eds.), *Encyclopedia of social work* (19th ed., pp. 424–433). Washington, DC: NASW Press.

Lindsey, D. (1994). *The welfare of children*. New York: Oxford University Press.

Miall, C. E. (2000). Adoption as family form. *Family Relations: Journal of Applied Family & Child Studies, 49* (4), 359–362.

Miller, T., Veltkamp, L., & Raines, P. (1998). The trauma of family violence. In Miller, T. *Children of Trauma: Stressful life events and their effects on children and adolescents* (pp. 61–76). Madison, CT: International Universities Press, Inc.

Mushlin, M. B. (1991). Foster care cannot protect children from physical abuse. In C. Wekesser (Ed.), *American children: Opposing viewpoints* (pp. 100–104). San Diego, CA: Greenhaven.

National Adoption Information Clearinghouse. (n.d.). Retrieved April 14, 2002, from http://calib.com/naic.

Pavao, J. M. (1998). *The family of adoption*. Boston, MA: Beacon Press.

Quam, J. (1995). Charles Loring Brace (1826–1890). In R. Edwards et al. (Eds.), *Encyclopedia of social work* (19th ed., p. 2575). Washington, DC: NASW Press.

Rosenthal, J. A. (1993). Outcomes of adoption of children with special needs. *The Future of Children, 3* (1), 77–88.

Rosenthal, J. A. & Groze, V. (1990). Special-needs adoption: A study of intact families. *Social Service Review, 64* 475–505.

Smith, S. L., & Howard, J. A. (1999). *Promoting successful adoptions: Practice with troubled families*. Thousand Oaks, CA: Sage Publications.

Tracy, E. M. (1995). Family preservation and home-based services. In R. Edwards et al. (Eds.), *Encyclopedia of social work* (19th ed., pp. 973–983). Washington, DC: NASW Press.

United Nations. (1989, November 20). *United Nations convention on the rights of children*. New York: Author.

U.S. Census Bureau. (2003). Children's living arrangements and characteristics: March 2002. U.S. Department of Commerce, Economics and Statistics Administration. Retrieved October 7, 2003 from www.census.gov/prod/2003pubs/p20-547.pdf.

U.S. Census Bureau. (2002) *Current population survey: 1988 to 2002 annual demographic supplements*. Chart retrieved March 24, 2003, from http://www.census.gov/hhes/www/img/incpov01/incomeeconchrt.jpg.

Watkins, S. A. (1990). The Mary Ellen myth: Correcting child welfare history. *Social Work, 35* (6), 500–503.

Wegar, K. (2000). Adoption, family ideology, and social stigma: Bias in community attitudes, adoption research, and practice. *Family Relations, 49*, 363–370.

White House Conference on Children in a Democracy (1942). *Final Report*, Washington, D.C., January 18–20, 1940 (Publication No. 272). Washington, DC: U.S. Government Printing Office. Reprinted in *Children and Youth: Social Problems and Social Policy*. New York: Arno Press.

Whittaker, J. K. (1995). Children: Group care. In R. Edwards et al., (Eds.), *Encyclopedia of social work* (19th ed., pp. 448–460). Washington, DC: NASW Press.

Wineman, D. (1995). Children's rights. In R. Edwards et al., (Eds.), *Encyclopedia of social work* (19th ed., pp. 465–475). Washington, DC: NASW Press.

Chapter 9

Health Care

OFTEN WE START IN ONE CAREER AND CHANGE TO ANOTHER. THIS was Liz's experience when she began her professional career as a nurse but after several years decided to switch to social work. Liz felt that her knowledge of the medical aspects of a client's condition blended beautifully with mental health considerations. Liz's belief is not unique; health care social workers know the importance to successful intervention of linking mind and body. Some contend that mind and body cannot be separated and each client must be treated individually with a focus on continued wellness and prevention. At a minimum, the health care social worker, who often works as part of an interdisciplinary team, brings knowledge and understanding of the special relation between the medical and the mental health of the client. In particular, the knowledge and skills used in linking the client to the environment are central to discharge planning and case management.

Health care social workers face great challenges in the new century. Issues of behaviorally based managed care, downsizing and reorganization of hospital social work staffs, services to insured and uninsured populations, and increased demand for brief interventions make health care a formidable setting for creative social work practice. Philosophy often comes into play: Do we provide health care to the homeless—and if so, to what extent? What about people in prison: do we provide health care to those serving life sentences with no possibility of parole? How do we ensure that people in rural and sparsely populated areas have access to high-quality health care? Should we move toward a national health insurance model? Should we finance alternative, nontraditional health interventions?

Health care is costly. You know that from your own experiences buying medication or paying for medical treatment. Health insurance is also costly. For example, the number of individuals without health insurance increased for a second year in 2002. This left an estimated 15.2 percent of the population or 43.6 million people without health insurance in 2002, with an increase of 2.4 million people since 2001 (Mills & Bhandari, 2003). Furthermore, in the U.S. children under age of 19, or 12.1 percent (9.2 million) were without health insurance in 2001 (Bahandari & Gifford, 2003). One reason why so many Americans, have no form of health insurance is the sheer expense! And there is no reason to believe that costs will decline or even level off in the near future.

In this chapter we introduce the numerous opportunities open to social workers who choose to practice in health care. Health care is one of the more complex

Name: Roni Levine

Place of residence: West Chester, PA

College/university degrees: West Chester University, BSW

Present position: Supports Coordinator for Chester County MH/MR Supports Coordination Unit

Previous work/volunteer experience: Devereus Kanner Center, American Red Cross, Pottstown Memorial Medical Center

Why did you choose social work as a career? I chose social work as a career to help other people. Seeing a smile on someone's face is my personal reward. Going through my first two years of high school I had no idea what I wanted to do. I started taking classes in psychology and sociology in order to find out what these fields would offer. I joined groups like peer counseling, drug, and alcohol prevention teams so that I could reach out to other students. I wanted to choose a major that offered services that would help others. I visited several schools, but decided that West Chester University was the right choice for me. They made me feel wanted and accepted in their program. I was treated by the school's professors the same way I had hoped to treat others.

What is your favorite social work story? When spending time thinking about my "favorite social work story" different situations come to mind. My most memorable story that I would like to share was about working with a woman in her late fifties who was dually diagnosed with mental retardation and mental health disorders. She was living in a group home with four other women and had displayed many behaviors that were getting worse over time. She was verbally and physically aggressive toward others. She was hospitalized six times in a six month period due to her behaviors. Each time she would go to the hospital the doctors would discharger her as they could not find anything wrong with her. Searching for placement in her county became very difficult as her reputation preceded her. Finally after everyone else turned her down I started to look for a placement outside her county. I found an agency that accepted her for who she was, and didn't judge her on her past actions. She has been there for three years now and has been very happy.

What would be the one thing you would change in our community if you had the power to do so? One of the things I would change in my community is the lack of compassion that exists for people that have mental health disorders. Working with people with these disabilities has given me a greater understanding of what their lives are like. I would have been better prepared to deal with these situations if the textbooks had offered more information about mental health disorders. All the knowledge and training I have received comes through on the job training with the population I work with. The way the general population look and stare at the mentally retarded show how they lack the knowledge about them. They do not take the time to get to them as individuals as I do.

arenas for social work. Many external issues and constituencies affect the delivery of health care social work. With all the challenges, however, the rewards from helping others in their time of need can be great.

HEALTH CARE SOCIAL WORK DEFINED

Health care social work, historically called "medical social work" and today "clinical social work" (not to be confused with the work of the private practitioner also referred to as a "clinical social worker," is one of the oldest, best-established fields of professional social work practice. Simply stated, health care social work practice deals with all aspects of general health. It enhances, promotes, and restores the highest level of social functioning for clients, families, and small groups when their abilities to do so are affected by actual or potential stress caused by illness, disability, or injury (Poole, 1995).

In health care practice, as in other areas of social work, the tasks performed are diverse and unique. Social workers serving in health care settings must be well trained in providing services to clients because they are competing in a service provision environment overcrowded with health care professionals. Moreover, today's health care social workers are exposed to all the turbulence and change of managed health care (Dziegielewski, 2004). In this environment, the insurance company dictates the level of service; no longer are recommendations from physicians or other professionals treated as "written in stone." Pressures to cut costs mean that health care service must be provided in the briefest, most effective manner possible (Dziegielewski, 1996, 1997, 2004). As a result, social work professionals, indeed all health care providers, must work in a versatile, flexible manner to complete tasks with limited resources. The varied tasks coupled with the dynamic environment complicate our simple definition of health care practice.

Did You Know...In 1918, the National Conference of Social Work in Kansas City helped to form the American Association of Hospital Social Workers. This was the first professional social work organization in the United States.

Tom Carlton, a major social work thinker and advocate in health care social work during the 1970s and 1980s, defined health care social work in its broadest sense as "all social work in the health field" (1984, p. 5). Carlton felt that social workers interested in this area must be prepared to do more than engage solely in direct clinical practice. His vision of health care practice includes program planning and administration; preparation, supervision, and continued training for social workers and other health care professionals; and social research.

So, let's complicate our definition. The term "health care social work" has historically been used interchangeably with the term *medical social work* but this obscures a subtle difference in meaning. In the *Social Work Dictionary*, medical social work is defined as a form of practice that occurs in hospitals and other health care settings. This type of practice facilitates good health, prevention of illness, and aids physically ill clients and their families in resolving the social and psychological problems related to disease and illness (Barker, 2003). Health care social work is more encompassing, indicating a type of practice that can take place in more than one setting.

Health care social workers often serve as members of professional **multidisciplinary** and **interdisciplinary teams**. Their role is essential in sensitizing the other team members to the social-psychological aspects of illness (Barker, 2003). Health care social workers are expected to address the psychosocial aspects of client problems. They are also expected to alert other team members to the psychosocial needs of clients and to ensure adequate service provision within the discharge environment. In performing these functions, social work professionals not only represent the interests of clients but often become the "moral conscience" of the health care delivery team. According to Leipzig, Hyer, Ek, et al. (2002), although provider satisfaction with interdisciplinary teamwork was often high, client satisfaction was low. Information such as this further reinforces the role of the social worker as one of the primary providers responsible for increasing communication and understanding for all involved.

The struggle to define exactly what health care social workers are expected to do reflects the changing nature of the health care system. Part of the struggle is trying to establish concrete cost-containing goals and objectives that clearly represent the diverse and often unique service provided. This inability to document a concrete service strategy has long been a thorn in the side of health care administrators, who need this information to justify and compete for continued funding. Nevertheless, simple descriptions of service provision vary, depending on the client population served and the services needed.

Health care social workers practice in a setting where doctors "fix what's broken" and do so with incredible speed and competence. As a result these workers are often expected to do the same. Given the complexity of the human situation, however, this task is not at all straightforward. In adapting to their diverse clients while anticipating changes in the health service environment, social work professionals must employ flexible and constantly updated skills.

A BRIEF HISTORY OF HEALTH CARE SOCIAL WORK

Medical social work can be traced back to the nineteenth-century public health movement. With urban growth, a result of industrialization, came overcrowding and the spread of disease. In Trattner's (1989) graphic words:

> American cities were disorderly, filthy, foul-smelling, disease-ridden places. Narrow, unpaved streets became transformed into quagmires when it rained. Rickety tenements, swarming with unwashed humanity, leaned upon one another for support. Inadequate drainage systems failed to carry away sewage. Pigs roamed streets that were cluttered with manure, years of accumulating garbage, and other litter. Slaughterhouses and fertilizing plants

contaminated the air with an indescribable stench. Ancient plagues like smallpox, cholera, and typhus threw the population into a state of terror from time to time while less sensational but equally deadly killers like tuberculosis, diphtheria, and scarlet fever were ceaselessly at work.

All in all, not a great place or time to live. It soon was evident that public sanitation programs were needed. The resulting laws and health care efforts helped doctors and related medical professionals to gain in stature (Segal & Brzuzy, 1998, p. 108).

Hospitals too changed dramatically during this era. Once a haven for the poor, the hospital became a "scientific center for the treatment of illness" where physicians were in control (Popple & Leighninger, 1990, p. 436). Medical social work was first practiced in 1900 in Cleveland City Hospital, when the workers helped to discharge from overcrowded wards patients with chronic conditions and homeless Civil War veterans (Poole, 1995). It subsequently developed as a specialization through the efforts of Dr. Richard Cabot and shortly thereafter Ida Cannon, a new graduate from Simmons College. Cabot in 1905 set up the first social service (work) department in a hospital. Though trained as a physician, Cabot recognized the unique and important contributions of social workers when he served as director of the Boston Children's Aid Society. The social worker's skill in linking social environment to disease, thought Cabot, would be extremely helpful in medical diagnosis. The social work department established at Boston's Massachusetts General Hospital is regarded as the debut of medical social work.

> *Activity…Have you ever been admitted to a hospital? While you were there did you see a social worker? If you didn't, would you have liked to? If you did, what services did he provide? Make a brief list of the services that you believe social workers can provide in the hospital setting.*

Health care social work today, as in Cabot's time, takes place in a "host" setting—that is, an organization whose primary purpose is something other than providing social work services. You'll find social workers in hospitals (a hospital accreditation requirement), neighborhood health centers, health maintenance organizations (HMOs), city public health departments, and nonprofit and for-profit health-related organizations. Our new aspect of today's health care social work is that it is now team based and interdisciplinary in nature. Social workers are part of a professional team that may include physicians, nurses, vocational rehabilitation workers, psychologists, and psychiatrists. Today's social worker must therefore understand and value the contributions that other professionals offer. For our clients and ourselves, we can no longer see matters solely through our individual professional lens.

UNDERSTANDING THE CURRENT HEALTH CARE ENVIRONMENT

Throughout the last quarter of the twentieth century, spiraling costs and growing numbers of uninsured people challenged the American health care system. And the crisis is hardly abating. According to Dziegielewski (2004) several reasons of direct interest to social workers have been cited:

1. The aging population needs more costly health care services.

2. Americans are resistant to paying additional fees for medical services.

3. The insurance industry is highly fragmented, with managers trained under different environmental conditions.

4. There is excessive pressure to fill an oversupply of hospital inpatient beds.

5. There is a focus on treating acute illness rather than a more holistic, wellness, or preventive perspective that could lead to more costly treatment.

6. Insufficient medical outcome data impair decision making.

7. Too many heroic attempts are made to implement expensive procedures without regard to quality of continued life.

8. Professionals try to be cautious and can order unnecessary tests and procedures to avoid the potential of malpractice suits.

Even though many of the underlying factors are difficult to change, predictions of vastly increased health care urgently require a response of one type or another.

During the early 1990s, politicians were responsive to the American public's demand for health care reform. During his first term in office, President Clinton, who had made a campaign promise to address this issue, a major task force chaired by his wife, Hillary, began to develop a national health care policy (Mizrahi, 1995). The task force considered numerous proposals for health care reform from single-payer systems to limited forms of universal coverage. The eventual proposal was not a single-payer approach but rather a type of "managed competition" in which purchasing alliances were formed that would have the power to certify health plans and negotiate premiums for certain benefit packages (*President's Health Security Plan*, 1993). Payment for these plans would be financed by employer-employee premiums. The actual consumer out-of-pocket cost would vary based on the benefit package chosen. The Clinton proposal eventually failed after concerted attacks by the health care industry and conservative members of the Congress. Some political commentators felt this had been the last chance to change the health care system, yet during the 2000 presidential campaign, health care resurfaced as a hot topic, with arguments over insurance coverage and a "patient's bill of rights."

Today, health care affordability remains a significant problem. According to Mills & Bhandari, (2003), the key demographic factors noted in limiting health care coverage are age, race, navitity and educational attainment. In terms of age, individuals between the ages of 18 and 24 were least likely to have coverage with only 70.4% having coverage in 2002. For uninsured individuals, Hispanics constituted 32.4% of the in 2002 and uninsured Blacks who reported a single race were 20.2%. For the foreign-born population those without health insurance (33.4%) were more than double those who were U.S. born (12.8%). In terms of education, it makes sense that the likelihood of being insured increases as educational levels increase.

As managed health care increases, health care social workers who participate in these types of reimbursement schemes must deal directly with managed care plans (Dziegielewski, 2004). Such dealings typically involve preauthorization for service by qualified providers; precertification for a given amount of care with concurrent review of treatment and services rendered; continued determination of need for hospitalization through a process of utilization review; and predischarge planning to ensure that proper aftercare services are identified and made available (Hiratsuka, 1990).

We don't want to paint a bleak picture but rather a realistic one. The continual changes and swirling controversies contribute to a turbulent health care environment. Declining hospital admissions, reduced lengths of stay, and numerous other restrictions and methods of cost containment are common threats that unite all health care social workers.

Did You Know...In current health care practice the term "patient" is being replaced. Originally, the adoption of the word "patient" by the medical community caused many social workers to stop using words such as "client" when referring to the people they served. The use and acceptance of the term "patient" is obvious when we read articles in the health care social work literature (Dziegielewski, 2004).

Today, with the shift away from the "medical sick role model" to the "wellness, concrete service, cost-effective approach," the term "patient" is in conflict with the wholeness and prevention strategy marketed by host health care organizations. Replacement terms include "client" (a term familiar to social work), "consumer" (to represent those receiving a service), and "covered persons" (reflecting those who have some type of medical insurance coverage). Those in favor of the euphemism "covered persons" argue that it is not used just to denote medical coverage but rather to convey a universal care perspective indicative of the security of medical coverage.

In summary, it is beyond the scope of this chapter to identify all issues central to health care reform. However, the five areas presented here provide fuel for thought about where reform efforts need to be focused. First, to reform the overall health care system meaningfully, there is a need for enhanced state-of-the-art information technology in all health care settings. For the most part, the health care sector has languished behind almost all other industries in adopting information technology. For example, many caregivers still record client data on paper documents that cannot be easily accessed by other providers in different settings—or sometimes even the same setting—which can result in errors and costly duplication of effort.

A second issue and probably the most daunting of health care challenges is the growing number of uninsured Americans, which now exceeds 40 million people. Methods of inclusion need to involve extending health coverage to all residents through the provision of tax credits designed to offset the costs of eligible participants' insurance premiums. Another way to confront this issue might be to consider expanding Medicaid and the State Children's Health Insurance Program to cover a broader range of participants. Among anticipated benefits are coverage of families under a single plan and access to a personal clinician, both of which increase the likelihood that patients will receive appropriate, timely care in the right setting.

A third area is malpractice reform. It has become commonplace to see debates over malpractice insurance and how some physicians are refusing to provide care based on what they perceive to be unreasonable rates. This debate and subsequent refusal to provide services has resulted in limited access to care for patients in some communities. On the other side, this professional fear of liability has impeded efforts to identify sources of error so that they can be prevented. Moreover, the tort system frequently does not result in injured patients getting compensated; those who do often experience long delays. One way to address this issue might be to have states create injury compensation systems outside of the courtroom that are client-centered and focused on safety. These systems would set reasonable payments for avoidable injuries and provide fair, timely compensation to a greater number of clients, while stabilizing the malpractice insurance market by limiting health care providers' financial exposure.

Another area of growing concern that needs attention has to do with changing times and the recognition of the quality and appropriateness of patient care, given the rising prevalence of chronic conditions such as diabetes and heart disease. Roughly 120 million Americans have one or more chronic conditions, many of which could have been prevented or delayed through education or other interventions that promote healthy behaviors. As stated earlier, current health care practices generally are focused on acute, episodic problems and do not effectively provide the ongoing treatment and coordination among multiple care providers and settings needed by those with chronic ailments. Moreover, health care still focuses largely on treatment rather than prevention. For example, half of all diabetics do not receive foot examinations to check for nerve damage, and smokers fail to receive counseling about quitting during three-quarters of all physician visits.

Last, is the need to enhance primary care facilities where the majority of clients enter the health care system and receive most of their care. The reliance on the primary care facility makes this type of facility critical to achieving goals in care of acute and chronic conditions, prevention, and health promotion. For example, in order to improve delivery, community health centers need to undertake initiatives to reinvent and substantially enhance primary care through new models of care delivery, support for patient self-management, and other strategies. The centers should build on their existing innovations in electronic record-keeping and management of chronic diseases, and they should also consider new incentives, such as enabling centers and their staffs to share in the rewards of the cost savings they generate by eliminating waste.

For the most part it is easy to see when confronted with challenges to unequivocally state "we are at a crossroads" or "we are facing a crisis." Yet social work is full of challenges, no matter what the workplace, whether it is health care or some other area of practice. And even the most experienced health care social worker has experienced the feeling that health care organizations can represent large bureaucracies that seem impossible to change. As such, we can become mired down at the crossroad, never moving, feeling others control our destiny—or we can begin to understand and identify what the problems are and explore potential solutions for change.

ROLES AND TASKS OF THE HEALTH CARE SOCIAL WORKER

According to the *Social Work Dictionary* health care workers can be defined in a generic sense as all "professional, paraprofessional, technical and general employees of a system or facility that provides for the diagnosis, treatment and overall well being of patients" (Barker, 2003, p. 192). Nevertheless, a clear distinction must be made between *health care workers* and *allied health care professionals.* Health care workers are nonprofessional service support personnel such as home health aids, medical record personnel, nurse's aides, orderlies, and attendants (Barker, 2003). Allied health care providers, by contrast, are generally professionals such as social workers, psychologists, audiologists, dietitians, occupational therapists, optometrists, pharmacists, physical therapists, and speech pathologists, among others.

It is as allied health care professionals that you will find social workers practicing in health care settings. Health care social workers appear to serve this area well because of their broad-based training in evaluating based on behavior the biological, psychological, and social factors that can affect a client's environmental situation—that is, the behavioral biopsychosocial approach. The beginning generalist (BSW) and advanced specialist (MSW) levels of education help to make the social work professional an invaluable member of the health care delivery team. The services that health care social workers provide can be divided into two major areas: direct practice and support or ancillary services.

Did You Know...The U.S. Veterans' Bureau, now the Department of Veterans' Affairs, began hiring social workers to work in its hospitals in 1926.

Where do physicians and nurses, the most recognizable health care providers, fit in? Physicians and nurses are not considered *allied* service providers. Because their services are necessary to any type of medical care, they are called "essential health care providers"—they are the major players in the host environment.

Direct Practice

Today, the role of the health care social worker is clearly established, and they can be found in every area of our health care delivery system. These practitioners typically provide a wide variety of services to clients and their families:

Case finding and outreach: Assist client to identify and secure the services they need

Preservice or preadmission planning: Identify barriers to accessing health care services

Assessment: Identify service needs and screen to identify health and wellness concerns

Direct provision: Secure concrete services such as admission, discharge, and aftercare planning

Psychosocial evaluation: Gather information on client's biopsychosocial, cultural, financial, situational factors for completion of the psychosocial assessment or social history

Goal identification: Establish mutually negotiated goals and objectives that address client's health and wellness issues.

Counseling: Help client and family to deal with their situation and problems related to health interventions needed or received

Short- and long-term planning: Help client and family to anticipate and plan for the services needed based on client's current or expected health status

Service access assistance: Identify preventive, remedial, and rehabilitative service needs and assist client and family to overcome potential barriers to service access

Education: Instruct client and family on areas of concern in regard to their health and wellness

Wellness training: Help client to establish a plan to secure continued or improved health based on a holistic prevention model

Referral services: Provide information about services available and make direct connection when warranted

Continuity of care: Ensure that proper connections are made among all services needed, taking into account the issue of multiple health care providers

Advocacy: Teach and assist clients to obtain needed resources, or on a larger scale advocate for changes in policy or procedure that directly or indirectly benefit the client (Dziegielewski, 2004).

Did You Know…In the 1920s and 1930s the U.S. military started to add social workers to its ranks. Military social workers usually work in mental health, health, and protective service settings.

The clinical services that health care social workers provide have clearly expanded far beyond the traditional core of **discharge planning**. Health care is a changing environment where even the classic definition of discharge planning has been altered. Social workers not only coordinate discharges, they also oversee the multidisciplinary or interdisciplinary teams of which they are members to be sure that clients are getting the services they need. Since discharges can involve numerous individual, family, and community factors, counseling services often must accompany these placements. Social workers are often called upon to provide this type of service. Furthermore, once the team agrees that a client is ready for discharge, it is often the social worker who is responsible for ensuring that transfer forms are completed, client and family education has been done, and the records that support continued care are ready for transfer (Mankita & Alalu, 1996).

Support Services

Social workers can also provide health-related services that are not considered direct practice. These support or ancillary services include staff supervision, administration, and community-based services:

Direct supervision: Provide direct professional social work supervision through direction, guidance, and education on case services and counseling

Consultation: Provide consultation services to other social workers and multidisciplinary and interdisciplinary teams

Agency consultation: Provide consultation to agency administrators on how to enhance service delivery to clients and organizations

Community consultation: Provide consultation services to communities to assist with the development of community-based services

Policy and program planning: Assist in formulation and implementation of health care policies and programs that will help to meet client needs

Program development: Assist the agency to refine and develop new and improved programs

Quality improvement: Assist the agency to ensure that continuous quality services are provided that meet standards of professionalism and efficiency

Service advocacy: Assist the agency to recognize the needs of clients

Service outreach: Identify unmet needs and services that are not available to clients; advocate for improved programs and services

At-risk service outreach: Identify clients at risk of decreased health or illness; advocate to secure services for them

Health education: Participate and instruct communities on developing and implementing health education programs

Agency liaison: Serve as liaison to the agency on behalf of the client, ensuring connections are made between client, supervisor, and community

Community liaison: Serve as a contact or connection between client, family, and community

Support services go beyond what we generally consider to be the core of health care social work. We must, nevertheless, recognize the importance of all practitioners who do this type of work day in, day out. These tasks and functions cannot be overemphasized, particularly in this era of managed care (see figure 1).

Direct Supervision. Staff supervision is a major support activity with a long and rich history in health care social work. Supervision requires specialized knowledge that builds on years of practice. As a result, you will find that most social workers performing supervision, in one form or another, have MSWs. On occasion, you may find a BSW worker in a supervisory role, but this is the exception.

Supervision is a complicated activity, but it is necessary for the professional growth of all social workers. Supervisors are mentors, teachers if you will, who can be sounding boards, share practice frustrations, and look at different ways of working with a particular client or group. Kadushin gave a more formal definition:

> An agency administrative staff member . . . is given authority to direct, coordinate, enhance, and evaluate on-the-job performance of supervisees for which work he [or she] is held accountable. In implementing this role the

Figure 1: Home healthcare worker examining a developmentally disabled senior who lives with his sister.

Activity...Cultural Diversity in the Medical Setting

Break into groups and discuss the following case. Prepare a plan on how to best assist the client situation described.

The social worker arrives in a client's hospital room to gather some routine admission information when she walks in on a couple having a very heated discussion. Jon is a 40-year-old Hispanic male who is in the hospital for routine same-day exploratory surgery. Jon's wife is visibly upset and crying. The social worker feels a bit awkward for intruding and asks if the couple would like her to leave. Jon motions that he would like her to stay, and begins to tell her that he is furious that his wife has decided to go on a trip alone to see her mother. When questioned as to whether he is disappointed because he wants to go with her, he quickly says no. He is angry because she made plans without getting his permission first. His wife states that she is sorry for not asking him first but she felt the decision had to be made quickly. The couple asks the social worker what her opinion is.

Taking into account a respect for cultural diversity and maintaining professional integrity, what types of responses and or assistance could the social worker provide? What types of responses should be avoided?

supervisor performs administrative, educational, and supportive functions in interaction with the supervisee in the context of a positive relationship. The supervisor's ultimate objective is to deliver to agency clients the best possible service, both quantitative and qualitatively, in accordance with agency policies and procedures (1976, p. 21).

Kadushin's definition applies to the field of health care social work, though with one very important addition. In health care work flexibility must be part of both practice and supervision. Repeated policy changes, and consequent organizational instability, often lead to reorganization, cutbacks, and ultimately reductions in the workforce (Braus, 1996). For the social worker, whether a new or an experienced practitioner, such uncertainty can be difficult to handle. Let's be honest—no one likes to be in an unsure work environment, where the rules may change from one day to the next. In health care, social workers must continually modify details of their practice. The health care social work supervisor also mediates, advocates, and brokers as part of staff supervision (Berkman, 1996). In mediating between supervisees and clients, coworkers, or the larger community, the supervisor should always try not to adopt the opinion of any side. Supervisors must be sensitive to their staff's ongoing struggles to create proactive client-directed services within the constraints set by payers. Supervisors too must balance the demands of their jobs with those of third-party payers. To say the least, the supervisor's role is difficult.

Flexibility, then, is key to competent supervision as well as good practice. The need to be flexible, however, and the environment that creates this need, is a major source of stress. Stress and its management are, therefore, important issues for both supervisor and staff.

Supportive supervision addresses such issues as stress, staff morale, and work-related anxiety and worry, which if left unattended, can lower job satisfaction and commitment to the agency. Supportive supervision builds worker self-esteem and emotional well-being. In the long run, it can reduce stress levels and thus the dissatisfaction that ultimately results in employee burnout (Resnick & Dziegielewski, 1996; Sheafor, Horejsi, & Horejsi, 1997).

As if system uncertainty were not enough for the health care supervisor, let's add another challenge to the job: lack of clarity in staff roles and responsibilities. In particular, what are the differences in the work carried out by BSWs and by MSWs?

Guidelines differentiating practice responsibilities between the BSW and the MSW are rarely clear (Levin & Herbert, 1995). You may find that what BSWs do in one setting is done only by MSWs in another. This lack of clarity about functions means that supervisors must be careful in assigning cases and tasks. Without clear definitions it is possible to assign tasks that are beyond the competence of the social worker, which compromises client care and worker well-being (Levin & Herbert, 1995). Supervisors must ensure that tasks assigned to BSWs are within their scope of practice. That another organization assigns a particular task to BSWs is no guarantee that the activity is appropriate for an entry-level practitioner. Rather, that organization may not be able to assign or even hire an MSW; but the task must be done, so it must be given to a BSW. Though professionally unsound, this task assignment can be made less so if the BSW is given consistent and persistent supervision.

Mediation, Advocacy, and Brokering. The health care social work supervisor also mediates, advocates, and brokers as part of staff supervision (Berkman, 1996). In mediating between supervisees and clients, coworkers, or the larger community, the supervisor remains neutral and does not adopt the opinion of any side (Shulman, 1993). Advice and direction are given on the best way to handle client care for the supervisee, the multidisciplinary or interdisciplinary team, the agency, and the community. Mediation requires the supervisor to recognize that conflicts that are not intentional and to help supervisees to address them in the most ethical, moral, and professional way possible.

The second role, advocacy, requires willingness on the parts of both supervisor and supervisees to assist with the development of needed services for clients, their families, and significant others, while not losing sight of the common ground that links them to administration (Shulman, 2002).

Did You Know…In the early days, hospital nurses generally performed medical social work services. These nurses were convenient choices for this employment because they were easily accessible, already knew agency procedure, and were aware of community resources. Later, however, when it was established that more specialized training in understanding social conditions was needed, the employment of social work professionals began.

Brokering, the third role, requires supervisor and staff to link the client with community services and other agencies. Remember, when most people come into a medical setting, such as a hospital, their stay is limited. The social worker must elicit a great deal of information on the client's environment, including social, emotional, and physical factors and their relation to the illness (remember, this is what Dr. Cabot saw as our great contribution to health care). The social worker

Name: Sam Hickman

Place of residence: Charleston, West Virginia

College/university degrees: Marshall University, BA
West Virginia University, MSW

Present position: Executive Director, NASW/West Virginia

Previous work/volunteer experience: Hospital social work
director; Federal Mental Health Disaster Program Grant
Director; Soil Conservation Service volunteer

What do you do in your spare time? I play and sing Appalachian folk music, coach
youth soccer, cook, garden, and bike.

Why did you choose social work as a career? My mother held social work/human services jobs while I was growing up. I often got to sit on the lap of the mental health
department director or juvenile court judge. When entering a part-time M.S.W. program
came up, it was a natural fit.

What is your favorite social work story? I have two that I would like to share. First,
after discussing nursing home care with a somewhat confused elderly woman, she looked
up at me from her hospital bed and said, "You damn Republican!" Second, last April at a
conference we organize, we passed the hat on the spur of the moment and raised over
$600 for storm victims in the southeast. We gave it to the Red Cross.

*What would be the one thing you would change in our community if you had the power
to do so?* I would pay respectable salaries to women who choose to stay home to care for
young children. I believe this is where healthy families begin.

---

may discover that a client needs a variety of follow-up support services to sustain
her or his family through the recovery period or through ongoing illness. Brokering is how the social worker seeks out these community-based services and develops a case plan that is tailored to the client.

Health Education and Health Counseling. Social workers were part of the
nineteenth-century public health education movement, also called the "Sanitation
Movement." Therefore, providing education and instruction is not new to social
work—though health care counseling was a rarity. Attention wasn't directed
toward counseling until training became institutionalized in colleges and moved to
an educational model.

Health care counseling is especially important with the increased participation
of social work professionals as educators in new health care areas that we might call
"nontraditional social work." These include smoking cessation and weight reduction, for example. The worker continues to teach new patterns of behavior but then
employs counseling theory and skills to help the client negotiate the period of
change. The worker calls on a range of skills and strategies ranging from support
to confrontation.

Administration. Administration and related tasks have not been considered core practice areas of health care social work. In fact, most prospective social workers shy away from studying administration, focusing instead on client-related courses. Don't believe us? Ask your classmates how many of them plan to major in or develop a specialization in administration. You'll probably find that everyone agrees someone should study administration—"but not me." Yet administration, particularly in health care, directly affects the types of services that are offered in a setting. The role that administration plays in strengthening direct practice cannot be overstated.

Social work administrators, like other health care administrators, must respond to often competing management philosophies. These conflicting styles can affect the provision of client care. For example, the social work administrator may receive a directive from the hospital central administration "to increase the participation of professional staff members in the organization's decision-making processes." The idea behind this directive is that greater involvement will strengthen commitment to the hospital. The social work administrator decides that "quality circles" and "total quality management" (TQM) will best achieve the culture that central administration is seeking. While the social work administrator is attempting to put TQM in place with quality circles among staff members, central administration announces that reimbursement from third-party payers and census data (e.g., patient-bed days) are down. The announcement is an unmistakable signal of financial pressure—remember, a hospital is a business and, like all businesses, needs to make a profit. So now the social work administrator must be concerned with generating significant patient numbers to justify and sustain the department. The goal is now to maximize reimbursement potential. If numbers are not increased, then the department will be forced to cut back on staff while raising workloads for those who stay. A "more with less" mentality takes hold while the edict to develop staff loyalty remains in place.

Sound frustrating? Doesn't make sense? You now understand why so many health care social work administrators feel trapped. Double-edged and conflicting messages sent by central administration or insurance companies make administration the most difficult, frustrating, and challenging aspect of health care work.

But the situation is not as dismal as it seems. Health care social work administrators can balance these pressures and influence the agency's **policy** decisions. Serving on agency committees or boards allows the administrator to help construct new policy directions and provides an opportunity to meet funding bodies in order to explain practice realities and discuss ways to enhance service delivery. This strategy is called "practice policy." It reflects the understanding that social work activities are born of policy decisions. As social workers, we must be informed about and involved in the development of organizational policy—our clients are stakeholders in the policy-making process. Our practice, knowledge, advocacy skills, and ability to mediate between conflicting parties are all contributions we social workers can make to the health care policy-making process.

Acute and Long-Term Care Settings

Social work has long been at the forefront in providing health care services to clients in acute care and long-term care settings. We find that the skills and theory that social workers bring to the workplace, again Dr. Cabot's observation holds true, are needed in today's acute care setting (Berkman, 1996). The health care social worker's roles and responsibilities in the acute care setting are clear:

◆ Provide assistance with treatment plans and compliance issues

◆ Assist clients and families with discharge planning and referral

◆ Provide counseling and support for clients and significant others in the areas of health, wellness, mental health, bereavement, and so forth

◆ Assist clients and their families ethically to make difficult decisions that can affect physical health and mental health

◆ Educate clients, their families, and significant others about psychosocial issues and adjusting to illness; assist in resolving behavioral problems

◆ Assist in identifying and obtaining entitlement benefits

◆ Secure nonmedical benefits; assist with risk management and quality assurance activities

◆ Advocate for enhanced and continued services to ensure client well-being

---

Did You Know…In 1928, the American College of Surgeons developed and included a minimum standard of service provision for social service—that is, social work—departments.

Long-term and restorative care settings may not be that familiar to you. Let's try some other names that you're more likely to recognize: rehabilitative hospitals and clinics, nursing homes, intermediate care facilities, supervised boarding homes, home health care agencies, hospices, and hospital home care units. These settings are usually multidisciplinary, and social workers provide services within the areas of assessment, treatment, rehabilitation, supportive care, and prevention of increased disability of people with chronic physical, emotional, or developmental impairments. Poole (1995) called for such health services to 1) be provided in the least restrictive environment possible, 2) support clients in autonomous decision making, and 3) maximize a client's level of physical, social, and psychological functioning and subsequent well-being.

Poole's recommendations may seem like common sense, and they are. They reflect the core values and ethics set out in the Code of Ethics, which remind us of how important it is to maintain sensitivity and respect for people served, to be aware of the individual's right and ability to make decisions for himself (in most situations), and to focus on client strengths and resources that can be maximized.

The phrase "long term" indicates that the client has a chronic condition that may affect his abilities. Unfortunately, many chronic conditions are unlikely to improve. But that doesn't mean the social worker and other team members give up hope or stop trying to ensure that the client receives the highest quality of professional treatment. We must be realistic, but optimistic. We should not hide information from clients or discount their feelings. Remember, we are all people who think, feel, and care.

Health care social workers employed in long-term care must develop specialized knowledge of various chronic conditions and learn to identify and assess signs and symptoms of the expected progression of various diseases (Dziegielewski, 2004). Such information is critical to being an effective practitioner with the client, family, and friends. For they (family, friends, and significant others) often need assistance to participate in the care of their loved ones (see, for example, figure 2). Many people don't know what to say or how to say it and, as a result, feel overwhelmed and even useless. We should never underestimate the importance of "others" in the healing or sustaining process. Considerable evidence exists that the involvement and support of family and friends contributes greatly to the overall wellness and satisfaction of all involved (Dziegielewski, 2004; Rubinstein, Lubben, & Mintzer, 1994).

One last thought: when addressing the needs of a client who suffers from a chronic condition the beginning professional should strive not to be afraid. Rely on what you have learned in school, and always be a compassionate person who uses skills and theory grounded in values and ethics that allow for the celebration of the entire human experience.

Figure 2: A daughter is about to give her father a haircut. The father and an adult son who was injured in an auto accident live together. Neither is able to drive and the other adult children take turns dropping by and helping out. Both the father and the son gain a sense of responsibility and accomplishment by taking care of each other.

Did You Know...Johns Hopkins Hospital established its first social work program in 1907. The first social worker to be employed there was Helen B. Pendleton (Nacman, 1977).

Hospital Emergency Room Social Work

Social work services are offered in many hospital emergency rooms across the country; yet, in this fast-paced environment the actual services provided can differ greatly. For the social worker assigned to the emergency room, this employment setting is generally perceived as a fast-paced setting. In this setting, crises, deaths, and severe client problems need to be assessed and addressed as quickly and efficiently as possible. The pressure for immediate action in this setting is intense, and the social worker must remain in a constant state of readiness prepared for whatever might come through the door next. According to Van Wormer and Boes (1997), working in the emergency room settings is different from other settings in the hospital because of the speed and intensity of which services must be assessed and provided. According to Ponto and Berger (1992) referrals to the emergency room social worker were often involved complex problems. Specific cases included: 1) acute psychiatric episode involving suspected or threatened self-inflicted injuries, anxiety attacks, or emergent psychotic episodes; 2) acute medical crisis involving long-term mental illness, chemical dependent individuals, homeless, or transient patients; 3) cases of domestic violence or rape; 4) suspected cases of child abuse or neglect, including sexual abuse; and 5) any traumatic injury or illness that involved the police or other agencies, including assault, sexual assault, domestic violence, intoxication, or temporary disabling conditions.

For many social workers in the emergency room setting, it is not uncommon to work as part of an interdisciplinary or multidisciplinary team. Teamwork in this setting often involves a variety of professionals comprised of physicians, nurses, respiratory technicians, health unit coordinators, x-ray technicians, nurse case managers, social workers, and other health care professionals. Furthermore, some emergency departments divide this team further into what is often termed a *case management sub-team or dyad* that utilizes the combined services of a nurse and a social worker (Bristow & Herrick, 2002). In this setting, the case management sub-team members work together to provide social services and discharge planning, and to ensure that continuum of care needs are met for each client served.

Historically, the presence of a social worker in the emergency room setting has been important from a supportive/clinical perspective as well as to provide direct case management and discharge planning services. Supportive services for helping clients include discharge planning or counseling services for the family support system of the identified client. In the emergency room, the problems clients seek treatment for are multifaceted and complex and the types of problems addressed are diverse, ranging from auto accidents to other types of accidental and non-accidental injuries. Many individuals may have acute or chronic episodes of an illness, first or repeated episodes of a physical or mental illness, or suicide attempts related to health and/or emotional issues.

According to Bristow and Herrick (2002), the services that social workers provided in this setting include psychosocial assessments, bereavement counseling and support, substance abuse assessment and referral, discharge planning, referrals for community resources, emotional support, and educating and advocating for patients. In addition, the emergency room social worker can assist with case management by gathering contact information for family and friends as well as finding additional means for meeting the client's health needs. Unfortunately, some believe the emergency room has become a dumping ground for those that lack insurance or are homeless. This group of individuals has a very unique set of circumstances requiring short-term intensive support designed to facilitate the discharge process and decrease the chance of recidivism (Dziegielewski, 2004). Since many individuals who seek care in the emergency room often lack or have inadequate health care coverage, this factor may force clients to seek emergency rooms as a means for obtaining non-emergency or episodic care (Spitzer & Kuykendall, 1994). Social work in the emergency department plays an important role in providing for the psychosocial needs of the patients in a time of crisis. Although this role is important, emergency room social workers warn that medical staff may overlook social work services because of their focus on the medical needs not the psychosocial needs of the client being served. Thus, to utilize the services of social workers in the emergency department better, it is vital that the emergency room staff as well as hospital administrators be educated about the role of the social worker in their department.

Home Care Services

Home care agencies have been providing high-quality, in-home services to Americans for more than a century and have remained an integral part of the provision of health services since 1905. Health care social workers help patients and their families cope with chronic, acute, or terminal illnesses and handle problems that may stand in the way of recovery or rehabilitation.

Home care refers to health care and the social services that are provided to individuals and families in their home or in community and other home like settings (Dziegielewski, 2004). Home care includes a wide array of services including nursing, rehabilitation, social work, home health aids, and other services. This rapidly expanding area of health care social work can be traced back as far as the early nineteenth century (Cowles, 2000; National Association for Home Care, 2000). In 1955, the United States Public Health Services endorsed a physician-oriented organized home health care team designed to provide medical and social services to patients within their home. The team consisted of a physician, nurse, and social worker (Goode, 2000). Since that time social workers have continued to provide social services in the home care setting, and this area of health care social work remains a diverse and dynamic service industry. The demand for home care services is increasing as hospital stays are decreasing.

For the most part, the majority of home care services are considered third party and reimbursable by Medicare, Medicaid, private insurance policies, health maintenance organizations (HMOs), and group health plans. These types of payments are determined by several factors, including client diagnosis and the types of services required. Medicare recipients are the largest group of clients needing home health care services. More frequently than not, the services they need involve social as well as medical supports, making the role of social work crucial in the field of home care. When psychosocial needs go unmet, clients are at risk of further health problems that can lead to physical deterioration, reduced independence, and eventually to the need for more intensive and expensive services (Berkman, Chauncey, Holmes, et al., 1999, p. 9). Cowles (2000) identified five categories of home care client problems: "(1) barriers to admission to the service; (2) problems of adjustment to the service; (3) problems of adjustment to the diagnosis, prognosis, or treatment/care plan; (4) lack of information to make informed decisions; (5) lack of needed resources; and (6) barriers to discharge from the service" (p. 176). Rossi (1999) described home care social workers' duties as the following: "(1) helping the health care team to understand the social and emotional factors related to the patient's health and care; (2) assessing the social and emotional factors to estimate the caregiver's capacity and potential, including but not limited to coping with the problems of daily living, acceptance of the illness or injury or its impact, role reversal, sexual problems, stress, anger or frustration, and making the necessary referrals to ensure that the patient receives the appropriate treatments; (3) helping the caregiver to secure or utilize other community agencies as needs are identified; and (4) helping the patient or caregiver to submit paperwork for alternative funding" (p. 335). McLeod and Bywaters (2000) validate the need for social workers in health care and report that there is substantial scope for social work involvement by working toward greater equality of access to existing health and social services. Equally important is to participate in shaping how social workers are viewed establishing their role as a knowledgeable, positive and supportive resource to support staff, co-workers, and administration (Neuman, 2000).

Hospice Social Work

Hospice care is a special way of caring for people who are terminally ill and their families. The goal of a hospice is to care for the client and the family with open acknowledgment that no cure is expected for client's illness. Hospice care includes physical, emotional, social, and spiritual care; usually a public agency or private company that may or not be Medicare-approved provides this service. All age groups are serviced including children, adults, and the elderly during their final stages of life (Facts and Figures, 2001). When working in the hospice setting, both in-patient and in-home services can be provided. In this setting the individual is prepared for a dignified death that is satisfactory to the person and to those who participate in the person's care (McSkimming, Myrick, & Wasinger, 2000).

In hospice the role of the social worker is crucial to the family planning process, and efforts are made to help family members deal with the client's illness and impending death in the most effective way possible. The social worker tries to facilitate open communication between patient and family and assess levels of stress—especially the ones that affect coping and prognosis. In addition, special attention is given to assessing the spiritual needs of the client and his/her family, and helping them continue to adjust and accept. In the hospice setting there is a strong interdisciplinary focus with a team approach that will continually assess environmental safety concerns. One of the first tasks of the social worker is to address grieving with an initial *bereavement risk assessment* for the caregiver, thereby assisting the patient and family to identify strengths that help cope with loss (Dziegielewski, 2004). Families are supported as time is allowed for the patient and family to progress through stages of grieving. Other duties of the hospice social worker involve updating bereavement care plans and assessing the type of bereavement program to be initiated upon death of the patient. Referrals are also provided for bereavement support services.

Life-Threatening Conditions and People with HIV/AIDS

Close to one million people in the United States are living with HIV or AIDS and over 42 million worldwide.

Did You Know…HIV is a worldwide illness. At the end of 2002, UNAIDS and the World Health Organization estimated adults and children living with AIDS in the following regions:

North America	980,000	Eastern Europe and Central Asia	1.2 million
Caribbean	440,000	South and South-East Asia	6 million
Latin America	1.5 million	Central Asia	1.2 million
Western Europe	570,000	East Asia	6 million
North Africa and Middle East	550,000	Australia and New Zealand	15,000
Sub-Saharan Africa	29.4 million		

Source: *http://www.who.int/hiv/facts/en/plwha_m.jpg*

Just what is HIV? HIV, which is an acronym for *human immunodeficiency virus*, is a virus that kills cells in your immune system. As the immune system weakens, our body becomes susceptible to various disease, many of which, including life-threatening diseases, infections, and cancers. This is what is referred to as AIDS or *acquired immunodeficiency syndrome*, the most advanced stage of HIV infection. Treated primarily through a drug regimen, the annual costs of treatment, in 1998, was $18,300 and of this, 55 percent was for medication, 15 percent for outpatient services and the remaining 30 percent for hospitalization (U.S. Department of Health and Human Services, 2003). The federal government's pri-

> *Did you know...In the United States,*
> *Every 13 minutes: Someone is infected with HIV.*
> *Every 13 minutes: Someone is diagnosed with AIDS.*
> *Every 34 minutes: Someone dies from AIDS.*

mary legislation that focuses resources and funding on HIV/AIDS is the Ryan White Care Act, which was first enacted in 1990.

HIV and AIDS cases can cut across all gender, racial, and ethnic boundaries. In 2000, less than 40 percent of the cases were related to men having sex with men (U.S. Department of Health and Human Services, 2003).

People with HIV/AIDS are vulnerable to economic threats as well. For example, in 2000, 63 percent of people in care were unemployed; 72 percent had annual household incomes of less than $25,000, and 46 percent had incomes of less than $10,000; only 32 percent had private health insurance; and 20 percent had no insurance at all, either public or private.

From a social work perspective, we recognize that HIV and AIDS is a life-threatening disease and that the worldwide medical community continues to search for a cure. In our practice we must ensure that the client with HIV/AIDS follows a strict medical regimen. We also work with the individual and his or her family and support group to fulfill their expectations of life, try to help these clients, as we would with any clients, to achieve their hopes, dreams and desires.

WHY DO IT?

By now you may be wondering why anyone would want to work in the changing, often unsettling, health care system. This is a fair question, so let's try to find an answer.

Social workers are among the many allied health professional groups that make up the health care "army." Given the interdisciplinary nature of today's work, it is incumbent for the social work profession to promote a clear understanding of its purpose and role in order to maintain a place in health care delivery. What we bring to the health care arena is vital. History shows this. Nevertheless, we must always define our role and be players in this process. Social workers cannot afford to let others decide what we can do with and on behalf of clients and their families.

The roots of health care social work, as part of the social work profession, lie in serving the poor and disenfranchised. As the medical arena has changed over the years so too has the role of the health care social worker.

And now, as the social environment changes, expectations for health care are becoming clouded. Is health care a right or a privilege? Should the government guarantee a minimum standard of health care for all people? Who would establish such a standard? What role should the insurance industry have in such deliberations? Should we develop a "patient's bill of rights" as a new initiative? (FYI: In New York City taxi cabs you will find a "rider's bill of rights." Interesting that taxi cab riders are provided certain guarantees but not people in the health care system!) While the public debates these issues, the day-to-day work of the social worker in health care is daunting. Flexibility is a prerequisite for helping our clients and for adjusting to the constantly renegotiated health care environment.

All health care social workers—whether in the role of clinical practitioner, supervisor, or administrator—face the challenge of understanding and anticipating health care trends. Each worker's skills must therefore be current, flexible to change, and proactive with clients. And yes, all health care social workers must also understand macroeconomics and its influence on health care delivery. The current economic environment is characterized by a shifting tension between quality of care and cost containment. While the goal of the social work profession is to provide high-quality care, these services are shadowed and ultimately influenced by cost containment strategies. Health care social workers are expected to include cost containment among their practice principles whether they serve as direct practitioners, professional supervisors, administrators, or community organizers (Caper, 1995).

The viability of health care social work rests on two points. First, medical settings must place greater emphasis on the macroperspective in health care. The social work profession must work actively to help the larger community understand its responsibility to create a cradle-to-grave health care system. Believing that the health care system will eventually solve its own problems is ludicrous. Health care social workers, whatever roles they choose for practice delivery, must take the lead in developing a more humane health care system that meets the needs of all people, regardless of their financial capabilities.

The second point that must be ingrained into all areas of health care social work practice is that advocacy leads to client empowerment. Health care social workers must change the mindset that managed care and the policies dictated by it are all bad. Social workers must recognize that there are benefits in a managed care system for both clients and providers. The strengths of managed care include enhanced and accountable mental health treatment; more positive client outcomes through concentration on specific goals and objectives in therapeutic treatment; time limits that can force emphasis on identifying external and environmental supports to allow continued therapeutic gains; avoidance of long-term therapy, with resulting decreases in long-term medication supplementation; and reduced health care costs for American businesses, which can only benefit the larger society (Browning & Browning, 1996).

We must recognize, however, that managed care also has many pitfalls. Health care social workers are therefore needed to advocate for clients. Workers must always stress development of new and needed services within the managed care framework. They must also teach clients how to obtain needed resources and help them to do so. On a larger scale, social workers are required—by our Code of Ethics—to advocate changes in policies or procedures that will directly or indirectly benefit clients.

Health care social work is far from easy. If you decide, nonetheless, that it's the area for you, the question is: How do you best respond to the challenge? You will often be tempted to switch areas and collect a paycheck in a less volatile setting.

Health care social work is suited to people who will relish the changing environment, want to maximize resources for clients, look to serve on boards and committees to influence policy and practice, and enjoy the idea that every day will be different. If that's you, the health care setting is worth considering.

SUMMARY

Health care social work is a dynamic, exciting, constantly changing field of practice. The past ten years have brought things never seen before. Experienced social workers are forced to address specific issues in an environment where the "rules" are evolving. Health care social work's history is an extensive one, deeply rooted in the activities of pioneers such as Ida Cannon and Richard Cabot. These early practitioners directly linked social work practice to the medical model considered the core of health care practice.

Today health care social workers continue to strive to restore the highest level of functioning for each client, family, small group, and community served. Health care social work remains central in building the profession. Starting long ago, to this day health care social work remains an important and vital force both in the profession and in communities across the country and around the world. People with medical illnesses often have other related problems and may need help re-establishing their routines once they arrive home from the hospital, or they may have trouble paying their bills. Families who lose a loved one may need counseling to process their grief, and those with hereditary conditions may need help sorting through their fears and concerns about the future. Health care social workers use a wide range of skills in all of these settings, employing both a family- and a systems-oriented approach to psychosocial care. They provide counseling, help families develop strengths and resources, and run programs for patients who have diseases such as AIDS and heart disease. The settings these workers occupy vary from acute short-term settings to extended care long-term settings. Regardless of the type of clientele served, or the area of practice, health care social work is a challenging and essential area of practice.

Today's health care system is imbued with knowledge, expertise, equipment, and technologies never before even dreamed of or thought possible. Within our lifetime we have seen transplants go from headline news to no news; diseases have been eradicated; life expectancy has dramatically increased. Yet we all know the health care system is challenged. Costs have risen, and continue to rise, to levels that require health insurance to help make care affordable. Even so, more than 40 million people are without health insurance. Scores of individuals and families day in and day out ask the simple question, "Do I put food on the table tonight or buy the prescription for my child?"

Let's for a moment consider what the health care system might be like—reflecting on Ida Maude Cannon's ideals and see how they would translate to a health care system at the outset of the twenty-first century. One way to consider "what might be" is to identify core principles that you feel are central to your organization's purpose. These principles are jelled together without bias or consideration of who is favored or not favored, and we need to begin to think about what is in the best interest of the whole. Some areas for future thought include:

1. Health care needs to be affordable to individuals and families, businesses, and taxpayers, and financial barriers to needed care need to be removed.

2. Health care needs to be as cost efficient as possible, spending the maximum amount of dollars on direct patient care.

3. Health care needs to provide comprehensive benefits, including benefits for mental health and long-term care services.

4. Health care needs to promote prevention and early intervention.

5. Health care provisions and services need to eliminate disparities in access to quality health care.

6. Health care needs to address the needs of people with special health care requirements, particularly for those within underserved populations in both rural and urban areas.

7. Health care needs to promote quality and better health outcomes.

8. Health care services need to be inclusive by having adequate numbers of qualified health care caregivers, practitioners, and providers to guarantee timely access to quality care.

9. Health care needs to provide adequate and timely payments in order to guarantee access to providers.

10. Health care services need to be comprehensive fostering a strong network of health care facilities, including safety net providers.

11. Health care services need to maximizes consumer choice in terms of health care providers and practitioners.

12. Health care services need to ensure continuity of coverage and care.

References

Bahandari, S., & Gifford, E. (2003). Children and health insurance: Current population reports: 2001. U.S. Census Bureau, (pp. 60–224). U.S. Department of Commerce, Economics and Statistics Division. Issued September 2003. Retrieved October 12, 2003 from: www.census/gov/pubs.

Barker, R. L. (2003). *The social work dictionary* (5th ed.). Washington, DC: NASW Press.

Berkman, B. (1996). The emerging health care world: Implications for social work practice and education. *Social Work, 41* (15), 541–549.

Berkman, B., Chauncey, S., Holmes, W., Daniels, A., Bonander, E., Sampson, S., & Robinson, M. (1999). Standardized screening of elderly patients' needs for social work assessment in primary care: Use of the SF-36. *Health and Social Work, 24* (1), 9–17.

Braus, P. (1996, February). Who will survive managed care? *American Demographics, 18,* 16.

Bristow, D. & Herrick, C. (2002). Emergency department: The roles of the nurse case manager and the social worker. *Continuing Care, 21* (2), 28–29.

Browning, C. H., & Browning, B. J. (1996). *How to partner with managed care.* Los Alamitos, CA: Duncliffs International.

Bruner, S. T., Waldo, R. R., & McKusick, D. R. (1992). National health expenditures: Projections through 2030. *Health Care Financing Review, 14,* 1–29.

Caper, P. (1995). The next shift: Managed care. *Public Health Reports, 110,* 682–683.

Carlton, T. O. (1984). *Clinical social work in health care settings: A guide to professional practice with exemplars.* New York: Springer.

Cowles, L. A., (2000). *Social Work in the Heath Field.* Binghamton, NY: Hawthorne.

Dziegielewski, S. F. (1996). Managed care principles: The need for social work in the health care environment. *Crisis Intervention and Time-Limited Treatment, 3* (2), 97–110.

Dziegielewski, S. F. (1997). Time limited brief therapy: The state of practice. *Crisis Intervention and Time-Limited Treatment, 3* (3), 217–228.

Dziegielewski, S. F. (2004). *The changing face of health care social work: Professional practice in the era of behaviorally based managed care.* New York: Springer.

Facts and Figures. (2001). *National Hospice and Palliative Care Organization.* Abstract retrieved February 20, 2002, from http://www.nhpco.org/public/articles/factsandfigures121001.pdf.

Goode, R. (2000). *Social work practice in home health care.* Binghamton, NY: Hawthorne.

Hiratsuka, J. (1990). Managed care: A sea of change in health. *NASW News, 35,* 3.

Kadushin, A. (1976). *Supervision in social work* New York: Columbia University Press.

Leipzig, R. M., Hyer, K., Ek, K., Wallenstein, S., Vezina, M. L, Fairchild, S., Cassel, C. K., & Howe, J. L. (2002). Attitudes toward working on interdisciplinary healthcare teams: A comparison by discipline. *Journal of Geriatric Society, 50,* 6, 1141–1148.

Levin, R., & Herbert, M. (1995). Differential work assignments of social work practitioners in hospitals. *Health and Social Work, 20* (1), 21–30.

Mankita, S., & Alalu, R. (1996, Spring). Hospital social work: Challenges, rewards. *New Social Worker,* pp. 4–6.

McLeod, E., & Bywaters, P. (2000). *Social Work, health and equality.* New York: Routledge.

McSkimming, S., Myrick, M., & Wasinger, M. (2000). Supportive care of the dying: a coalition for compassionate care-conducting an organizational assessment. *American Journal of Hospice & Palliative Care, 17* (4), 245–252.

Mills, R.J., & Bahandari, S. (2003). Health insurance coverage in the United States: 2002. Current Population Reports. U.S. Census Bureau, (pp. 60–223). U.S. Department of Commerce, Economics and Statistics Division. Issued September 2003. Retrieved October 12, 2003 from www.census/gov/pubs.

Mizrahi, T. (1995). Health care: Reform initiatives. In R. Edwards et al. (Eds.), *Encyclopedia of social work* (19th ed., Vol. 2, pp. 1185–1198). Silver Spring, MD: NASW Press.

Nacman, M. (1977). Social work in health setting: A historical review. *Social Work in Health Care, 2* (4), 407–418.

National Association for Home Care. (2000). *Basic statistics about home care.* (pp. 1–25). Retrieved February 11, 2002 from www.nach.org.Consumer/hcstats.html.

Neuman, K. (2000). Understanding organizational reengineering in health care: Strategies for social work's survival. *Social Work in Health Care, 31* (1), 19–32.

Ponto, J. M., & Berger, W. (1992). Social work services in the emergency department: A cost benefit analysis of an extended coverage program. *Health & Social Work, 17,* 1, 67–75.

Poole, D. (1995). Health care: Direct practice. In R. Edwards et al. (Eds.), *Encyclopedia of social work* (19th ed., Vol. 2, pp. 1156–1167). Washington, DC: NASW Press.

Popple, P., & Leighninger, L. (1990). *Social work, social welfare and American society.* Needham, MA: Allyn and Bacon.

The President's health security plan. (1993). New York: Times Books/Random House.

Resnick, C., & Dziegielewski, S. F. (1996). The relationship between therapeutic termination and job satisfaction among medical social workers. *Social Work in Health Care, 23* (3), 17–35.

Rice, D. (1995). Health care: Financing. In R. Edwards et al. (Eds.), *Encyclopedia of social work* (19th ed., Vol. 2, pp. 1168–1175). Washington, DC: NASW Press.

Rossi, P. (1999). *Case management in healthcare*. Philadelphia: W. B. Saunders.

Rubinstein, R. L., Lubben, J. E., & Mintzer, J. E. (1994, March). Social isolation and social support: An applied perspective. *Journal of Applied Gerontology, 13* (1), 58–72.

Segal, E., & Brzuzy, S. (1998). *Social welfare policy, programs, and practice*. Itasca, IL: Peacock.

Sheafor, B. W., Horejsi, C. R., & Horejsi, G. A. (1997). *Techniques and guidelines for social work practice* (4th ed.). Needham Heights, MA: Allyn and Bacon.

Shulman, L. (2002). Developing successful therapeutic relationships. In A. R. Roberts & G. J. Greene (Eds.), *Social workers' desk reference*. (pp. 375–378). New York: Oxford University Press.

Spitzer, W. J., & Kuykendall, R. (1994). Social work delivery of hospital-based financial assistance of services. *Health and Social Work, 19*, 4, 295–298.

Trattner, W. (1989). *From poor law to welfare state: A history of social welfare in America* (4th ed.). New York: Free Press.

UNAIDS (2002). *Adults and children estimated to be living with HIV/AIDS as of end of 2002*. Retrieved October 5, 2003 from http://www.who.int/hiv/facts/en/plwha_m.jpg.

U.S. Department of Health and Human Services, Health Resources and Services Administration. (2003). *The AIDS Epidemic and the Ryan White CARE Act Past Progress, Future Challenges 2002–2003*. Health Resources and Services Administration, HIV/AIDS Bureau 301.443.1993. Retrieved October 5, 2003 from http://hab.hrsa.gov.

Van Wormer, K. & Boes, M. (1997). Humor in the emergency room: A social work perspective. *Health and Social Work, 22* (2), 87–92.

Chapter 10

Mental Health

SOCIAL WORKERS ARE THE NATION'S LARGEST PROVIDERS OF MENtal health services. Today in the United States it is estimated that there are 35,000 physicians currently in psychiatric practice, 70,000 psychologists, 50,000 marriage and family therapists, and approximately 200,000 social workers (Comer, 2002). Furthermore, these professionals are often the only mental health care providers serving residents of the poorest, most rural communities (NASW, 1998).

In mental health practice social workers are essential service providers helping individuals meet their daily needs. Social workers practicing in this area engage in numerous services and functions, including mental health counseling in community mental health centers, private practice, psychiatric hospitals and psychiatric units, long-term care facilities, courts, and prisons; case management; discharge planning, intake or admission evaluation; high social risk case finding; patient education, support and advocacy; crisis intervention; and interdisciplinary collaboration. Services are provided to all clients and their families, and all the major psychiatric disorders are addressed, including schizophrenia, affective and mood disorders such as depression, neuropsychiatric disorders, eating disorders, personality disorders, phobias, substance abuse, childhood disorders, and organic psychoses (NASW, 1990).

The mental health social worker has either a baccalaureate or a master's degree from an accredited school of social work. Social work in general is not a highly paid profession, but of all the practice areas workers in mental health fare well. According to NASW, social workers at the BSW level who work in mental health earned about $20,000 to $30,000 a year (NASW, 1998); those with MSWs earned a salary of approximately $41,290 to $45,660 in 1999 (Linsley, 2003).

Did You Know...Massachusetts General Hospital in Boston pioneered hospital and psychiatric social work, starting a social service department in 1905, and hiring social workers to work with patients who suffered from mental illness in 1907 (NASW, 1998).

When a social worker employed in a local mental health clinic outside of Orlando, Florida, was asked how she felt about her job, she said she could describe it best as "challenging, rewarding, and most of the time quite frustrating." She believed that the role of the mental health social worker is complicated because allegiances must be divided, and always placing the needs of the client first forced her to maintain a delicate balance between the needs of the family, the society, and

Name: Carolyn Heymann

Place of residence: Indiana

College/university degrees: Indiana University, MSW

Present position: Mental Health and Addiction Specialist

Previous work/volunteer experience: Worked with clients that suffer from addictive disorders

What do you do in your spare time? Flower/landscape gardening, writing, family

Why did you choose social work as a career? I believe that "if you give a person a loaf of bread you feed them a meal, teach that person how to plant wheat and bake bread, you feed them for a lifetime." That model assumes the recipient is physically and mentally able to sow the grain, follow instructions, and has an oven available. I chose to assist those who cannot and do not.

What is your favorite social work story? One Friday afternoon I was working in the crisis department when a lady came in with a bag of clothing stating her doctor had told her to get over to the Psychology Pavilion as soon as possible. She didn't know why, except that she had told him she finally had to confess that she hadn't been taking her anxiolytics and painkillers as prescribed. "He was in the process of writing another prescription, and I just had to tell him." I asked if she had been abusing prescription narcotics. She explained that what she had been trying to tell the doctor for months was that he was prescribing too many meds in excessive dosages and she had been decreasing intake to the point that she no longer needed them. "I don't know why he sent me here. I haven't been taking any meds and I am fine."

What would be the one thing you would change in our community if you had the power to do so? Within the social work community I would like to see social workers apply principles of acceptance, tolerance, compassion, and nondiscrimination to those with brain disease or addictions.

the agency. Clients who are mentally impaired often cannot handle their own affairs, making it essential for the social worker to ensure that the client's rights are not violated.

The mental health social worker must also be well aware of "duty to warn." If a client is perceived as a "danger to self or others," action is taken to protect any person or persons who may be at risk. "Duty to warn" may force a social worker to violate the confidence of the client in order to protect others in the immediate environment or, if threatening suicide, to protect the client. Therefore, mental health social work practitioners must always strive for balance between the *rights* of the client and the needs of the client and her family. Social workers must be advocates for clients who are mentally impaired; these clients will often be provided services through facilitation and referral because they are rarely capable of representing themselves.

Many beginning social work professionals are attracted to the area of mental health because they aspire to do therapy with the clients they serve. NASW (1990) described the essential components of psychosocial psychiatric services as 1) the completion of timely psychosocial screenings, 2) timely psychosocial assessments, 3) comprehensive psychosocial assessments, 4) timely contacts with family and significant others, 5) teamwork on interdisciplinary or multidisciplinary teams. These highlight how important it is for the social work professional to understand diagnosis and assessment, particularly because most social workers serve as advocates, facilitating and ensuring as part of the interdisciplinary team that the client gets the services needed.

In this chapter we introduce the role of social worker in mental health. In particular, we introduce the completion of a multidimensional psychosocial assessment that allows the social worker to gather information needed to understand the client and her environment. In closing we examine several potential areas of practice for the social worker interested in working in the area of mental health.

MULTIDIMENSIONAL PSYCHOSOCIAL ASSESSMENT

In the area of mental health the profession of social work did not develop in isolation. In order to survive and compete in the mental health practice environment many social workers have adapted to the dominant culture. This means that the practice approaches and methodologies employed by social workers at all levels meet the same expectations, as other mental health professional's address. These expectations generally relate to reimbursement for service. For example, outcome measures, which dictate service reimbursement, have become mandatory (Dziegielewski, 2004). Moreover, it is not uncommon for social workers to feel forced to reduce services to some clients, focusing their efforts instead of those covered by insurance or able to pay privately. For those who cannot pay, services may be terminated if they seem too costly (Dziegielewski & Holliman, 2001; Ethics Meet Managed Care, 1997). Accurate psychosocial assessment is therefore a critical tool for all mental health and health care social workers because it documents a client's needs and can support the efficiency of a chosen intervention. Such assessments not only open the door for services, they also determine who will receive them and what will be provided.

Currently, many social workers work with clients who suffer from mental illness, from the BSW-level practitioner who is active in case management, initial assessment, and discharge planning to the master's-level social worker who is an active participant in completing assessments and diagnoses. Whatever his level of practice, a social worker must be aware of the tools and expectations characteristic of the field. The importance of the initial psychosocial assessment should not be underestimated; it provides the foundation and the framework for any future intervention.

Assessment is defined as "the process of determining the nature, cause, progression and prognosis of a problem and the personalities and situations involved

Mental Illness Can Strike Anyone and the Consequences Can Be Devastating: A True Case Story

Forth Worth—Jane fell so far so fast. A woman of education with a soft spot for the underdog, Jane combined a master's degree in social work with a compassion for the homeless that propelled her into Austin's power circles. She drove an expensive car, lived a full life, and was devoted to a loving family.

And she lost it all as a victim of mental illness.

The petite, blue-eyed blonde who once turned heads was beaten to death Saturday, left alone on a dirty sidewalk among those she once helped. At age 43, she died penniless and homeless all her worldly goods in two plastic grocery bags.

For those who knew Jane, the tragic end was no surprise. Jane suffered from bipolar and personality disorders that left her without a family, unable to work, and on the street. "It is sad to say, but we feared something like this would happen," said her friend for 12 years. "She was so out of control, and no matter how hard we tried to help, she wouldn't take it."

Early Saturday, Jane was found slumped over in front of Mental Health–Mental Retardation Services day resource building. An autopsy showed she died from blunt force injuries to her head. Her killer remains a mystery, and there are no new leads in the case. Witnesses told police they saw Jane talking to an unidentified man about an hour before she was found dead, said the homicide detective.

A composite of the man has been posted on fliers and tacked up around the shelters and known hangouts for local indigents. "He could be a witness or a suspect, and right now we just want him for questioning."

Jane's daughter said the fact that her mother wouldn't accept help from loved ones adds to her sadness. "A lot of people ask me, 'Why didn't you help? Why didn't you do anything?' Well, what they don't know is that it is harder than that," her daughter said.

Jane's former social work professor, who taught and served as a mentor, said Jane is proof that mental illness can tear apart lives. "I don't think the general public knows just how vicious mental illness is. It can destroy you. . . It destroyed her to the end."

Her daughter stated that most of her family hadn't seen Jane for two years. Her mother had avoided seeing loved ones but managed to keep in touch through phone calls and letters. She described her mother as someone who had inner and outer beauty, a person with a great sense of humor who was articulate and who made sure the family went to church. "During the summer she used to make me volunteer. She was just that way. She really cared about others. But the mental illness tore our relationship apart," her daughter said.

"I had a real good conversation with her, a week ago," her daughter continued. "It was the best we had in a long time. I was beaming for days afterward. . . . I think, since it was the last time we talked that is was a gift from God."

News about Jane's slaying unnerved the night shelter residents, who expressed fear that the killer might be among them.

"Women who are street-wise know how to protect themselves," said the executive director of the shelter. "Unfortunately, Jane didn't. Jane did not fit the stereotypes of a homeless person. She was educated and not addicted to drugs or alcohol. But the mental illness left her destitute. Jane didn't say anything to anybody. She kept to herself and roamed all over the city. I was really crushed when I heard what happened to her. She didn't deserve this."

"About 60 percent of the homeless in this country suffer from some form of mental illness, and about 40 percent have a substance abuse problem," said the chief of mental health and addiction services. Jane was first diagnosed with depression when she was about 18, relatives and friends said. She was in and out of treatment facilities much of her life, beating the illness long enough to fall in love, get married, and raise a family.

At some point, Jane, who was adopted, sought out her birth mother. The reunion proved devastating when her mother rejected her, friends said. The illness resurfaced and her marriage failed. She divorced her husband and lost custody of her daughter.

She remarried and enrolled in college while in her 30s. Her friend remembered the days when they went to the state capitol to lobby for welfare reform and how easily Jane fit into the social work community and the jobs that followed.

But Jane left the work she loved in 1993, when she learned she was pregnant with her second child. After the birth, manic depression took its toll, relatives and friends said. The marriage failed and her second husband took custody of her son, who is now 4.

Those close to her said those events may have triggered her depression and mood swings. And by the spring of 1996, Jane found comfort living on the streets, traveling between Forth Worth, Las Vegas, and San Diego.

Her friend tracked her down at a psychiatric facility in Forth Worth and found Jane staring blankly at daytime television through a fog of medication. She said, "Hi, what are you doing here?" And I said, "To see you. What are you doing here?" And she said, "Well, this is where I belong." This memory left her friend feeling helpless and frustrated.

"Jane used to work hard to help people who had fallen through the cracks and were unemployed or near homeless," her friend said. "She was a good person who took everything to heart. . . . To me, this is proof that if it can happen to Jane, it can happen to the rest of us." (Modified from Craig, 1998; names were either deleted or changed and text was abridged.)

therein; the social work function of acquiring an understanding of a problem, what causes it, and what can be changed to minimize or resolve it" (Barker, 2003, p. 30). Social workers assume that any type of assessment begins with the first client-worker interaction. The information that the social worker obtains determines the requirements and direction of the helping process. The mental health social worker gathers information about the present situation, elicits history about the past, and anticipates service expectations for the future. This assessment should always include creative interpretations of alternatives to best assist the client to get the services needed (Dziegielewski, 2002).

In mental health assessment, as in all social work assessments, the client is regarded as the primary source of data. In most cases, the client is questioned directly, either verbally or in writing. Information about the client is also derived from direct observation of verbal and physical behavior and interaction patterns between the client and other interdisciplinary team members, family members, significant others, or friends. Viewing and recording these patterns of communication can be extremely helpful in later identifying and developing strength and resource considerations (see figure 1). In addition, background sheets, psychological tests, and tests to measure health status or level of duty functioning may be used.

Furthermore, in keeping with social work's traditional emphasis on including information about other areas, the worker talks with family members and signifi-

Figure 1: This woman was previously hospitalized for schizophrenia. With family support she was able to live outside of an institution, enjoy her grandneice, and live a fuller life.

cant others to estimate planning support and assistance. It might also be important to access secondary sources such as client's medical record and other health care providers.

To facilitate assessment, the social worker must be able to understand the client's medical situation or at least know where to go for information and help. Knowledge of certain mental health conditions, as well as common accompanying conditions, can only help the social worker to provide needed services or to decide when and where to refer the client to other health professionals for continued care. A key point: no social worker should ever be afraid to ask others to clarify concepts in regard to a client's care, especially when unsure about how the information may enhance understanding of the client.

Five expectations guide the initiation of assessment in the health and mental health setting (Dziegielewski, 2004).

1. Clients must be active and motivated in the treatment process: As in almost all forms of intervention, the client is expected to be active. The client must often expend serious energy in attempting to make behavioral changes. Clients therefore must not only agree to participate in the assessment process but must be willing to embark on the intervention plan that will produce behavioral change. Social workers usually practice verbal therapy; however, clients who are unmotivated or unwilling to talk or discuss change strategies may require more concrete goals and objectives to bring about specific behavior change.

2. The problem must guide the approach or method of intervention used: Social workers need to be aware of different methods and approaches to practice. No preferred approach should guide the choice of intervention. Sheafor, Horejsi, and Horejsi (1997) also warned about the opposite extremes, however: social workers becoming over involved and wasting valuable time in trying to match a particular problem to a particular theoretical model or approach. Health and mental health social workers must never lose sight of the ultimate purpose of the assessment process, that is, to complete an assessment that helps to establish a concrete service plan that addresses the client's needs.

Activity...Review the definition of assessment, and look at the reasons given for social workers to participate in this function. Discuss these issues with your classmates and decide where you believe it is essential for social workers in health care and mental health to participate in assessment. Explain both what you see as reason for participation and what you see as problems that might be caused by taking this active stance as a member of an interdisciplinary team.

3. The influence of values and beliefs should be made apparent in the process: Each one of us, professional or not, is influenced by her own values and beliefs. These beliefs are the foundation of who we are. In the professional practice of social work, however, it is essential that these personal beliefs and values do not affect the assessment and subsequent intervention process. A social worker must clearly identify from the onset of treatment those of his individual values, beliefs, and practices that can influence treatment outcomes. For example, what if an

unmarried client in a psychiatric hospital has tested positive for pregnancy? The social worker assigned to her case personally believes that abortion is wrong, and even though the client does not have the capability to be a parent the worker cannot in good conscience recommend abortion as an option. The client is unsure about what to do yet knows her own limitations and wants to explore every possible alternative. For the social work professional this can be a difficult case, but the ultimate assessment and intervention strategy must be based on the client's needs and desires, not the social worker's. Therefore, guided by the profession's Code of Ethics, the social worker tells the client of his prejudice and refers her to someone who can be more objective in exploring abortion as a possible course of action.

Most social work professionals agree that clients have the right to make their own decisions. Clients exercise this right especially when they are aware of their situation and want to participate in their own health care plans. Whatever their own feelings, mental health social workers must do everything possible to ensure this right and to keep their personal opinions from impairing a proper assessment.

In addition, the beliefs and values of the members of the interdisciplinary team must be considered. Social workers need to recognize value conflicts that arise among the other team members and make team members aware of how their personal feelings and opinions might keep them from exploring all possible options for a client. This is not to suggest that social workers are more qualified to address this issue or that they always have an answer; it means that social workers should strive to assist these professionals and should always keep before the team the goal of best serving the client.

4. Issues of culture and race should be addressed openly in the assessment and treatment: Social workers need to be aware of their own cultural heritage as well as the client's to create the most open and receptive environment possible. Dziegielewski (1997) suggested that the social work professional:

    1. Be aware of her cultural limitations

    2. Be open to cultural differences

    3. Recognize the integrity and the uniqueness of the client

    4. Use the client's learning style, including his own resources and supports

    5. Implement a behavior biopsychosocial approach to practice within an integrated, nonjudgmental format.

Did You Know…The fourth edition of the Diagnostic and Statistical Manual of Mental Disorders (DSM-IV), *the major reference for the diagnosis of mental disorders and related mental health conditions, stresses that cultural factors must be considered before establishing a diagnosis. DSM-IV emphasizes that delusions and hallucinations may be difficult to separate from general beliefs or practices related to a client's culture or lifestyle. Social workers do not take behavior arising from a client's cultural beliefs however 'socially inappropriate' it may seem as evidence of mental disorder. To help professionals to deal with the cultural aspects of mental health, an entire appendix of the DSM-IV-TR describes and defines culturally bound syndromes that might affect the diagnosis and assessment process (American Psychiatric Association, 2000). All social workers must know how cultural and ethnic factors can affect assessment.*

5. Assessment must focus on client strengths and highlight the client's own resources: Clients have enormous difficulty identifying and planning to use their own strengths. People in general tend to focus on the negative and rarely praise themselves for the good they do. For many social workers use of a **strengths-based assessment** is considered critical (Sheafor, 1988). For so many clients, especially those with mental health problems, their judgments of the world around them as well as what they think of themselves can become clouded. An all-or-nothing approach may result that them feeling lost, alone, and ineffective in what they have done or tried to do. Therefore, it is the role of the social worker to assist the client in identifying positive behaviors and accomplishments.

In today's high-pressure health and mental health environments, social workers cannot spend time exploring issues that don't contribute to the client's well-being. They must quickly utilize a strengths-based assessment by helping the client to identify her own strengths. Most treatment is time limited these days, so individual resources are essential for continued growth and maintenance of wellness after the formal treatment period has ended. Although there are many different time-limited approaches to practice, most social workers agree that their first task is to clearly identify the client's strengths to use them as part of the treatment planning process. Focusing on a client's strengths helps to empower the client to make changes in her life.

Person-in-Environment: A Systematic Approach to Assessment

In mental health practice today many forms of formal assessment can assist in the development of a treatment plan. One system of assessment that has recently

Figure 2: Members of the Berrien County Association of Retarded Citizens (ARC) gather for a photo after a Fourth of July field trip with a social worker to a town on Lake Michigan. These citizens live either in group homes or with families.

gained favor with social workers is the **Person-in-Environment Classification System**, also known as "the PIE." Designed primarily for advanced MSW-level practice, the PIE was underwritten by an award given to the California chapter of NASW from the NASW Program Advancement Fund (Whiting, 1996). Knowledge of the PIE is relevant for all mental health social workers regardless of educational level because of its emphasis on situational factors.

In the PIE the process of assessment is built around two major premises that are basic to all social work practice: recognition of social considerations and the person-in-situation stance. The PIE responds to the need to identify the problems of clients in a context that mental health and health professionals can easily understand (Karls & Wandrei, 1996a, 1996b):

> [It] calls first for a social work assessment that is translated into a description of coding of the client's problems in social functioning. Social functioning is the client's ability to accomplish the activities necessary for daily living (for example, obtaining food, shelter, and transportation) and to fulfill major social roles as required by the client's subculture or community (Karls & Wandrei, 1996a, p. vii).

The PIE provides the following:

◆ A common language with which social workers in all settings can describe their client's problems in social functioning

---

Tips on Information Recording and Documentation

Social workers must document their assessment plans clearly. Although it is beyond the scope of this book to discuss documentation techniques in detail, the following tips introduce the most important aspects of accurate and timely record keeping.

1. Always document justification for the "service necessity" of what you do.

2. Be sure to document clearly purpose, content, and outcome in every note you write—regardless of the type of note or reason for making the entry.

3. Always sign your name, credentials, and so forth, at the end of every note you write. Be sure to include the date and time the service was provided in every note. Don't forget to put in the record the amount of time spent with the client.

4. All those who review records for billing say that the biggest problems are lack of information and inaccurate information in the record.

5. Always document problem behaviors in terms of frequency, intensity, and duration.

6. Always be able to benchmark progress.

7. Use a black pen (whose ink does not run), and never reproduce notes for others.

8. If you do not document it, it did not happen.

◆ A common capsule description of social phenomena that can facilitate treatment or ameliorate problems presented by clients

◆ A basis for gathering data to be used to measure the need for services and to design human service programs to evaluate effectiveness

◆ A mechanism for clearer communication among social work practitioners and between practitioners, administrators, and researchers

◆ A basis for clarifying the domain of social work in human service fields (Karls & Wandrei, 1996a)

The PIE is an excellent tool for advanced social workers; beginning professionals are not ready nor will they be expected to use this complex assessment tool. As you progress through human behavior and practice courses you will become more familiar with this technique, its advantages, and its uses in mental health practice. It's enough now to observe that PIE provides an important vehicle to understanding the many factors that affect a client's behavior, which is an important part of the assessment process.

The PIE system is user friendly because it classifies clients' problems into four distinct categories, or "factors." For the purpose of this chapter we have presented an abbreviated version of this assessment system. This information is not meant to be all-inclusive; rather it is intended to help introduce beginning social work professionals to the knowledge base underlying the use of the PIE and to its relevance to formalized mental health assessment.

DSM-IV-TR

Another important tool for social workers in the mental health arena that you should be aware of is the *Diagnostic and Statistical Manual of Mental Disorders* (DSM-IV-TR; American Psychiatric Association, 2000). The DSM is considered an advanced tool for social work practice. Its use is covered in graduate courses, and in some schools, entire courses are devoted to the study of the DSM. For a more detailed explanation of the DSM-IV-TR and its relation to the PIE in practice see Dziegielewski (2004).

THE BEHAVIORAL BIOPSYCHOSOCIAL APPROACH TO SOCIAL WORK PRACTICE

Social work practice in assessment and intervention should recognize three factors: the *bio*medical, the *psycho*logical, and the *social* (Carlton, 1984; Dziegielewski, 2004). A social worker that understands the **biopsychosocial approach** to health and mental health practice strives to ascertain for each client the appropriate balance among biomedical, psychological, and social considerations. Balance, however, doesn't mean that these factors are treated as equal for every client. The particular situation experienced by the client determines where emphasis must be placed and what area must be addressed first. In today's practice environment, with its insistence on observable, a measurable outcome, the mental health social worker addresses the biopsychosocial factors in the client's life through the *behavioral* aspects of the client's condition.

Activity...Here is a sample treatment plan for a client who is suicidal. Taking a behavioral biopsychosocial approach, what do you think of this plan? What are its strengths and its limitations for the client being served?

Sample Treatment Plan for Suicidal Ideation/Behavior

Definition: Suicide is a human act of self-inflicted, self-intentional cessation. Simply stated, it is the wish to be dead with the act that carries out the wish.
Suicide ideation: thinking about suicide. *Suicide verbalization:* talking about suicide.
Parasuicide: attempting suicide.

Signs and Symptoms to Note in the Record (be sure to document any of these signs in the record):
Changes in eating and sleeping; changes in friends and social programs.
Changes in grades, job status, or love relationships; changes in usual daily activities.
Constant restlessness or unshakable depression; neglected appearance or hygiene.
Increase in drug or alcohol use; giving away of material possessions.
Recurrent thoughts or preoccupation with death; recent suicide attempt.
Ongoing suicidal ideation and any previous or present plans; history of suicide attempts in the family.
Sudden change in mood that is not consistent with life events; past suicide attempts and what was done.
History of drug abuse.

Goals:
1. Stabilize suicidal crisis.
2. Place client at appropriate level of care to address suicidal crisis.
3. Reestablish a sense of hope to deal with the current life situations.
4. Alleviate suicidal impulses and intent and return to higher (safer) level of functioning.

Objective	Intervention	Time Frame*
Client will report no longer feeling the need to harm self.	Assess for suicidal ideation and concrete plan of execution. Then make appropriate disposition/referral.	
Client will discuss suicidal feelings and thoughts.	Assist client to develop awareness of negative self-talk patterns and encourage positive images and self-talk.	
Identify positives in current life situation.	Complete no-suicide contract. Address behaviors to complete when having suicidal thoughts or impulses.	
Help client to identify consistent eating and sleeping patterns.	Educate client in deep-breathing and relaxation techniques. Assist client in developing coping strategies.	
Take medications as prescribed and report any inconsistencies or side effects.	Monitor for medication use and misuse, and confer with treatment team on a regular basis.	
Complete assessments of functioning.	Arrange or complete administration of the test. Determine level of depression or suicide precaution. Assess and monitor suicide intervention.	

*Time frame is to be individualized to the client.

For example, if a client is newly assessed as having schizophrenia while also being HIV positive, many issues must be addressed. At first the emphasis may be placed on the biomedical or biological area. The client needs immediately to be told that the medical test for HIV is positive and to be given information about what a positive test means. The task can be complicated by the client's mental condition. The schizophrenia may produce periodic breaks from reality, such as hallucinations and delusions that keep him from accurately interpreting medical information. The client may have difficulty understanding how far the disease has progressed and what can be expected medically, for example. Nevertheless, every attempt must be made to help the client to understand the medical aspects of his condition and what being infected with this virus actually means. It is critical to ensure the client understands terms such as "t-cell count" and how important future self-protection from illness and opportunistic infectious disease is.

Once the biomedical area is addressed, emphasis may shift to the social and psychological aspects of the client's condition. Since HIV is clearly communicable, the client must realize quickly that his behavior could have significant effects on people in his support system. Early education about how the virus is transmitted can be critical. Since HIV is most often sexually transmitted, the client's past and present sexual partners must be considered. Himself or with help, the client must face telling loved ones about what has happened and what it will mean for future social relations.

Furthermore, the client may be frightened by the changes in his mental status and be unsure of how to control the symptoms related to schizophrenia. First, the client must understand what is happening. Second, the client must be helped to realize what schizophrenia means for him and for those he comes in contact with. Important information must be shared with family and friends. The social perspective of the biopsychosocial approach focuses on the individual client together with his family, significant others, and friends, on how best to protect them but also to involve them in problem solving. The psychological perspective focuses directly on the fears and concerns of the individual, on how to help him to understand his mental health and the emotions he exhibits.

Biomedical or Biological Factors to Be Considered in Mental Health Assessment

Area	Explanation
General medical condition	Describe the physical illness or disability from which the client is suffering.
Overall health status	Client is to evaluate her self-reported health status and level of functional ability.
Overall level of functioning	Describe what the client is able to do to meet her daily needs. Concrete tasks are assessed and documented for focus on future change effort.
Maintenance of continued health and wellness	Measure the client's functional ability and interest in preventive medical intervention.

Social Factors to Be Considered in Mental Health Assessment

Area	Explanation
Social/societal help-seeking behavior	Is the client open to outside help? Is the client willing to accept help from those outside her immediate family or the community?
Occupational participation	How does the client's illness or disability impair or prohibit functioning in the work environment? Is the client in a supportive work environment?
Social support system	Does the client have support from neighbors, friends, or community organizations (church membership, membership in professional clubs, etc.)?
Family support	What support or help can be expected from relatives of the client?
Support from significant other	Does the significant other understand and show willingness to help and support the needs of the client?
Ethnic or cultural affiliation	If the client is a member of a certain cultural or religious group, will affiliation affect medical treatment and compliance issues?

As you can see, if a client is dual diagnosed helping can become very complicated. In our example, the dual diagnosis of HIV and schizophrenia means that the client may be losing touch with reality and how his behaviors can harm others at a time when this knowledge is especially important.

Once the immediate needs of the client and his family have been addressed, the focus of intervention should shift to the functional/situational factors affecting the individual client. A functional assessment allows the social worker to determine the level at which the client is capable of responding to a concrete intervention-based plan.

It is essential that assessment and intervention be related to the needs and abilities of the client. The social worker expects assessment to help the client better understand himself, and the factors identified during the procedure are shared with the client to assist in self-help or continued skill building. At first, the assessment process is used to examine the situation and initiate the helping process; later it contributes to an intervention plan.

MENTAL HEALTH AND WORKING WITH THE FAMILY IN ACUTE CARE SETTINGS

As early as 1903 at Massachusetts General Hospital, Dr. Richard C. Cabot realized the importance of addressing psychosocial factors in medical illness. From this

Psychological Factors to Be Considered in Mental Health Assessment

Area	Explanation
Life stage	Describe the development stage in life at which the individual appears to be functioning.
Mental functioning	Describe the client's mental functioning. Complete a mental status measurement. Can the client participate knowledgeably in the intervention experience?
Cognitive functioning	Does the client have the ability to think and reason about what is happening to her? Is the client able to participate and make decisions in regard to her own best interest?
Level of self-awareness and self-help	Does the client understand what is happening to her? Is the client capable of assisting her level of self-care? Is the client capable of understanding the importance of health and wellness information? Is the client open to help and services provided by the health care team?

early perspective the assigned duties of the medical social worker included focusing on the economic, emotional, social, and situational needs of patients and their families (Cabot, 1919). To accomplish the assigned tasks in the late 1800s and early 1900s, health care social workers were required to have adequate medical knowledge, an understanding of disease and factors that affected mental health, and a firm comprehension of public health. With the medical advances of the late 1950s the social worker was expected to bridge ". . . the gap between the hospital bed, the patient's home and the world of medical science" (Risley, 1961, p. 83).

In the area of health and mental health today the role of the social worker continues much along the same path, with extensive consideration being placed on also meeting the needs of client and his or her family members. Although the family members are not the actual client being served, it is not uncommon for services to be provided to them that include education, supportive interventions, and referrals as well as reporting problematic social conditions, assisting and ensuring treatment compliance with the established medical regime, and providing linkages between the acute care setting and the appropriate community agencies. Other areas of service provision in these acute health care settings include case consultation, case finding, case planning, psychosocial assessment and intervention, case consultation, collaboration, treatment team planning, group therapy, supportive counseling, organ donation coordination, health education, advocacy, case management, discharge planning, information and referral, quality assurance, bereavement, and research (Holliman, 1998; Holliman, Dziegielewski & Data, 2001).

Name: Elizabeth Hosnedl

Place of residence: Sodus, Michigan

College/university degrees: Eastern Michigan University, BSW

Present position: Assistant to MSHDA Section 8 Housing Agent in Berrien County Instructor for Basic and Advanced Drunken Driving Courses at the Berrien County Health Department

Previous work/volunteer experience: Home Health worker, SW for Area IV Agency on Aging, Program Coordinator and Director of ARC (Association for Retarded Citizens), Berrien County, Assessment Specialist for Shoreline Consultation assessing indigent and MA persons for drug and alcohol treatment. Volunteer at Benton Harbor Soup Kitchen and ARC Bowling League.

Why did you choose social work as a career? Actually, social work chose me! After a ten-year hiatus, I was working on finishing my English degree while working as an apartment manager. I was not really enthused about teaching, and didn't know what else I could do with an English degree, so I tried an introductory social work class. The types of work described and the different situations we discussed in that class were a very good fit to my personality, and I knew that was where I belonged. In the last seventeen years, I have been very fortunate to have worked with several different populations. I'm a very hands-on person, and social work gives me the opportunity to work one-on-one with clients in very practical ways that show immediate change.

What is your favorite social work story? One gentleman came in to Shoreline very reluctantly looking for treatment. He was forty-seven years old but looked seventy. He was forty pounds underweight, had no teeth, and had a broken jaw that could not be repaired, because they could not get him sober long enough to sedate him for surgery. His skin was waxy and yellow, and my co-workers and I thought he would be dead before he made it to treatment a week later.

Six months later, a good-looking man walked in the door, smiling and the picture of physical health. None of us recognized him, but it was the same man! Obviously, he had done the hard work, but I was in the right place at the right time to set him on the path.

What would be the one thing you would change in our community if you had the power to do so? If I could change one thing in Berrien County, it would be to give all levels of government from the city council on up to the governor the experience I have had with the recovery community. Drugs and alcohol have devastated large segments of this county, and it's only getting worse. In terms of man hours and money dedicated to programming, recovery is at the bottom of the list. It seems that the funders don't realize the multitude of problems they could solve if they would just work on reducing addiction.

In this fast-paced environment social workers are, like other health care professionals, being forced to deal with numerous issues that include declining hospital admissions, reduced lengths of hospital stay, and numerous other restrictions and methods of cost containment (Braus, 1996; Dziegielewski, 2002). Struggling to resolve these issues has become necessary based on the inception of prospective payment systems, managed care plans, and other changes in the provision and funding of health care (Lens, 2002; Ross, 1993; Simon, Showers, Blumenfield, Holden, & Wu, 1995). Previous research has linked not receiving services to increased rates of high-risk patient relapse (Christ, Clarkin, & Hull, 1994; Hudson, 2001; Lockery, Dunkle, Kart, & Coulton, 1994). The goal of discharge planning is often the arrangement of an appropriate follow-up service plan for return to a lesser level of care. Many times the role of the social worker is assumed to end once the client is discharged from the facility (Simon et al., 1995).

A significant issue to consider when dealing with mental health issues of the client is the psychological and social burden that is often placed on the client's family. This burden can in turn either lead or exacerbate higher rates of mental health problems (Bauman, Drotar, Leventhal, Perrin, & Pless, 1997). From an environmental or situational (mezzo) perspective, the families of the client are left at increased risk for psychological disturbances.

When dealing with the family of a mentally ill client the role of the social worker needs to be flexible and diverse. Often family members may have different expectations of what they perceive as their role in the inpatient and discharge process (Blumenfield & Epstein, 2001; Davidson, 1990). These different expectations may lead to blurring and overlap of the services provided. It is crucial for the social worker to examine the family member's sense of personal well-being, ability to self-care, or level of family and environmental support as many times these factors become essential to the discharge of the client. If these personal/social and environmental issues are not addressed, the mentally unstable client may be put at risk for harm. When an client is discharged home to a family that does not want him or her, the mentally ill client is more at risk of abuse and neglect. Family members can feel a situation is hopeless placing them at greater risk for depression or even suicide. The social worker must always recognize the importance of culture and environmental factors as paramount to efficient and effective practice. Examples of situations when cultural and environmental factors play a part in patient care is when the family members of a sick infant objects to a blood transfusion for religious reasons or when the family refuses life support because it is viewed as disturbing the natural life progression. The de-emphasis or denial of this consideration can result in the delivery of substandard care.

In today's environment of behaviorally based managed care, capitation, fee for service, and decreased number of hospital inpatient beds, health care social work continues to hold a place in the acute care hospital setting. According to Kadushin and Kulys (1994) and Dziegielewski (2004), the challenge for acute medical hospitals is to combine the humanitarian objective of practice with the hospitals' agenda for cost control and rationing of resources.

In addressing the mental health needs of family members the current focus on health and wellness and the decreased stigma associated with the treatment of mental health problems has clearly created and increased in service requisition (Epstein & Aldredge, 2000; NASW, 1996; Lyons, Howard, O'Mahoney, & Lish, 1997).

Often family members need assistance and the acknowledgment and addressing of family problems can help to improve and maintain quality of life for the mentally ill client and his or her support system. The functions of the mental health social worker in this setting include psychosocial evaluations (assessment for the treatment plan), casework (counseling and supportive intervention), group work (education and self-help), information and referral, facilitation of community referrals, team planning and coordination, and client and family education, as well as advocacy for clients on their behalf within the setting or beyond that with local state and federal agencies (NASW, 1995b). In addition, with the numerous service cutbacks and cost-effectiveness strategies, many social workers are now being required to expand their duties. Many are being asked to serve as financial counselors to ensure that the client and the service agency will receive adequate reimbursement for services needed. These services can involve assisting clients to apply for outside insurance carriers to cover additional services not directly covered under current policy.

Berkman (1996), Dziegielewski, (2004), and Holliman (1998) all believe that social workers have essential skills and practice techniques that are needed in today's acute care mental health settings. The social worker remains integral in providing assistance with treatment plans and compliance issues; assisting clients and families with discharge planning and referral; providing counseling and support for clients and significant others in the areas of health, wellness, mental health, bereavement, and so on; assisting clients and their families to make ethical and morally difficult decisions that can affect health and mental health; educating clients, their families, and significant others to psychosocial issues and adjusting to illness; assisting in resolving behavioral problems; assisting in identifying and obtaining entitlement benefits; securing non-medical benefits; assisting with risk management and quality assurance activities; and, last, advocating for enhanced and continued services to ensure continued client well-being.

DEINSTITUTIONALIZATION AND THE MENTALLY ILL IN THE CRIMINAL JUSTICE SYSTEM

The practice of deinstitutionalization, which resulted in the closing of many federal and state mental health facilities, has had devastating effects on the provision of mental health services, including those in the criminal justice system. More and more social workers interested in the area of mental health have begun to accept positions in this area. What is most concerning is that an alarming 16 percent of those in state prisons and local jails have been diagnosed as mentally ill (Ditton, 1998). Additionally, these individuals are 53 percent more likely to be incarcerated for a violent offense, and, according to year 2000 population statistics, this would equate to 296,176 incarcerated individuals with a diagnosed mental illness.

Functional/Situational Factors to Be Considered in Mental Health Assessment

Area	Explanation
Financial status	How does the health condition affect the financial status of the client? What income maintenance efforts are being made? Do any need to be initiated? Does the client have savings or resources to draw from?
Entitlements	Does the client have health, accident, disability, or life insurance benefits to cover her cost of health service? Has insurance been recorded and filed for the client to assist with paying of expenses? Does the client qualify for additional services to assist with illness and recovery?
Transportation	What transportation is available to the client? Does the client need assistance or arrangements to facilitate transportation?
Placement	Where will the client go after discharge? Is there a plan for continued maintenance when services are terminated? Is alternative placement needed?
Continuity of service	If the client is to be transferred to another health service, have the connections been made to link services and service providers appropriately? Based on the services provided has the client received the services she needs during and after the treatment period?

Furthermore, extending this trend into the year 2002, incarcerated individuals could exceed 718,000 individuals suffering from a diagnosed mental illness. Beck and Maruschak (2001) also found a large incarcerated population with mental illnesses utilizing a survey that found that, in 1,394 of 1,558 U.S. adult correctional facilities, 1 in 8 state prisoners were receiving mental health services and 1 in 10 were provided with psychotropic medications. The majority of the facilities were able to provide psychiatric assessment (65 percent), therapy and/or counseling by trained mental health professionals (71 percent), and the distribution of psychotropic medications (73 percent).

For social workers, the greatest challenge yet to come is how to help these facilities to recognize and address the medicinal needs as well as mental health treatments needed for those diagnosed mentally ill. Furthermore, the problem can actually extend beyond the prisons, as what will happen to the mentally ill persons once they are released from jail or prison either through probation, parole, or their own recognizance? Prison systems designed purely to house rather than also treat mentally ill inmates will fall short when the mentally ill offender is finally released back into the community.

The implementation of deinstitutionalization provides a perfect example of how a political and economic proposal that is not thoroughly explored prior to implementation can have devastating effects on those caught in the system. Many professionals in the area firmly believe that deinstitutionalization has resulted in utilizing the prison system as a holding tank for those with serious mental disorders and that prisons have thus become a replacement for the mental hospitals that have been closed (Butterfield, 1998). Furthermore, the mental health services that are provided within the prison system are limited because of the lack of public concern for rehabilitation with offenders. Regardless of the exact reason, the number of mentally ill offenders is growing in our prisons and jails and within the probation and parole system.

Moreover, this movement to close state mental health facilities and treat chronic offenders in the community has left many mentally ill homeless and without care (Grob, 1995). Additionally, individuals with mental illness may also be unfairly arrested and jailed because their behaviors present a danger or risk to those around them. This is further complicated by the fact that the most appropriate placements, such as mental health centers in the community, may be either unwilling or unable to help due to the chronically mentally ill's indigent status and subsequent inability to pay for services (Harrington, 1999). This problem requires the joining of law enforcement officers and mental health professionals.

To help address this issue, social workers have advocated for the development of case management services as a humane, effective, and efficient way to address the growing issue of the mentally ill offender in the community (Mechanic, 1998). Additionally, through assertive case management, and through collaboration between mental health providers and the criminal justice system, joint problem solving is encouraged. This increased education and coordination can lead to reduced hospital stays, improved living situations, and improved social relationships for the mentally ill offender (Calsyn, Morse, Klinkenberg, Trusty & Allen, 1998). Mechanic and McAlphine (1999) further support this stance by seeking more appropriate placement for the mentally ill through assertive case management with the presumption that this type of service could bring about beneficial results at a low cost (compared with the cost of incarceration) to the community.

Similar to problems occurring in the health care system, recidivism or the readmission of individuals within the penal justice system has presented a serious concern (Hiller & Knight, 1996). Hiller and Knight asserted that the rates of mental illness within the community-based setting were consistent with those of the rest of the correctional system, and that some offenders may be more at risk than others for re-arrest (especially those with comorbidity involving depression and substance abuse).

For mental health social workers in this area a partnership between criminal justice professionals and social workers is blossoming. This collaboration could result in early identification and treatment of the mentally ill, which ultimately lessens the burden on the criminal justice system (Conly, 1999; Harris & Koespell, 1998; Lovell & Rhodes, 1997). Without such a partnership, mentally ill offenders will continue to be rotated from mental health centers to jails in a cycle that causes further disease deterioration and increased criminality (Harrington, 1999). Jails are not trained to be mental hospitals, and the short period of incarceration compounds the problem because the mentally ill offender has no chance to stabilize or receive necessary treatment (McDonald & Teitelbaum, 1994). Therefore, planned efforts to achieve better community treatment would result in fewer costly hospital stays and less jail time for the mentally ill offender.

Another important concept leading to this advocacy for service unification of the two disciplines revolves around societal cost, financial and otherwise. Spending for behavioral health care is falling behind other types of health care, and the quality of care is suffering (Mechanic & McAlpine, 1999). With deinstitutionalization, many of the mentally ill were diverted into substance abuse programs, which the federal government funded because the community programs were unprepared to handle the influx of patients (Grob, 1995). Those seriously mentally ill individuals who were not placed in residential treatment facilities were criminalized because the mental health providers were actively involved with treating societal coping skills (Harrington, 1999).

Yet this union of the disciplines will never succeed unless both disciplines acknowledge the importance and strongly advocate for collaboration and information sharing between the various professionals as well as the organizations involved in the process (Dawes, 1996). Since there is no single system or organization that can meet all of the conditions needed for optimal treatment of the mentally ill (Schnapp & Cannedy, 1998), sharing information is critical. Collaboration fosters more supportive and integrated planning as well as policy development and facilitation of the highest degree of complete and accurate information for decision making (Dawes, 1996).

SPECIAL CONSIDERATIONS: MENTAL HEALTH AND THE DUAL DIAGNOSIS

No matter what the population or field of practice in which social workers are employed, they are increasingly confronted with the dually diagnosed client. This means that clients can have more than one mental health problem and each must be equally addressed in the intervention process. In order for mental health social workers to work successfully with dually diagnosed clients, they must be cognizant of client problems, diagnostic assessments, clinical interventions, and current case studies. For example, clients with psychiatric and comorbid substance use disorders often exhibit extremely poor compliance for outpatient treatment (Booth et al., 1992; Carey & Carey, 1990; Daley & Zuckoff, 1998; Matas et al., 1992). This leaves these individuals vulnerable to a variety of negative clinical ramifications, including problems with relapse and rehospitalization, that in turn could relate to higher service utilization and cost (Bartels et al., 1993; Clark, 1994; Bartels et al., 1992; Cournos et al., 1991).

Although addressing the needs of a client with more than one mental health problem will be covered in more depth in your clinical courses, the client with a dual diagnosis can often be misdiagnosed and/or given inadequate treatment due to the limited time frame allowed for inpatient care. Resources and at times intervention strategy is shaped and influenced by cost containment, with an emphasis placed on time-limited, outcome-oriented interventions (Moggi et al., 1999; Dziegielewski, 2002). In managed health care, adequate funding is rarely made available for treatment programs specializing in integrated treatment models.

Daley and Zuckoff (1998) highlight the following adverse effects that can transpire for noncompliant, dually diagnosed clients:

♦ Poorly compliant clients are more likely to experience clinical deterioration of their psychiatric condition, relapse to alcohol or other drug use, and return to the hospital as a result of severe depression, suicidality, homicidality, mania, or psychotic decompensation.

♦ Missing outpatient appointments often leads to failure to renew medication prescriptions, which in turn contributes to exacerbations of psychiatric and substance use symptoms.

♦ Poor treatment compliance causes the loss of supportive relationships and contributes to frustration among family members and professionals, who find themselves watching helplessly as the client deteriorates.

♦ Due to increased risk of hospitalization, poor outpatient compliance leads to increased costs of care as a result of more days spent in expensive inpatient treatment facilities.

Mental health social workers must be educated and trained in the treatment of clients who suffer from more than one mental health problem and or condition. For the dually diagnosed client, treating one condition without recognition of the comorbid or contributing factors is not considered acceptable.

SUMMARY

Whatever we call them, psychosocial assessments performed by mental health and health care social workers are essential. Assessment is the critical first step in formulating a plan for intervention. It thus sets the tone and framework for the entire mental health social work process. In order to compete in today's mental health environment social work professionals must play a twofold role: 1) to ensure that high-quality service is provided to the client and 2) to ensure that the client has access and is given an opportunity to see that her mental health needs are addressed. Neither of these tasks is easy, nor will they make a social worker popular in today's environment. Mental and other health services must now be delivered with limited resources, and the pressure to reduce services is intense. Social workers must know the assessment and treatment planning tools that are used in the field and be able to use them. Assessment and treatment planning are together the first step in providing services, a step that social work professionals cannot afford to neglect.

Numerous tools and methods exist to assist social workers in the mental health assessment process, and the PIE is only one example of what is available. These forms of systematic assessment can provide social workers with frameworks for practice. We should always use such tools cautiously, however; as you will learn in practice courses yet to come, many social workers fear that these methods can place labels on clients that are very difficult to remove. These fears are well founded, but they shouldn't cause social workers to shun assessment. Indeed, the fact that social workers are aware of such dangers makes their participation in assessment essential. In addition, the social worker brings a wealth of information to the interdisciplinary team about a client's environment and family situation. Social workers, who focus on building on the skills and strengths of the client, are well equipped to help design a treatment plan that is realistic and effective. Although assessments completed today appear to have a more narrow focus, it is essential that utility, relevance, and salience be maintained (Dziegielewski, 2004). Because social workers practice in numerous health and mental health settings and perform many different duties, it is not surprising that the processes of assessment and treatment planning show great diversity. Assessment and subsequent treatment plan development depend on a multiplicity of factors, including client need, agency function, practice setting, service limitations, and coverage for provision of service. Many times the scope of assessment and intervention must be narrowed in response to reductions in economic support. Therefore, overall practice in the mental health setting must continually be examined to ensure high quality. If the process of helping is rushed, superficial factors may be highlighted and significant

---

Mental Health Social Work Practice in the New Millennium:
Questions to Guide Assessment and Intervention Success

1. Are you able to document a DSM-IV multiaxis diagnosis?

2. Can you show that the identified condition is treatable with a realistic chance of success?

3. Have you developed specific goals and objectives for the treatment of the client?

4. Do you provide a clear rationale for the level of care, modality, types of intervention, and duration of treatment?

5. Is there a process for updating and periodic review of goal and objective attainment?

6. Is the client involved in the treatment development process?

7. If treatment is to be longer than originally expected, is a rationale for extension provided?

8. What specific things will happen to indicate that treatment goals and objectives have been met?

9. Is the intervention plan utilized consistent with social work values and ethics?

---

ones overlooked. All social workers regardless of the mental health care setting must establish services that are quality driven, no matter what the administrative and economic pressures may be.

Questions to Think About

1. Based on the information provided in this chapter, what do you see as the future role for mental health social workers in the assessment process?

2. Do you believe that the PIE will continue to gain in popularity in health and mental health settings with practitioners other than social workers?

3. Do you believe that a complete assessment and treatment planning framework is needed to guide social work practice and will continue to be required for reimbursement in order for social work services to increase?

References

American Psychiatric Association. (2000). Diagnostic and statistical manual of mental disorders (4th ed.) Text revison. Washington, DC: Author.

Barker, R. L. (2003). *The social work dictionary* (5th ed.). Washington, DC: NASW Press.

Bartels, S. J., Drake, R. E., & McHugo, G. J. (1992). Alcohol abuse, depression, and suicidal behavior in schizophrenia. *American Journal of Psychiatry, 149,* 394–395.

Bartels, S. J., Teague, G. B., Drake, R. E., Clark, R. E., Bush, P., & Noordsy, D. L. (1993). Substance abuse in schizophrenia: Service utilization and costs. *Journal of Nervous Mental Diseases, 181,* 227–232.

Beck, A., Maruschak, L., (2001) *Mental health treatment in state prisons, 2000.* Washington, D.C., US Department of Justice, Office of Justice Programs, Bureau of Justice Statistics NCJ188215.

Berkman, B. (1996). The emerging health care world: Implications for social work practice and education. *Social Work, 41,* 541–549.

Blumenfield, S. & Epstein, I. (2001). Introduction: promoting and maintaining a reflective Professional staff in a hospital-based social work department. *Social Work in Health Care, 33* (3/4), 1–13.

Booth, B. M., Cook, C. A. L. & Blow, F. C. (1992). Comorbid mental disorders in patients with AMA discharges from alcoholism treatment. *Hospital and Community Psychiatry, 43,* 730–731.

Braus, P. (1996, February). Who will survive managed care? *American Demographics, 18,* 16.

Butterfield, F. (1998, March 5). Prisons replace hospitals for the nation's mentally ill. *New York Times,* pp. A1, A26.

Calsyn, R., Morse, G., Klinkenberg, W., Trusty, M., Allen, G., (1998) The impact of assertive community based treatment on the social relationships of people who are homeless and mentally ill, *Community Mental Health Journal, 34,* 6, 579.

Carlton. T. O. (1984). *Clinical social work in health care settings: A guide to professional practice with exemplars.* New York: Springer.

Clark, R. E. (1994). Family costs associated with severe mental illness and substance use: A comparison of families with and without dual disorders. *Hospital and Community Psychiatry, 45,* 808–813.

Comer, R .J. (2002). Forward. In Sifton, D.W. (Ed.) *PDR: Drug guide for mental health professionals* (pp. V–VI). Montvale, NJ: Thompson Medical Economics.

Conly, C. (1999). *Coordinating community service for mentally ill offenders: Maryland's community criminal justice treatment program.* Washington, D.C.: US Department of Justice, Office of Justice Programs, National Institute of Justice.

Cournos, F., Empfield, M., Horwath, E., McKinnon, K., Meyer, I., Schrage, H., Currie, C., & Agosin, B. (1991). HIV seroprevalence among patients admitted to two psychiatric hospitals. *American Journal of Psychiatry, 148,* 1225–1230.

Craig, Y. (1998, August 19). Victim dived from La Madeline lunches to homeless. Star-Telegram.com.

Christ, W. R., Clarkin, J. F., & Hull, J. (1994). A high risk screen for psychiatric discharge planning. *Health and Social Work, 19* (4), 261–270.

Christ, G. H., Siegel, K., & Weinstein, L. (1995). Developing a research unit within a hospital social work department. *Health and Social Work, 20,* 60–69.

Daley, D. C. & Zuckoff, A. (1998). Improving compliance with the initial outpatient session among discharged inpatient dual diagnosis clients. *Social Work, 43* (5), 470–474.

Dawes, S. (1996) Interagency information sharing, expected benefits, manageable risks, *Journal of Policy Analysis and Management, 15* (3), 377–394.

Ditton, P. (1999). *Mental health and treatment of inmates and probationers. Washington, D.C., US Department of Justice, Office of Justice Programs, Bureau of Justice Statistics Special Reports NCJ 174463.* Washington D.C.: Department of Justice.

Dziegielewski, S. F. (1997). *Clinical, advanced, intermediate: Preparation for the clinical licensure exam.* Tuscaloosa, AL: Siri Productions.

Dziegielewski, S. F. (2004). *The changing face of health care social work: Professional practice in the era of managed behavioral health care* (2nd ed.). New York: Springer.

Dziegielewski, S.F. (2002). *DSM-IV-TR ™ in action.* New York: Wiley and Sons.

Dziegielewski, S.F. & Holliman, D. (2001). Managed care and social work: Practice implications in an era of change. *Journal of Sociology and Social Welfare. XXVIII,* 2, 125–138.

Ethics meet managed care. (1997, January). *NASW News, 42* (1), 7.

Epstein, M. W. & Aldredge, P. (2000). *Good but not perfect.* Boston: Allyn and Bacon.

Forum of ESRD Networks. (1995, March). *The end stage renal disease network system* [brochure]. Los Angeles, CA: ESRD Clearing House.

Grob, G., (July/August, 1995) The paradox of deinstitutionalization, *Society, 32,* 51–59.

Harrington, S., (May/June, 1999). New bedlam: Jails not psychological hospitals now care for the indigent mentally ill. *Humanist, 59,* 9–13.

Harris, V., Koespell, T., (1998) Re-arrest among mentally ill offenders, *Journal of the American Academy of Psychiatry and the Law, 26,* 3, 393–402.

Hiller, M., Knight, K., (June, 1996) Compulsory community-based substance abuse treatment and the mentally ill criminal offender, *Prison Journal, 76* (2), 180–185

Holliman, D. (1998). Discharge planning in Alabama hospitals. DAI-59-09A 3647 Ann Arbor: UMI: Unpublished Dissertation.

Holliman, D., Dziegielewski, S.F., & Datta, P. (2001). Discharge planning and social work practice. *Journal of Health Care Social Work. 32,* 3, 1–19.

Kadushin, G., & Kulys, R. (1994). Patient and family involvement in discharge planning. *Journal of Gerontological Social Work, 22,* 171–199.

Lovell, D., Rhodes, L., (1997) Mobile consultation, crossing correctional boundaries to cope with disturbed offenders, *Federal Probation, 61* (35), 40–45.

Karls, J. M., & Wandrei, K. M. (Eds.). (1996a). *Person-in-environment system: The PIE classification system for social functioning problems.* Washington, DC: NASW Press.

Karls, J. M., & Wandrei, K. M. (1996b). *PIE manual: Person-in-environment system: The PIE classification system for social functioning problems.* Washington, DC: NASW Press.

Linsley, J. (2003). Social work salaries: Keeping with the times? *The New Social Worker, 10,* 1, 1–5.

Lockery, S., Dunkle, R., Kart, C., & Coulton, D. (1994). Factors contributing to the early re-hospitalization of elderly people. *Health and Social Work, 19* (3), 182–191.

Lyons, J. S., Howard, K. I., O'Mahoney, M. T., & Lish, J. D. (1997). *The measurement and management of clinical outcomes in mental health.* New York: Wiley.

Matas, M., Staley, D., & Griffin, W. (1992). A profile of the noncompliant patient: A thirty-month review of outpatient psychiatry referrals. *General Hospital Psychiatry, 14,* 124–130.

McDonald, D., Teitelbaum, M., (1994) Managing mentally ill defendants in the community. *Washington, D.C., US Department of Justice, Office of Justice Programs, National Institute of Justice,* 11.

Mechanic, D., (November/December, 1998) Emerging trends in mental health policy and practice: managed care provides the potential for a more balanced system in the post-institutional era of mental health care, *Health Affairs, 17,* 82–98.

Mechanic, D., & McAlpine, D., (September/October, 1999) Mission unfulfilled: potholes on the road to mental health parity, *Health Affairs, 18* (5) 7–21.

Moggi, F., Ouimette, P. C., Finney, J. W., Moos, & Rudolf, H. (1999). Effectiveness of treatment for substance abuse and dependence for dual diagnosis patients: A model of treatment factors associated with one-year outcomes. *Journal of Studies on Alcohol, 60* (6), 856.

NASW. (1990). NASW clinical indicators for social work and psychosocial services in the acute psychiatric hospital [Pamphlet]. Washington, DC: Author.

NASW. (1998). Centennial information: Celebrating 100 years of social work practice [Pamphlet]. Washington, DC: Author.

National Association of Social Workers (NASW). (1995a). *A brief look at managed mental health care* [Brochure]. Washington, DC: NASW Press.

Orlin, L. & Davis, J. (1993). Assessment and intervention with drug and alcohol abusers in psychiatric settings. In Straussner, S. L. A. (Ed.), *Clinical work with substance-abusing clients.* New York: Guilford Press.

Risley, M. (1961). *The house of healing.* London: Hale.

Sheafor, B. W., Horejsi, C. R., & Horejsi, G. A. (1997). *Techniques and guidelines for social work practice* (4th ed.). Needham Heights, MA: Allyn and Bacon.

Simon, E. P., Showers, N., Blumfield, S., Holden, G., & Wu, X. (1995). Delivery of home care services after discharge: What really happens. *Health and Social Work, 20,* 5–14.

Whiting, L. (1996). Foreword. In J. M. Karls & K. M. Wandrei (Eds.), *Person-in-environment system: The PIE classification system for social functioning problems* (pp. xiii–xv). Washington, DC: NASW Press.

Further Reading

Adkins, E. A. (1996). Use of the PIE in a medical social work setting. In J. M. Karls & K. M. Wandrei (Eds.), *Person-in-environment system: The PIE classification system for social functioning problems* (pp. 67–78). Washington, DC: NASW Press.

Dziegielewski, S. F. (1996). Managed care principles: The need for social work in the health care environment. *Crisis Intervention and Time-Limited Treatment, 3* (2), 97–110.

Fischer, J., & Corcoran, K. (2000). *Measures for clinical practice: A sourcebook* (3rd ed.). New York: Free Press

Chapter 11

The Elderly

LET'S BEGIN BY EXPLORING YOUR THOUGHTS ABOUT AGING. TRY TO
answer these questions about getting older (Garner et al., 1997):
1. For me, getting older means . . . MATURING, GROWING

2. Close your eyes and imagine yourself at various ages. What do you see?
   a) At age 60, I am . . . a GRANDMA
   b) At age 70, I am . . .
   c) At age 80, I am . . .
   d) At age 90, I am . . . DEAD
   e) At age 100, I am . . . DEAD

3. Name a person age 65 or older whom you admire or have admired. DR. HORLICK
   What is so special about this person? PERSONALITY, HUMOR
   How can this person be a role model for you? ENCOURAGING, STRIVES...

No one escapes the aging process. In fact, from the moment we're born we all begin to age. During the aging process, as in all phases of human growth and development, people must adjust to changes in their life circumstances. Unfortunately, many of these changes are viewed negatively in our society. Declines in physical functioning, changes in physical appearance, loss of income, retirement, and loss of partner and social supports are all associated with aging. But not everyone experiences these shifts. Most professionals agree that to understand aging, we must look at more than just a person's chronological age—that is, how old he is. The study of the elderly therefore embraces varied life circumstances and issues and must consider physical and psychosocial factors (Dziegielewski, 2004; 2002; Dziegielewski & Ricks, 2000; Strawbridge, Camacho, Cohen, & Kaplan, 1993; Segrin, 1994).

Did You Know...One myth about aging is that "all older people are alike" and should therefore display predictable patterns of age-related behavior. However, this has not been proved; if anything, the opposite appears true: "as people get older they are less alike" (Peterson, 1994, p. 46).

Over the years, however, use of a chronological age cutoff has been the most common way to decide who is "elderly." You may know people who shortly after their 50th birthdays began to receive retirement information from various groups.

Name: Ramsi Wilkes

Place of residence: Birmingham, Alabama

College/university degrees: University of Montevallo, BSW

Present position: Admissions Coordinator, Galleria Oaks Guest Home

Previous work/volunteer experience: Discharge planner in a rehab hospital (Healthsouth) and retirement community

What do you do in your spare time? I participate in church activities, and I like music.

Why did you choose social work as a career? It was a way to act compassionately for others and make a difference. I was drawn to geriatrics from personal experience and I believed service in this area represented my Christian beliefs.

What is your favorite social work story? I will never forget working with a terminally ill client who was receiving hospice services. She lived in the supervised housing facility where I worked. I was with her when she was dying, and she told me what she was seeing and experiencing. She told me she saw angels in her room while she breathed her last breaths. She described everything about them and pointed them out. Spine tingling!

What would be the one thing you would change in our community if you had the power to do so? I would encourage more people to work with seniors and to learn to respect them more.

A number of major airlines offer "senior discounts" to people age 55 or older. The Senior Golf Tour minimum age is 50, as is the entry age to various states' senior games, that is, athletic contests. Most professionals agree that the definition of "senior" status began with the Economic Security Act of 1935 and was based on the German precedent, which established 65 years as the appropriate age for benefits to begin (Brieland et al., 1980). And indeed, this simple definition is administratively useful because it establishes clear eligibility standards for programs such as Social Security.

> *Did You Know...When the Economic Security Act was passed in 1935, age 65 marked the 95th percentile of the U.S. age distribution. By 1986, age 65 marked the 76th percentile (Wolinsky & Arnold, 1988). Therefore, the share of the U.S. population age 65 and over has increased and it is expected to continue growing dramatically.*

Although looking at chronological age is the simplest approach for administrators and policy planners, it is deficient when used alone because it cannot reflect changes in the composition of the aged population. These changes have made the elderly a much less homogeneous group. One long-term change is based on gender. As Americans continue to enjoy longer and longer life spans and lower death rates, elderly women in particular have benefitted. About sixty years ago there were equal numbers of men and women age 65 and over; since then, however, the proportion of men in this population has declined (Rhodes, 1988). Population projections support that this trend has continued. According to the 2000 census the greatest population increases occurred in 50- to 54-year-olds (55 percent), 45- to 49-year-olds (45 percent), and 90- to 95-year-olds (45 percent). Furthermore, each 5-year age group 75 and over has increased 20 percent (U.S. Census Bureau, 2001). Today there are an estimated 35 million people aged 65 or older in the United States (Federal Interagency Forum on Age Related Statistics, 2000). Therefore, earlier predictions of life expectancies that people who reach age 65 will live to approximately 83 for women and 80 for men remain realistic (Morgan & Kunkel, 1998).

Another factor that undermines any simple definition of "elderly" is the wide range of ages of people who can be included in this designation (Belsky, 1988).

Some people, for example, live well into their 90s and even beyond. Unfortunately, these elderly individuals tend to have significantly more health problems than the younger elderly in their 60s and 70s, and it is almost impossible to compare the two groups. To address this problem, the elderly population can be divided into the young-old, the medium-old, and the old-old (Rhodes, 1988). For purposes of simplicity we will use the terms "elderly" and "aged" to refer to all people age 65 or older.

During the late 1990s, the social work community was encouraged by the John A. Hartford Foundation, a national foundation that supports gerontological efforts, which financially supported the development of both MSW and BSW educational initiatives in aging (http://www.jhartfound.org/). In schools and departments of social work, gerontology field placements, elective courses, and concentrations (at the graduate level) were developed as a direct result of the Hartford support. The Council on Social Work Education has developed a national gerontological project, SAGE-SW (Strengthening Aging and Gerontology Education in Social Work), which in turn has supported national social meetings focusing on gerontology, and gerontological educational modules. And in 2001, a second major national foundation, the Randolph Hearst Foundation, awarded five schools of social work each a $500,000 endowment to support scholarships in gerontology.

Efforts such as these by the CSWE and the Hartford and Hearst Foundations have spurred social work educators to embrace gerontology as a key educational area and practice domain. In this chapter we introduce you to the topic of aging, a normal and universal stage of human development. As the number of elderly citizens rises today, so does the need for social work services. Fortunately, many services provided to the aged are considered human rights and are not subject to the means testing so common elsewhere in the social service arena. We highlight issues and trends essential to an understanding of the elderly population.

AGING: WE CANNOT ESCAPE IT

The number of aged people is rising. According to Galambos and Rosen (2000), in the twentieth century the number of elderly more than tripled. Three reasons have been suggested for this increase. The first is simply the large portion of the population that will be reaching old age. Prior to World War II, large numbers of young immigrants came to America, most legally, and as such reflected in the national statistics, and others illegally, and therefore not counted. Many of these immigrants (legal and illegal) are now reaching retirement age. This group will be augmented as people born after World War II between 1945 and 1955, often called "baby boomers," age into retirement (Rhodes, 1988). According to the U.S. Census (2000) these numbers continue to rise, and it is estimated that in 2030 one out of every five people living in the United States will be over the age of 65 (Council on Social Work Education/SAGE-SW, 2001).

This means that one in every five individuals will be 65 years or older (Morgan & Kunkel, 1998). In particular, the proportion of the total population that is age 75 and over is expected to grow well into the twenty-first century. The increase in the numbers of elderly people is evident throughout the American population and currently . the elderly make up the fastest growing age group in the United States.

Activity...Explore the concept of aging by visiting the Census Bureau web site www. census.gov/population/www/socdemo/age.html. Compare trends on the national level and in your home state or county. For information from an international perspective try www.census/gov/ipc/www/idbnew.html.

The second factor underlying the growth in the number of aged individuals is the number of births in relation to the number of deaths. The trend in recent years has been fewer births and longer and healthier lives resulting in lower death rates (Rhodes, 1988; Morgan & Kunkel, 1998). It is predicted that death rates will continue to decline, leaving more aged individuals in society, especially among the old-old, or those over age 75 (see figure 1).

The third, most obvious reason for growth in the elderly population is the strides made by the scientific community in understanding and promoting the factors that support longer and healthier life spans (Belsky, 1988; Rhodes, 1988; Mosher-Ashley, 1994). The study of aging did not become popular until the end of the 1930s (Shock, 1987). This increased attention to the elderly was related to three major events: 1) the implementation of the Economic Security Act, 2) the development of a scientific basis for the study of the aged, and 3) the dramatic population trends involving elderly people.

By the late 1930s, the United States was experiencing the aftermath of many major social changes. As World War I had ended many people were thrust into poverty. The Great Depression made destitute so many people who had never been poor before. Faced with these newly and "unusually" impoverished fellow citizens, American society showed increased willingness to help certain disadvantaged groups. This sentiment was felt particularly toward older people and young children (Frank, 1946). At the same time, the country still held a strong work ethic; regardless of age or circumstances every person was expected to be a productive part of society. It was during this period that the public, among whom social work-

Figure 1: Rosa is an older woman who lives with her daughter and receives help from a visiting social worker.

ers were active, began to insist that government take the necessary steps to ensure that the elderly and children did not, through their inability to work, become burdens on society (Axinn & Levin, 1982).

The Economic Security Act of 1935 was a societal response to the problem of widespread unemployment caused by the Great Depression. The act mobilized an unprecedented redistribution of income within society. As a result of this legislation, elderly citizens were provided with a government-assisted income, because they were officially designated as unemployable (Axinn & Levin, 1982). Their new guaranteed income helped to make this "worthy" group prosperous enough to command additional professional and societal attention.

Also in the 1930s, an improved scientific basis for the study of the aged developed. The year 1942 saw the publication of *Problems of Aging* by E. Cowdry, a collection of papers by eminent scientists from many disciplines that represented the first compilation of "scientific data on aging" (Shock, 1987, p. 34). Following Cowdry's publication, the first issue of the *Journal of Gerontology* appeared in January 1946. This journal claimed to be the first in the field of gerontology designed "to provide a medium of communication and of interpretation in our efforts to gain a much surer knowledge of human growth and development" (Frank, 1946, p. 3). It represented the Gerontological Society, whose primary interest was to assist the elderly "against the present almost brutal neglect of the aged, by which many have been misused" (Frank, 1946, p. 3). These two publications highlighted the point that science and technology could assist in preventing the loss of this valuable resource. Now, over a half-century later, a large body of literature reflects the popularity of aging as a subject of study. Numerous books, textbooks, and classes are offered in this area. Furthermore, such professionals as chemists, physicians, economists, dentists, psychologists, and social workers have all contributed to existing knowledge about the aging population.

Did You Know...The social work profession has a long-standing interest in aging. This interest was expressed as early as 1947 at the National Conference of Social Work. Issues in aging were also included in the 1949 Social Work Yearbook *(Lowry, 1979).*

Finally, the third reason for increased attention to the concept of the elderly in the late 1930s lay in population trends within this group. The late 1930s saw growing numbers of elderly individuals (Axinn & Levin, 1982; Morgan & Kunkel, 1998), which caused much concern because these people were not considered capable of contributing to the national economy in terms of work (Frank, 1946; Axinn & Levin, 1982). Many people now worry that programs created under the Economic Security Act to assist this population may no longer suffice. This fear is inspired primarily by expected increases in the elderly population and the extended life spans that these elderly people will enjoy. Given the open advocacy and concern expressed for the elderly today, a sense of cautious optimism has developed; yet resistance continues to new programs to address the needs or our elderly population (Dziegielewski, 2004; Morris, 1993).

THEORETICAL FRAMEWORKS FOR PRACTICE WITH THE ELDERLY

A cornerstone of all social work programs is the acknowledgment of the influence of human growth and development theory. This theoretical framework became popular in the 1970s because its broad approach takes into account the benefits and challenges that individuals encounter as they mature in life. The personality of an individual is assumed to be consistent with the way life tasks are developed and managed throughout his lifetime (Rhodes, 1988). For social workers borrowing from this psychological theory, the most comprehensive and widely used work is that of Erikson (1959). Erikson described eight different stages of human development:

Basic trust vs. mistrust

Autonomy vs. shame and doubt

Initiative vs. guilt

Industry vs. inferiority

Identity vs. identity diffusion

Intimacy vs. self-absorption

General activity vs. stagnation

Integrity vs. despair

He believed that once an individual had completed all of these stages successfully, she would accept her self and take responsibility for her own life. In the last developmental stage, integrity versus despair, an individual's life goals reach finalization, and reflection and contemplation become important tasks. Ryff (1982), among others, expanded on Erikson's last developmental stage by including such tasks as adjusting to the fact that the individual no longer supplements the sense of identity through work. Therefore, the individual becomes accepting of the physical limitations imposed by the aging process, and learns to cope with the concept of death while embracing spirituality.

Social workers must help elderly people to maximize the positive experiences in their lives while minimizing the negative ones. Creating an environment where successful aging can occur is essential. Unfortunately, we all have to face objective losses in the body and the mind, but the way we feel about and react to these losses helps to lay the foundation for future acceptance (Marsiske, Franks, & Mast, 1998; Roberts & Dziegielewski, 1995).

Disengagement Theory

Disengagement theory was introduced by Cumming and Henry (1961) and focused on the "normal" process of withdrawal from the social environment to which an aging person belonged. The aging person initiates withdrawal from the usual life events and acknowledges his impending death, reduced physical energy, or poor health. The process of disengagement is considered beneficial to both the individual and society. According to proponents of this theory, the role of the social worker is to help the client to disengage from mainstream society. This allows a natural transition by physically separating the individual from mainstream life, thus fostering an adjustment period to his absence. Disengagement is viewed as an inevitable process that every aging individual must undergo. Further, if a person resists this natural process of "letting go," then problems in adjustment to the elderly years would develop (Cumming & Henry, 1961).

To date, most social workers, although aware of this theoretical perspective, do not embrace it wholeheartedly. This is especially true since the research on disengagement theory has been controversial and contradictory. The relationship between disengagement and the activity level the elderly individual will engage in after leaving mainstream society is unclear (Rhodes, 1988). Previous studies suggested that the role elderly individuals assume after disengagement depends on the behavior patterns they had established over their lifetimes (Maddox, 1964; Sills, 1980). Furthermore, some individuals do not separate but instead stay engaged by changing the focus of their activities. In closing, more research is needed to determine whether disengagement really is a natural part of the aging process.

Activity Theory

Activity theory assumes that the elderly have the same social and psychological needs as middle-aged people. The concepts of activity theory were introduced before disengagement theory, but activity theory was not formalized until 1972 with the work of Lemon, Bengston, and Peterson. These authors were among the first to test activity theory in relation to reported life satisfaction. They hypothesized that as activity increased, life satisfaction would also increase; and conversely, as role loss increased, life satisfaction would decrease. Basically, getting older is characterized by the desire to remain middle aged. Therefore, in order for aging to be successful, the elderly individual needs to continue activities similar to those that were important in middle age (Lemon, Bengston, & Peterson, 1972).

Proponents of this theoretical framework believe that professional intervention involves helping the client to continue an active existence. For example, a social worker might encourage an elderly person to do volunteer work as a way to replace previously paid employment. To date, most social workers working with the elderly are aware of this theory and of its influence on ideas about the aging process; however, most agree that more research is needed before activity theory can be used as a framework for practice. In particular, additional research is needed to establish a direct link between level of activity and life satisfaction (Hoyt, Kaiser, Peters, & Babchuk, 1980; Rhodes, 1988).

Whatever theoretical practice framework is used, more empirical research is needed to establish the utility of developmental theories in working with all populations including the elderly (Dziegielewski & Roberts, 2004 (in press); Dziegielewski & Powers, 2000; Dzigielewski, Shields, & Thyer, 1998; Rhodes, 1988). Ryff (1982) argued that research must attempt to isolate the factors that result in accomplishment of Erikson's developmental stages and to examine the factors that actually allow elderly individuals to achieve optimal levels of performance. It is important to add another caution about these theories, namely, their apparent middle-class and sexist biases.

Human growth and development theories have largely displaced older theories about how the elderly adjust to their changing societal role. Historically, in our quest to understand the aging process and the milestones that elderly people attain, social workers entertained the concepts of disengagement and activity. These theories postulate that activity and disengagement from traditional life experiences are normal and natural parts of the aging process. While research has not proved these theories to be comprehensive enough to explain all life changes experienced by the elderly (Rhodes, 1988), their influence on social work practice remains. Social workers need to be aware of these perspectives on aging and how they can affect elderly clients. Whether these theories are valid or not, the fact that many professionals and lay people believe them may strongly affect their expectations and behavior. Uncritical adherence to these ideas may keep practitioners from thinking about alternative explanations for clients' behavior and from trying innovative problem-solving techniques.

The Pain in My Elbow

A 90-year-old man visits a physician for pain in the elbow joint of his right arm. After the client explains his symptoms to the physician, the physician says, "You are 90 years old. It's possible that the pain is merely related to your age, and there may be no plausible medical explanation for your pain." After hearing this theory the patient thought for a moment and asked, "If your idea is tenable, why doesn't my other elbow hurt? After all, it's the same age."

HEALTH, MENTAL HEALTH, AND THE ELDERLY

How often have you heard someone describe an aged loved one as dying "of old age"? How often have you heard professionals encourage this notion? How often have you seen or heard of an elderly person who consulted a physician about a certain ache or pain only to be told that the pain was simply related to old age?

Dying of old age is a myth that should not be propagated. Social work professionals must give elderly clients the respect they deserve, allowing them to state their concerns in a nonjudgmental atmosphere. No one ever died of old age. There are many causes of illness in the elderly, including such serious conditions as heart disease, cancer, and stroke (Rhodes, 1988), but death due to these or other medical conditions should never be dismissed as dying of old age. This attitude can lead to actual diseases going undetected because symptoms characteristic of disease may be attributed by both client and physician to the aging process itself (Anderson & Williams, 1989). The elderly deserve the same professional treatment as any other age group, and social work professionals have a role in educating and helping elderly individuals to secure the specific health services they need.

Did You Know...In an archival study of records on 298 clients treated by a mental health center, three types of issues predominated among elderly clients: 1) family conflicts, 2) poor physical health, and 3) feeling that they were not in control of their lives (Mosher-Ashley, 1994).

The U.S. Senate Special Committee on Aging (1981) reported that 45 percent of elderly people experience limitation of activity due to some type of chronic condition. As a result the elderly are important consumers of health care.

Hospital use by the elderly received a strong boost in 1965 with the initiation of Title XVIII (Medicare), which provided health insurance for the elderly, a high-risk group in terms of vulnerability to illness and poverty (Axinn & Levin, 1982). Medicare was one of the amendments to the Economic Security Acct of 1935. Obviously, as people get older they are more likely to need health care services; yet since 1965 and the implementation of Title XVIII, the increase in health care consumption at age 65 has been dramatic. The Medicare program brought health care within the means of many elderly people who could not afford it otherwise; physicians and hospitals also benefitted from the greater assurance of payment for providing needed health care services. The benefits to health care recipients and providers, however, came at a particularly high price for the federal government. As the cost of services continued to escalate, the government became determined to control Medicare expenditures (Starr, 1982).

In 1983, Congress mandated a radical change in the payment structure for hospital care to rescue the Hospital Insurance Trust Fund from imminent bankruptcy (Lee, Forthofor, & Taube, 1985). The original system required Medicare to pay whatever hospitals charged for a particular service. Faced with these various and fluctuating costs the government wanted to achieve uniformity and predictability. To control costs and develop an equitable payment system, Diagnostic Related Groups (DRGs) were developed (Begly, 1985).

The DRG system groups together individuals who have similar diagnoses, regardless of age or general health status. Each diagnostic category is assigned a particular standard of care, including length of stay, for which the government is willing to pay—for example, gallbladder removal is allowed seven days of hospital treatment. This new system thus has a fixed payment schedule and hospitals know how much money they will receive for each individual. Unfortunately, for elderly people, who are more fragile and often have chronic or complicating conditions, this system is problematic. Little incentive exists for hospitals to accept patients who might require extended stays. When hospitals do accept elderly patients, many social workers have noted that they are discharged as quickly as possible. Quick discharges are problematic because many of the sick elderly have low incomes and few supports in the community for extended care assistance (Blazyk & Canavan, 1985). Facilities such as nursing homes are often reluctant to take these recently discharged individuals, in their less medically stable conditions. Nursing home professionals are strained when these new patients require much more care and observation; in many cases an increase in staff to accommodate the additional needs of these new patients never occurs. The result in the long run can be readmission, which is costly for the individual and for the hospital (Berkman & Abrams, 1986).

Medicare—and insurance reimbursement in general—is of particular interest to social workers because they are the ones who generally handle the discharge and placement of elderly clients in both nursing home and hospital settings. Social workers must be aware of community supports for discharge back into the community and the availability of any special treatment or services. Discharging elderly people home may place great stress on the family and extended care staff. In discharges back to the community, family stress is often a major contributing factor to long-term care admission (Pratt, Wright, & Schmall, 1987). Measures should be taken to allow families to communicate needs, problem solve, and participate in support groups. Social workers provide an excellent entry point for supportive and educational services to both elderly clients and caregivers. Similarly, placing an elderly client who needs a great deal of individual care into a long-term care facility can create great stress for the staff. Support groups and regular in-service training on how to treat these clients is mandatory. If additional staff are needed to facilitate placement, social workers should recommend such support.

From the individual perspective, developing a chronic health condition is generally an elderly person's worst fear because it can impair activity and unaided mobility (Rhodes, 1988). The chronic conditions from which the elderly often suffer are either physical (biological or physiological) or mental (psychological) in nature. We make this distinction only for simplicity's sake; it is important to note that physical and mental health conditions are often related and interdependent. For example, a physical event such as a stroke may develop into the mental health condition dementia.

---

*Did You Know...A "chronic" condition is generally defined as a disease of long duration, following a long, drawn-out progression (*Taber's Cyclopedia Medical Dictionary, *1977). An "acute" condition, on the other hand, generally has a rapid, severe onset and a short duration (*Taber's Cyclopedia Medical Dictionary, *1977). Elderly people are affected more often by chronic than by acute conditions.*

Physical Health Conditions

"Probably no factor is of more immediate concern to older people than physical health" (Maldonado, 1987, p. 99). Many elderly people fear the loss of individual, unaided activity or perceived independence. Of all physical health conditions, heart disease remains the leading cause of death among those age 65 or older, followed by cancer, stroke, chronic obstructive lung disease, pneumonia and influenza, and diabetes. For those individuals aged 85 or older heart disease was responsible for 40 percent of all the deaths (Federal Interagency Forum on Age Related Statistics, 2000). Although these conditions (excluding cancer) are considered acute, patients often gradually fall prey to chronic conditions such as paralysis and mental impairment resulting in some type of dementia making dementia as the 6th leading cause of death among the elderly (Federal Interagency Forum on Age related Statistics, 2000). Other major chronic conditions that result in the restriction of activity include rheumatism and hearing and vision impairments.

Among vision conditions, cataracts and glaucoma are most common. Social workers should always encourage elderly clients suffering from vision impairments to receive regular check-ups to aid in detecting such conditions before permanent damage results. It is also important for social workers to consider how decreased vision can affect the counseling relationship. For example, an elderly client may not want to admit that he cannot easily read written material or navigate in a particular setting.

Special attention should also be paid to possible hearing loss in clients. Someone who seems withdrawn and unresponsive to conversation may simply be suffering from hearing loss and may be hearing only part of what is said and hypothesizing the rest. If the response is not appropriate, it can seem like confusion. Family members, in particular, may believe their aged relative is becoming confused or simply ignoring them, and confusion in the elderly tends to increase the stress felt by family members about their aged relative (Dziegielewski, 1990;1991; Smallegan, 1985).

Name: Carol Ana Naylor

Place of residence: Kalamazoo, Michigan

College/university degrees: Western Michigan University, BA, MSW

Present position: Full-time social worker on the senior ACT team, Senior Services, Inc., part-time crisis worker at Gryphon Place, a local helpline.

Previous work/volunteer experience: Advocate at ACT of Kalamazoo, lead summer respite worker at Family and Children's Services, direct care worker at Living Ways, volunteer Big Sister at Family Resource Center, volunteer trainer at Gryphon Place.

Why did you choose social work as a career? Quite simply, I feel good when I am helping others. After college, I worked at several jobs as I struggled to find my niche in the world. Working with people was the common denominator in my employment, whether it was waitressing or retail management. Oddly, those jobs seemed to fit naturally into a career in social work. I realized one day that in order to be happy I required something more of myself. Five years ago I made it my mission to become a social worker in the area of mental health. Everyday, I love going to work because I know that what I do matters: it matters to my clients, to my community, and it matters to me.

What is your favorite social work story? When I was an intern at the Battle Creek Veterans Administration Hospital, I spent eight weeks as a substance abuse counselor. This rotation required me to work with down-and-out, chronically alcoholic veterans. I felt helpless counseling many of these men. While I knew they appreciated my insights and active listening skills, I still felt doubtful that I was offering them anything of real value. One vet in particular seemed like a hopeless case. After he left the program, I assumed he would go right back to his previous life of drinking, poverty, and liver problems. Weeks later, I received a note from my supervisor. He included a note from the veteran stating that he felt I had heard him and respected him. He was doing well at a halfway house near his home community. I had no idea until then just how powerful it can be simply to listen and to respect someone. For me, it all relates back to the basic concept of treating people with dignity, which is what social work is all about.

What would be the one thing you would change in our community if you had the power to do so? I feel strongly about the rights of people with chronic mental illness. There has always been a stigma attached to the mentally ill: many people fear, loathe, or discount them. Society often seems not to know what to do with them. I would remove that stigma. I dream of a world where acceptance is abundant—acceptance of all our various colors, sizes, appearance, and harmless eccentricities.

In closing, social work professionals should always be aware that the elderly are often shocked and embarrassed by changes in their health, and these feelings may lead to denial. All of us can understand reluctance to admit individual inadequacy. Counseling and interviewing should include initial assessment to determine whether health concerns are affecting the interview process.

Mental Health Process

Elderly individuals suffer many life circumstances that can affect their mental health. It is virtually impossible to age and not have traumatic life-changing experiences. Common stressful life events include widowhood, social and occupational losses, and physical health problems. In addition, criminal victimization is listed as a critical factor in the area of health risks (Federal Interagency Forum on Age Related Statistics, 2000). Taking the sheer number of life tragedies that elderly people have faced, it would seem logical that they would seek more mental health services than other population groups; however, this is often not the case. Many elderly individuals do not openly seek mental health services. One reason is the method of delivery. When living in the community elderly psychiatric clients generally go to community mental health centers for check-ups and medication; many of the elderly refuse these services because they don't want to leave their homes (Dziegielewski, 2004).

Depression. Depression is a common mental health problem of the elderly, one frequently associated with physical symptoms and illness. According to the 2000 conference report by the Federal Interagency Forum on Age related Statistics women between the ages of 65 and 84 are more likely than men to have severe depressive symptoms. Once an individual reaches the age of 85, however, the levels of depression seem to become equal regardless of gender. Although it is obvious that depression exists, there is little consensus among researchers regarding the prevalence of this condition and how to recognize it in the aged (Ban, 1987; Dziegielewski, 2002; Reynolds, Small, Stein, & Teri, 1994). The existence of depression among the elderly is especially unfortunate, because although it is often treatable, it has been noted that few of the elderly actually seek treatment for this or any other mental health condition (Maldonado, 1987; Belsky, 1988). Furthermore, depression is believed to be related to the disproportionately high suicide rate among the aged population (Ban, 1987; Perkins & Tice, 1994).

Commons signs and symptoms of depression include feelings of sadness, loneliness, guilt, boredom, marked decrease or increase in appetite, lack or increase in sleep behavior, and a sense of worthlessness (American Psychiatric Association, 2000). When depression arises in response to life circumstances, it is called "situational." Situational depression is a particular risk for the elderly because they generally endure many tragedies including loss of loved ones, jobs, status, and independence and other personal disappointments. Feelings of depression can be triggered by such experiences as bereavement for a deceased loved one or frustration with a medical condition (Dziegielewski, 2002; Marsiske et al., 1998).

Social work intervention and counseling can help elderly clients to deal with situational depression and achieve greater life satisfaction. For example, social workers can teach elderly people how to control the frequency of their depressive thoughts and to use relaxation techniques, such as imagery and deep muscle relaxation, to calm down during anxious times. Concrete problem solving and behavioral contracting can be used to help the elderly client change problem behaviors. Whenever possible, family members should be included in treatment contracting because they can provide support and assist in recording and observing behaviors that the elderly client is seeking to change.

Caution should always be used, however; not all cases of depression in the elderly are situational. Some cases of depression may arise directly from internal causes; this is called "endogenous" depression. Furthermore, the etiology of depression in the elderly is not always distinct; depression may be the result of a combination of situational and endogenous factors. For example, many chronic medical conditions are often accompanied by depression. These include hypothyroidism, Addison's Disease, Parkinson's disease, Alzheimer's disease, and congestive heart failure. It is also possible that symptoms of depression are by-products or side effects of medication taken for another condition (Belsky, 1988; Dziegielewski & Leon, 1998) or are, in fact, symptoms of something else. The American Psychiatric Association (2000) has warned that the diagnosis of depression in the elderly can be particularly problematic because the symptoms of dementia in its early stages and those of depression are very similar. Symptoms such as loss of interest and pleasure in usual activities, disorientation, and memory loss are common to the two conditions. There is one big difference, however. Although many signs and symptoms are the same, the person in the early stages of dementia will rarely improve as a result of treatment.

For the beginning social work professional, working with clients who are depressed can be frightening. You may feel very uncertain about what to do and also worry greatly that the client might try to harm herself. This makes it a practice necessity to gather as detailed a social, medical, and medication history as soon as possible. In addition, depressed elderly clients should always be referred for medical examination in order to rule out any physical reasons for depressive symptoms. Depression is most dangerous when it is unrecognized. When implemented, treatment for depression in the elderly is as effective as with other age groups (Dziegielewski, 2002; Reynolds et al., 1994).

Discharge Options. The current trend is for many mentally impaired elderly who cannot be handled at home or in the community to be discharged to long-term care facilities. This practice has increased as a result of the deinstitutionalization that over the past thirty-three years has shrunk state mental health hospitals to one-third their former capacity, and thus reduced one important placement option (Dziegielewski, 2004; Talbott, 1988). In response to the consequent need for more constricted placement, many privately run long-term care facilities, including adult congregate living facilities (boarding homes) and intermediate- and skilled-level care nursing homes, have been opened. In the past thirty years the number of nursing homes alone has increased dramatically in the United States (Dziegielewski, 2004; Morgan & Kunkel, 1998). These homes provide a discharge option for mentally impaired elderly clients that other population groups do not have. Most patients admitted to long-term care facilities are over age 65.

Dziegielewski (2004) warns that long-term care facilities, although convenient, are inappropriate placement options for the mentally impaired elderly because they generally do not provide mental health services. Dziegielewski (1990 and 1991) along with Talbott (1988) argued that very few long-term care facilities provide psychosocial interventions, and medication is often the sole method of treatment. Beginning social work professionals must exercise caution when placing a client in a long-term care facility, especially if the client needs mental health services. Each facility is different. Social workers need to be aware not only of what long-term facilities exist in an area but which services these different facilities offer to the mentally impaired elderly client.

Many elderly people fear functional activity loss. Social workers must be aware of this fear, regardless of whether such loss has actually occurred. Such worries have a real foundation. Since many elderly individuals suffer from chronic conditions, the probability that their condition will improve is low.

Our society tends to deny that problems may be terminal. Family members, and some professionals, may tell aged people that they'll get better rather than helping them to develop ways to cope (Dziegielewski, 2004). It is important for social work practitioners to be knowledgeable about common chronic conditions, their signs and symptoms, their expected progression, and when and where to refer clients for additional treatment. Furthermore, there is considerable evidence that the involvement and support of family members is important in creating a general sense of well-being in the elderly (Rubinstein, Lubben, & Mintzer, 1994; Dziegielewski, 2004). Therefore, the role of the social worker is essential in educating aged clients and their family members to cope with and understand changes that will occur. A comprehensive assessment of the individual, taking into account health conditions and environmental factors, is critical.

EMPLOYMENT CHANGES OF THE ELDERLY AND SOCIAL WORK PRACTICE

Today, problems associated with unemployment in the United States are inspiring social work professionals to look seriously at the social and economic consequences of being without a job (Rife & Belcher, 1994). At the same time, a growing abundance of low-paying and minimum wage jobs are not being filled. Having to address these problems has brought to the attention of the public the specific experiences of certain groups such as older adults. Currently, the trend toward early retirement, in conjunction with the diminishing number of youths entering the workforce (as a result of lower birthrates), has created interest in the elderly as a potential source of labor to help fill this gap. Elderly people, who are living longer and healthier, remain viable employees and constitute an underutilized labor pool that should not be ignored (Federal Interagency Forum on Age Related Statistics, 2000, Mor-Barak & Tynan, 1993). In addition to societal need, many elderly individuals who enjoy good health see continued employment as desirable. For example, an archival study conducted by Mosher-Ashley (1994) on 298 mental health outpatient records found that elderly men between ages 60 and 98 described loss of "work role" as a major area of personal concern. Furthermore, with today's economic turbulence and changes in traditional family structure, elderly people may be expected to take more active roles in supporting their extended families (Duke, Barton, & Wolf-Klein, 1994). Staying active is so important that at the 2000 conference forum the Federal Interagency on Age Related Statistics found that social activity and staying active was a key factor in continued health status (see figure 2).

The Working Elderly

Sadly, if an elderly person does decide to return to work there is no guarantee that a job will be obtainable. Even with the protective legislation that exists, such as the ban on mandatory age-based retirement, age discrimination can and does take place (Sterns, Barrett, Czaja, & Barr, 1994). Many times it occurs when prospective employers refuse to make necessary adjustments for elderly employees (Sterns et al., 1994; Mor-Barak & Tynan, 1993).

Until recently, social security rules created an unnecessary barrier for seniors who wished to work. Seniors who worked full or part time and earned income over

Figure 2: An 80-year-old at the ecumenical social center after an exercise class. This is a drop-in center that offers seniors lunch and a variety of activities.

Social Security Retirement Benefits

At one time people used to talk about retiring at age 65. Well, retirement age has increased for most people, as seen in this table. Can you retire at any age? Sure, but if you retire earlier than "full retirement age" your monthly social security check will be reduced. An eligible person may begin receiving retirement checks at age 62 or delay receiving checks while working past retirement age. Note that the longer you wait to collect your benefits, the larger your monthly checks will be.

Year of Birth	Full Retirement Age (years)	Total Reduction of Benefits If Retire Early[a]
1937 or earlier	65.5	20%
1940	65.5	22.5
1943–54	66.5	25.5
1960 and later	67.5	30.5

Source: See www.ssa.gov.

[a]Early retirement is age 62. An advantage of early retirement is that you collect your benefit for a longer period (if you live). The disadvantage is that your monthly check is permanently reduced by some percentage for the remainder of your life.

a certain level were penalized for working by having their social security checks reduced. The U.S. Congress continues to address this issue while proposing strategies that would decrease and/or eliminate this penalty and allow seniors to earn as much as they can while maintaining their retirement checks (see figure 3).

To assist elderly clients returning to the workforce social work professionals strive to perform the following three tasks. First, social workers must encourage elderly clients to update or learn new skills so that they can remain competitive throughout their careers. This consideration is especially important with the rapid technological advances occurring today, as well as the use of computer and automation technologies in most occupational settings. For an elderly client learning and maintaining these types of skills can be frightening. This apprehension creates the need for the next point of social work intervention.

Second, social workers must work with employers to make job sites more worker friendly while linking elderly clients to larger support systems. Programs are often needed to accommodate older workers. These may include work schedule modifications such as sharing one job between two or more workers, flextime schedules, and reduced work weeks. Furthermore, programs that are designed to build worker skills, motivation, and self-confidence need to be made available either by the employer through in-house programs or in community through community-based programs (Mor-Barak & Tynan, 1993). Assistance programs such as the "job club" described by Rife and Belcher (1994), which utilized a specialized job assistance strategy, provide an excellent practice environment in which social workers can help older workers to become reemployed.

Figure 3: This couple has just celebrated their 50th wedding anniversary. It is often difficult for them to make Social Security income cover all their expense and they get help from their children.

Caregiving in the Community

Social workers must be aware that caregiving assistance may be needed to allow elderly clients to leave the home and continue working. Caregiving can be as serious an issue for elderly couples as for younger couples. In addition, often the family member identified for this caregiving role is the female (Conway-Guistra, Crowley & Gorin, 2002). A recent studies found that caregiving supportive services are valuable in easing the burden on caregivers (Dziegielewski & Ricks, 2000). For all extended families, the need for eldercare services will become a reality (Dziegielewski, 2004). Provision of elder daycare services similar to child daycare services can help these families. Social workers should advocate for companies to consider adding eldercare as a standard option in employee benefit packages.

The Elderly in Retirement

Retirement from the workforce has been viewed in different ways over the years. Attitudes toward retirement have changed with changes in social, emotional, political, and cultural climates. To illustrate how the view of retirement has changed, we present a brief history of the role of the aged in the labor force, drawn from Dziegielewski and Harrison (1996).

Activity…Go to the Social Security Administration web page www.ssa.gov and using the on-line retirement planner estimate your monthly social security benefit check. What do you find? Is this what you thought you would get? Can you live on this amount of money?

The early twentieth century saw a shift from an agrarian to an urban industrial economy in the United States (Axinn & Levin, 1982). In agrarian society, all family members were viewed as contributing members of a cohesive unit. The family was responsible for meeting all the needs of its individual members, including elderly family members. Industrialization, however, changed this perspective, establishing different expectations and roles. The decline in individual business and farm ownership meant that many people had to obtain incomes from outside sources (Atchley, 1976).

During these years (1890–1912), one member's income was not enough to support the entire family, and often work outside of the home by all family members, including women, children, and the aged, became mandatory (Axinn & Levin, 1982). The participation of all these groups in the labor force did not last long, however. Family members left the workforce for primarily two reasons: 1) With industrialization fewer workers were needed in the production of output. 2) An influx of new immigrants made far more workers available (Morrison, 1982). Women, children, and the elderly were therefore no longer needed in the workforce. It was in this era that elderly people began to receive attention from the public. Morrison (1982) attributed this increased interest to the growth in the elderly population and to worries that this large population might compete for limited jobs with younger workers.

The Economic Security Act of 1935 was the first time the government had acknowledged responsibility for providing the elderly with an income that did not depend on continuing participation in the labor market. "The Social Security Act . . . set up a national system of old age insurance . . . which legitimized retirement at age 65" (Morrison, 1982, p. 9). This act supported limited, although permanent, economic guarantees to elderly individuals. Social security helped to ensure that retirement benefits would moderate the reduction in income that workers faced when they left the labor market, and it helped to establish 65 years as the encouraged or expected retirement age (Morrison, 1982).

The lives of the aged have not changed radically over the past fifty years; what has changed, however, is our view of the elderly and how society acts upon this view. In working with elderly clients, social workers need to be aware of the following aspects of retirement, and how they can affect the lives of the aged. Over the short span of forty years, retirement has become an important concern of the American people; almost every day, articles and commentaries appear in publications throughout the country on the economic, social, and psychological consequences of retirement. It is clear that this interest in retirement has been heightened by the rising costs of public and private retirement benefits and by doubts as

Activity...Retirement involves both endings and beginnings. Take a look at your own retirement and think about your endings and beginnings.

Endings: *What will your life be like when you retire? Think about your paycheck, alarm clock, commute . . .*

What Will End	Will You Miss It?	
	Yes	No
1._____	_____	_____
2._____	_____	_____
3._____	_____	_____
4._____	_____	_____

Beginnings: *What will you miss from your work environment and what can you replace with it? For example, you might miss managing projects, and replace it with volunteering in a program that requires management skills.*

Miss	Replace
1._____	_____
2._____	_____
3._____	_____
4._____	_____
5._____	_____

Source: Garner et al. (1997).

to whether these costs can be sustained in the future (Morrison, 1982; Dziegielewski & Harrison, 1996). As the baby boomers approach retirement age, concern centers specifically on the ability of the social security system to handle the inevitable growth in the number of beneficiaries.

Helpful Point...When working with clients approaching retirement have them contact the Social Security Administration to get a copy of their lifetime earnings report. They should do this each year to verify the amount earned and credited toward their retirement. Any problems can be corrected with documentation of salary. But it's best to catch errors early rather than waiting until retirement.

Social work intervention can be critical in helping an aged client make a successful transition from the role of worker to the new role of retiree. It is important, however, that the social worker clearly communicate to elderly clients what role he will play in the delivery of services, because the provision of such services may be poorly understood (Scharlach, Mor-Barak, & Birba, 1994). For example, preretirement planning is just one of the services a social worker can provide to assist in the transition process. Through counseling and more specific assistance the social worker can help aged clients to plan for the role adjustment they will face. It is important to remember that many people gain their status or identity through working (Mosher-Ashley, 1994). They enjoy the work they do and don't want to give up the internal and external rewards they derive from it. Some elderly people can afford to retire but choose not to because of the value placed on working for money in this society (Davidson & Kunze, 1979). Ekerdt (1986) concurred that the importance of the work ethic in our society should not be underestimated. He recommended that elderly people reaching retirement plan their leisure time as carefully as they planned their work time; otherwise, their self-esteem may suffer. Social workers need to be sensitive to this aspect of work in order to help elderly individuals to find other activities that they will find fulfilling.

In planning leisure time, the degree and type of activity that a client can perform (and afford) must be considered. Worker and client can together create a list of possible options and discuss each option in a problem-solving, decision-making manner. Once they have chosen an appropriate leisure activity they can develop an individual contract. The contracting of leisure time activity can give the client "permission" to engage in something that does not work and can provide structure to an otherwise ambiguous period in life.

Finances are another factor that may deter an elderly individual from entering retirement (Dziegielewski & Harrison, 1996). Fear of not having enough income or of being inundated with medical bills and having difficulty securing health insurance may cause an elderly person to avoid facing retirement. A social worker must be aware of the resources available to his elderly client and must help the client to obtain adequate financial counseling. Places of employment often will provide such counseling on request. Insurance brokers can be consulted about health and life insurance. These brokers are usually able to discuss numerous policy options because they represent several different companies.

Always remember when conducting retirement counseling that people often resist change and avoid what they cannot predict. Many people approaching retirement have grown comfortable in their careers and established job patterns that are integral parts of their lives. Elderly clients need to be made aware of the options available to them in retirement, especially in regard to leisure activities.

Preretirement services offered to prospective retirees is an area of social work intervention that should probably be expanded because currently many people preparing to retire avoid or do not engage in this type of planning (Rhodes, 1988) and social work practice offers few preretirement services (Dziegielewski & Harrison, 1996). Most social work interventions in this area come after the fact and are supportive in nature. Montana (1985) stated that preretirement counseling is necessary because it can help elderly people to decrease their anxiety about what retirement will bring. Social workers can take a more active role in preretirement counseling by telling clients about its importance, as well as about how to plan for the future and what to expect in the way of benefits and activities. Attitude toward retirement can be very important in determining life satisfaction during retirement (Rhodes, 1988).

COMMUNITY CARE AND CASE MANAGEMENT WITH THE ELDERLY

Case management is a collaborative process that assesses, plans, implements, coordinates, monitors, and evaluates the options and services required to meet an

> *Did You Know...Two general terms are often used in the medical community to describe the process of getting older. The first, "aging," is defined as the condition of growing older regardless of chronological age; the second, "senescence," is used to characterize the later years in a life span (Peterson, 1994).*
>
> *Furthermore, normal aging can be divided into two types: "intrinsic aging," which refers to the characteristics and processes common to all elderly people of a given gender, and "extrinsic aging," which refers to the factors that influence aging in varying degrees and that can affect individuals differently—for example, lifestyle patterns and exposure to environmental influences. "Normal aging is defined as the sum of intrinsic aging, extrinsic aging, and idiosyncratic or individual genetic factors in each individual" (Peterson, 1994, p. 46).*

individual's health needs, using communication and available resources to promote quality, cost-effective outcomes (Mullahy, 1998). Case management services seek to ensure that all clients receive the services that they need in a system that sometimes appears fragmented and difficult to navigate. The tasks in case management can vary; for the most part, however, they include the concrete tasks of completion of psychosocial assessments, initiation and implementation of advanced directives, assistance in connecting to resources and insurance verification for hospital stays, provision of community resources, and completing referrals for services and durable medical equipment. Case management also includes more supportive services such as crisis intervention support services and assisting clients with medication understanding and compliance (Hawkins, Veeder, & Pearce, 1998). All of these services are designed to help the individual maintain his or her current status in the community.

For the elderly, community-based care and case management services often begin with assessing the "person-in-situation." For example, to stay in the community safely, what type of support system does the elderly individual have? When support systems are severely limited or do not exist, a client can refuse to consider more restrictive care. Therefore, it is a delicate issue when a client living in the community refuses to go to a nursing home when they are unable to handle their own activities of daily living (ADLs) or their own affairs.

In the broadest sense, the social work case manager is the person who makes the health care system work, influencing both the quality of the outcome and the cost (Mullahy, 1998). Roles are diverse but perhaps the case manager can facilitate an earlier more supported and stable discharge when a client has been hospitalized, negotiate a better fee from a medical equipment supplier, or encourage the family to assume responsibility for assistance with the day-to-day care for their elderly relative. In addition, the social worker can serve as a catalyst for change by seeking solutions that promote improvement or stabilization rather than simply monitoring patient status (Mullahy, 1999). Often the social worker may have to arrange home health care for the patient, arrange for nursing home placement, arrange for medical equipment, arrange for hospice, arrange transplants, or simply arrange transportation for the patient (Nelson & Powers, 2001). To ensure that individual worth, dignity, and safety are always maintained, the social worker must take into account the client's desires, the client's family's desires, the needs of the client, and the potential for future growth in this environment.

ABUSE, NEGLECT, RISK OF EXPLOITATION AND AGING

Individuals with the cognitive impairment disorders such as dementia are at increased risk of elder abuse. Violent behaviors between caregivers and care recipients can occur as well as self-neglect, requiring the case be reported to adult protective services. Drifthnery (2000) examined abuse, neglect, and exploitation of the elder population and found that factors such as self-imposed neglect, endangered behaviors, financial mismanagement, and environmental dangers as well as physical illness and/or disability, with a mental health conditions such as alcohol or other substance abuse could support cases of elderly abuse. Choi and Mayer (2000) believe that one way to decrease this problem is to open up more community-based care opportunities such as case management. In the community care setting, social workers are encouraged to provide education to the elderly, their families, and the public to prevent elder maltreatment. Also, greater advocacy to increase funding for prevention, detection, support, and intervention in elder abuse and neglect is needed. This trend is just beginning, as law enforcement agencies have just begun to see the need to develop programs to investigate and identify crimes against the elderly. According to the U.S. Department of Justice Bureau of Justice Statistics, in 1999, 3.8 of every 1,000 persons 65 and older were victims of elderly crime. An elderly person swindled out of more than $50,000 is a typical financial crime of the aging population. Unfortunately, many elderly victims, especially those who live alone, worry that reporting crime could bring embarrassment, along with additional harassment. Even worse, victims think concerned family members could use the incident as leverage to put them in a nursing home. Social workers need to review warning signs, such as when the elderly withdraw large sums of money from bank accounts, and family members or financial institutions should watch for these transactions. Agencies and victim support services are ill prepared to deal with an increase in victims. Advocacy against crimes against the elderly is necessary and urgent.

ASSESSING SUICIDE AND PLANNING FOR DEATH

Today, suicide rates among the elderly are on the rise, particularly among elderly men, and some authors believe these rates are underreported.

> Among the general population, the suicide rate is 12.4 per 100,000 persons; the suicide rate for older people is higher than in the general population with a rate of 20 per 100,000 being recorded in 1990. Persons aged 65 and older compromise 12.5 percent of the population and account for 20.9 percent of the suicides annually (Perkins & Tice, 1994, p. 438).

The American Association of Suicidology supports this contention, reporting that this rate is approximately 18.1 percent. This organization also reports that in

2000 suicide rates ranged from 12.6 percent or 100,000 persons aged 75 to 84. For the elderly, this makes the rate almost double when compared to the overall U.S. rate.

Did You Know…Suicide is the eighth leading cause of death in the United States and accounts for over 30,000 deaths each year.

There is probably no conclusive reason for these trends, but one possibility is that stress levels among the elderly are so high that usual methods of coping and problem solving are ineffective (Canetto, 1992). Furthermore, the elderly appear to be more dissatisfied with their functional abilities because of ill health and its effects (Reynolds et al., 1994). Finally, the tremendous number of life stressors that the elderly may experience in a short amount of time—for example, death of spouse, relatives, or friends and changes in social status and employment status—cannot be overemphasized (Dziegielewski, 2004).

Suicide rates are usually considered indicative of the mental health, satisfaction, and well-being of a population. But society doesn't always view suicide among the elderly in the same way as suicide involving young people. For example, the increase in suicide rates among adolescents has raised much alarm and led many to a call for solutions. At the same time, however, suicide is sometimes accepted as an understandable option for elderly people who feel lost, trapped, and alone (Kastenbaum & Coppedge, 1987). As proposed by Kastenbaum and Coppedge (1987) it remains the case that suicide for the frail and sick elderly may even be encouraged by the reduction of health care benefits and the rationing of "limited health care options" to aged individuals.

A No-Suicide Contract

Social work professionals often help clients to complete these contracts even when clients have no actual plans to harm themselves. This is not a legal contract; it is merely done to help the client feel that there is a plan and that the plan is being monitored.

I _____ agree that I will not harm myself in any way and that I do not have any plans to do so. If I start to feel as though I might want to try to harm myself, I agree to immediately call [insert the name and number of a 24-hour hotline or emergency room the client can call].

Signed [client's name signed here]

Witness [Social worker's name here] [Phone number for agency/social worker]

Family Witness [if possible get a family member to witness]

The death of a partner presents a particular coping problem because it may require the elderly survivor to assume new, unfamiliar duties: balancing a checkbook, driving, shopping for groceries, and so forth. These new tasks and the adjustments they imply, in conjunction with the loss of a life partner, can place unbelievable stress on the elderly. They may feel isolated from married friends and fear possible dependence on family or friends. Widowhood particularly affects elderly women because they generally outlive their male partners (Federal Interagency Forum on Age Related Statistics, 2000). Female widowhood may not be directly linked to suicide, however, because suicide rates are higher for elderly men than for elderly women. Nevertheless, Wan (1985) warned, widowhood is likely to have negative effects on the survivor, including impairment of physical, psychological, and social well-being. Suicide among the elderly is almost always a result of major life stresses and accumulated losses; therefore, widows and widowers have a high probability of committing suicide. Research indicates that the first year after the death of a spouse is the hardest time of adjustment (Wan, 1985; Belsky, 1988). During this especially stressful period, social workers should keep aware of a client's abilities or problems in coping with grief.

The social worker plays an essential role with potentially suicidal elderly clients. First, if a client, young or old, expresses a wish to commit suicide and has a concrete plan, steps to ensure hospitalization must be taken immediately. The person needs to be in a safe place. Unfortunately, criteria for hospital admission are not always clear, and the social worker may not know how likely the client is to turn thoughts into actions (Dziegielewski & Harrison, 1996). In any case, some type of counseling must take place. For dealing with aged clients Perkins and Tice (1994) emphasized a counseling strategy that focuses on client strengths. In this method client and social worker identify the client's preexisting coping and survival skills in order to help the client to accept the role of survivor. This approach, in conjunction with crisis services and bereavement counseling, can help the elderly client to regain control of her life.

Much of the confusion in our society regarding death can be linked to the atmosphere of denial, secrecy, and fear that we have created around this inevitable part of life (LaRue, 1985). Many people attempt to ignore or avoid this fact, at least until it affects them indirectly. For example, have you prepared for your own death? Do you have a will? Is your family aware of your wishes? For most of us the answer is no. Our reasons vary from "I'm too young to worry about that now" to "I have plenty of time." Now consider, if you the helping professional said no, what do you think your clients will answer? By the way, if you did say no, you're not alone; but don't take too much comfort in this—it's evidence that you need to address these issues in your own life.

No one rationally desires to be dying or to have a terminal illness. Indeed, most people resist even the idea of being ill. For some people, however, regardless of age, there comes a time when they truly do want to die (High, 1978). Among the elderly, many fear the chronic conditions that can make them dependent on family and or friends. Family members too fear this new relation, daunted by the prospect of making decisions about a loved one, especially in regard to continuing or terminating life. The elderly person and family members often turn to science and medicine for the answers. Physicians, as representatives of the scientific and healing community, are sought out and expected to supply answers and make decisions. Unfortunately, many physicians, taught from the day they enter medical school to preserve life, may feel unprepared to deal with the psychosocial aspects of dying (Nolan, 1987). Trained to help people avoid death, many health care professionals see their role as avoiding death (Dziegielewski, 2004). It is the social worker, often as part of an interdisciplinary team, who will be asked to help the client or family to cope with death.

Before a social worker can successfully help a client and her family to deal with death, several issues should be addressed. First, the social worker must explore his own feelings about death. Many social work practitioners, like their medical counterparts, are uncomfortable with the subject of dying (LaRue, 1985). It may help for the social worker to discover how death is viewed in other countries and religions (Dziegielewski & Harrison, 1996). The Roman Catholic Church, for example, has been very responsive in helping individuals to prepare for death (LaRue, 1985). By examining alternative conceptions of death and the legitimization of the role of death, social workers can disperse some of the mysticism that surrounds death in this country. Once the social worker feels comfortable talking about death these concepts need to be discussed with the client as well as family members.

Second, the social worker must know what resources and services available in the community might assist elderly clients in preparing for death. One example is the Hospice program. Hospice, which is funded by Medicare, offers services to people suffering from terminal illnesses who are expected to live six months or less (Dziegielewski, 2004). This and similar programs do not focus on prolonging life beyond its natural end. In providing services through such programs the social worker serves on an interdisciplinary team designed to help the client and family members to prepare for natural death.

Finally, the social worker should learn about living wills and decide whether such a measure is appropriate for the client. Most people are aware of the need for, and some do complete, a will that declares who is to receive their money, property, and other possessions. However, the concept of a living will is less familiar (Dziegielewski, 2004; Paterson, Baker, & Maeck, 1993). Simply stated, a living will allows a person to document, in advance, his or her preferences relating to the use or avoidance of life-sustaining procedures, in the event of a terminal illness. This type of documentation is especially helpful to family members burdened with making such decisions when an elderly relative is mentally incapacitated. Without it, they may avoid making any decision because they feel that doing so gives them too much control and responsibility.

SUMMARY

We all face the prospect of growing old. Yet the elderly often suffer as the result of societal attitudes that devalue old age. Our society fears aging and promotes any number of attempts to beat the effects of old age on the human body and the mind. Such prejudices spring from both rational and irrational fears. Rational fears about worsening health, the loss of loved ones, and declining social status can be intensified by negative stereotypes of the elderly. And irrational fears about changes in physical appearance, loss of masculinity or femininity, and perceived mental incompetence are not unusual. For elderly people, misinformation and myth, as well as real biological, psychological, social, and economic challenges, can impede self-help and the pursuit of individual contentedness.

Aging in today's society creates complexities both in policy and in the human experience. Advances in medicine allow people to live longer. You will find many families that have three generations of "seniors": the granddaughter in her late 50s, the father in his early 80s, and the grandmother in her 100s. Talk about perplexing family dynamics!

As we age and live longer, we will spend more years in retirement. Once a short period of time, maybe ten to fifteen years, retirement now can last forty and even fifty years. Income, health care, socialization, loneliness and happiness, and support are among the many areas that policymakers and senior advocates struggle with today.

At a minimum, social workers need to examine their own attitudes about aging and how these attitudes can affect their practice with elderly clients and their families. We should be keenly aware of the types of discrimination that can occur, and we must never contribute, directly or indirectly, to any discriminatory practices based on age. All helping professionals need to recognize that each aged person is a valuable resource in our society. Our role is to provide services and advocacy that will help the elderly to maximize their life satisfaction and well-being.

References

American Psychiatric Association. (2000). *Diagnostic and statistical manual of mental disorders: Text revision* (4th ed.). Washington, DC: Author.

American Association of Suicidology. (2000). About Suicide: Elderly fact sheet. Retrieved October 25, 2003 from www.suicidology.org

Anderson, F., & Williams, B. (1989). *Practical management of the elderly*. Boston: Blackwell.

Atchley, R. (1976). *The sociology of retirement*. New York: Halsted.

Axinn, J., & Levin, H. (1982). *A history of the American response to need*. New York: Harper and Row.

Ban, T. A. (1987). Pharmacological perspectives in therapy of depression in the elderly. In G. L. Maddox & E. W. Busse (Eds.), *Aging: The universal experience* (pp. 127–131). New York: Springer.

Begly, C. (1985). Are DRGs fair? *Journal of Health and Human Resources Administration, 8,* 80–89.

Belsky, J. (1988). *Here tomorrow: Making the most of life after fifty*. Baltimore: Johns Hopkins University Press.

Berkman, B., & Abrams, R. (1986). Factors related to hospital readmission of elderly cardiac patients. *Social Work, 31* (2), 99–103.

Besdine, R. W. (1994, February). Successful aging for all? *Patient Care*, pp. 7–8.

Blazyk, S., & Canavan, M. (1985). Therapeutic aspects of discharge planning. *Social Work, 30,* 489–495.

Brieland, D., Costin, L. B., & Atherton, C. R. (1980). *Contemporary social work* (2nd ed.). New York: McGraw-Hill.

Brody, E. M., Brody, S. J. (1987). Aged: Services. In A. Minahan (Ed.), *Encyclopedia of social work* (pp. 106–126). Silver Spring, MD: NASW Press.

Canetto, S. S. (1992). Gender and suicide in the elderly. *Suicide and Life Threatening Behavior, 22*, 80–97.

Choi, N. G. & Mayer, J. (2000). Elder abuse, neglect, and exploitation: Risk factors and prevention strategies. *Journal of Gerontological Social Work, 33* (2), 5–25.

Cowdry, E. V. (Ed.). (1942). *Problems of aging: Biological and medical aspects*. Baltimore: Williams and Wilkins.

Council on Social Work Education/SAGE SW. (2001). *Strengthening the impact of social work to improve the quality of life for older adults and their families: A blueprint for the new millennium*. Alexandria, VA: Council on Social Work Education.

Cumming, E., & Henry, W. (1961). *Growing old: The process of disengagement*. New York: Basic Books.

Davidson, W. R., & Kunze, K. (1979). Psychological, social and economic meanings of work in modern society: Their effects on the worker facing retirement. In W. C. Sze (Ed.), *Human life cycle* (pp. 690–717). New York: Jason Aronson.

Driisthnery, F. (2000). Work history and U.S. elders. *Transitions into Poverty*, November 30, 2000.

Duke, W. M., Barton, L., & Wolf-Klein, G. P. (1994). The chief complaint: Patient caregiver and physician's perspectives. *Clinical Gerontologist, 14* (4), 3–11.

Dziegielewski, S. F. (2004). *The changing face of health care social work: Professional practice in behaviorally based managed care*. New York: Springer.

Dziegielewski, S. F. (2002). *DSM-IV-TR™ in action*. New York: Wiley.

Dziegielewski, S. F. (1990). *The institutionalized dementia relative and the family member relationship*. Unpublished PhD dissertation. Florida State University, Tallahassee.

Dziegielewski, S. F. (1991). Social group work with family members of elderly nursing home residents with dementia: A controlled evaluation. *Research on Social Work Practice, 1* (4), 358–370.

Dziegielewski, S. F., & Roberts, A. R. (2004, In Press). Evidence-based practice. In A. Roberts & K. Yeager (Eds.), *Handbook of practice-focused research and evaluation*. New York: Oxford University Press.

Dziegielewski, S. F. & Powers, G. T. (2000). Procedures for evaluating time-limited crisis intervention. In A. Roberts (Ed.), *Crisis intervention handbook* (2nd ed.). New York: Oxford University Press.

Dziegielewski, S. F., Shields, J. & Thyer, B. A. (1998). Short-term treatment: Models and methods. In J. Williams & K. Ell (Eds.), *Advances in mental health research: Implications for practice*. Washington, D.C.: NASW Press.

Dziegielewski, S. F. & Harrison, D. F. (1996). Counseling the aged. In D. F. Harrison, B. A. Thyer, & J. Wodarski (Eds.), *Cultural diversity in social work practice* (2nd ed.). Springfield, IL: Thomas.

Dziegielewski, S. F. & Leon, A. M. (1998). Psychopharmacology and the treatment of major depression. *Research on Social Work Practice, 8* (4), 475–490.

Dziegielewski, S. F. & Ricks, J. (2000, July–September). Adult daycare for mentally impaired elderly and measurement of caregiver satisfaction. *Activities, Adaption and Aging, 24* (4), 51–64.

Ekerdt, D. J. (1986). The busy ethic, moral continuity between work and retirement. *Gerontology, 26*, 239–244.

Erikson, E. (1959). Identity and the life cycle. In *Papers by Erik H. Erikson*. New York: Universities Press.

Federal Interagency Forum on Aging-Related Statistics. (2000, August). *Older Americans 200: Key indicators of well-being*. Federal interagency forum on aging-related statistics, Washington, D.C.: U.S. Government Printing Office.

Frank, L. (1946). Gerontology. *Journal of Gerontology, 1*, 1.

Garner, J., et al. (1997). *Ernst & Young's retirement planning guide*. New York: Wiley.

Galambos, C. M., & Rosen, A. (2000). The aging are coming and they are us. In S. M. Keigher, A. E. Fortune, & S. L. Witkin (Eds.). *Aging and social work: The changing landscapes* (pp. 13–19). Washington, DC: NASW Press.

Hawkins, J., Veeder, N., & Pearce, C. (1998) *Nurse social worker collaboration managed care: A model of community case management*. New York: Springer.

High, D. (1978). Quality of life and care of the dying person. In M. Blaes & D. High (Eds.), *Medical treatment and the dying: Moral issues* (pp. 65–84). Salem, MA: Hall.

Hoyt, D. R., Kaiser, M. A., Peters, G. R., & Babchuk, N. (1980). Life satisfaction and activity theory: A multi-dimensional approach. *Journal of Gerontology, 35*, 935–981.

Kasterbaum, R., & Coppedge, R. (1987). Suicide in later life: A counter trend among the old-old. In G. L. Maddox & E. W. Busse (Eds.), *Aging: The universal human experience*. New York: Springer.

LaRue, G. A. (1985). *Euthanasia and religion*. Eugene, OR: Hemlock Society.

Lee, E., Forthofor, R., & Taube, C. (1985). Does DRG mean disastrous results for psychiatric hospitals? *Journal of Health and Human Services Administration, 8*, 53–78.

Lemon, B. L., Bengston, V. L., & Peterson, J. A. (1972). An exploration of activity of aging: Activity types and life satisfaction among in-movers to a retirement community. *Journal of Gerontology, 27*, 511–583.

Lilienfeld, D. E., & Perl, D. P. (1994). Projected neurogenerative disease mortality among minorities in the United States. *Neuroepidemiology, 13*, 179–186.

Lowry, L. (1979). *Social work with the aging: The challenge and promise of later years*. New York: Harper and Row.

Lusky, R. (1986). Anticipating the needs of the U.S. elderly in the twenty-first century: Dilemmas in epidemiology, gerontology and public policy. *Social Science Medicine, 23*, 1217–1227.

Maddox, G. (1964). Disengagement theory: A critical evaluation. *Gerontologist, 4*, 80–82.

Maldonado, D. (1987). Aged. In A. Minahan (Ed.), *Encyclopedia of social work* (pp. 95–106). Silver Spring, MD: NASW Press.

Marsiske, M., Franks, M. M., & Masat, B. T. (1998). Psychological perspectives on aging. In L. Morgan & S. Kunkel (Eds.) *Aging: The social context* (pp. 145–182). Thousand Oaks, CA: Pine Forge Press.

Montana, P. (1985). *Retirement programs: How to develop and implement them*. Englewood Cliffs: NJ: Prentice-Hall.

Mor-Barak, M. E., & Tynan, M. (1993). Older workers and the work place: A new challenge for occupational social work. *Social Work, 38*, 45–55.

Morgan, L., & Kunkel, S. (1998). *Aging: The social context*. Thousand Oaks, CA: Pine Forge Press.

Morris, R. (1993). Do changing times mean changing agendas for the elderly? *Journal of Aging and Social Policy, 5* (3), 1–6.

Morrison, M. (1982). *Economics of aging: The future of retirement*. New York: Van Nostrand Reinhold.

Mosher-Ashley, P. M. (1994). Diagnoses assigned and issues brought up in therapy by older adults receiving outpatient treatment. *Clinical Gerontologist, 15* (2), 37–64.

Mullahy, C. (1998). *The case manger's handbook.* Gaithersburg, Maryland: Aspen Publishers.

National Council on Aging. (1981). *Aging in the 80s: America in transition.* Washington, DC: Author.

Nelson, J. & Powers, P. (2001). Community case management for frail, elderly clients: The nurse case manager's role. *Journal of Nursing Administration, 31* (9), 444–450.

Nolan, K. (1987). In death's shadow: The meanings of withholding resuscitation. *Hastings Center Report, 17,* 9–14.

Paterson, S. L., Baker, M., & Maeck, J. P. (1993). Durable powers of attorney: Issues of gender and health care decision making. *Journal of Gerontological Social Work, 21,* 161–177.

Perkins, K., & Tice, C. (1994). Suicide and older adults. The strengths perspective in practice. *Journal of Applied Gerontology, 13,* 438–454.

Peterson, M. (1994). Physical aspects of aging: Is there such a thing as normal? *Geriatrics, 49* (2), 45–49.

Pratt, C., Wright, S., & Schmall, V. (1987). Burden, coping and health status: A comparison of family caregivers to community dwelling institutionalized Alzheimer's patients. *Social Work, 10,* 99–112.

Reynolds, C. F., Small, G. W., Stein, E. M., & Teri, L. (1994, February). When depression strikes the elderly patient. *Patient Care,* pp. 85–101.

Rhodes, C. (1988). *An introduction to gerontology: Aging in American society.* Springfield, IL: Thomas.

Rife, J. C., & Belcher, J. R. (1994). Assisting unemployed older workers to become reemployed: An experimental evaluation. *Research of Social Work Practice, 4,* 3–13.

Roberts, A. R. & Dziegielewski, S. F. (1995). Basic forms and applications of crisis intervention and time-limited cognitive therapy. In A.R. Roberts (Ed.). *Crisis intervention and time-limited cognitive treatment,* pp. 5–30. Newbury Park: Sage Publications.

Rubinstein, R. L., Lubben, J. E., & Mintzer, J. E. (1994). Social isolation and social support: An applied perspective. *Journal of Applied Gerontology, 13,* 58–72.

Ryff, C. D. (1982). Self-perceived personality change in adult-hood and aging. *Journal of Personality and Social Psychology, 42,* 108–115.

Scharlach, A. E., Mor-Barak, M. E., & Birba, L. (1994). Evaluation of a corporate sponsored health care program for retired employees. *Health and Social Work, 19,* 192–198.

Segrin, C. (1994). Social skills and psychological problems among the elderly. *Research on Aging, 16,* 301–321.

Shock, N. W. (1987). The International Association of Gerontology: Its origins and development. In G. L. Maddox & E. W. Busse (Eds.), *Aging: The universal experience,* pp. 21–43. New York: Springer.

Sills, J. S. (1980). Disengagement reconsidered: Awareness of finitude. *Gerontologist, 20,* 457–462.

Smallegan, M. (1985). There was nothing else to do: Needs for care before nursing home admission. *Gerontologist, 25,* 364–369.

Specht, R., & Craig, G. T. (1982). *Human development: A social work perspective.* Englewood Cliffs, NJ: Prentice-Hall.

Starr, P. (1982). *The social transformation of American medicine.* New York: Basic Books.

Sterns, H. L., Barrett, G. V., Czaja, S. J., & Barr, J. K. (1994). Issues in work and aging. *Journal of Applied Gerontology, 13,* 7–19.

Strawbridge, W. J., Camacho, T. C., Cohen, R. D. & Kaplan, G. A. (1993). Gender differences in factors associated with change in physical functioning in old age: A six-year longitudinal study. *Gerontologist, 33* (5), 603–609.

Taber's cyclopedia medical dictionary. (1977). Philadelphia: Davis.

Talbott, J. (1988). Taking issue. *Hospital and Community Psychiatry, 39,* 115.

U.S. Census Bureau. (2001). *Aging in the United States: Past, Present, and Future.* Washington, D.C.: U.S. Government Printing Office.

U.S. Senate Special Committee on Aging. (1981). *Development in aging, 1981* (Vol 1). Washington, DC: U.S. Government Printing Office.

Wan, T. (1985). *Well-being for the elderly: Primary preventive services.* Lexington, MA: Lexington Books.

Wodarski, J. & Dziegielewski, S. F. (2002). *Human Growth and Development: Integrating Theory and Empirical Practice.* New York: Springer.

Wolinsky, F. D. & Arnold, C. L. (1988). A different perspective on health and health services utilization. In G. L. Maddox & M. P. Lawton (Eds.), *Annual review of gerontology and geriatrics* (Vol. 8, pp. 77–94). New York: Springer.

Chapter 12

Domestic Violence

CONSIDERABLE ATTENTION HAS BEEN PAID TO THE FACT THAT OUR society is "violent." In 1994, *Time* magazine reported that women are as likely to be killed by their partners as by any other kind of assailant (July 4, 1994, p. 21). Today, as the population continues to increase so does the incidence of domestic violence against women (Wilke & Vinton, 2003). According to Rennison and Welchans (2000), after utilizing the National Crime Victimization data it was estimated that five times as many women as men were victims of domestic violence. In addition, there is believed to be extensive minor abuse that is perpetrated by both males and females within intimate relationships (Wilke & Vinton, 2003). Furthermore, there is a growing body of research that has linked threats and coercion by the batterer as a means of keeping the individual from leaving the situation. Threats can include harming children, relatives, or even the individual's pets (Faver & Strand, 2003). Nevertheless, many women who experience abuse by partners remain resistant toward placing charges (Siegler, 1989). Although domestic violence is not purely a crime against women, millions of women are affected by this cyclic pattern of abuse. The numbers are astounding: each year 2,000 to 4,000 women are beaten to death, and more than half the women in the United States report that at some point in the love relationship they have been abused either physically or emotionally by their partners (Liutkus, 1994). Studies indicate that in any given year anywhere between one-third and one-half of women murdered in the United States have been killed by a boyfriend, spouse, or ex-mate (Schneider, 1994; Litsky, 1994) whereas 10 percent of the men murdered in America have been killed by a female partner, usually in self-defense (Statman, 1990). As many as half of the couples living in the United States are estimated to have experienced violence in their relationship (Gelles, 1979).

> *Did You Know...Domestic Violence and the treatment of such has been recognized as a public health problem. In a 2003 study of 522 individuals in CA, 79.4% of the participants agreed and supported the need for more domestic violence prevention programming (Sorenson, 2003).*

Finklehor (1988) reported that 12 percent of spouses surveyed stated that they had experienced at least one violent incident with their mates in the past year and 28 percent reported experiencing violence throughout the course of the marriage.

Name: Magaly Ortiz

Place of residence: Miami, Florida

College/university degrees: Barry University, BS in Psychology, University of Central Florida, MSW

Present position: MSW intern/student and MSW Student Association President

Previous work/volunteer experience:
Case Manager for a sexual trauma recovery center

What do you do in your spare time? I like to exercise, dance, and spend time with family and friends.

Why did you choose social work as a career? One of the things that helped me decide to become a social worker was my parents' divorce, which was a very difficult experience for me. While technically my parents were not taken away from me, I can relate to the fear of losing one's family. In this way, I can empathize and relate on a more personal level with clients who are children of divorced parents.

What is your favorite social work story? I have not been in the field long enough to have many stories, but one that comes to mind occurred when I was an intern working with sexually abused children. I remember the satisfaction of watching a child begin and end her healing journey. It was exciting for me to see the progress and success that children can make with treatment. It was at this time that I knew I was in the right field.

What would be the one thing you would change in our community if you had the power to do so? I would like to change the decision-making power that managed care has on the treatment that our clients receive. Insurance companies make the decisions about how much time a client needs to recover from a mental illness or trauma; however, they do not have the education to determine the medical attention necessary. Therefore, if I had the power to change anything, I would like medical doctors and professionals to be the evaluators in determining the treatment a client should receive.

The American Medical Association estimated that over four million women each year are victims of assault by their partners each year (National Clearing House for the Defense of Battered Women, 1995). Approximately 20 percent of female visits to emergency rooms are the result of battering, and more generally, assault by a partner—domestic violence, date rape, and so forth—accounts for 70 percent of all admissions. With abuse being addressed more and more in emergency rooms, many states now allow the police to arrest a suspected abuser without a warrant when evidence exists of an injury serious enough to require emergency medical care (Statman, 1990). The legal treatment of domestic violence can be complicated because laws in regard to domestic violence vary from state to state and often differ between municipalities in the same state (Statman, 1990). Over the past fifteen years the problem of domestic violence and legal system intervention, as well as the roles of assessment and social work practice, have gained wide recognition within the social work profession.

Domestic violence has deep roots. Women have historically been characterized as subordinate to men. Numerous theological teachings, Judeo-Christian as well as Moslem, foster the belief that women must submit to men. Roman law defined the status of women as subject to the wishes and desires of their husbands because women were regarded as personal possessions of men (Siegler, 1989). Throughout history father-to-son transmission of wealth has been common, and a woman's property has fallen under the control of her husband after marriage. Under English common law, a woman had no legal existence apart from the relation with her spouse. For example, if a woman was raped, only her father or her husband could claim compensation from the perpetrator (Siegler, 1989).

> *Did You Know...In 1883 the state of Maryland outlawed wife abuse after acknowledging that violence against women was assault. In 1910 thirty-five states followed this lead and adopted the view that the battering of women is equivalent to assault (Siegler, 1989).*

The advent of the feminist movement in the 1960s and 1970s greatly altered the perception of violence perpetrated against women. The prevailing psychoanalytic view, which asserted that battered women were masochistic and gained sexual excitement from beatings, was challenged (Costantino, 1981; Gelles & Harrop, 1989). Recent theories of violence toward women take the view that battering is rooted in patriarchal society (Srinivasan & Davis, 1991) and that imbalances in power between men and women leave women vulnerable to abuse. The problem is thus redefined as a social issue rather than an individual pathology. Sociological perspectives investigate domestic violence in the context of social stress, learned violent response, and cycles of perpetuated family violence (Gutierrez, 1987). Feminist perspectives identify battering as a means of obtaining social control and maintaining social oppression (Gutierrez, 1987). Indeed, it wasn't until the feminist movement of the 1970s that the battering of women was recognized as a problem that required attention (Siegler, 1989).

In this chapter we discuss the problems of domestic violence. We emphasize that social workers must not—and must teach others not to—blame those involved in domestic abuse. It is a nationwide problem that can affect anyone, of any age, race, creed, or income. Interventions with survivors of domestic violence must be interdisciplinary in nature. Social workers must cooperate closely with other service providers, including members of the criminal justice system.

DOMESTIC VIOLENCE DEFINED

What exactly is domestic violence? We use the word "violence" because "this is not a question of minor arguments or disputes but, rather, intentional hostile and aggressive physical or psychological acts" (Dwyer, Smokowski, Bricout, & Wodarski, 1996). Definitions of violence range from "the use of physical force by one person against another" (Siegler, 1989) to "pushing, slapping, punching, kicking, knifing, shooting, or the throwing of objects at another person" (Gelles, 1987, p. 20). In its most simple form **domestic violence** is defined as any physical act of violence directed at one partner or the other (Edleson, 1991).

A broader concept, **abuse** refers to any behavior that harms the target, including psychological, emotional, and nonviolent sexual abuse (Siegler, 1989). Although the magnitude and severity of domestic abuse varies, it generally also involves violent acts perpetuated against a partner in a relationship, in the presumed safety and privacy of the home (Dwyer et al., 1996).

CHARACTERISTICS OF THE ABUSED AND THEIR ABUSERS

In discussing survivors of abuse two points must be emphasized. First, social workers must be careful never to blame the victim for domestic violence. Unfortunately, both society at large and the abuser may assert that the violence itself is evidence that the victim must have done something wrong. It is important to ensure that both the victim and her family understand that blaming the victim for what is happening simply reinforces the problem. Second, social workers need to be aware that female abuse survivors may blame themselves for the abuse. The may have illusions of being able to control the abuser's behavior and so feel great shame at allowing themselves to be abused (Dziegielewski & Resnick, 1996).

Several studies—admittedly on small samples—indicate that women who are battered have experienced childhood family violence, witnessed parental abuse, and were often abused as children (Siegler, 1989; Gelles & Cornell, 1990; Tolman & Bennett, 1990). Characteristics of women who feel trapped in abusive relationships include 1) low self-esteem, 2) lack of self-confidence, 3) a tendency to withdraw from marital disputes and stress, 4) increased feelings of depression, hopelessness, and frustration, 5) proneness toward drug and alcohol abuse and dependency, and 6) suicide attempts and successful suicidal and homicidal behavior (Liutkus, 1994).

Blaming The Victim and the Case of Hedda Nussbaum

Societal contempt was clear in the case of Hedda Nussbaum, who made the cover of *Newsweek* in 1988. Her live-in boyfriend, Joel Steinberg, charged with murdering the couple's adopted 6-year-old daughter, had beaten her face and body. The abuse in this relationship was documented as beginning in March 1978 and ending November 1987, when Hedda asked Steinberg for permission to get help for their abused child. Unfortunately, the child was already dead from the beating she had received. In the aftermath many people blamed Hedda for her failure to save the child. The *Washington Post* described as sickening that the state and its key witness could collude to use "victimization" as an excuse for Hedda's lack of judgment and inaction (Jones, 1994, p. 175). Many people could not believe that the beatings that Hedda received and the fear she developed as a result of the abuse left her incapable of intervening for the life of her daughter, let alone her own.

No one knows exactly why a woman stays in a violent relationship, but numerous reasons have been postulated. The abused woman may believe that her spouse will reform. She may doubt her ability to manage alone. She may fear the stigma of divorce and of being left "alone." She may worry about what will happen to her and her children if she leaves—poor employment options and the possibility of homelessness (half of homeless women in this country are fleeing from domestic violence; Mullins, 1994), as well as difficulty finding adequate daycare for her children (Dziegielewski & Resnick, 1996; Dziegielewski, Resnick, & Krause, 1996; Gelles & Cornell, 1990).

Among all these possibilities, it has been speculated that the greatest deterrent for women is the fear of economic hardship and inadequate care for their children. For women this fear is very well founded. Many women, by accepting primary responsibility for home and children, place themselves at a disadvantage as wage earners. Their economic dependence can serve to preserve abusive situations by reducing opportunities for leaving them. On average for all women, not just abused women, marital separation often leads to a significant drop in a woman's standard of living within the first year. To complicate this further, child support payments are often not made regularly, and consistent alimony payments are rare even when they are awarded (Davidson & Jenkins, 1989). Economic disparity alone amply explains why women stay in abusive relationships. Social and economic factors overall clearly indicate the need for therapeutic intervention that is progressive and addresses protection, prevention, and economic support.

A high correlation exists between substance abuse and domestic violence (Liutkus, 1994; Siegler, 1989; Tolman & Bennett, 1990; Stith, Williams, & Rosen, 1990). It is important to note that in such cases spouse abuse is very often mutual. Husbands and wives have both been found to initiate repetitive, violent interactions; however, the consequences of male physical violence are usually more profound (Siegler, 1989; Stith et al., 1990). Men who physically abuse their partners expect their partners to be subordinate to them (Stith et al., 1990). Abusive males generally adhere to traditional, stereotypic gender or sex roles and use violence to maintain power and control over the family (Petretic-Jackson & Jackson, 1996).

Men who abuse have low self-esteem, low assertiveness, and a low sense of self-efficacy and have often been exposed to childhood family violence (Tolman & Bennett, 1990). These men are especially prone to feelings of helplessness, powerlessness, and inadequacy. Abusers are often pathologically jealous, prone to addiction, and passive, dependent, and antisocial (Gelles & Cornell, 1990). Histories of sexual aggressiveness and violence toward others, poor impulse control, isolation, and poor relationship skills are also common traits (Finklehor et al., 1988). Educational level, occupational status, and income are customarily low, and in fact, unemployment or underemployment increases the likelihood of battering (Siegler, 1989; Gelles & Cornell, 1990).

Pregnancy can put a tremendous stress on a relationship, and is indeed also a factor that increases the rate of battering (Siegler, 1989; Rizk, 1988). Liutkus (1994) reported that 37 percent of pregnant women seeking obstetrical care reported battering during the term of their pregnancies. Those who abuse often tell social workers that they were provoked to violence (Edleson & Tolman, 1992; Pence, 1989). Although claims that "she drove me to it" are often made to justify abusive behavior, research suggests that such provocation is rare (Ganley, 1989). Many professionals believe that these claims likely reflect the abuser's denial of responsibility for his actions and must be challenged and refuted in order for him to progress in treatment (Edleson, 1991).

Did You Know...Although there is no consensus about the causes of domestic violence, Straus (1980) identified the following characteristics in cases of spousal abuse:
- ◆ *Husband employed part time or unemployed*
- ◆ *Spousal concerns about economic security*
- ◆ *Two or more children*
- ◆ *Spousal disagreements over children*
- ◆ *Spouses from violent families*
- ◆ *Couples married less than ten years*
- ◆ *Spouses under 30 years of age*
- ◆ *High levels of family and individual stress*
- ◆ *Spouses verbally aggressive*
- ◆ *Frequent alcohol use*
- ◆ *Residence in a neighborhood less than two years*
- ◆ *Family not part of an organized religion*
- ◆ *Wife a full-time homemaker*

When working with batterers there are two primary types of intervention often used. The first is perpetuator groups and the other is couples counseling. In the groups designed specifically for men who batter, relationship issues and the power and control relationship is clearly defined. For example, Pence and Paymar (1993) use a tool called the "Power and Control Wheel," which helps the individual identify methods of coercion such as threats, economic abuse, intimidation, emotional abuse, minimizing, denying and blaming, isolation, male privilege, and children. In couples counseling, nonviolence and equality are stressed. In this type of equality, Pence and Paynar (1993) stress negotiation and fairness, nonthreatening behavior, respect, honesty and accountability, trust and support, responsible parenting, shared responsibility, and economic partnerships.

HELPING SURVIVORS OF ABUSE

To this point we have stressed that domestic abuse is a societal and a family problem and thus needs attention from social workers trained in both macro- and micropractice. However, no practitioner should forget that "a domestic violence incident [is also] a crime and, as with other crimes, the responsibility of taking legal action against an offender should rest with the justice system" (Goolkasian, 1986, p. 3). To best help survivors of abuse social workers must be skilled in cooperating and coordinating with representatives of the criminal justice system, from police officers to prosecutors and judges.

The Criminal Justice System

To understand how the legal system treats survivors of abuse three major areas merit consideration (Parker 1985, presented in Siegler, 1989). The first is the ideology of privacy, whereby an individual's home is viewed as a private place. Acts that happen in the home are considered to have occurred in a sacred place. As long as the couple stay together in the same house the husband cannot be ordered to change his behavior (Siegler, 1989). Many judges will not evict a man from his home because they believe the old adage that "a man's home is his castle" and they believe that evicting him from his home would leave him homeless (Abbott, 1996; Mullins, 1994).

Did You Know…A woman could not legally refuse her spouse conjugal rights until the 1970s, when some states legally recognized the concept of marital rape.

The second area is the gap between written law and contemporary practice. Traditionally, the justice system has been unwilling to intercede or intrude in family matters, and society has preferred it that way. Survivors of abuse can feel helpless trying to persuade police officers and the courts to take action to control their partners; police officers, for their part, are often frustrated by women who refuse to press charges when incidents occur. In recognition of this weakness in the law the federal **Violence Against Women Act** of 1994 (VAWA) was designed to improve the response of the criminal justice system to violent crimes against women (National Resource Center, 1994).

The purpose of the VAWA is to create policies to prevent domestic violence. The VAWA treats domestic violence as a major law enforcement priority and funds improved services to victims of domestic violence. Title II of the bill, the Safe Homes Act, increases federal funding for battered women's shelters and related programs. It also provides a federal crime statute for spouse abuse committed during interstate travel (Mullins, 1994). By creating emergency and long-term solutions for battered women's housing and survival needs, the VAWA is an important step in the government's commitment to preventing domestic violence.

The third area is the complexity and lack of integration of existing legal remedies. The laws that currently exist are complex, contradictory, and at times unenforceable. The law regards property division, divorce, child custody, financial obligations, and criminal culpability as separate matters. In domestic violence cases, however, many of these issues overlap, yet because they must be addressed separately important considerations are overlooked. Although new domestic violence statutes have reduced this confusion and increased integration between jurisdictions, an abuse survivor should still have a legal representative to successfully negotiate the system (Siegler, 1989).

Police discretion in the assistance they provide used to be the most essential part of police work at the domestic violence scene. Today, however, this is changing; in many states police are now required to process charges. Policies that favor

Name: Joya Hovde

Place of residence: Cumming, Georgia

College/university degrees: Georgia State University, BSW

Present position: Child Protective Service Investigator with Hall County DFCS

Previous work/volunteer experience: 2003 Council on Social Work Education Member, 2002 NASW GA Legislative Action Committee, 2002 Georgia State University, College of Health and Human Services, Student Services Committee, 2001 Georgia State University, BSW Social Work Club, Director of Fundraising, and Philanthropy and President in 2002. 1999 MOMs Club of Smyrna, Subcommittee Chair, Community Outreach and Administrative Vice President in 2000.

What do you do in your spare time? In my spare time, I race remote controlled gas powered cars with my husband and son, play with our four dogs, make homemade jams and jellies, research the current social work literature, and attend conferences.

Why did you choose social work as a career? For me, social work just made sense. I enjoy empowering individuals to look beyond the reality of today and embrace the possibility of tomorrow.

What is your favorite social work story? February 18, 2002 in Atlanta, GA. It was NASW GA Student Lobby Day at the capital. Approximately 200 students, teachers, and other professionals from around the state of Georgia presented a united front at the capital. At noon we gathered together on the capital steps awaiting the end of the daily legislative session, in order to take a picture with the Speaker of the House Terry Coleman, Representative Nan Orrock, and Representative Sally Harrell. At the bottom of the steps was Governor Perdue. I walked up to Governor Perdue, introduced myself and asked him if I could introduce him to 200 voting social workers from around the state of Georgia, all of whom were representing NASW Georgia. The look on his face was priceless. Even though it was not on his schedule, Governor Perdue graciously took a picture with the members of NASW Georgia chapter represented on the capital steps that day.

What would be the one thing you would change in our community if you had the power to do so? I would change the perception of the individual members of the community and help them realize that the power within a democratic society lies with the voting majority.

My favorite quote is: "It is not the hand that signs the law that holds the power, it is the hand that casts the ballot." —*Harry S. Truman*

---

the arrest of abusers continue to spread even though the short-term effects of arrest on getting abusers to stop abusive behavior in the future are unknown (Roberts, 1996c). Frisch and Caruso (1996) warned, however, against the opposite extreme: even the most complete legal plan to address an abused woman's needs is useless if those responsible for carrying it out have no enforcement power.

The Role of the Social Worker

Mullarkey (1988) identified five areas in which social workers can join the criminal justice system and prosecutors to assist domestic violence survivors. Mandatory arrest policies and warrantless arrests can detain the abuser, but they do not address the entire problem (Roberts, 1996c). First, the social worker can help the system to understand the client by completing a detailed and accurate assessment thus providing more information about the type of abuse, the history of abuse, and the circumstances and repercussions of the abuse. Using this additional information the social worker can attempt to identify the most dangerous cases, screen survivors for treatment, and evaluate and predict potential treatment outcomes (Saunders, 1992). The social worker can also help the client to understand the system. Abused women have varied needs for legal services, social services, and psychological services. A well-documented community-wide approach, coordinated by the social worker, can help to integrate the efforts of mental health, social service, judicial, and law enforcement agencies for the benefit of abused women (Roberts, 1996c).

The second type of assistance the social worker can provide is education. Social workers have an obligation to educate, and to be educated by, system participants such as police telephone operators and dispatchers, police officers and staff, prosecutors, judges, and those directly involved such as the survivors, the abusers, and family and support system members. They need to be aware of pro-arrest and mandatory arrest policies and what they involve, as well as the potential of electronic monitoring as part of a coordinated community effort (Roberts, 1996c).

Social workers need to educate and train police telephone operators, dispatchers, and police officers. Operators and dispatchers are the first to receive the call for help and the officer is usually the first on the scene. This education and training should include telephone training for screening and assessment, basic techniques of police safety, and dispute management and crisis intervention techniques, as well as the ability to provide referral links with the social service worker (Fusco, 1989). Training sessions in these skills can influence police officers to take seriously their role in protecting the abused woman (Roberts, 1996c).

When conducting training the social worker is responsible for creating an atmosphere for a team intervention that reflects respect, support, cooperation, and feedback. Moreover, the social worker plays a crucial role in advocating for the rights of the client, particularly in ensuring equality of access, discouraging sex-role stereotyping, explaining the social and emotional effects of discrimination, and identifying the dynamics of victimization and other relevant psychosocial factors (Martin, 1988).

In addition to training frontline workers, education and training also should be provided to court clerks, case managers, legal advocates, and judges (Roberts, 1996a). Professionals in the legal system often focus on conviction as the primary means for accomplishing justice. The pain that the abuser has caused the female survivor, her children, and her family may be overlooked. The social worker therefore has a twofold task: the social worker needs, first, to educate people in the legal system about the dynamics and issues within the abusive situation and, second, to remind everyone to address the psychosocial effects that have occurred regardless of the legal outcome.

Activity...It is important to understand the difference between physical and psychological abuse and how best to handle the two types of situations. Break into groups and take the two case examples below. Decide whether they involve physical abuse or psychological abuse. As a social worker presented with this situation, how would you best intervene to help? What referrals would you make in each situation and for whom would the referral be made?

Scenario 1: *A verbal dispute between a husband and wife resulted in the husband threatening to get a knife and stab the wife if she tried to leave the house with the children. For fear that her husband might act on the threat, the wife did not leave.*

Scenario 2: *During an altercation a husband and wife yelled and pushed each other repeatedly. Upon being pushed down the husband hit his head, cutting it on an end table, and the wife later developed bruises on her shoulder and arms where her husband had grabbed her in anger.*

The third role that the social worker can assume is to be a "safe individual" whom the survivor can trust and feel comfortable with. One dynamic in abusive relationships is for women to become isolated from their family and friends. They have often been taught to fear and avoid contact with others outside the abusive relationship. This isolation is problematic even when a woman has started to receive relief from the legal system. This woman must face her abuser and others who may threaten retaliation if the abuser faces conviction and possible incarceration. Anticipating this outcome of the legal process may leave the survivor feeling a mixture of relief and guilt, and these contradictory emotions can hamper her testimony and make her look like an unreliable witness. To represent herself in the best possible light the survivor needs to feel supported in this process. The prosecutor is usually rushed, however, and cannot build the rapport needed to get the survivor to trust her; therefore, the social worker can be a critical bridge between the prosecutor and the survivor.

The fourth role the social worker embraces is that of advocate. This role has always been critical for social work professionals, and advocating for the survivor within the legal system through all stages of the criminal process is essential. Social workers have the right to serve as advocates for the survivor, even before an arrest is made or while a case is awaiting trial or on appeal (Mullarkey, 1988). The role of the survivor's advocate (a.k.a. victim's advocate) is to assist the client in acting as her own representative whenever possible (Martin, 1988). When it is not possible—perhaps because the survivor is too distraught or is incapacitated by the fear of retribution—the advocate can speak with the client's permission. Many states now permit the survivor or the survivor's advocate to address the judge at sentencing (Mullarkey, 1988).

The successful advocate for a domestically abused woman must address two important tasks. The first is recognizing and preparing for the complexities of the legal system. The social worker needs to make himself aware of the variety of system components that are involved—in particular, law enforcement procedures, prosecution, and corrections. The second task is advocacy with family members and the support system to which the client will return. Many myths and beliefs about the survivors of domestic violence are ingrained in our society (Roberts, 1996b), and clients may be forced to confront myths subscribed to by family and friends.

The social worker can assist the survivor in this by telling people in the support system 1) about the strengths of the survivor, 2) the reason it was necessary for her to leave the abusive relationship, and 3) the reason she should put a formal end to abuse and request legally sanctioned punishment for the abuser.

The fifth role the social worker plays is expert witness. The social worker can provide professional information to clarify the meaning of the survivor's behavior (Saunders, 1992; Martin, 1988). Although social workers welcome any opportunity to assist their clients, they may worry that acting as a witness will compromise their duty to protect their client's legal rights. Counseling sessions and written notes may contain information that the social worker does not want to share because its disclosure might harm the survivor's case. For example, many times the survivor is angry with the abuser and voices this anger in an attempt to gain emotional distance from the abuser. The social worker should nevertheless always take careful case notes, though well aware that these notes can be subpoenaed by a court of law. "The constitutional guarantee to confront accusers provided by the sixth amendment can be interpreted by any competent court to override any privacy statute or shield law" (Mullarkey, 1988, p. 49).

Without a court order, social workers are not required to speak to defendants, attorneys, or investigators outside of the courtroom. Mullarkey (1988) recommended that when social workers are summoned to court they recognize the importance of 1) appearing and being professional and nonpartisan, 2) answering all questions directly or fully, 3) immediately asking for clarification of unclear

---

Activity...In the classroom, break into small groups of three or more students. As a group look at the six goals for domestic violence programs listed below and choose the three most important goals. Compare your group's choices with those of the other groups. Was it difficult for your group to agree? Why? Why not?

Goals for Domestic Violence Programs

1. To ensure safe surroundings for survivors and their children
2. To increase access to material resources—income, housing, food, etc.
3. To establish and enhance legal supports
4. To build social contacts and support networks for survivors and their children
5. To change societal beliefs about domestic violence
6. To create a model for relationships of shared power and leadership (adapted from Roche & Sadoski, 1996).

questions, 4) going over possible questions with the prosecutor before testifying, and 5) ensuring that every note, professional conversation, and report they have prepared is discoverable by the defendant and his legal representatives.

PRACTICE APPLICATION: THE ROLE OF THE WOMEN'S SHELTER SOCIAL WORKER

Susan and her husband have been together for ten years. During that time she has been beaten severely and treated in the local hospital emergency room. Much

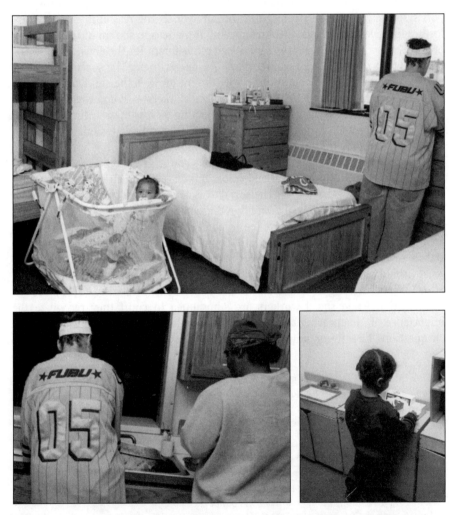

Figures 1a, b, c: These are photographs taken in a shelter for women and children who are victims of domestic abuse. The bedroom with two beds and two bunk beds may be used for one or two families. The women are cleaning up after lunch in the communal kitchen. The child is in a play area. The center is staffed by childcare workers who care for the children while mothers go to work, look for work, or go to counseling.

of the abuse between the couple is reported to be mutual; however, Susan's husband has never been hospitalized for her return attacks. On several occasions Susan has called the police to intervene, but when they arrived on the domestic violence scene, she usually refuses to press charges. Susan has stated that she once began to press charges but soon dropped them when her husband called from jail to tell her that he loved her and to beg her forgiveness. The police are being dispatched to the scene so often that they refer to Susan and her husband by their first names.

Susan has tried to leave her husband several times but he always tracks her down and persuades her to return. Susan's family is well aware of the abuse. Both Susan's mother and her sister have started to refuse her calls asking for help. Susan often calls them when she and her husband are fighting, asking for an "understanding ear or a safe place to stay." Her family is frustrated because no matter what they do Susan always seems to return to the abusive situation. Also, whenever they do take Susan in, her husband arrives and tries to intimidate her mother. Susan's mother doesn't think her health is strong enough to handle the repeated stress.

On a referral from her employer, Susan has confided in a shelter social worker that she feels lost and abandoned. During the second session Susan tells the social worker that she wants to kill her husband. When asked how she would do it, Susan immediately breaks down and cries that she would probably be better off killing herself. The event that precipitated Susan's crisis is a fight that she and her husband had the previous night. Susan's husband insisted that she climb a ladder and help him paint the house. Susan refused because she is four months pregnant and is afraid of heights. Her husband then hit her with the ladder across her back.

Based on the information Susan provides the social worker is able to make the following assessment. First, Susan is being beaten regularly. Second, she fears for her life and is threatening to take the life of another. Third, Susan has alienated her family and has no support system available to her. Last, she is threatening to take her own life. The social worker feels that immediate intervention is essential to help Susan to adjust to her current situation without violence to herself or others. First, the social worker explores the possibility of inpatient admission. Since Susan has no medical insurance and none of the local facilities have an empty bed, the worker forms another plan.

The social worker helps Susan gain admission to the local shelter for abused women. Shelter personnel are notified of Susan's possible desire to end her life and a suicide watch is implemented. Intensive individual and group counseling resources are made available. With the help and support of the social worker an order of protection is filed. Susan decides to press charges against her husband, and asks the social worker to help her to state her case to an attorney; the social worker agrees. Susan does press charges this time and her husband is sentenced to two years in prison with the possibility of parole in six months. After she regains the recognition and assistance of her family, Susan moves to another city and stays with her aunt. Before leaving, Susan has started making plans to give up her child for adoption.

Discussion. In this case the social worker played a twofold role. First, the social worker found a safe environment where the client received help in dealing with her crisis. The social worker also provided counseling and supportive services. Second, the social worker helped the client to create and carry out a plan of action in her dealings with the legal system. Women who have been abused by their spouses or partners need supportive services. In addition, they need the assistance of this country's legal institutions. These women need to know the following: 1) that legal services are available to them, 2) that supportive services such as those provided by a social worker are available, and 3) that the combined use of these services will alleviate and eventually resolve the situation. The role of the social work professional is crucial. Whether working within the criminal justice system itself or outside the system in an ancillary agency, the social worker can make a true difference for a survivor of domestic abuse.

SUMMARY

Women who survive abuse need all the services and protection that law enforcement can provide. They also need to be treated with respect. Social workers play a crucial role by providing the following services to survivors of abuse. First, they complete detailed assessments that give information about the type of abuse, the history of abuse, and the circumstances and repercussions of the abuse. Second, they actively educate and are educated by law enforcement and justice system participants and people directly involved, such as survivors, abusers, and family and support system members. Third, they act as safe individuals whom survivors can trust. Fourth, they advocate for survivors through all stages of the criminal prosecution. Last, they assist prosecutors and aid survivors by acting as expert witnesses.

Social workers must strive to develop a team approach with the legal professionals involved. These professionals must be trained to view domestic assault situations as appropriate and routine targets of police intervention. Representatives of the legal system and social workers can work together, each an integral part of the intervention team. The criminal justice system can be an effective force in decreasing violence against women. Both short-term emergency support and long-term support services are needed (Davis, Hagen, & Early, 1994). Counseling, social service assistance, and protection must be carefully coordinated and available to the abuse survivor twenty-four hours a day (Fusco, 1989; Roberts, 1996c). Morning or next-day referrals are a poor substitute for an immediate response to the crisis. Social work professionals need to be available to work directly with police and to start intervention services at the crisis scene or as soon after the incident as possible. Our current system of referral "after the fact" is not meeting the needs of many survivors of abuse.

The domestic violence shelter can offer an "immediate" safe place for women who wish to escape an abusive situation. Unfortunately, however, the number of existing shelters is far from adequate (Dziegielewski et al., 1996). There are few shelters convenient for women in rural areas, and attempts to establish emergency shelters for battered women in cities still meet a variety of obstacles. Before a facility is granted approval a review of proposed property use by community boards and city planners is required in many cities. However, this requirement may compromise the confidentiality of the women and children who depend on the emergency shelter for services and so risk their safety. In addition, many community residents object to having emergency shelters in their neighborhoods because they believe such facilities are disruptive (Mullins, 1994).

Social workers must participate in and help to establish brief time-limited practice strategies (Dziegielewski, 1996, 1997). Also, schools of social work must address this topic and help the beginning social work professional to feel academically prepared (Danis, 2003). The purpose of these programs and policies is to immediately ease the severity of domestic violence as well as to develop long-term solutions to the need for emergency housing and financial support systems. One advance in this direction was the 1994 Violence Against Women Act.

Until recently, our society and our laws have treated the preservation of the family as paramount. Fortunately, this is changing. We must break from our history of preserving the family at any cost—even the cost of exposing women to abuse. Because social workers practice across the public and private sectors, they have enormous potential for influencing approaches to the problem of violence against women (Martin, 1988; NASW, 2003). The profession must demand changes in our laws and legal system that will prevent domestic violence. Social workers clearly recognize the importance of counseling and supportive services. However, to plan for the future, they must never lose sight of the importance of social policy change in assisting the survivors of domestic violence.

References

Abbott, A. A. (1996). Epilogue: Helping battered women. In A. R. Roberts (Ed.), *Helping battered women: New perspectives and remedies* (pp. 235–239). New York: Oxford University Press.

Constantino, C. (1981). Intervention with battered women: The lawyer social worker team. *Social Work, 26*(6), 456–460.

Davis, L., Hagen, J., & Early, T. (1994). Social services for battered women: Are they adequate, accessible, and appropriate? *Social Work, 39* (6), 695–704.

Danis, F. S. (2003). Social work response to domestic violence: Encouraging news from a new look. *Affillia, 18*, 177–191.

Dwyer, D. C., Smokowski, P. R., Bricout, J. C., & Wodarski, J. S. (1996). Domestic violence and woman battering: Theories and practice implications. In A. R. Roberts (Ed.), *Helping battered women: New perspectives and remedies* (pp. 67–82). New York: Oxford University Press

Dziegielewski, S. F. (1996). Managed care principles: The need for social work in the health care environment. *Crisis Intervention and Time-Limited Treatment, 3* (2), 97–110.

Dziegielewski, S. F. (1997). Time-limited brief therapy: The state of practice. *Crisis Intervention and Time-Limited Treatment, 3* (3), 217–228.

Dziegielewski, S. F., & Resnick, C. (1996). Crisis intervention in the shelter setting. In A. R. Roberts (Ed.), *Crisis management and brief treatment* (pp. 123–141). Chicago: Nelson Hall.

Dziegielewski, S. F., Resnick, C., & Krause, N. B. (1996). Shelter based crisis intervention with abused women. In R. Roberts (Ed.), *Helping battered women: New perspectives and remedies* (pp. 159–171). New York: Oxford University Press.

Edleson, J. L. (1991, June). Note on history: Social worker's intervention in woman abuse, 1907–1945. *Social Service Review*, pp. 304–313.

Edleson, J. L., & Tolman, R. M. (1992). *Intervention with men who batter: An ecological approach*. Newbury Park, CA: Sage.

Favor, C. A., & Strand, E. B. (2003). Domestic violence and animal cruelty: Untangling the web of abuse. *Journal of Social Work education, 39* (2), 237–253.

Finkelhor, D. (1988). *Stopping family violence*. Newbury Park, CA: Sage.

Frisch, L. A., & Caruso, J. M. (1996). In A. R. Roberts (Ed.), *Helping battered women: New perspectives and remedies* (pp. 102–131). New York: Oxford University Press.

Fusco, L. J. (1989). Integrating systems: Police, courts and assaulted women. In B. Pressman, G. Cameron, & M. Rothery (Eds.), *Intervening with assaulted women: Current theory, research and practice* (pp. 125–135). Hillsdale, NJ: Erlbaum.

Ganley, A. L. (1989). Integrating feminist and social learning analyses of aggression: Creating multiple models for intervention with men who batter. In P. L. Caesar & L. K. Hamberger (Eds.), *Treating men who batter*. New York: Springer.

Gelles, R. J. (1979). Violence in the American family. *Journal of Social Issues, 35* (1), 15–39.

Gelles, R. J. (1987). *The violent home*. Thousand Oaks, CA: Sage.

Gelles, R. J., & Cornell, C. P. (1990). *Intimate violence in families*. Thousand Oaks, CA: Sage.

Gelles, R. J., & Harrop, J. W. (1989). Violence, battering, and psychological distress among women. *Journal of Interpersonal Violence, 4* (4), 400–420.

Gutierrez, L. M. (1987, Summer), Social work theories and practice with battered women: A conflict-of-values analysis. *Affilia*, pp. 36–52.

Jones, A. (1994). *Next time she'll be dead: Battering and how to stop it*. Boston: Beacon.

Litsky, M. (1994). Reforming the criminal justice system can decrease violence against women. In B. Leone, B. Szumski, K. de Koster, K. Swisher, C. Wekesser, & W. Barbour (Eds.), *Violence against women*. San Diego, CA: Greenhaven.

Liutkus, J. F. (1994, April). Wife assault: An issue for women's health. *Internal Medicine, 7*, 41–53.

Mancoske, R. J., Standifer, D., & Cauley, C. (1994). The effectiveness of brief counseling services for battered women. *Research on Social Work Practice, 4* (1), 53–63.

Martin, M. (1988). A social worker's response. In N. Hutchings (Ed.) *The violent family: Victimization of women, children, and elders*. New York: Human Science Press.

Mullarkey, E. (1988). The legal system for victims of violence. In N. Hutchings (Ed.), *The violent family: Victimization of women, children, and elders* (pp. 43–52). New York: Human Science Press.

Mullins, G. P. (1994). The battered woman and homelessness. *Journal of Law and Policy, 3* (1), 237–255.

National Association of Social Workers (NASW). (2003). Family violence policy statement. In *Social work speaks*. Washington, D.C.: NASW Press.

National Clearinghouse for the Defense of Battered Women. (September, 1995). Statistics Packet 3rd Ed. Retrieved October 26, 2003 from www.actabuse.com/dvstats

National Resource Center on Domestic Violence and the Battered Women's Justice Project. (1994, September). The Violence Against Women Act 1994. Available from the National Resource Center, 6400 Flank Drive, Suite 1300, Harrisburg, PA 17112-2778.

Pence, E., & Paymar, M. (1993). *Education groups for men who batter*. New York: Springer.

Petretic-Jackson, P. A., & Jackson, T. (1996). Mental health interventions with battered women. In A. R. Roberts (Ed.), *Helping battered women: New perspectives and remedies* (pp. 188–221). New York: Oxford University Press.

Rennison, C. M., & Welchans, S. (2000). *Intimate partner violence*. Retrieved August 3, 2003 from http:///www.ojp.usdoj.gov/bjs/pub/pdf/ipv.pdf

Rizk, M. (1988, April). Domestic violence during pregnancy. In *Proceedings Family Violence: Public Health Social Work's Role in Prevention* (pp. 19–31). Pittsburgh, PA: Department of Health and Human Services, Bureau of Maternal and Child Health.

Roberts, A. R. (1996a). Court responses to battered women. In A. R. Roberts (Ed.), *Helping battered women: New perspectives and remedies* (pp. 96–101). New York: Oxford University Press.

Roberts, A. R. (1996b). Introduction: Myths and realities regarding battered women. In A. R. Roberts (Ed.), *Helping battered women: New perspectives and remedies* (pp. 3–12). New York: Oxford University Press.

Roberts, A. R. (1996c). Police responses to battered women: Past, present and future. In A. R. Roberts (Ed.), *Helping battered women: New perspectives and remedies* (pp. 85–95). New York: Oxford University Press.

Roche, S. E., & Sadoski, P. J. (1996). Social action for battered women. In A. R. Roberts (Ed.), *Helping battered women: New perspectives and remedies*. New York: Oxford University Press.

Saunders, D. G. (1992). Woman battering. In R. T. Ammerman & M. Hersen (Eds.), *Assessment of family violence: A clinical and legal source book*. New York: Wiley.

Schneider, E. M. (1994). Society's belief in family privacy contributes to domestic violence. In B. Leone, B. Szumski, K. de Koster, K. Swisher, C. Wekesser, & W. Barbour (Eds.), *Violence against women*. San Diego, CA: Greenhaven.

Siegler, R. T. (1989). *Domestic violence in context: An assessment of community attitudes*. Lexington, MA: Heath.

Sorenson, S. B. (2003). Funding public health: The public's willingness to pay for domestic violence prevention programming. *American Journal of Public Health, 93* (11), 1934–1938.

Srinivasan, M., & Davis, L. V. (1991). A shelter: An organization like any other? *Affilila, 6* (1), 38–57.

Statman, J. B. (1990). *The battered woman's survival guide: Breaking the cycle*. Dallas: Taylor.

Stith, S. M., Williams, M. B., & Rosen, K. (1990). *Violence hits home: Comprehensive treatment approaches to domestic violence*. New York: Springer.

Straus, M. (1980). A sociological perspective on the causes of family violence. In M. R. Green (Ed.), *Violence and the family* (pp. 7–31). Boulder, CO: Westview.

Tolman, R. M., & Bennett, L. W. (1990). A review of quantitative research on men who batter. *Journal of Interpersonal Violence, 5* (1), 87–118.

Wilke, D. J., & Vinton, L. (2003). Domestic violence and aging: Teaching about their intersection. *Journal of Social Work Education, 39* (2), 225–235.

Chapter 13

The Political Arena

THINK FOR A MOMENT ABOUT POLITICS AND THE GLAMOUR OF being an elected politician. Think about the movie *Mr. Smith Goes to Washington*, in which Jimmy Stewart plays a young, idealistic politician who goes to Washington to represent the people and do what is right. As he embraces this mission he truly believes that government is the friend of all the people, works for all the people, and represents all the people. He believes that elected leaders are simply an extension of our neighbors who act on our behalf and place the community's need above their personal interests. Their overriding purpose is to help achieve what is best for the country. Do you hold this view of politics and the government? We suspect not. It's likely that few people today believe that Mr. Smith's idealistic vision accurately depicts the motivations of politicians in the late twentieth and early twenty-first centuries.

For many of us the political arena is not an enticing place. Politics may conjure up ideas of backroom deal making, abuses of rank and power, payoffs, and other unethical activities. Political scandals and allegations of wrongdoing over the past few years have reached every level of political office and branch of the government. It's not surprising if you hold politics in low esteem.

Before going any further, let's clarify what we mean by politics. Certainly, politics and the political arena include all elected offices and the officials who fill them, at the local, county, state, and federal levels. This arena is often referred to as "electoral politics." This classification, however, doesn't include what some would call "informal politics," which involves politically charged or motivated behavior in organizations, agencies, and even on social work practice teams. How often have you heard someone say "the politics here stink" or "they're just playing politics" or "you have to understand the politics of the situation"? Therefore, what we refer to as "politics" is diverse and embraces many of our day-to-day activities. Indeed, Haynes and Mickelson (1991) have gone further, contending that "all social work is political" (p. 21). In this chapter we look at electoral politics and its relation to social work practice. Our discussion examines political strategies that we hope can serve as a primer for social workers on politics and political activities.

WHY POLITICS AND SOCIAL WORK?

First, let's take a brief look at the political arena and its relation to social service agencies. What guides the activities of social workers in agencies? Workers are

Name: Carrie Marie Sullivan

Place of residence: Boston, Massachusetts

College/university degrees: Florida International University, BA, Boston College, MSW

Present position: Community Affairs Director for Massachusetts State Senator Dave Magnani.

Previous work/volunteer experience: Mentor at Miami-Dade Halfway House, and at a Child Enrichment Center for foster care children in Miami, Florida, Community Liaison at a child-care resource center in Cambridge, Massachusetts, volunteer cook at a soup kitchen for the homeless in Ft. Lauderdale, Florida.

What do you do in your spare time? Almost five years ago, I became actively involved with saving abandoned dogs from shelters throughout the eastern United States. Three years ago, I began my own rescue organization specializing in saving and re-homing dogs, mostly, Labrador Retrievers. To date, I have placed over 300 dogs, that were destined to die in shelters, into loving homes.

Why did you choose social work as a career? The study of human relations has always interested me and I really enjoy working with people. When I found out that I could obtain an MSW concentrating in community organization and public policy, I knew immediately that I wanted to work in public office. As a social worker, I understand social problems and I am committed to social justice. I know how policies affect individuals and communities and I see the opportunity to make changes on a broader scale. Social workers make the best politicians because they are committed to improving the quality of life for people.

What is your favorite social work story? Everyday, I speak with people who feel helpless. When I first started working in government, I received a call from an elderly woman who could no longer afford to pay her bills. Like most senior citizens, this woman was on a fixed income and because of rising property taxes, she was being taxed right out of her home. After hearing the fear in her voice, I made a few phone calls and was able to put her in touch with a local agency that, in turn, was able to help her. A few weeks later, I received a thank-you card from this woman thanking me for helping her maintain her dignity and independence.

What would be the one thing you would change in our community if you had the power to do so? There are so many people who lack empowerment and do not know that they have a voice. I would empower these people to speak their feelings and to fight for what they believe in. People also seem to have a limited perception of the social work profession, therefore, I would also encourage people to be more open-minded and to realize that the profession of social work is within every facet of life.

not able to take liberties in their practice and provide any type of service they see fit. An agency's function clearly dictates what the practitioner can do with and on behalf of a client. Let's say, for example, that a practitioner in a child welfare agency wants to offer group therapy to senior citizens in a local housing project. The intervention may be worthy, but the agency is likely to decide that a senior's group falls outside its purpose and function.

An agency's function is set forth in its mission statement and operationalized by its policies. Policies do not just spring forth; rather they are the result of a political process, be it an agency board of directors or an elected body such as a state legislature. And who are these people? Are they social workers? Are they really expert enough in human services that they should be shaping social work practice? Unfortunately, many people who develop social policies have little, if any, direct social work experience, and few have an educational background in social work. When professional social workers choose to avoid the political aspects of the field, one outcome is inevitable: people who are not social workers will govern social work practice.

Activity...Find out how many social workers there are in your state legislature, both the house and senate. You can do this by checking with your state's secretary of state's office. Then look at the house and senate committees that oversee social problems; they may have titles like Committee on Health and Human Services. Now, look to see how many committee members are social workers. Now look at their staffs how many staff members are social workers? What do your findings tell you about the development of social policies in your state?

SOCIAL WORK VALUES AND POLITICAL ACTIVITY

Some social workers allow negative images of politics and political activity to outweigh their responsibility to engage in the political arena. Yet the NASW Code of Ethics clearly states our obligations and political responsibilities in two separate places in section 6, "The Social Worker's Ethical Responsibilities to Society":

Social workers should facilitate informed participation by the public in shaping social policies and institutions. (sec. 6.02)

Social workers should . . . advocate for changes in policy and legislation to improve social conditions in order to . . . promote social justice. (sec. 6.04(a))

CSWE accreditation standards also support the profession's political involvement. To be accredited BSW and MSW programs must include in their curricula such political content as knowledge of political systems, including how policies are formulated and how their content can be influenced. The Curriculum Policy Statement states specifically:

Students must be taught to analyze current social policy within the context of historical and contemporary factors that shape policy. Content must be presented about the political and organizational processes used to influence policy, the process of policy formulation, and the framework for analyzing policies in light of the principles of social and economic justice (CSWE, 2001, pp. 9, 11).

Why do the Code of Ethics and the CSWE accreditation standards emphasize practitioner involvement in the political arena? First and foremost, remember that the definition of social work includes working to bring about a just community built on the tenets of social and economic equality. Second, many of the problems experienced by clients are created by forces external to the client and can be remedied only through amended social policy or additional funding for social services. Third, the best advocates for change are those who deal with problems day in and day out. Through direct practice, social workers see firsthand the debilitating effects of problems on clients.

A HISTORICAL OVERVIEW OF POLITICAL ACTIVITY BY SOCIAL WORKERS

Social work has had three separate but significant waves of political involvement: the Progressive Era of the nineteenth century, the 1930s New Deal, and the 1960s War on Poverty. In each of these periods, social work's involvement in politics mirrored the profession's growth and internal conflict over mission, scope, and function. In all three periods, leaders disagreed about the causes of social problems and how best to solve them. The Progressive movement was attractive to many social workers and provided a political focus for their philosophical beliefs and commitments. Jane Addams and Florence Kelley, among others, used the political system to address social problems. Settlement house workers seemed to be more partisan than other social workers. Weismiller and Rome (1995) have noted that settlement workers ran political campaigns, organized neighborhoods to support particular candidates, lobbied, and worked on welfare reform. On the other hand, Mary Richmond, a leader in the COS movement, believed that social workers should be nonpartisan and confine their efforts to helping clients to resolve their individual issues (Weismiller & Rome, 1995).

The Great Depression of the 1930s created ample opportunity for social workers to again venture into the political arena. Schools of social work were more organized than their forerunners during the Progressive Era and macrocontent, which touched on political concerns, was included in the curriculum. The federal government's Children's Bureau and Women's Bureau provided social workers with a setting in which to address social issues. In fact, many parts of the Economic Security Act of 1935 were written by social workers (Weismiller & Rome, 1995). The profession was beginning to accept political activism as an appropriate response to crisis; however, it still did not embrace political activity as an appropriate long-term social work methodology (Haynes & Mickelson, 2002).

The third wave of political activism by social workers came in the 1960s. With the emergence of the Peace Corps and VISTA, a domestic version of the Peace Corps program, and the burgeoning civil rights movement, social workers actively promoted a political agenda. Community organization, both as a practice and an educational specialization, took shape in the late 1950s and 1960s. This activity challenged social workers to view systems from the much broader macroprospective. Federal dollars were funneled to initiatives that encouraged neighborhoods and local people to engage in problem solving and community action.

Within the profession, debate continued on the role and scope of political activity. Weismiller and Rome (1995) have reported that NASW members in one study agreed to pay increased dues if it brought about greater political activity by members. Yet this somewhat over zealous characterization didn't nearly affect the entire profession, and members continued to debate the merits of efforts at the political level, particularly in light of the massive problems facing individuals and families.

Did You Know...A social worker, Senator Barbara Mikulski (D-Maryland), was a keynote speaker during the 1992 Democratic National Convention.

In 1976, NASW organized its first conference on politics, in Washington, DC. Aimed primarily at social work political activists, the meeting gathered NASW members from around the country for a political training institute. NASW then supplemented this national meeting with regional institutes. NASW continues to sponsor these meetings approximately every two years.

The 1990s seemed to be a watershed decade for social workers involved in electoral politics. Never before in the profession's history were social workers and their professional organizations as active in political campaigns as in the last decade of the twentieth century. "Lift Up America" was the NASW's 1992 Presidential Project theme, augmented by numerous national, regional, and state election activities (Landers, 1992); and NASW's political action committee, Political Action for Candidate Election (PACE), endorsed more than one hundred candidates for national office (Hiratsuka, 1992) and contributed approximately $200,000 to national campaigns while state PACE committees dispensed in excess of $160,000 to state and local candidates (D. Dempsey, personal communication, November 30, 1992; Dempsey, 1993).

In 1991, NASW reported that 113 social workers held elected office (Weismiller & Rome, 1995); by 1992, 165 known social workers in forty-three states had won a variety of races (NASW, 1992); and by 1998, there were more than 200 known social workers holding political office in the nation! They held elected office at all levels of government from city council to the U.S. Senate. With each succeeding election, individual social workers and their professional associations gained new experiences, built on previous knowledge, and strengthened themselves as active players in the political arena. And as recently as 2003, 175 social workers nationwide held a variety of local, state and federal offices (see table 1).

Table 1: Social Workers in State and Local Office 2003

State	Name	Party	Title	District	City/Council/School
AK	Bettye Davis	D	State Senator	District K	East Anchorage
AK	Rose Beck	N/P	City Council Member		Homer
AL	Ethel Hall	D	State Board of Education	District 4	
AL	Luke Cooley	R	Probate Judge		Houston County
AL	Peggy Givhan	R	District Judge		Montgomery County
AR	Janice Judy	D	State Representative	District 92	Fayetteville
AR	Jim Medley	R	State Representative	District 64	Fort Smith
AZ	Peter Rios	D	State Senator	District 23	Hayden
AZ	Jorge Luis Garcia	D	State Senator	27	Tucson
CA	Erica Quijada-Barrera	N/P	School Board Member		Compton
CA	Alice Lai-Bitker		Board of Supervisors	District 3	Alameda County
CA	Patty Berg	D	State Assemblywoman	District 1	Sebastapol
CA	Gail Jones	N/P	School Board Member	Area 6	Alameda County
CA	Gloria Cortez Keene	N/P	Board of Supervisors	District 1	Merced County
CA	Victoria Deane	N/P	School Board Trustee	Area 4	Sacramento County
CA	Lara Larramendi Blakely	N/P	Mayor		Monrovia
CO	K. Jerry Frangas	D	State Representative		Denver
CT	Toni Edmunds-Walker	D	State Representative	District 93	New Haven
CT	Christopher Donovan	D	State Representative	District 84	Meriden
CT	Kenneth Green	D	State Representative	District 1	Hartford
CT	Edith Prague	D	State Senator	District 19	Norwich
CT	Kathleen Fox	D	Town Meeting Member		Branford
DC	Tommy Wells	N/P	School Board Member	District 3	Washington, DC
DE	Ted Blunt	D	City Council President		Wilmington
FL	Mandy Dawson	D	State Senator	District 29	Fort Lauderdale
FL	Edward B. Bullard	D	State Representative	District 118	Miami
FL	Daisy W. Lynum	D	City Council/Mayor Pro Tem	District 5	Orlando
FL	Suzanne Gunzburger	D	Commissioner		Broward
GA	Barbara Mobley	D	State Representative	District 58	DeKalb County
GA	Sally Harrell	D	State Representative	District 54	DeKalb County
HI	Haunani Apoliona	N/P	Office of Hawaiian Affairs		U. of Hawaii
IA	Susan Kosche Vallem	N/P	Hospital Board of Trustees		Waverly
IA	Mark Smith	D	State Representative	District 43	Marshalltown
IA	Geri Huser	D	State Representative	District 42	Altoona
IA	Robert "Robin" Thomas	N/P	Extension Service Council		Des Moines/Burlington
IA	Romaine "Ro" Foege	D	State Representative	District 29	Mt. Vernon
IA	Donna L. Smith	D	CountySupervisor	District 27	Dubuque
IA	Rachelle Colson LaMaster		School Board Member		Washington Community
IA	Maggie Tinsman	R	State Senator	District 41	Davenport
IL	Karen R. Adamczyk	N/P	School Board President	District 92	Will County
IL	Susan Rose	N/P	Alderman		Elmhurst
IL	Helen Schaeffer	N/P	Park District Board		Park Ridge
IL	Ken Dunkin	D	State Representative	District 5	
IL	Christine Radogno	R	State Senator	District 41	Cook County

Table 1: Social Workers in State and Local Office 2003 — (*Continued*)

State	Name	Party	Title	District	City/Council/School
IN	Debra Marsh-Niccum		Township Trustee		Cass County
KS	Nancy Kirk	D	State Representative	District 56	Topeka
KY	Jim Wayne	D	State Representative	District 35	Louisville
KY	Tina Ward-Pugh	D	Councilwoman	District 9	Louisville
KY	Paul Bather	D	State Representative	District 43	Louisville
KY	Dolores Delahanty	D	Commissioner	District C	Jefferson County
KY	Susan Westrom	D	State Representative	District 79	Lexington
LA	Nancy Broussard	D	School Board Member	District K	Iberville Parish
LA	Lori Williams	R	City Council Member		Denham Springs
LA	Irma Dixon	D	Public Service Commissioner	District 3	New Orleans
LA	Sol Gothard	D	Appellate Court Judge	District 5	New Orleans
LA	Martha G. Forbes	D	State Central Committee		Baton Rouge
LA	Cheryl Mills	D	School Board Member	District 1	Orleans Parish
LA	Dianne Peabody	D	School Board Member	District 4	St. Francesville
MA	Vincent A. Pedone	D	State Representative	District 15	
MA	Judith Zabin	D	Town Meeting Member		Lexington
MA	Helen Cherlupsky	D	School Committee Member		Brookline
MA	Carolyn Perry	D	Planning Board Member		Sunderland Cnty/City
MA	Sarah "Sally" Parker	D	Town Meeting Member		Arlington
MA	Karen Browning	D	Town Meeting Member	Precinct 6	Belmont
MA	Sallye Bleiberg	D	Town Meeting Member	Precinct 3	Belmont
MA	Douglas Peterson	D	State Representative	District 8	Swampscott
MA	Henrietta Davis	D	Vice Mayor		Cambridge
MA	Sara Henesey		School Board Member		Hingham
MA	Mary DeChitto		School Board Member		Swampscott
MD	Agnes Welch	D	City Council Member	District 4	Baltimore
MD	Salima Siler Marriott	D	State Delegate	District 40	Baltimore
MD	Melony Ghee Griffith	D	State Representative	District 25	Prince George's County
ME	Michael F. Brennan	D	State Senator	District 27	Falmouth
ME	Lynn Bromley	D	State Senator	District 30	South Portland
ME	Joseph C. Brannigan	D	State Representative	District 35	Portland
ME	Thomas J. Kane	D	State Representative	District 16	Saco
ME	Marie Laverriere-Boucher	D	State Representative	District 18	Biddeford
MI	Burton Leland	D	State Senator	District 5	Detroit
MI	Barbara Levin Bergman	D	Commissioner	District 8	Washtenaw County
MI	Ellen Ryder-Petre	R	Township Trustee		Thomas
MI	Jacquelin Washington	D	Board of Governors		Wayne State University
MI	Maryann Mahaffey	N/P	City Council		Detroit
MI	Sharon Gire	D	State Board of Education		Clinton Township
MN	Rafael Ortega	N/P	CountyCommission Chair	District 5	Ramsey County
MN	Ranna LeVoir	N/P	Board of Education		Maple Lake
MN	Julie Ann Sjorstand	N/P	Board of Education		Lancaster
MN	Becky A. Montgomery	N/P	School Board Chair		St. Paul
MN	Sheldon Johnson	DFL	State Representative	District 67B	St. Paul

Table 1: Social Workers in State and Local Office 2003—(*Continued*)

State	Name	Party	Title	District	City/Council/School
MN	Rita Elfering	N/P	Board of Education		
MN	Neal Cheng Thao	N/P	Board of Education		St. Paul
MN	Kathleen Blatz	N/P	Chief Justice, Supreme Court		St. Paul
MO	Margaret Donnelly	D	State Representative	District 73	St. Louis
MS	Mamie Chinn	D	Justice Court Judge		Canton
MS	Joe T. Grist, Jr.	D	State Representative	District 23	
MS	Dr. Gemma Beckley	D	City Council Member		Holly Springs
MS	Carrie Moulds	D	Alderman		Lucedale
MS	Catherine Jones	D	School Board Member		Starkville
MT	Rosalie "Rosie" Buzzas	D	State Representative	District 65	Missoula
MT	Jolie Fish		City Council Member		Columbia Falls
NC	Edith Wiggins	N/P	Town Council Member		Chapel Hill
NC	Benjamin Ruffin	N/P	Board of Governors		U. of North Carolina
NC	Louise Woods	N/P	Board of Education	District 4	Charlotte/Mecklenberg
NC	Wilhelmina Rembert	N/P	Board of Education		Charlotte/Mecklenberg
NC	Stephen Wilkens	D	Town Commissioner		Hudson
NC	Carl Mumpower	R	City Council		Asheville
NC	Jacquelyn Gist	N/P	Alderman		Carrboro
ND	Tim Mathern	D	State Senator	District 11	Fargo
NH	James MacKay	R	State Representative	District 39	Merrimack County
NH	Barbara Richardson	D	State Representative	District 26	Cheshire County
NJ	Louise Murray	N/P	School Board Member	Morris	Morristown
NM	Mary Jane M. Garcia	D	State Senator	District 36	Dona Ana
NV	Myrna Williams	D	Commissioner	District E	Clark County
NV	Gary Waters	N/P	State Board of Education		
NV	David E. Humke	R	Commissioner		Washoe County
NY	Betty Williams	N/P	Civil Court	District 7	Brooklyn
NY	Fran Knapp	D	CountyLegislator		Dutchess County
NY	Joseph Sanfilippo	D	City Council Member	District 4	Binghamton
NY	Lydia Chang	N/P	School Board Member	District 30	Queens
NY	Angela Petty	D	City Council Member	Third Ward	Rome
NY	Henrietta Lodge	N/P	School Board President		Pawling
NY	C. Virginia Fields	D	Borough President		Manhattan
NY	Vito Lopez	D	State Assembly	District 53	Kings County
NY	Patricia Eddington	D	State Assembly	District 3	Patchogue
NY	Symra Brandon	D	City Council Member	District 1	Yonkers
NY	Earlene Hill Hooper	D	State Assembly	District 18	Hempstead
NY	Katharine O'Connell	D	Common Council, Majority Ldr		Syracuse
OH	Barbara A. Sykes	D	State Representative	District 44	
OH	Tina Skeldon Wozniak		City Council		Toledo
OH	David C. Crowley		City Council		Cincinnati

Table 1: Social Workers in State and Local Office 2003—(*Continued*)

State	Name	Party	Title	District	City/Council/School
OH	Jack Ford		Mayor		Toledo
OH	Patricia Britt	D	City Council Member	Ward 6	Cleveland
OK	Ann Simank	D	City Council Member	Ward 6	Oklahoma City
OR	Carolyn Tomei	D	State Representative	District 41	
PA	Joan Cashin	D	Borough Council Member		Wyalusing
PA	Allyson Y. Schwartz	D	State Senator	District 4	
RI	Michael Reeves	D	School Committee		Coventry
RI	Rita Williams	D	City Council		Providence
RI	Stephen S. Mueller	D	School Committee		West Kingston
RI	Roger Picard	D	State Representative	District 51	Woonsocket
RI	Ellen Crosby-O'Hara	D	City Council Member		Cranston
SC	Gilda Cobb-Hunter	D	State Representative	District 66	Orangeburg/Dorchester
SC	Cynthia Sweigart	N/P	School Board Member	District 5	Richland/Lexington
TN	Michael Miller	N/P	Commissioner		TN Department of Children's Services
TN	Tommie Brown	D	State Representative	District 28	Chattanooga
TX	Dolores Briones	N/P	County Judge		El Paso
TX	Jim Murphy	N/P	School Board Member		Canyon
TX	Elliott Naishtat	D	State Representative	District 49	Austin
TX	Vilma Luna	D	State Representative	District 33	Corpus Christie
VA	James A. Fitzsimmons	N/P	School Board Member	District 4	Shenandoah County
VT	James Leddy	D	State Senator		South Burlington
VT	Ann Pugh	D	State Representative		South Burlington
VT	Janet Munt	D	State Senator		Burlington
VT	Michael Fisher	D	State Representative		Lincoln
WA	Pat Thibaudeau	D	State Senator	District 43	Seattle
WA	Eric Pettigrew	D	State Representative	District 37	Southeast Seattle
WA	Connie Ladenberg		City Council Member		Takoma
WA	Mary Lou Dickerson	D	State Representative	District 36	Seattle
WI	Jim Ryan		Village President		Hales Corners
WI	Willie Johnson, Jr.		County Supervisor		Milwaukee
WI	John Jose Lopez	N/P	School Board Treasurer		Madison
WI	Mark Schmitt	N/P	Board of Supervisors	District 24	Eau Claire County
WI	Wendy Volz-Daniels	N/P	Village Trustee		Campbellsport
WI	Joan Groessl	N/P	City Council Member		Algoma
WV	Cathy Gatson	N/P	Circuit Clerk		Kanawha County
WV	Jon Blair Hunter	D	State Senator	District 14	Morgantown
WV	Barry Locke		City Council Member		Shinnston
WV	Donna Reid Renner	D	State Delegate		Fairmont
WV	Becky Jones Jordon		School Board Member		Kanawha County

Source: https://www.socialworkers.org/pace/state.asp

All too often social workers do not think of themselves as "politicians" being elected to a political office. Yet, men and women (see table 2) and people of color (see table 3) hold a variety of offices. Although most elected social workers hold the MSW degree (75%), BSWs hold state and local offices as well (see table 4).

ELECTORAL AND LEGISLATIVE POLITICS

Political social work has two sides that are intricately related and both of which are important to the social work profession's realization of its goals. First,

Table 2: Social Workers in Elected Offices by Gender/Office, 2003

	Women	Men	Total
U.S. Congress	4	2	6
State Legislature	34	10	44
County/Borough	13	4	17
City/Municipal	34	28	62
School Board	26	9	35
Other	8	2	10
Total	119	55	174

Table 3: Social Workers in Elected Offices by Race/Ethnicity/Office, 2003

	African American	Asian American/ Pacific Islander	Caucasian	Hispanic/ Latino	Unknown
U.S. Congress	2	3	1		
State Legislature	14	42	5	3	
County/Borough	2	1	7	3	4
City/Municipal	9		21	1	11
School Board	6	2	19	1	7
Other	1	1	7		1
Total	34	4	99	11	26

Table 4: Social Workers in Elected Offices by Credential/Office, 2003

	BSW	MSW	DSW	Unknown
U.S. Congress		6		
State Legislature	12	46	3	3
County/Borough	2	13	0	2
City/Municipal	5	35	2	
School Board	2	25	4	4
Other	9	8	0	
Total	22	135	9	9

Figure 1: Workers in the Michigan Citizens Action office. This is a nonprofit policy group.

social workers identify and support candidates who are friends of the profession and support our issues. By making contributions and working in candidates' campaigns, social workers are able to help pro-human service candidates to win elections. We call this phase "electoral politics." Second, social workers collaborate with elected officials on policy proposals during the legislative process. We call this phase "lobbying."

Political activity is generally viewed through the lobbying lens. Richman (1991), Haynes and Mickelson (1991), Mahaffey and Hanks (1982), and Wolk (1981), among others, emphasize the lobbying side of politics. Little attention is paid to electing candidates to public office. Deemphasizing electoral politics violates two important legislative lessons, however:

Lesson 1: Lobbying is much easier with supporters and friends of social work than with its detractors and antagonists.

Lesson 2: Lobbying for prevention proposals is a much better use of energy than lobbying against negative proposals and rectifying previous legislative errors.

You might view the political process as a cycle (see box 1). In a rational model, the political life cycle begins with candidate identification, then progresses through participation in electoral politics, educating the candidate on social work issues and advocating certain positions, lobbying the candidate to support the profession's stance, and back to candidate identification and reelection. The real-life political cycle is not so rational, and you may in fact enter the process and begin your efforts at any given point. Suppose, for example, that legislation regarding abortion is up for debate in the state senate. First, you attempt to educate your legislator on the issue from a social work perspective; the representative decides not to support your view. You soon realize that a new elected official is needed to better serve the interests of your district and the profession, and you begin to seek an alternative candidate for the next election. And the cycle continues.

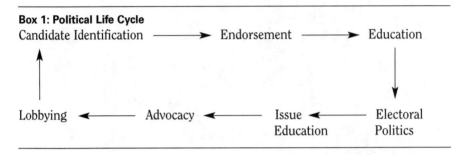

Box 1: Political Life Cycle
Candidate Identification ⟶ Endorsement ⟶ Education

Lobbying ⟵ Advocacy ⟵ Issue Education ⟵ Electoral Politics

Elected officials, while primarily responsible to their constituencies, are also open to input from their campaign supporters. Active campaign support establishes a positive relation between the office holder and the social work community. When this is achieved, rather than having to adopt a defensive lobbying posture— protecting what we have from social work antagonists—social workers are able to influence the development and enhancement of social services through public policy. Conversely, when we don't have friends in the legislative body, social workers must put most of their efforts into attempting to block of modify coercive public policies.

Social Work Organizations and Electoral Politics

Education Legislative Network. In 1971, the *Education Legislative Network* (ELAN) was organized by NASW as a vehicle to bring together divergent and often contentious social work groups, in particular, clinical and macrolevel social workers. The premise of ELAN was that a united work community would strive together for the good of the whole and as it did so separate groups would become more friendly toward each other, thus creating broader support for each group's issues.

As a beginning effort, ELAN was successful in educating NASW members on a number of national policy issues. ELAN used a progressive strategy in which NASW members were 1) informed on issues and 2) encouraged to lobby their elected representatives in Washington. It became obvious, however, that more friendly elected leaders were needed. Concurrent with the association's first organized political efforts, political action committees took on greater importance in American politics overall. In 1976, NASW organized PACE, which served as the association's national effort to raise money and endorse candidates for national office who supported the profession's agenda.

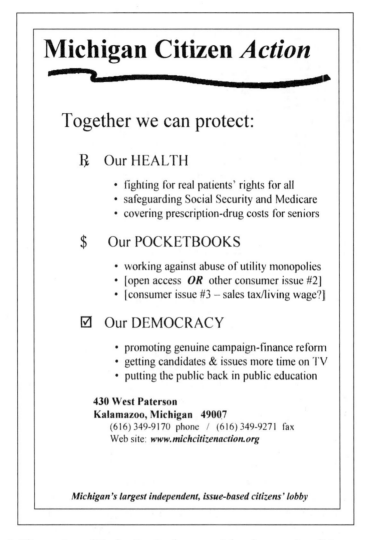

Michigan Citizen *Action*

Together we can protect:

℞ Our HEALTH

- fighting for real patients' rights for all
- safeguarding Social Security and Medicare
- covering prescription-drug costs for seniors

$ Our POCKETBOOKS

- working against abuse of utility monopolies
- [open access *OR* other consumer issue #2]
- [consumer issue #3 – sales tax/living wage?]

☑ Our DEMOCRACY

- promoting genuine campaign-finance reform
- getting candidates & issues more time on TV
- putting the public back in public education

430 West Paterson
Kalamazoo, Michigan 49007
(616) 349-9170 phone / (616) 349-9271 fax
Web site: ***www.michcitizenaction.org***

Michigan's largest independent, issue-based citizens' lobby

Figure 2: Flier urging political action to change social and economic policies.

Political Action for Candidate Election. PACE has a threefold purpose. First, it endorses those candidates who are most supportive of social work issues. Second, PACE sometimes makes campaign contributions to endorsed candidates. And third, PACE educates NASW members about candidates and encourages electoral participation.

National PACE is limited to endorsing and contributing to national candidates, that is, candidates for the presidency, the U.S. House of Representatives, and the U.S. Senate. A board of trustees, each of whom is appointed by the national NASW president, governs PACE. The board, with consultation from NASW members and state chapters, screens candidates for national elections, endorses candidates, and

Name: Anita C. Cruzan LCSW, CCM.

Place of residence: Springfield, Missouri

College/university degrees: Southwest Missouri State University, BSW

Present position: Community Resource Coordinator/Trainer, Special Health Care Needs Unit of the Missouri Department of Health and Senior Services. I provide training, technical assistance, and mentoring to contracted service coordinators who work with children with special health care needs.

Previous work/volunteer experience: Service Coordinator for children with special health care needs, Service Coordinator for individuals with HIV/AIDS, and Service Coordinator for disabled adults and the elderly.

Why did you choose social work as a career? My introductory sociology class in college was the first class that I truly enjoyed and seemed to understand completely—it all made sense to me. From that beginning I took the introductory social work class and decided this career was a perfect fit for me and it remains so after twenty-five years. Social work allows me to have a positive impact on the lives of others, and at the same time, it reminds me of how fortunate I am to have the life I do.

What is your favorite social work story? I worked as an investigator of elderly abuse and neglect hotline calls. I received a report of an elderly woman with a gun who was upset with her husband. I met two police officers at the home and stood behind them as they knocked on the front door. The officers appeared casual, as if this were a routine matter. The woman came to the door and admitted she did have a gun and was having marital problems. The officers asked to see the gun and she readily complied. The officers continued to act nonchalant, possibly because the woman appeared so calm. The woman returned to the front door carrying a shotgun! The officers came to full attention and asked to see the gun. When they opened it up they discovered it was indeed loaded. The woman voluntarily allowed the officers to remove the gun. I began to provide social work services to this family to assist with the stress that triggered this event. The lesson I learned was that for your own safety you should always be aware of your surroundings and what is going on around you; situations may change rapidly and you need to be prepared to respond.

What would be the one thing you would change in our community if you had the power to do so? Have people redefine their priorities. We all seem to be rushing here and there because we think we need to do so much and have so much. We all need to stop and smell the roses more.

in some but not all instances makes financial contributions. Following endorsement of a candidate, NASW members in the candidate's state or district are encouraged to work in the candidate's campaign and make additional campaign contributions.

Even as the national PACE effort grew in strength, NASW recognized the truth of former House Speaker Tip O'Neil's (D-Massachusetts) statement "All politics is local." NASW therefore encouraged state chapters to organize their own PACE units to endorse local and statewide candidates and raise funds for their campaigns.

By 1998, every state had a PACE unit working to help candidates who support social work positions. The state PACE units are structured in a manner similar to the national PACE: each has a board of trustees, appointed by the state chapter president, and each screens and endorses candidates. The efforts and activities of the state PACE units are separate from each other and from the national PACE; there is no formal mechanism or means for accountability to the national professional association.

In theory, a state PACE unit could work against the interests of NASW by endorsing candidates who do not support the social work positions outlined at the national level. If this happened there would be no recourse for the NASW or the chapter membership. As trustees, the board members are ultimately responsible for all endorsements and for disbursements of campaign contributions, and they are accountable only to themselves. Nevertheless, the nationwide network of social work PACE units provides an important opportunity to identify, support, and work to elect individuals who can be advocates for social work issues and friends of the profession.

According to the Political Affairs Office of NASW, national PACE contributions placed PACE in the top ten of the more than 2,000 PACs contributing to that year's election (D. Dempsey, personal communication, November 30, 1992; Dempsey, 1993). While the national PACE's level of activity seems impressive, Colby and Buffum (1998) did not find the NASW membership to be especially active or concerned with PACE activities, and few dollars were raised by the association outside of the money collected as part of membership dues. (PACE dollars are raised by a "negative dues check-off" that requires NASW members to check off on their annual dues bills that they do not want $10.00 of their dues to be donated to PACE. If the box is left unchecked, $10.00 is transferred to PACE.)

Did You Know...A number of graduate and undergraduate academic programs offer courses focusing on politics and social work. The University of Houston School of Social Work implemented a graduate specialization in politics and social work, and the University of Connecticut sponsors an institute on political social work.

PACE Endorsement Process. Each state unit as well as the national PACE develops its own endorsement process and procedures. Remember that the state PACE units are not tied to each other or to the national PACE; they are separate entities, each with its own set of by-laws. A state's PACE unit is separate even from the state's NASW chapter.

Colby and Buffum (1998) found what seems to be a typical format for state endorsement (but recognize that not all states follow this procedure). The board puts together a survey that is distributed to all candidates (see box 2). Candidates are given a specified period in which to respond; if a survey is not returned

Box 2: Examples of Candidate Survey

Currently, Texas is ranked 49th of the 50 states and the District of Columbia in the delivery of health and human services.At the same time, Texas also ranks near or at the top of all states in terms of severity of many health and social problems, including teen pregnancy, school dropouts, the number of AIDS cases, infant mortality, and the lack of rural health care.

During the Spring Texas Legislative Session, numerous bills were introduced to address these issues. As with most states, however, the ongoing state deficit forced cuts in social services. Public education to housing and health care were all cut. Yet the legislature spent three special sessions, at a cost of $1.5 million per session, to redraw Congressional district maps in order to eliminate Congressional seats held by democrats and increase the number of Republicans in the U.S. House of Representatives. Obviously the majority of the membersin the Texas Legislature were more concerned about political self-interests rather than providing for the public good.

Do you support or oppose the following initiatives?

Support   Oppose

_____   _____ 1. Legislation that would allow parents to take up to three months' leave without pay from their jobs to care for a seriously ill child, spouse, or parent or for the birth or adoption of a child.

_____   _____ 2. Increased funding for Aid to Families with Dependent Children (AFDC).

_____   _____ 3. Legislation ensuring that all at-risk students have access to pupil services (including school social workers, school psychologists, and counselors).

_____   _____ 4. Legislation that would prohibit the use of corporal punishment in Texas public schools.

_____   _____ 5. Legislation that would ensure that pregnant women have full access to prenatal care.

_____   _____ 6. Legislation that would ensure that children in need receive regular preventive health care and treatment.

_____   _____ 7. Include funding in Texas' budget to supplement federal funds for Head Start.

_____   _____ 8. Include funding to supplement federal funds for the Supplemental Food Program for Women, Infants and Children (WIC).

_____   _____ 9. Legislation increasing the availability of affordable, quality childcare, preschool, and early childhood development programs.

_____   _____ 10. Legislation that opposes mandatory HIV testing of all health care workers who perform invasive procedures.

_____   _____ 11. A state income tax in order to adequately fund state services.

_____   _____ 12. Increased funding for the Texas Department of Human Services Child Protective Services Unit to hire professional social workers in order to provide higher quality services to children at risk and raise the minimum standards of training and qualifications for frontline workers.

_____   _____ 13. In the event the Supreme Court overturns Roe v. Wade, legislation protecting the freedom of choice and access to reproductive health care for women and families.

_____   _____ 14. Legislation that increases the availability of affordable housing in the state.

_____   _____ 15. Legislation amending the Texas Commission on Human Rights Act of 1991 and requiring state agencies to implement Affirmative Action programs and workforce diversity programs.

_____   _____ 16. Making a substantial investment in initiatives to reform and improve services to children and families involved in protective services, mental health, and the juvenile justice system.

On a separate piece of paper, please answer the following questions:

1. If elected, (a) what would be your main legislative priorities, and (b) what committee assignments would you seek?
2. Are you, any member of your family, or a close personal friend a professional social worker?
3. Many of the health care licensing and certification acts are under Sunset Review, and the legislature will have to re-enact these laws during the next regular session. Social work certification is one of the laws under Sunset Review. NASW/Texas is interested in strengthening this law by refining the definition of social work practice and regulating under the law only those practitioners who hold BSW and MSW degrees. Will you support the continued regulation of social workers? Would you support the narrowing of the law to only regulate social workers who hold professional degrees? Would you support a license for social workers?
4. Why are you seeking our endorsement? If endorsed, how would you use our endorsement?

Source: National Association of Social Workers/Texas PACE Candidate Questionnaire, 1992.

a telephone call to the candidate's office is made asking to have the survey completed. If the candidate is seeking reelection, the board will also review the incumbent's voting record. Finally, members of local NASW units are asked to provide input to the process. Some state PACE units also hire professional lobbyists to help assess candidates. Professional lobbyists work the legislative halls every day, attempting to convince legislators to vote one way or another on specific legislation. As a result they often have a more detailed understanding of candidates than PACE trustees.

Based on the information it accumulates from the survey, the board decides which candidates to endorse. Once endorsements are made, the board then determines whether a financial contribution will be made. The board looks at many issues in deciding whether to make a contribution: Is the candidate opposed in the election? Does the candidate need the money? If unopposed, does the candidate need help in retiring a campaign debt? There are no correct answers to these questions; they simply serve as discussion points to help the trustees to make a final decision.

Financial contributions are governed by state law. Typically states cap the amount an organization may contribute to a candidate for a specific election or election cycle. Also, the level of office—for example, state representative versus governor—affects the limits on contribution size.

Did You Know…"Bundling" is a campaign loophole that allows organizations to get around legal financial caps on contributions. For example, a state PACE unit may contribute the maximum amount for a person running for the state house, say $500.00. When presenting the PACE check, additional checks from individual NASW chapter members are given at the same time (thus the idea of a bundle of checks). So a candidate may receive $500.00 from the organization and, say, thirty checks each for $50.00, for a total of $2,000. In effect, the organization, with member support, has increased its level of financial support to the candidate. And the candidate is more likely to remember a $2,000 contribution than individual $50.00 checks.

Once endorsements are made and the level of contributions determined, NASW members are informed of the PACE decisions. Checks are presented directly to the candidate by social workers from the candidate's district; this provides an opportunity for local social workers to make a direct connection with the candidate and to strengthen the relations for future lobbying efforts.

Activity…Contact your state PACE unit through NASW. Find out who serves on the PACE board of trustees. What is the track record of PACE endorsements? Do endorsed candidates get elected? How many Republicans, Democrats, or candidates from other political parties were endorsed in the last election? How much money was contributed to the candidates?

Social Workers and Political Campaigns

Volunteers and paid campaign staff provide critical support to a candidate's electoral bid. Commitments to a candidate and her ideas is the only prerequisite. It doesn't matter where the individual's competence lies: a campaign has room for a volunteer to perform an array of tasks—answering phones, preparing bulk mailings, putting up yard signs, and canvassing neighborhoods.

Social workers, in particular, can contribute many skills typical of their profession to a political campaign. These include planning decision-making, consensus building, group management, research, assessment, relationship building, crisis intervention, and communication. In terms of roles, or functions, that social workers perform, eight are appropriate for political campaigns:

Role	Tasks
Advocate	Speaks on behalf of the candidate and represents his position to various constituent groups
Teacher/educator	Instructs staff and volunteers about campaign strategy and issues; in conjunction with advocacy, educates potential supporters about the candidate
Mobilizer	Energizes staff and volunteers; prioritizes and assigns individuals to needed campaign activities
Consultant	Provides expertise in problem solving and strategizing; helps candidate and staff to develop strategies for the campaign
Planner	Identifies key community players and activities; assesses strengths of potential relationships and overall prospects for electoral victory
Caregiver	Provides emotional support to candidate, his family, friends, staff, and supporters (relations can become strained)
Data manager	Develops and implements a data structure that allows for quick and easy access; designs a user-friendly system for staff, volunteers, and candidate
Administrator	Develops and implements a well-operating campaign structure that is functional and not overwhelming; keeps the structure simple, efficient, and consistent with the candidate's best interests

The following are a few simple things that social workers can do to strengthen the presence of the social work profession in a political campaign.

Spend time at a campaign office. Traditionally a campaign begins on Labor Day and concludes with the general election in November, generally a ten- to eleven-week period. A campaign relies on volunteers to staff an office, with much of the work taking place during evenings and on weekends. Organize ten to fifteen social workers and commit to providing a volunteer for one night each week at the campaign office for the duration of the campaign. Say you selected Tuesday evening; this can become known as Social Work Night to the candidate and key staff. The potential value to future lobbying efforts of even such a brief commitment is incalculable. The candidate will be much more open and sympathetic to a group that worked throughout the campaign.

Use buttons and t-shirts. Make a modest investment to purchase buttons or t-shirts printed with a simple slogan. Social workers for (candidate's name)—what an effective message! Be sure to wear the buttons or t-shirts on Social Work Night/Day at the campaign office. Let others know who you are and where you stand.

Host a fundraiser. All candidates need money to run a campaign. A bare-bones, efficient run for the state house costs at least $25,000. Plan a fundraising event with other social workers. Be sure to coordinate the event with the candidate's campaign staff—there is usually one person who is responsible for scheduling the candidate's time. Make the event brief—the candidate has no extra time during the heat of a campaign and often needs to be in four places at once. Try to make the event fun as well. Be creative. For example, one interesting fundraiser was a "nonevent fundraiser" that people donated $25.00 *not* to attend! If you host an event with the candidate present, be sure to wear your buttons or t-shirts.

Realize the importance of election day. Election day is the longest day in the campaign. With polls opening as early as 6:00 a.m. in some states and closing as late as 8:00 p.m., campaign volunteers work up to eighteen hours! Volunteers are needed to work near the polling places, passing out candidate literature; put up last-minute candidate yard signs; provide voters with transportation to the polls (be sure to wear your buttons or t-shirts and to talk about your candidates with those you are driving); and staff the campaign office answering phones and dealing with last-minute glitches and crises. When the polls close, go to the candidate's headquarters or wherever the party is being held. You deserve to celebrate after all the energy you've put into the campaign. And be sure to wear your buttons or t-shirts.

Lobbying for Social Work Legislation

Lobbying is an act of persuasion in which you educate someone about an issue with the goal of gaining their active support. Recognize one key principle of lobbying: you are the expert with key information.

Lobbying takes many different forms. Typical activities include writing letters, making telephone calls, making personal visits, and giving public testimony. Each is an effective and important part of the lobbying process. With computer technology, letter writing is not very difficult—a mass mailing to the legislature doesn't take too much longer to compose than a single letter. Telephone calls may be more costly, especially if you don't live in the state capital, but they take far less time. Personal visits are expensive if you don't live in or near the state capital, and they also require a great deal of time for what are generally brief meetings; but face-to-face meetings are effective. No matter which form of lobbying you select be sure to be brief, dignified, sincere, and, most important, respectful.

Letter writing. Write early, before the legislator has made up her mind. Make the letter one page or less, legislators don't have time to read dissertations! Get to the point quickly and be concise. Attach handouts to support the key points. Make sure you educate, educate, and educate the legislator on the issue. If you are writing about a specific bill, be sure to include the bill number. Note how the legislation will affect the legislator's district, mention the names of key supporters of your position from the district or from the legislator's campaign, provide reasons to support the bill, and request an answer to your letter indicating how she plans to vote on the issue. Be sure to say thank you at the beginning and the end of the letter, and be sure to use the appropriate salutation (see box 3).

Telephone calls. You'll probably talk with a legislative aide, so don't take it personally if you don't speak with the legislator. Also, if there is a phone blitz on the bill you're calling about, the aide may be rather short with you and may cut you off in the middle of your presentation. Again, don't take it personally.

Be brief and to the point; try to take less than three minutes. Make notes before you call and practice what you want to say. Introduce yourself and mention your address, especially if you are from the legislator's home district. Follow the same principles as in letter writing: identify the bill number and describe how it will affect the legislator's district. Ask how the legislator plans to vote on the issue; if the person you speak to doesn't know, ask when you can call back to learn of the decision. End by thanking the legislator or aide for his time and support.

Personal visits. Personal visits are probably the most time-consuming, frustrating, and potentially the most effective form of lobbying. Meetings are as a rule very brief, lasting from a few to no more than fifteen minutes. They usually take place in the legislator's office, but don't be surprised if you find yourself walking down the hall accompanying the representative or senator to a meeting while you lobby for a few short minutes. Most often you'll meet with an aide, but if you have a good relationship with the legislator—in particular, if you were a good campaign volunteer—you'll probably be able to meet with the elected official. You'll need to be pleasant, brief, concise, and convincing. Discuss only one legislative issue during your meeting. Be sure to follow up with a phone call and a letter of appreciation.

These meetings may be short in time, but many a social worker has found that they have been able to change a politician's stance on an issue as a result of a face-to-face meeting. Your sincerity, knowledge, and compassion about the issue speak volumes to politicians.

Public testimony. In general, when considering legislation a committee must allow opportunities for public input. Such testimony usually lasts less than five

Box 3: Salutations for Letter Writing

Governor
1. Writing:
   The Honorable (full name)
   Governor of (State)
   Address

   Dear Governor (last name)

2. Speaking: "Governor (last name)"

Lieutenant Governor
1. Writing:
   The Honorable (full name)
   Lieutenant Governor of (state)
   Address

   Dear Lieutenant Governor (last name)

2. Speaking: "Lieutenant Governor (last name)"

Speaker of the House
1. Writing:
   The Honorable (full name)
   Speaker of the House
   Address

   Dear Mr./Madame Speaker:

2. Speaking: "Mr./Madame Speaker"

State Senator
1. Writing:
   The Honorable (full name)
   The (State) State Senate
   Address

   Dear Senator (last name)

2. Speaking: "Senator (last name)"

State Representative
1. Writing:
   The Honorable (full name)
   The (State) House of Representatives
   Address

   Dear Mr./Ms. (last name)

2. Speaking: "Representative (last name)" or "Mr./Ms. (last name)"

minutes per speaker. The committee will have rules that govern the testimony's length—check them out beforehand by contacting the committee's staff person in the legislative offices.

Be sure your testimony is in a typed or word processed format, distribute copies to the committee members, and be sure to have a few extra copies available for others who are interested in your comments. Make sure your name, address, and phone numbers are easily found on the cover page of your testimony in case someone wishes to get in touch with you after the hearing.

Don't be surprised if the legislators ask you no questions after your presentation. There may be twenty to thirty people offering testimony, each speaking three to five minutes. Asking questions only prolongs the process. If a question is asked, be sure of your answers. Don't make up an answer; if you aren't sure what the answer is, tell the committee you'll find out and get back to their staff person within twenty-four hours. And be sure you do! Nothing is more damaging to your credibility in the legislature than to give inaccurate or misleading information or to make a promise and not follow up.

Finally, *don't argue with the legislators!* You are a guest in their workplace. You are there to convince and make friends, not to argue and make enemies. Your legislative opponent today may be your key supporter tomorrow on another issue. Don't burn your bridges.

COMMUNITY ORGANIZATION: LINKING THE POLITICAL TO THE COMMUNITY

To best link the political to the needs of the community, a strategy must first be outlined. By "strategy" we mean the action options that are open to the social worker to help reach the change goals identified. Rothman, Erlich, and Tropman, (1995) remind us that this must start by researching the history and the evolution of strategies that have been applied in the past. After all, the old adage "history can repeat itself" could complicate any type of intervention plan. Second, the social worker must explore the societal climate or environment. What is important to the individuals that live in the community? What are the values, the norms and the expectations of the constituents to be served? To discover this, the community itself must be examined. The stakeholders must be identified. Small groups, both formal (such as church members) and informal (such as neighborhood support systems) within this community will affect the change efforts to be implemented. These players must be identified and all efforts must be ensured to make sure that their needs are addressed. In community organization, the needs and wishes of the community always provide the cornerstone for all helping efforts. Therefore, it is important not to have helping efforts thwarted by individual or institutional agendas that do not operate for the best efforts of the community. To completely describe the fundamentals of this type of practice is beyond the scope of this chapter. Although it is a critical part of social work macro practice, more specialized training and education is encouraged before a beginning social worker should embark in this type of practice.

SUMMARY

"Despite residual skepticism about the appropriateness of political work, there has been a resurgence of political action in recent years" among social workers (Weismiller & Rome, 1995, p. 2312). Courses in schools of social work, ongoing efforts by national and state PACE units, direct participation in political campaigns, and the election of social workers to political office are among the many ways social workers are developing much-needed political savvy.

We have learned through many, often painful, experiences that attempts to influence the development of public policy must begin well before the legislative process. Identifying and working for the election of people who are in favor of human services initiates the lobbying effort; having the right people in place makes lobbying that much easier.

Moreover, elected officials are influenced by groups that "vote regularly and are active in the electoral process" (Parker & Sherraden, 1993, p. 27). Social workers and their membership organizations are making significant contributions to political campaigns. As campaign workers, social workers are able to translate their agency-based practice expertise to the political arena.

Social work practice is directly affected by politics. Who can call themselves social workers and practice as such, program eligibility requirements, and the types and levels of services are but a few of the critical decisions made by elected politicians. Every two years, more than 450,000 offices are up for election, involving some one and a half million candidates (Beaudry & Schaeffer, 1998). These elected officials are for the most part not social workers. While the number of social workers holding elected office increased by over 90 percent in the 1990s, decisions made by non-social workers continue to have enormous impact on social workers and clients alike. Social workers face a simple choice: remain on the sidelines while others make decisions that determine how the social service community operates, or participate aggressively at all levels of political activity in order to open the door for progressive lobbying efforts. Simply put, social workers can sit in the audience watching others or can be pivotal actors who build on the rich experiences of political campaigns.

References

Beaudry, A., & Schaeffer, B. (1986). *Winning local and state elections: The guide to organizing your campaign*. New York: Free Press.

Colby, I., & Buffum, W. (1998). Social work and political action committees. *Journal of Community Practice, 5* (4), 87–103.

CSWE Commission on Accreditation. (2001). *Educational policy and accreditation standards*. Alexandria, VA: CSWE.

Dempsey, D. (1993, March 10). Letter to chapter presidents. Washington, DC: NASW.

Haynes, K., & Mickelson, B. (2003). *Affecting changes* (5th ed.). New York: Longman.

Hiratsuka, J. (1992). 114 more races backed. *NASW News, 37* (9), 1, 10.

Landers, S. (1992). NASW steps up efforts to elect Clinton. *NASW News, 37* (9), 1.

Mahaffey, M., & Hanks, J. (Eds.). (1982). *Practical politics and social work and political responsibility*. Silver Spring, MD: NASW.

NASW Political Affairs Office. (1992, April). *The political social worker*. Washington, DC: NASW.

Parker, M., & Sherraden, M. (1992). Electoral participation of social workers. *New England Journal of Human Services, 11* (3), 23–28.

Richman, W. (1991). *Lobbying for social change*. New York: Haworth.

Rothman, J., Erlich, J. L., & Tropman, J. E. (1995). *Strategies for community intervention*. Itasca, IL: Peacock.

Weismiller, T., & Rome, S. H. (1995). Social workers in politics. In R. L. Edwards et al. (Eds.), *Encyclopedia of social work* (19th ed., pp. 2305–2313). Washington, DC: NASW Press.

Wolk, J. (1981). Are social workers politically active? *Social work, 26* (4), 283–288.

Part IV

Expanding Horizons for Social Work

Chapter 14

International Social Welfare

OUR WORLD IS A GLOBAL COMMUNITY. WE MUST THINK ON A LARGE scale about our interests, concerns, influences, and obligations, for the community in which we live stretches far beyond the confines of our geographic neighborhood. Today, we call this phenomenon globalization, the creation of an international system that affects domestic economies, politics, and cultures (Midgley, 1997).

Most of us would agree that we live in a global neighborhood. Twentieth-century history has shown how regional conflicts and disasters can quickly escalate into global ones. The Great Depression of the 1930s, for example, was felt worldwide and not only in the United States where the early effects were concentrated.

Later in the 1930s, after the German and Japanese war machines had conquered many of their neighbors, the United States, which had originally assumed an isolationist position, became one of the leading allied nations. The collapse of the Berlin Wall in November 1989 signaled upheavals in many communist bloc nations that have had significant social and economic consequences around the world. In 1998, weakening in the Asian and Russian economies led to stock market gyrations in the financial centers of the world. Certainly, other examples of global effects exist, and the message is clear: what happens across the oceans affects all of us, no matter where we live.

Did You Know...According to the World Bank, 3 billion people in the world live on less than $2.00 each day.

We also can learn from other societies and cultures about how to strengthen our own approach to social living. We can study how other countries approach social problems and think about how their successes may work in our communities. Some people believe that the United States has nothing to learn from the rest of the world about technology, education, and other social advancements. But this is not true! "Social scientists agree that knowledge can be increased by investigating phenomena in other societies and by testing propositions in different social, economic, and cultural contexts" (Midgley, 1995, p. 1490). The study of international social welfare is an imperative that will move us beyond our many self-imposed barriers and allow all of us to be better off in a cooperative, world community.

Name: Matthew Colton

Place of residence: Swansea, Wales, United Kingdom

College/university degrees: Keele University; BA with honors (First Class) in Applied Social Studies, Diploma in Applied Social Studies, Certificate of Qualification in Social Work, Oxford University, D.Phil.

Present position: Professor and Head of Applied Social Studies (Social Work), University of Wales, Swansea

Previous work/volunteer experience: Social work teacher and researcher, social worker mainly with children and families

What do you do in your spare time? I don't have any spare time as such. Outside of my work, most of my time is spent with my wife, two children, and extended family. I really enjoy family activities and take an active interest in my children's hobbies and interests.

Why did you choose social work as a career? From an early age, my parents nurtured and encouraged me to have respect and concern for others, particularly those who are troubled or oppressed. My mother died when I was 9 years old. I think that this experience deepened my compassion and empathy for those whose lives are especially difficult, and my concern for social justice.

What is your favorite social work story? There are so many! For example, I was once called to the home of a client who wished to make a complaint about her social worker. Having introduced myself on the doorstep, I was beckoned in by the old woman whom I was there to see. The house was dimly lit and overrun with cats.

"How can I help?," I asked when we were seated.

"She [the social worker] doesn't like my cats," complained the woman. "Wants me to kill them all. Told me to hit them with a spade."

"Hit them with a spade?" I asked, somewhat puzzled. Then it dawned on me. My colleague had, in fact, advised the woman to have the cats spayed.

What would be the one thing you would change in our community if you had the power to do so? I would like to see a genuine commitment to tackling social exclusion. This would include practical measures to reverse the increasing polarization in British society between the poor and the affluent as well as measures to combat child poverty—which has tripled over the past two decades—and institutional racism.

Yet American social workers have been ambivalent in their commitment to the international arena. In fact, Midgley (1997, p. 63) has contended that the profession is not "fully prepared" to meet international challenges and opportunities and must be more aggressive in benefiting from international opportunities. In other words, just as the world experiences globalization, so too must the social work profession.

In this chapter we touch on the many international facets of social work. Though we cannot delve into details of cultural differences and economic and demographic trends, we hope to raise your awareness of these issues. By the end of the chapter you'll recognize that social work is a global profession, facing the persistent challenge of promoting social and economic justice.

HOW DO WE COMPARE DIFFERENT NATIONS?

When making international comparisons, it is helpful to have a framework for grouping nations based on similarities. Otherwise, comparisons may not be meaningful. For example, very little can be learned from comparing the economic systems of the United States and Nepal. The vast political, economic, social, and cultural differences between these two nations makes such a comparison virtually impossible.

One framework is based on a nation's technological level. Three levels are identified: preindustrial, industrial, and postindustrial (Bell, 1973). This framework can be visualized as a core with circles, or "concentric zones," surrounding the core. Core nations include those in western Europe and North America; a semi-periphery surrounds the core; and the semi-periphery is then encircled by the periphery (Chatterjee, 1996). The semi-periphery includes former communist nations and selected nations in Asia and South America. The periphery includes the remaining Asian and South American countries and Africa. Chatterjee called these three groups of nations the first world, the second world, and the third world (see box 1).

The World Bank, an international organization that promotes economic development and productivity to raise the standard of living in less developed nations, uses a different framework. The World Bank categorizes nations into six regions:

Box 1: The World System

First World: Also known as the core, it includes North America, western Europe, Australia, and Japan. It is wealthy, capitalist, industrial, and based on the traditions of a market economy and individualism.

Second World: Somewhat outside the core, it consists of eastern Europe, central and northern Asia, and Cuba. It is neither wealthy nor poor, socialist, selectively industrial, and based on the traditions of a planned economy and collectivism. A substantial part of the second world has been attempting to convert to a market economy since 1991.

Third World: It includes nations mostly in Africa, southern and Southeast Asia, and South America. It is mostly poor, often nationalist, selectively industrial to preindustrial, and based on a mixed economy and regional loyalty.

Source: Chatterjee (1996, p. 46).

South Asia, Middle East and North Africa, Latin America and the Caribbean, Europe and Central Asia, East Asia and the Pacific, and the Africa Region (see box 2).

We've described two frameworks here, but there are a number of alternative approaches to comparing nations. The purpose of our work is to be able to organize the world's countries in order that our discussions are consistent and appropriate. In other words, we want to compare apples with apples, not apples with peaches!

Box 2: Regions of the World as Defined by the World Bank

South Asia: Afghanistan, Bangladesh, Bhutan, India, Maldives, Nepal, Pakistan, Sri Lanka.

Middle East and North Africa: Algeria, Bahrain, Egypt, Iran, Jordan, Kuwait, Lebanon, Morocco, Oman, Qatar, Saudi Arabia, Syrian Arab Republic, Tunisia, Yemen, United Arab Emirates.

Latin America and the Caribbean: Antigua and Barbuda, Argentina, Belize, Bolivia, Chile, Colombia, Costa Rica, Dominica, Dominican Republic, Ecuador, El Salvador, Grenada, Guatemala, Guyana, Haiti, Honduras, Jamaica, Mexico, Nicaragua, Panama, Paraguay, Peru, St. Kitts and Nevis, St. Lucia, St. Vincent and the Grenadines, Suriname, Trinidad and Tobago, Uruguay, Venezuela.

Europe and Central Asia: Albania, Armenia, Azerbaijan, Belarus, Bosnia and Herzegovina, Bulgaria, Croatia, Czech Republic, Estonia, Georgia, Hungary, Kazakhstan, Kyrgyz Republic, Latvia, Lithuania, Former Yugoslav Republic of Macedonia, Moldova, Poland, Romania, Russian Federation, Slovak Republic, Slovenia, Tajikistan, Turkey, Turkmenistan, Ukraine, Uzbekistan.

East Asia and the Pacific: Cambodia, China, Fiji, Indonesia, Kiribati, Korea, Lao People's Democratic Republic, Malaysia, Marshall Islands, Federated States of Micronesia, Mongolia, Myanmar, Palau, Papua New Guinea, Philippines, Samoa, Solomon Islands, Thailand, Tonga, Vanuatu, Vietnam.

Africa: Angola, Benin, Botswana, Burkina Faso, Burundi, Cameroon, Cape Verde, Central African Republic, Chad, Comoros, Congo, Democratic Republic of Congo, Republic of Côte d'Ivoire, Djibouti, Equatorial Guinea, Eritrea, Ethiopia, Gabon, The Gambia, Ghana, Guinea, Guinea-Bissau, Kenya, Lesotho, Liberia, Madagascar, Malawi, Mali, Mauritania, Mauritius, Mozambique, Namibia, Niger, Rwanda, São Tomé and Principe, Senegal, Seychelles, Sierra Leone, Somalia, South Africa, Sudan, Swaziland, Tanzania, Togo, Uganda, Zambia, Zimbabwe.

Question: What countries are missing from the list and why? Connect with the World Bank's web page (www.worldbank.org) for additional information and read the organization's purpose for the answer.

Source: www.worldbank.org.

Let's use Chatterjee's classification to demonstrate how a framework can be applied to make international comparisons. As shown in box 3, Chatterjee identified social issues and then tabulated how the first, second, and third worlds respond to them. Chatterjee also took the application a step further by asking the following questions about the three worlds and then compiling responses, listed in box 4.

Box 3: Welfare Trends on Selected Issues in the Three Worlds

Issue	First World	Second World	Third World
Housing	Public housing for the poor; some rent control or subsidy	Rationed housing for all	No such concept
Education	State supported; uneven in the United States	State supported	State efforts do not reach all
Income maintenance	Almost all countries	Almost all countries	Almost none except in Singapore, South Korea, Taiwan, and Hong Kong
Health care	Almost all countries except the United States; rising costs	Almost all countries; supplies and equipment problematic	Crisis-based care to the poor from charitable clinics or hospitals

---

Did You Know... The World Bank estimates that 900 million adults worldwide are illiterate. Four hundred million 6- to 17-year-olds are not in school and 225 million of them are girls.

1. Once a person has been socially defined as not employable, can he/she ask the state for help?

2. Once a person has been socially defined as employable but is unemployed, can he/she ask the state for support?

3. Once a person has been socially defined as employed but is marginally employed, can he/she ask the state for support?

4. If the state is providing support, is it means tested?

5. If the state is providing support, it is related to past or potential future earnings?

6. If the state is providing support, it is a flat rate or with a minimum or maximum, or is it linked to an index of fluctuating living costs?

7. Is the state committed to seeing that each citizen receives a basic package of health care, or has it engaged other qualified parties to do so?

8. Is the state committed to seeing that each citizen receives a basic education? If so, has it set up a formal structure to provide such education itself, or has it engaged other qualified parties to do so?

9. Is the state committed to seeing that each citizen receives basic housing? If so, has it set up a formal structure to provide such housing, or has it engaged other parties to do so?

10. Is the state committed to providing protection to various vulnerable groups (children, elderly, developmentally disabled, and mentally ill)? If so, has it set up a formal structure to provide such protection, or has it engaged other qualified parties to do so?

11. Have one or more occupational groups emerged within the state, which are self-appointed advocates for vulnerable groups and are seeking increased professionalization? (1996, p. 78)

Box 4: Comparison of Eleven Welfare State Variables

Question	First World	Second World	Third World
1.	Yes	Mostly yes	Mostly no
2.	Yes	Mostly yes	No
3.	Mostly yes	Mostly yes	No
4.	Mostly yes	Mostly yes	Does not apply
5.	Mostly yes	Mostly yes	Does not apply
6.	Mostly yes	Mostly yes	Does not apply
7.	Yes except in US	Yes	No
8.	Mostly yes	Mostly yes	No
9.	Mostly yes	Yes	No
10.	Yes	Mostly yes	No
11.	Yes	Partially yes	Partially yes

Source: Chatterjee (1996, p. 80).

RECENT HAPPENINGS AND THE WORLD TODAY

The violence caused by the recent turn of events starting with the incident on September 11, 2001, remains unprecedented in American history. The American people have traditionally been expected to adjust to new social environments, maintain good personal and occupational standing, and face pressures related to supporting friends and family. The United States, along with the rest of the world, was shocked and stunned as the terrorist attacks of September 11, 2001, unfolded. Following the attacks, debates relating to terrorist activity within the United States and the vulnerabilities inherent within American society began to emerge. Fears that terrorists could cross our extensive borders, the relative ease in which immigrants can disappear into American society, and the global and open nature of lifestyles Americans have come to depend upon leave the society susceptible to terrorist threats and attacks (Dziegielewski & Sumner, 2002). Furthermore, the threat of biological warfare abounds.

In the United States terrorism is defined by the Department of Defense as "the calculated use of violence or the threat of violence to inoculate fear; intended to coerce or to intimidate governments or societies in the pursuit of goals that are generally political, religious or ideological" (Terrorism Research Center, 2000). Terrorism is a crime that targets innocent and unsuspecting victims, and its purpose is to heighten public anxiety. Also, although acts of terrorism may seem random, they are actually planned by the perpetrators whose main objective is to publicize their attacks. The growing threat of terrorism and terrorist activity is expanding across the United States, and success in combating it will require agencies to implement proactive approaches and strategies (Terrorism Research Center, 2000).

The vulnerabilities in American society realized through the events of September 11, 2001, have initiated preemptive approaches for combating terrorists and further terrorism. For example, this event has caused the United States to explore the entry millions of legal and illegal immigrants enter the country each year. It has also caused security measures at airports and other ports of entry to be reinforced. Also, law enforcement in the United States has been exposed as vulnerable with limited communication and information sharing between federal, state, and local agencies, especially in cases where jurisdictions and charters overlap. In the United States, population groups are often centralized, allowing for large concentrations of people to inhabit relatively small areas, and these large population areas capture the attention of terrorists because of the possibility of larger casualty rate (Terrorism Research Center, 2000).

The Unites States is a global community where, in 1991 alone, there were 455 million entries by immigrants and international travelers via air, land, and sea. By 1993, that number had increased to 483 million entries; in 1995 alone, at the ports of entry to the United States, the 4,000 Immigration inspectors intercepted almost 800,000 persons who were ineligible for admission into the United States. Furthermore, there is no estimate available as to the number of those who were able to escape detection (Hays, 1996; McDonald, 1997; Badolata, 2001; Gibb, 2001). This has caused many Americans to look inside the country's boundaries for threats to their own health and safety.

Imbedded within this fear are psychological reactions that can be prolonged and intense, more so than by those following natural types of disaster (Myers, 2001). Terrorist attacks, by their very nature, are designed to instill fear, anxiety, and uncertainty within a population (Badolata, 2001). For example, the New York City skyline changed in a matter of hours when the World Trade Center buildings collapsed and only a pile of smoking debris was left and remains a constant reminder of the devastation of that day. Another psychological effect of terrorism is the threat to personal safety and security for both citizens and responders. Areas that were previously believed to be safe suddenly become unsafe, and this feeling of insecurity can be instilled in an individual for an extended period of time. The September 11th attacks were different from other terrorist acts because of the magnitude and suddenness of the tragedy, the vast loss of life on American soil, the ability of citizens to follow the events of the attack through extensive media coverage, and the method of using airplanes, considered to be a common and "safe" mode of transportation, as a means of destruction (Dyer, 2001).

Since the astronauts first circled the moon and took one of the most exciting pictures of the planet Earth, there has been an awareness that all people on the planet are connected.

But from our perspective, the earth is a very large home. If anything, we find great diversity among the earth's people, governments, and experiences. And yet within this great diversity, despite the looming threat of terrorism, we know that there are still common social problems that afflict people day in and day out. Poverty, homelessness, mental illness, inadequate housing, hunger, poor health care, physical violence, and neglect are among the many problems that know no geographic borders.

Social problems are enormous from a worldwide perspective. Although poverty, for example, has declined in parts of South Asia and the Middle East and North Africa, three billion people live on less than $2 each day. About one-third of the world's developing population is poor. According to the United Nations Africa Recovery Program, 172 of every 1,000 African children died before reaching age 5, 2.4 million African children under age 15 are HIV positive, and 12.1 million African children are AIDS orphans (Fleshman, 2002). In most countries, social exclusion is closely linked to economic, health, and educational disparities.

Did You Know...The World Bank estimates that 70 percent of women infected with HIV are between ages 15 and 25.

The infant mortality rate is an indicator of a nation's health care, in particular, of its comprehensiveness and ability to cover the poor and non-poor alike. It counts the number of children under age 1 who die per 1,000 live births. The U.S. rate in 1997 was 6.6—that is, 6.6 infants died for every 1,000 born (Brunner, 1997). Infant mortality was lower in seventeen nations than in the United States (see table 1).

At the other extreme, in 2003 infant mortality exceeding 110 per 1,000 live births can be found in Mozambique (199), Angola (193), Sierra-Leone (146), Afghanistan (142), Liberia (132), Niger (123), Somalia (120), Mali (199), Tajikistan (113) and Guinea-Bissau (110). Central Intelligence Agency (2003) (World Factbook, http://www.cia.gov/cia/publications/factbook/fields/2091.html).

Life expectancy is a second indicator of a nation's well-being. Life expectancy is a numerical estimate of the average age a group of people will reach. U.S. life expectancy in 2003 was 77.1; forty-six nations have higher expectancies (see table 2).

Many other indicators show that the United States lags behind other countries. While some people may be surprised at how the United States ranks worldwide in

Table 1: National Infant Mortality Rates Lower than U.S. Rate (6.80), 2003

World Rank	Nation	Mortality Rate (per 1,000)
225	Japan	3.30
224	Sweden	3.42
223	Iceland	3.50
222	Singapore	3.57
221	Finland	3.73
220	Norway	3.87
219	Andorra	4.06
218	Germany	4.23
217	Netherlands	4.26
216	Austria	4.33
215	Switzerland	4.36
214	France	4.37
213	Slovenia	4.42
212	Macau	4.42
211	Spain	4.54
210	Belgium	4.57
209	Luxembourg	4.65
208	Australia	4.83
207	Liechtenstein	4.85
206	Guernsey	4.85
205	Canada	4.88
204	Denmark	4.90
203	United Kingdom	5.28
202	Gibraltar	5.31
201	Ireland	5.34
200	Czech Republic	5.37
199	Jersey	5.43
198	Northern Mariana Islands	5.52
197	Malta	5.62
196	Monaco	5.63
195	Hong Kong	5.63
194	Portugal	5.73
193	San Marino	5.97
192	New Zealand	6.07
191	Greece	6.12
190	Aruba	6.14
189	Man, Isle of	6.17
188	Italy	6.19
187	Guam	6.46
186	Faroe Islands	6.52
185	Taiwan	6.65
184	United States	6.80

Source: Central Intelligence Agency (2003). World Factbook (http://www.cia.gov/cia/publications/factbook/fields/2091.html)

Figure 1: Chona and her grandmother at their home in the mountains of Northern Luzon in the Philippines. They live with the bare necessities and medical help is scarce. The grandmother's feet show the effects of a lifetime of work in the rice fields.

these areas, the findings suggest that nations can both learn a great deal from and assist each other.

HOW DO WE LOOK AT INTERNATIONAL SOCIAL WELFARE?

The literature detailing international social welfare issues is, to say the least, interesting and stimulating. Themes that you'll find consistently in international social welfare journals include peace and social justice, human rights, and social development. These areas are critical for all social workers to understand. In fact, CSWE accreditation standards require that these topics be included in both baccalaureate and graduate social work programs. Our fascination with international issues transcends our educational mandates, however, and is evident in our day-to-day conversations. How often have we heard people compare the United States with other countries? Typically, the conversation will include a statement such as "The poor in the United States have it easy compared with the poor in India." Statements of this sort form the basis of comparative social welfare discussions.

Table 2: National Life Expectancies Greater Than U.S. Expectancy (77.10), 2003

World Rank	Nation	Life Expectancy (years)
1	Andorra	83.49
2	Macau	81.87
3	San Marino	81.43
4	Japan	80.93
5	Singapore	80.42
6	Australia	80.13
7	Guernsey	80.04
8	Switzerland	79.99
9	Sweden	79.97
10	Hong Kong	79.93
11	Canada	79.83
12	Iceland	79.80
13	Cayman Islands	79.67
14	Italy	79.40
15	Gibraltar	79.38
16	France	79.28
17	Monaco	79.27
18	Liechtenstein	79.25
19	Spain	79.23
20	Norway	79.09
21	Israel	79.02
22	Jersey	78.93
23	Faroe Islands	78.90
24	Greece	78.89
25	Aruba	78.83
26	Netherlands	78.74
27	Martinique	78.72
28	Virgin Islands	78.59
29	Malta	78.43
30	Germany	78.42
31	Montserrat	78.36
32	New Zealand	78.32
33	Belgium	78.29
34	Guam	78.27
35	Austria	78.17
36	United Kingdom	78.16
37	Saint Pierre and Miquelon	78.11
38	Man, Isle of	77.98
39	Finland	77.92
40	Jordan	77.88
41	Luxembourg	77.66
42	Guadeloupe	77.53
43	Bermuda	77.41
44	Saint Helena	77.38
45	Ireland	77.35
46	Cyprus	77.27
47	Unites States	77.10

Source: Central intelligence Agency (2003). World Factbook.

Did You Know...Each year, according to the World Bank, 2 million or more girls are subjected to genital mutilation with upwards of 115 million girls worldwide having undergone genital mutilation. This practice is found in 26 African countries (including the Middle East), a few Asian countries, and is increasingly practiced in Europe, Canada, Australia, and the United States. Egypt, Ethiopia, Kenya, Nigeria, Somalia, and the Sudan account for 75 percent of all cases. In Djibouti and Somalia, 98 percent of girls are mutilated.

Midgley identified five basic types of international social welfare studies:
◆ Comparative studies of social need
◆ Comparative studies of social policies and human services
◆ Typologies of welfare states
◆ Studies of the genesis and functions of social policy
◆ Studies of the future of the welfare state (1995).

Comparative studies of social need are reports that collect and assess a variety of social and economic data from different countries. These reports are usually quantitative in nature and present tabular data on a variety of topics. Typical studies include data on income, education, birthrates, poverty, and migration.

Comparative studies of social polices and human services are most often qualitative or descriptive presentations of issues. The topics explored are similar to those addressed by comparative studies of social needs, but the discussion includes

Figure 2: Girls on their way home from school in a remote mountain area of the Philippines where the New People's Army is rebelling against the government. Roads are almost nonexistent in this part of the country.

Figure 3: Japanese students in a school for persons with developmental disabilities. Like most Japanese students, they wear uniforms. The school teaches trade skills (woodworking, plumbing, bricklaying) as well as life skills. Art, music, and physical education are taught. The school has a large gym and swimming pool. Many of the students train for the Special Olympics.

analysis of political issues, funding patterns, eligibility standards, types of services, and provision or delivery of services.

Typologies of welfare states discuss the ideological and philosophical bases for the welfare systems of different countries. Typology studies, which are generally qualitative or descriptive, can shed light on a nation's view of people and social issues and, at the same time, provide important insight into the direction of its social welfare program. According to Midgley (1995), the most common typology is the Wilensky and Lebeaux conceptual model of residual versus institutional social welfare (see chapter 2 for a discussion of this framework).

Studies of the genesis and functions of social policy are closely related to welfare typology studies. They focus on three areas: how welfare organizations emerged, what forces affect the development of social policy, and what are the functions of social policy in the society (Midgley, 1995). Such studies may be either quantitative or qualitative. They form the theoretical basis for social welfare endeavors.

Studies of the future of the welfare state have become more common recently. Midgley (1995) believed this happened in response to international criticism of social welfare and worldwide attempts to rethink national social welfare commitments and responsibilities. Such reports integrate the other four types of welfare studies and forecast the future.

INTERNATIONAL SOCIAL WELFARE ASSOCIATIONS

Many social work practitioners and students are surprised to learn that numerous, long-standing social welfare associations exist around the world. The number of international social welfare associations greatly expanded following World War

II, primarily to help rebuild war-torn countries and to assist poor countries in gaining greater economic stability (Healy, 1995). Healy (1995) classified international associations into three groups: 1) United Nations structures, 2) U.S. government agencies, and 3) private voluntary bodies.

United Nations Structures

The United Nations was originally organized in 1945 to provide a forum to help to stabilize and maintain international relations and to give peace among nations a more secure foundation. By 2002, 202 nations were members an increase of 43 new members since 1990 (http://www.un.org/Overview/growth.htm). The United Nations is probably most recognized for its peacekeeping forces, which have been deployed throughout the world to help mediate conflict. In addition to its peacekeeping mission, however, the United Nations conducts a variety of activities, with 80 percent of its work taking place in developing nations. Typical of these services are programs for children, environmental protection, human rights, health and medical research and services, poverty and economic development, agricultural development, family planning, emergency and disaster relief, air and sea travel, use of atomic energy, and labor and workers' rights.

Did You Know...The United Nations spends about $10 billion each year or $1.70 for each of the world's inhabitants. At the end of March 2003, member nations owed the UN $1.182 billion for previous years' dues, of which the United States alone owed $532 billion (47 percent in total and 45 percent of the regular budget).

While the United Nations is involved in an array of activities, seven specific agencies address social welfare issues:

United Nations Children's Fund: Probably the best known UN social welfare program, it provides a variety of child-directed services in such areas as health, child abuse, neglect and exploitation, child nutrition, education, and water and sanitation. UNICEF received the Nobel Peace Prize in 1965 for its efforts on behalf of children.

World Health Organization: This specialized UN agency focuses on worldwide health issues. It works to establish international health standards in a variety of areas, including vaccines, research, and drugs; it monitors and attempts to control communicable diseases; and it has a special focus on primary health care.

UN High Commission for Refugees: The commission oversees protection, assistance, and resettlement aid. In 1981, it was awarded the Nobel Peace Prize for its work with Asian refugees.

Economic and Social Council: The council coordinates a number of economic and social activities, with specific commissions for focusing on social development, human rights, population, the status of women, and drugs.

Department of Policy Coordination and Sustainable Development: Under the auspices of the UN Secretariat, the leading body of the United Nations, this department coordinates the development of welfare policies and activities.

UN Developmental Programme: This program provides technical assistance grants to developing member nations. Its primary area of support is in agriculture, though grants also support health, education, population, employment, and other related human service programs.

UN Population Fund: This agency collects worldwide population data and implements family programs, including education and contraception.

Did You Know...The United Nations and its organizations have been awarded the Nobel Peace Prize on six separate occasions—1954, 1965, 1969, 1981, 1988, and 2001. In addition, seven people affiliated with the United Nations have received the Nobel Peace Prize—1945, 1949, 1950, 1957, 1961, 1974, and 2001.

The United Nations provides many other social welfare services. Typical activities include conferences and conventions, as well "special years" dedicated to a specific issue. Conferences focus on very specific themes. In 1990, for example, the United Nations sponsored the World Summit for Children; in 1992, the UN Conference on the Environment (Brazil); and in 1995, the Fourth World Conference on Women (Beijing). Special years included the 1994 International Year of the Family and the 1999 International Year of Older Americans.

U.S. Government Agencies

The United States carries out a variety of international social welfare efforts through federal agencies:

Administration for Children and Families: A subsection of the Office of Public Affairs, this agency is the primary conduit for international affairs and social work. Activities include meetings, research, professional exchanges, and cosponsorship of welfare programs. (See www.acf.dhhs.gov.)

Office of Refugee Resettlement: This office coordinates resettlement of refugees in the United States. Since 1975 over two million people have been assisted in the United States because of persecution in their homelands due to race, religion, nationality, or political or social group membership. (See www.acf.dhhs.gov/programs/orr/.)

Social Security Administration: This agency examines social insurance programs worldwide. (See www.ssa.gov.)

U.S. International Development Corporation: This corporation has two responsibilities: international private investment and operating the Agency for International Development (AID). AID provides funding for international projects and is very concerned about AIDS, child welfare, population growth, and basic education. AID has given money to welfare groups, including NASW, to sponsor international programs. (See www.info.usaid.gov.)

Peace Corps: First organized in 1961, the Peace Corps sends American volunteers to different nations to assist in a variety of social, economic, and agricultural projects. (See www.peacecorps.gov.)

U.S. Information Agency: This agency sponsors international leaders from around the world to participate with their colleagues in the United States. The agency also sponsors Americans to study abroad. (Healy, 1995).

Private Voluntary Bodies

Private or nongovernmental groups provide a variety of services and activities throughout the world. Human service organizations such as the YMCA and YWCA sponsor direct services and programs. In addition, nonprofit organizations consult with international agencies and groups about human service issues.

INTERNATIONAL PROFESSIONAL SOCIAL WELFARE ORGANIZATIONS

There are a variety of international social welfare organizations around the world. Some are social work membership associations, similar to the NASW. Others are national and regional educational associations, similar in purpose and function to CSWE.

Three primary worldwide organizing bodies cross national boundaries and encourage partnerships: the International Federation of Social Workers, the International Association of Schools of Social Work, and the International Council on Social Welfare.

International Federation of Social Workers

The International Federation of Social Workers (IFSW) was founded in 1956 to promote social work on the world stage. IFSW is divided into five geographical regions: Africa, Asia and the Pacific, Europe, Latin America and the Caribbean, and North America. Membership is open to one professional social work association in each country. In 1998, seventy national member associations represented more than 460,000 social workers (see box 5 and appendix F). Individuals and organizations may join IFSW as well as take part in the Friends Program. As a friend, a social worker receives the IFSW newsletter, published three times annually, policy papers, and a discount on registration for IFSW international and regional conferences.

IFSW sponsors meetings throughout the world (see box 6). In addition to its biennial international meetings, IFSW sponsors regional meetings that focus on specific area issues; participant costs are much lower for these meetings. Between 1966 and 2002, there have been sixteen regional meetings in Europe, eleven meetings in Asia and the Pacific, and four meetings in Africa. Both regional and worldwide gatherings provide social workers from around the world with a chance to share research findings as well as program ideas.

Box 5: Members of the IFSW, 2003

Argentina	Federacion Argentina de Asociaciones de Profesionales de Servicio Social, www.trabajosocialarg.org.ar
Australia	Australian Association of Social Workers, www.aasw.asn.au
Austria	Österreichischer Berufsverband Diplomierter SozialarbeiterInnen, www.sozialarbeit.at
Bahrain	Bahrain Society of Sociologists
Bangladesh	Association of Social Workers (ASW) Bangladesh
Belarus	Belorussian Association of Social Workers, www.basw.unibel.by
Benin	Syndicat National des Techniciens Sociaux du Benin, csabenin@intnet.bj
Bolivia	Colegio Nacional de Trabajadores Sociales de Bolivia
Brazil	Conselho Federal de Serviço Social (CFESS), www.cfess.org.br
Bulgaria	Bulgarian Association of Social Workers
Canada	Canadian Association of Social Workers, www.casw-acts.ca
Chile	Colegio Asistentes Sociales de Chile, www.cmet.net/profesional
China	China Association of Social Workers
Colombia	Federación Colombiana de Trabajadores Sociales (FECTS)
Croatia	Croatia Association of Social Workers
Cuba	Sociedad Cubana de Trabajadores Sociales de la Salud
Cyprus	Cyprus Association of Social Workers (CyASW)
Czech Republic	Association of Social Workers in Czech Republic
Denmark	Danish Association of Social Workers, www.socialrdg.dk; HK/ Kommunal—Danish Union of Commercial and Office Employees/ Local Government, www.hk-kommunal.dk; National Federation of Social Educators (SL), www.sl.dk
Dominican Republic	Asociacion Dominicana de Trabajadores Sociales Profesionales (ADOTRASOP)
Faroe Islands	Faroe Islands Association of Social Workers
Finland	Union of Professional Social Workers Talentia, www.talentia.fi
France	Association Nationale des Assistants de Service Social (ANAS), http://anas.travail-social.com
Germany	Deutscher Berufsverband für Sozialarbeit e.V, www.dbsh.de
Ghana	Ghana Association of Social Workers (GASOW)
Greece	Hellenic Association of Social Workers, www.skle.gr
Hong Kong	Hong Kong Social Workers Association, www.hkswa.org.hk
Hungary	Szociális Munkások Magyarországi Egyesülete
Iceland	Iceland Association of Social Workers, www.soc-work.is
India	National Coordinating Committee of Professional Social Workers (NCCPSW)
Ireland	Irish Association of Social Workers, www.iasw.eire.org
Israel	Israel Association of Social Workers, www.isassw.org.il
Italy	Associazione Nazionale Assistenti Sociali, www.assnas.it
Japan	Japanese Association of Certified Social Workers (JACSW), www.jacsw.or.jp; Japanese Association of Social Workers (JASW), www.jasw.jp; Japan Association of Social Workers in Health Services (JASWHS); Japanese Association of Psychiatric Social Workers (JAPSW), www.mmjp.or.jp/psw/

Box 5: Members of the IFSW, 2003—(*Continued*)

Kenya	Kenya National Association of Social Workers
Korea	Korean Association of Social Workers, www.kasw.or.kr
Kuwait	Kuwait Association of Social Workers
Kyrgyz Republic	Association of Social Workers of the Kyrgyz Republic, http://asw.gratis.kg
Latvia	Latvian Association of Professional Social and Care Workers; Union of Municipal Social Workers in Latvia
Lebanon	Association des Assistants Sociales du Liban
Lesotho	Lesotho Social Workers
Lithuania	Lithuanian Social Workers' Association
Luxembourg	Association Nationale des Assistantes d'Hygiène Sociale, Assistantes Sociales et Infirmières Graduées du Luxembourg, www.anasig.lu
Macedonia	Union of Social Workers' Associations of Macedonia
Malaysia	Malaysian Association of Social Workers
Malta	Maltese Association of Social Workers
Mauritius	Mauritius Association of Professional Social Workers(MAPSOW)
Mongolia	Mongolian Association of Social Workers
Morocco	Association Marocaine des Assistants et Assistantes Sociales
The Netherlands	Nederlandse Vereniging van Maatschappelijk Workers (NVMW), www.nvmw.org
Netherlands Antilles	Organisashon di Trahadornan Sosial Uni (OTSU)
New Zealand	Aotearoa New Zealand Association of Social Workers, www.anzasw.org.nz/
Nicaragua	Asociacion Nicaraguense de Trabajadores Sociales "Mildred Abaunza"
Niger	Association Nigerienne es Travailleurs Sociaux (ANTS)
Nigeria	Nigeria Association of Social Workers
Norway	Norwegian Union of Social Educators and Social Workers (FO), www.fobsv.no
Peru	Colegio de Asistentes Sociales del Peru
Philippines	Philippine Association of Social Workers, Inc. (PASWI)
Poland	Polish Association of Social Workers, www.ptps.ops.pl
Portugal	Association of Trained Social Workers—APSS, www.apss.web.pt
Romania	Romanian Association for the Promotion of Social Work (ARPAS); Romanian Social Workers Association
Russia	Russian Union of Social Pedagogues and Social Workers
Singapore	Singapore Association of Social Workers, www.sasw.org.sg
Slovak Republic	Association of Social Workers in Slovak Republic (ASPS), www.asps.sk
Spain	Consejo General de Colegios Oficiales de Diplomados en Trabajo Social y Asistentes Sociales, www.cgtrabajosocial.es
Sri Lanka	Sri Lanka Association of Professional Social Workers
Sweden	Akademikerförbundet SSR, www.akademssr.se; SKTF (Swedish Union of Local Government Officers), www.sktf.se
Switzerland	Schweizerischer Berufsverband Soziale Arbeit (SBS) and Association suisse des professionels de l'action sociale (ASPAS), www.sbs-aspas.ch

---

Box 5: Members of the IFSW, 2003—(*Continued*)

Tanzania	Tanzania Association of Social Workers
Thailand	Social Workers' Association of Thailand
Turkey	Association of Social Workers in Turkey, www.shudernegi.org.tr.tc
Uganda	National Association of Social Workers of Uganda (NASWU)
Ukraine	Ukrainian Association of Social Pedagogues and Specialists in Social Work
United Kingdom	British Association of Social Workers, www.basw.co.uk
Uruguay	Asociacion de Asistentes Sociales del Uruguay (ADASU)
United States	National Association of Social Workers, www.socialworkers.org
Zimbabwe	National Association of Social Workers

Box 6: Meetings Sponsored by IFSW

1966	Helsinki	1988	Stockholm
1970	Manila	1990	Buenos Aires
1974	Nairobi	1992	Washington, DC
1976	Puerto Rico	1994	Colombia
1978	Tel Aviv	1996	Hong Kong
1980	Hong Kong	1998	Jerusalem
1982	Brighton	2000	Montreal
1984	Montreal	2002	Harare
1986	Tokyo	2004	Australia

IFSW also provides critical leadership in the pursuit of human rights for individual social workers, social work students, and social service workers. In 1988, IFSW established a Human Rights Commission with members representing each region. The commission works with a number of international human rights groups including Amnesty International.

Did You Know...The headquarters for IFSW is located in Berne, Switzerland, and can be reached at Tel (41) 31 382 6015, Fax (41) 31 381 1222, or via e-mail: secr.gen@ifsw.org

Another noteworthy activity of IFSW is its research and publication of policy papers that explore social issues that social workers face day in and day out. In addition to the following issues, policy papers are planned to explore indigenous people and international adoptions:

Advancement of women	Welfare of elderly people
Child Welfare	Health
HIV-AIDS	Human rights
Migration	Peace and disarmament
Protection of personnel	Refugees
Rural communities	Self-help
Youth	

International Association of Schools of Social Work

As the name suggests, the International Association of Schools of Social Work (IASSW) is the focal point for social work education around the world. IASSW does not set international accreditation standards for social work education, rather it promotes social work education and the development of high-quality educational programs around the world. In a 1928 worldwide meeting, attended by more than 3,000 people from forty-two different nations, the participants agreed that social work was a mechanism that could professionalize and achieve better outcomes from charitable activities (Hokenstad & Kendall, 1995). The following year IASSW was organized, and today membership is open to national associations, such as CSWE, and their specific educational programs. By 1995 IASSW membership totaled 450 schools from 100 countries (Hokenstad & Kendall, 1995). Member schools are divided into six regions—Asia, Africa, Europe and Middle East, Latin America and Caribbean, North America, and Oceania—which facilitates development of regional educational initiatives.

Did You Know…The journal International Social Work *is sponsored jointly by the International Association of Schools of Social Work, the International Federation of Social Workers, and the International Council on Social Welfare.*

IASSW sponsors a biennial meeting, the International Conference of Schools of Social Work, and supports a variety of educationally directed projects. In addition, the association publishes a newsletter and texts. IASSW has also published, with CSWE, a very useful guide to social work programs around the world. The guide—Rao and Kendall (1984)—lists social work programs in different countries, admission standards, and an overview of curricula. While this publication is out of date, it does provide an interesting look at the diversity of social work education around the world. For example, in some African countries you'll find a "certificate" or "state diploma" awarded after the completion of three years of postsecondary study. In Asia, undergraduate and graduate programs are similar in structure to those in America. Hokenstad and Kendall (1995) have written that national traditions and ideologies make it impossible to generalize about social work education in Europe. Structures differ greatly, from length of time to complete a degree program to the content studied.

International Council on Social Welfare

The International Council on Social Welfare (ICSW) is a "global non-governmental organization which represents a wide range of national and international member organizations that seek to advance social welfare, social justice and social development" (www.icsw.org). The primary thrust of the council is to promote social and economic development activities that will reduce poverty, hardship, and vulnerability. The council was founded in Paris in 1928, and today its office is located in London, England. Like IFSW and IASSW, the council holds a biennial conference as well as regional meetings.

ICSW is subdivided into five regions—Africa, Asia and Pacific, Latin America and Caribbean, North America, and Europe. In 2003 ICSW was active in more than fifty countries (www.icsw.org).

NASW AND CSWE INTERNATIONAL INITIATIVES

National Association of Social Workers

NASW is active in pursuing and promoting international relations. The association is guided by its International Activities Committee, which was formed in 1986. The international committee seeks to adopt a variety of mechanisms to increase the globalization of NASW.

As part of its international outreach activities, NASW has sponsored international meetings and travel opportunities. For example, in 1992 NASW, as part of that year's annual meeting, cohosted the World Assembly, the biannual international conclave of social workers, in Washington, D.C. During the 1980s and 1990s, many state NASW chapters forged partnerships with social workers and associations in other countries. In fact, by 1992 twenty-one state chapters had formal relationships with other associations around the world. In addition, the national association and a number of state chapters have sponsored study tours in various countries around the world.

Council on Social Work Education

CSWE is also extremely active in international circles. Organizationally, the council includes an International Commission, which was established in 1978. The commission's focus is on enhancing international opportunities in the social work curriculum. While linking CSWE with international groups, such as IASSW, the

---

Box 7: Sample of International Social Welfare Organizations and their Web Sites

HelpAge International	www.helpage.org
Inclusion International	www.inclusion-international.org
International Catholic Migration Commission	www.icmc.net
International Council of Jewish Women	www.icjw.org.uk
International Council on Jewish Social and Welfare Services	(no web; phone: 41-22-344-9000)
International Federation of Aging	www.ifa-fiv.org
International Federation of Red Cross and Red Crescent Services	www.ifrc.org/what/health/archi/homepage.htm
International Federation of Settlements and Neighborhood Centers	http://datenbanks.spinnenwerk.de/ifs
International Organization for Migration	www.iom.int
International Planned Parenthood Federation	www.ippf.org
International Social Service	www.iss-ssi.org/index.htm
Salvation Army	www.salvationarmy.org

commission strongly advocates that schools internationalize curricula and provide students with worldwide opportunities. In 1998 CSWE, its International Commission, and a number of schools of social work sponsored an international meeting that primarily examined issues related to the Caribbean Basin.

A number of social work programs offer international student exchanges, field placement opportunities, and study tours. These opportunities are usually announced through NASW News, state NASW newsletters, or fliers sent to departments and schools. The following list is just a small sample of the activities that social work programs have undertaken; check directly with your own social work program about any international opportunities it offers:

University of North Carolina–Chapel Hill: study tour of Ireland, Wales, and Scotland

University of Houston: academic exchange program with City University of Hong Kong and travel courses to Wales and China.

University of Central Florida: summer course in Mexico

Florida State University: summer course in England and Spain

International Acronyms

EC	European Community
ECE	Economic Commission of Europe
EFTA	European Free Trade Association
EU	European Union
Eurostat	European Statistical Office
FAO	Food and Agriculture Organization
GATT	General Agreement on Tariffs and Trade; succeeded by WTO
IBRD	International Bank for Reconstruction and Development; usually called the World Bank
IDA	International Development Association
IFAD	International Fund for Agricultural Development
IFC	International Finance Corporation
IMF	International Monetary Fund
NATO	North Atlantic Treaty Organization
OPEC	Organization of Petroleum Exporting Nations
UNDP	United Nations Development Programme
Unesco	United Nations Educational, Scientific, and Cultural Organization
UNICEF	United Nations Children's Fund
UNIDO	United Nations Industrial Development Organization
USAID	United States Agency for International Development
WFP	World Food Programme
WHO	World Health Organization
WTO	World Trade Organization

East Carolina State University: summer course in Bristol, England

University of South Carolina: study tour of Greece

SUMMARY

The events of September 11, 2001, and the fear of terrorism have created a climate never before experienced in this country. These events, however, cannot be used as an excuse to turn away from the issues so germane to the globalization of our society. Problems of substance abuse, child abuse and neglect, spouse battering, poverty, inadequate mental health and health care, and the 'isms' of race, age, and gender continue to be found in every region of the world. And social workers too are found throughout the world, helping individuals, families, and communities to confront these and other social issues.

We experience globalization every day. We can cross the oceans in a matter of hours; we can talk to a friend in another nation simply by dialing a telephone. Through e-mail we can send messages around the world to any number of people in mere milliseconds.

Social work and social welfare are part of this fast-paced, ever-changing world. Yet social work students in the United States have limited exposure to international issues (Hokenstad & Kendall, 1995). Certainly, CSWE and NASW encourage, in a variety of ways, exposure to the international scene as part of the professional experience. But should we be doing more? And if so, how?

The social work educational curriculum is already packed with required content. It is easy to say "International content is required in all social curricula," but at what expense? Will existing content need to be dropped or modified? Are social work educators and practitioners willing to decide whether international content, while important in our world today, is necessary for effective social work practice?

Social work practitioners often claim that they are stretched to the limit by work obligations and wonder how they could continue to manage the rigors of work if required to move into the international arena. As one practitioner stated:

> Don't get me wrong, I'm very concerned about poverty in India and the clear mistreatment of people based on a caste system. BUT I just don't have enough time in a day to do what needs to be done for my child welfare clients. What is important for me is that my kids are able to get back with their families and no longer feel the pain of abuse and neglect.

Attending an international meeting is often a surprise for the American social worker. It's not uncommon to hear social workers from around the world speak in negative terms about the American social work community. Many believe that American social workers do not value the international experience. Whether true or not, they perceive that American social welfare journals discriminate against international authors by declining to publish their manuscripts. They feel that U.S. social work programs do not value international journals and texts, an idea reinforced by the absence of international materials among required readings in social work courses.

There is some truth to allegations that American social workers are ignorant of the international social welfare arena. We are surprised to learn that there are social work organizations similar to NASW and CSWE throughout the world. Yes, we are surprised to discover that social work extends beyond the borders of North America and some parts of Europe.

But rather than berate the profession and each other, we need to commit ourselves to professional globalization. In the classroom, we need to look at issues and conduct discussions in an international context. That doesn't mean that the focus of all efforts should be international, but it does mean that we should consider topics through an international lens, when appropriate.

But what are some specific things we can do? First, we can support NASW in its organizational efforts on a national level as well as in the state chapters and local units. Dedicating one monthly meeting to an international issue with either a guest speaker or a film will enhance our efforts. Second, while more ambitious than looking for a guest speaker, we can try to organize with NASW or utilize a study-travel tour offered by a social work program. Third, we can work to develop a sister program with an international social welfare association or school that can lead to professional exchanges for practitioners and students alike. Fourth, each year most colleges sponsor an "international week" on their campuses. The local social work student group can sponsor an activity that highlights international social welfare.

What we do is limited only to our creativity. But before doing anything we must first commit to the belief that we live in a global community. We need to embrace the notion that our work influences and is influenced by the global community. Then, and only then, will we be able to confront the social ills that plague the world and have any chance of achieving social justice for all people no matter where they live or what their social and economic status.

References

Bell, D. (1973). *The coming of post-industrial society*. New York: Basic Books.

Badolata, E. (2001). How to combat terrorism: Review of United States terrorism policy. *World and I, 16* (8), 50–54.

Brunner, B. (Ed.). (1997). 1998 *Information please almanac*. Boston: Information Please.

Chatterjee, P. (1996). *Approaches to the welfare state*. Washington, DC: NASW Press.

Dyer, K. (2001). *What is different about this incident?* [Online]. Available: http://www.kirstimd.com/911_health.htm.

Dziegielewski, S. F. & Sumner, K. (2002). An Examination of the American Response to Terrorism: Handling the Aftermath Through Crisis Intervention. *Brief Treatment and Crisis Intervention. Winter 2* (4), 287–300.

Fleshman, M. (2002). A troubled decade for Africa's children. *Africa recover. 16*(1), 6.

Gibb, N. (2001). Homeland Insecurity. *Time, 158* (19), 40–54.

Hays, R. (1996). *INS passenger accelerated service system*. [Online]. Available: http://www.biometrics.org/ REPORT/INSPASS.html.

Healy, L. (1995). International social welfare: Organizations and activities. In R. L. Edwards et al. (Eds.), *Encyclopedia of social work* (19th ed., pp. 1499–1510). Washington, DC: NASW Press.

Hokenstad, M. C., & Kendall, K. A. (1995). International social work education. In R. L. Edwards et al. (Eds.), *Encyclopedia of social work* (19th ed., pp. 1511–1520). Washington, DC: NASW Press.

McDonald, W. (1997). Crime and illegal immigration: Emerging, local, state, and federal partnerships. *National Institute of Justice Journal*, 232, 21–25.

Midgley, J. (1995). International and comparative social welfare. In R. L. Edwards et al. (Eds.), *Encyclopedia of social work* (19th ed., pp. 1490–1499).

Midgley, J. (1997). Social work in international context: Challenges and opportunities for the 21st century. In M. Reisch & E. Gambrill (Eds.), *Social work in the 21st century* (pp. 59–67). Thousand Oaks, CA: Pine Forge Press.

Myers, D. (2001). Weapons of mass destruction and terrorism: Mental health consequences and implications for planning and training. Presented at the Weapons of Mass Destruction/Terrorism Orientation Pilot Program, August 2001. [Online]. Available: http://www.icisf.org/Acrobat%20Documents/TerrorismIncident/WMD_Myers.htm.

Rao, V., & Kendall, K. (Eds.). (1984). *World guide to social work education*. New York: CSWE.

Terrorism Research Center. (2000). Chapter 8, Combating Terrorism: *U.S. Army Field Manual*. [Online]. Available: www.terrorism.com.index.html.

Chapter 15

Conclusions

YOU CAN TELL A GREAT DEAL ABOUT SOME BOOKS JUST FROM THEIR titles. Margaret Truman's *Murder at the CIA*, for example, is a murder mystery set within the government. Woodward and Bernstein's *All the President's Men* is a work exploring a president, Nixon in this case, and his staff. On the other hand, titles may mislead you. *Hunt for Red October* is not a story about fall in New England. Salinger's classic *Catcher in the Rye* is not a baseball story about the exploits of Yankee legend Yogi Berra.

In social work, you can also tell a lot from book titles. Look at the following titles and think about what they say to you:

♦ *Social Work, a Profession of Many Faces* (Morales & Sheafor, 1997)
♦ *The Professional Altruist* (Lubove, 1965)
♦ *Social Work, the Unloved Profession* (Richan & Mendelsohn, 1973)
♦ *The Drama of Social Work* (Bloom, 1990)
♦ *Unfaithful Angels* (Specht & Courtney, 1994)

Each title should tell you something about the authors' view of the profession. Morales and Sheafor find social workers involved in a number of settings providing an array of services. Lubove recognizes social workers as people who want to help others but looks beyond the philanthropic model, to someone who is professionally trained in this important art and science. *Social Work, the Unloved Profession* depicts the somewhat negative view that the larger community holds of social work, one in which the profession's activities are not held in high regard. Finally, *Unfaithful Angels* is a critical look by two social workers at the social work profession in which the authors strongly assert that professionals have abandoned advocacy efforts on behalf of the poor in favor of for-profit and private psychotherapeutic services.

These titles taken collectively—each viewed as part of a whole—can inspire an interesting, thought-provoking discussion. And while the main purpose of a text is to educate and inform, a text should also get its readers to think about the subject matter in a more critical, insightful manner.

So, what does the title of our book suggest? After reading the chapters, have you learned something new about the social work profession? Do you have a better understanding of the profession, its varied practice methodologies, and the issues faced by today's practitioners?

The primary purpose of this book is to help you, the reader, to develop a better understanding of social work as a profession. While we've certainly tried to highlight the many exciting and intriguing areas of social work for the beginning social work professional, this presentation is based on reality and we've been as realistic as possible about the state of the profession as it enters its second century.

THE TIME TO DECIDE IS APPROACHING

From the outset, we've made some assumptions about you as the reader of this text and as a beginning social work professional. First, we believe you are reading this book because it's assigned for a class. We realize this isn't the evening, weekend, or vacation book of choice! Second, we think you are taking a social work course that's called "Introduction to Social Work," or something similar, because you're interested in learning more about the field. Actually, whatever the course title may be, the class you are taking is probably one of the first social work courses in a series of prospective majors. Third, we've assumed that while you or some of your classmates may have had some experience with social work professionals, for the most part you agreed when we said that most people do not really have a detailed understanding of the social work profession, including its mission, purpose, and function. Fourth, some of you are seriously exploring social work as a possible career and have registered for this course with that purpose in mind. For others of you, however, this may have been the course that was available at the time or you may have heard that the instructor was really interesting.

Trying to address all of the needs implicit in these assumptions was sometimes daunting, but it was an effort we enjoyed making. It feels good to have put together a text that meets the social work accreditation standards, helps people to gain a clear understanding of the social work profession, supports the faculty member's direction in a course, and helps the individual student to make a career decision: is social work for me?

Making a career decision is not easy, nor should it be. We'll be very forthright with our advice to you: Don't make yourself miserable with worry. What you decide today doesn't obligate you for the rest of your life, or even through next week! You can change your mind at any time about your career goals. It's not unusual for college students to change majors a number of times before completing their baccalaureate studies.

To be fair, it's true that family, friends, and college teachers and counselors put unnecessary pressure on today's students. Why is it so important to select a major by the end of your sophomore year? When you say that you're going to college, why is the first question you hear "What's your major?"

The reasons vary. Family and friends are probably excited that you're pursuing a college education, and naturally they're interested in what courses you plan to take and what career path you'll follow. Those of us who teach in higher education see the potential major as a means to sustain the field. Academic programs are under constant pressure, in many institutions intense pressure, to maintain student enrollments. Declining student enrollments jeopardize continuation of a major. Look at what happened to sociology at a number of colleges in the 1980s: it was discontinued as a major, nontenured faculty were released from their jobs, and tenured faculty members were moved to other departments.

Only a few years ago, the preference was for a student to get a liberal arts education as an undergraduate. To be considered educated a person must have studied a variety of subjects in the arts, sciences, and humanities in an effort to develop a broad, worldly view of people and their settings. The idea was that a liberal thinker, in the literal rather than the political sense, is better suited to participate in society. Some occupations were satisfied with this broad-based education. People could get good jobs without having majored in a specific area. Training for a specific position or workplace happened on the job. People who chose to continue their studies in a specialized field did so in graduate programs.

By contrast, today undergraduate students, some even at the time of application, are asked to declare their majors. Is it fair to ask someone who is just beginning her college education to select a career? Well, we could argue the merits and drawbacks of this practice till we're all blue in the face. The fact is that you must select a major or be cast into the land of the general major (different colleges have different terms for this group; it usually captures all students who haven't chosen a career path).

Most readers of this text have probably made some decisions about social work by this point. We won't take sole credit for influencing the decision-making process. In your course, class discussions, guest speakers, and other instructional strategies, in addition to this text, have helped you to make your decision, or at least a partial decision.

The Non-Social Work Major

We want to offer a few words to those of you who have decided that social work is not for you. First, we're glad you've made a decision that is right for you at this time. Don't be disappointed that social work is not your profession of choice as you may have thought originally. By looking at yourself in the light of information gleaned from this course, you are taking a very important step in your life. And you can always revisit your decision. In career choices the door never closes for good: you can always reconsider your options.

We hoped you have a better understanding and appreciation of social work and the issues that drive our profession. While you feel social work is not your career choice, you can nevertheless help to strengthen the social welfare system. You are better informed about a number of social issues and a number of myths that shroud public policy. When you hear others attack social welfare, listen carefully to what is being said and respond with accurate information. You can be part of the myth-busting squad that dispels misinformation. Let people know the facts about poverty, child welfare, mental health, and the many other areas discussed in the text. Stay informed about the issues: read the daily newspapers and visit social welfare web sites for updated information. Information and facts are among the most powerful tools you can have at your disposal. You can also be invaluable as a social service volunteer. The vast majority of social agencies need people of one kind or another. All it takes is one phone call to a specific agency asking if it needs help. Or if you just want to volunteer a few hours a week and the agency setting doesn't matter, call your local volunteer service agency. They will place you in the most needy agency at which your skills and expertise can make a contribution.

The Social Work Major

Well, you are about to enter a very structured educational experience. Remember what we learned about CSWE accreditation demands in chapter 2? (If not, you may want to reread that chapter, especially before your final examination!) Your academic schedule is pretty much set for the remainder of the program. Courses are sequenced by semester or quarter. You can look at your program's student handbook or ask the course instructor or your academic advisor to review the academic program.

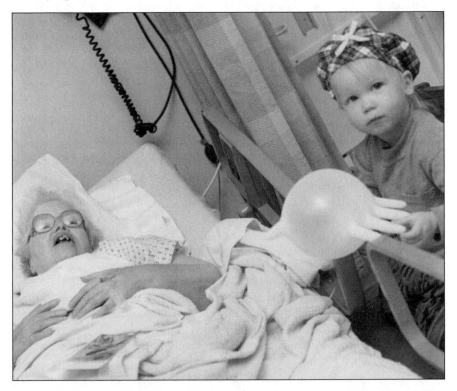

Figure 1: This woman has suffered serious physical illness and can no longer live at home. Her care needs were more than the staff at a nursing home could provide and she was moved to a hospital. Her grandniece and other family members visit her in the hospital.

A few features of your program are set in granite, with little room for modification or negotiation. We also want to raise some considerations you need to keep in mind.

1. The program will take two years of full-time study. You will not be able to graduate in one year. We have found over the years that some students spend an inordinate amount of time challenging and trying to change a structured educational program. They often become angry with the faculty and program, calling them inflexible. Before signing on the dotted line as a social work major be sure to check the curriculum model and its specific requirements, including length of time to complete the program. Can you meet these structural requirements? If not, meet with a social work advisor and determine whether your needs can be accommodated. Don't select the major without first checking all possible scenarios. Plan your schedule carefully and make any necessary arrangements, such as childcare or employment, in order that you can complete all the program requirements (see item 3 below on field placement). Check whether your program has a part-time option in which you can take longer to complete your course of study.

2. Academic credit will not be given for any life experiences, according to CSWE accreditation standards. There are no ifs, ands, or buts on this point. Academic credit is awarded for successful completion of specific college courses. It doesn't matter if you were in the Peace Corps for two years or worked in an agency for five years—no credit can be awarded for these activities.

3. You will have a field placement, which is strategically scheduled in your academic program to allow demonstration of specific knowledge and skills learned in the classroom. You will not be able to take the field course any sooner in the program. Nor can your field course be waived in recognition of previous work experience. Remember, the CSWE life credit requirement applies to all facets of the educational program, including field placement. Check with the field coordinator to discuss any worries you may have; if you aren't able to work in any agency or require some special situation, it is best to let the field coordinator know this as early as possible in order to find a site that meets your needs. You'll need to be flexible in field placement selection. A program will work with you to find the best site to meet your academic needs, but the final field assignment rests with the social work program. We've heard students say that their placement must be in a certain agency, in order to get a job. While programs are concerned about employment, the primary issue in field assignment is your learning—employment comes later.

Some programs may have limited resources to meet all or even some of your field placement needs. Some students haven't received BSW degrees simply because they did not complete field placements because the placements were not during the evening when the students were able to work.

4. Remember: Your peers in social work courses are in the same place you are. Although everyone's circumstances are different—some are older or younger, some have agency experience while others have none—these differences really have minimal importance: all of you are evolving as you begin the process of becoming a professional social worker. No one is better off than anyone else as a result of life experiences. Don't be intimidated by what others say or do or how they come across in class.

5. The purpose of your educational program is to prepare you for entry-level generalist social work practice. It is not to prepare you for a specialization. Nor is it the program's purpose to get you into a graduate program. Your course instructor and academic advisor care primarily about your development as a beginning social worker.

6. Don't approach an instructor and say that you need an A in the course in order to get into graduate school. There's a saying in Texas that fits this type of situation: That dog won't hunt! You certainly have the right to talk with a faculty member about a grade and how it was reached, but it doesn't do any good to be argumentative. The instructor's responsibility is to assess your answers and summarize the quality of your responses with a grade. Grading is not easy—to say the least—and many teachers struggle to ensure that their grades are fair and consistent. Rather than arguing your position, be a social worker: clarify the situation and seek a remedy if you feel one is needed. Can you redo the assignment? Is there extra credit work you can do for the course? And so on. If you feel that your grade is incorrect, check out the student grievance policy in the program. But, we emphasize, use this only as a last resort.

Remember that your faculty members were once students and, like you, at one time or another felt that an instructor had graded them unfairly. We also know that the vast majority of the time, the instructor's assessment is correct; it's just that as students we don't like to get negative information. The key is to look at what the assessment is saying: What didn't you do on the assignment? What could you have done to get your point across more clearly?

Remember, your goal should be the same as your faculty's goal for you: to develop competence and expertise in entry-level generalist social work practice. Your energy should be directed toward developing critical knowledge and skills necessary for effective practice.

Two questions, then, to ask around grades: 1) How will my challenging a grade for a paper, test, or final exam make me a better social work practitioner? 2) Is there an error in the grading that I can demonstrate to the course instructor that justifies the assignment of another grade?

THE FUTURE AND YOU

We are now in a new century and the second hundred years of social work practice. As an up-and-coming social worker, the foundation for the twenty-first century will be laid by your efforts. What you do and say will shape the profession for years to come.

As we bring the text to a close, we want to spend our remaining time looking at two questions. First, knowing what you do about social work, what do you want the profession to look like in the years to come? And second, what changes do you foresee in the social welfare system?

Social Work as a Profession: Future Considerations

You've seen how social work evolved from volunteer effort geared toward the poor to a multifaceted profession working with a variety of client groups. Education was initially limited to on-the-job training, with no oversight of work other than the agency's internal safeguards. Men were the supervisors while women were the caseworkers. Today, education is formal, for some too rigid, and set within colleges and universities. There is public regulation in every state for some, but not all, levels of social work practice. And women, throughout the first hundred years of the profession, made critical contributions to the theory, practice, and politics that make social work what it is today. In the twenty-first century, we find women holding critical positions, leading the profession in academic, professional associations, and in social welfare agencies.

The profession's first century required commitment, passion, and vision in order to achieve its current stature. While we've come a long way, as the poet Robert Frost wrote, we have miles to go before we sleep.

So what are some areas the profession should move into more aggressively? Let's put forth a few ideas to consider:

1. Social work in the twenty-first century is in a pivotal position to create positive social change. Social workers hold elective office at the local, state, and national levels. But we need more of our colleagues to run for office. Who better to write laws about families, children, the poor, the sick, and those at risk, but social workers? Why should lawyers hold a monopoly on political office? Let our opponents call us "bleeding heart liberals." If being a bleeding heart means that we stand for health care for all people, shelter for the homeless, food for the hungry, and education for all children, then call us bleeding hearts. Wouldn't you love to run against an opponent who claims to oppose care of sick children, to want homeless seniors to live unprotected on the streets, to want people, in particular children, to starve, and to oppose making all of our children the best educated in the world? In other words, the profession must use its assets. Our assets are people skills and knowledge.

2. The profession must somehow work together and present a unified front. We need special interest groups and membership associations in order to focus on specialized practice matters. But we are fast approaching, if we haven't already reached, a crossroad where practice membership associations are in conflict with each other and with the overall interests of the profession.

A case in point is public regulation of social work practice. NASW is a staunch advocate of regulation for BSW and MSW levels of practice. The national and state clinical social work membership groups oppose licensing of practice other than clinical practice. Why? Because clinical practitioners fear losing fee-paying clients. They will deny this and point to other factors, but they oppose licensing that will protect all members of the public, not just those who are insured.

How do we bridge the gulf between these two groups? NASW, nationally and in the states, is an important power than can help clinical social worker membership societies achieve their goals. Tension between members of these two groups is not healthy for the profession or, more important, for the public and the clients we serve. Social work membership groups must find common ground if we are to become even more effective in our public efforts.

3. We must seek out more BSWs to join NASW. There are too few BSW members in the association. As a result, BSW practice interests are not fully represented at all levels of the association. Annual membership dues certainly are expensive—in particular, for lower-paid BSWs—and NASW has taken this into account in the dues structure. But efforts to attract BSWs must go far beyond lower dues. MSWs must make BSWs feel like accepted and important members of the profession. Elitism and professional ethnocentrism will only weaken our efforts.

Social work programs can play a critical role by involving BSW students in NASW. First, programs can promote membership. Student dues are relatively inexpensive and are far outweighed by the association's benefits. Second, social work programs, together with state chapters and local units, can look at developing student units that hold meetings on campus. Third, social work programs can work with local NASW units to hold meetings on campus—many students are place bound and have no way to get to a meeting.

The key is for professional groups and social work programs to be aggressive in recruiting students, then to value BSW students as future members, and finally to involve them in association activities.

4. In chapter 14, we spent time exploring the international social welfare arena. Social work is a worldwide profession that helps people, families, communities, and social systems to deal with issues that cut across national boundaries.

As practitioners in the twenty-first century, your work, more than at any other time in the world's history, will influence and be influenced by the international community. The phrase "think globally, act locally" probably best captures the direction we must go. Yet social workers, for the most part, have little exposure to international social welfare. International course content is sparse in both undergraduate and graduate programs. There are exceptions, of course; some schools sponsor study-abroad programs, offer educationally directed travel programs, or have a greater international emphasis. Yet most social work programs do little more than offer brief mentions as part of a course or courses.

Professional associations also work to promote international issues. Again through study tours and publications, we become more aware of the international community. But is this enough? We don't think so. We support the goal of global understanding and activism. Expanding our understanding will help us to be knowledgeable members of the world community. Our global learning and understanding of others will help us to better appreciate the strength and potential of seemingly different people while developing greater awareness of the struggles that will need to be engaged. Global activism builds on knowledge. Once we understand others we are in a better position to offer effective assistance and support.

There are many mechanisms we can implement to pursue the goal of global understanding and activism. Obviously, the expansion of BSW and MSW curriculum content would help us toward this goal. International content in each course and an additional specific international course would help enhance our knowledge base. We can also become more creative in our approach. Social work educational programs can sponsor annual activities that highlight one or two aspects of international social welfare. Professional associations, both at the national and state levels, can sponsor international activities each year. Hosting continuing education workshops, dedicating parts of association newsletters to international issues, and developing dedicated international handouts and brochures will help us to become more global.

The American Social Welfare System: The Future

What a fascinating history we have in social welfare! The overview in chapter 2 was just that, an overview. Even from that brief foray, we could see emerge the beliefs that underpin the current U.S. social welfare system.

First, the poor and people in need are "different" from the rest of us. Some say the poor are morally inferior and lazy; others might say the poor are poorly educated and lack the motivation to change. Second, welfare services are best organized by nongovernmental entities. Americans have always been reluctant to support federal involvement in the social welfare system. Social agencies, churches, volunteer associations, and informal networks are more acceptable vehicles for social welfare. Third, social welfare is not an entitlement but rather a temporary support given only to the most worthy. Over time, women, infants, children, the aged, and people with disabilities have fallen into the category of the "worthy" poor. Fourth, work is the primary way to achieve self-sufficiency. All anyone needs is a job, not even a good-paying job at first, because the early experience will lead to future, higher paying jobs.

Now, these views are not necessarily those of most social workers, but they do express the expectations of much of the American public. In chapter 2 we discussed the modern welfare system and in chapter 7 the 1990s welfare reform package. And with the presidential election of 2000, a new welfare concept came across the national scene: "compassionate conservatism." These discussions showed how well ingrained into the American welfare system these four beliefs are.

So, where does the American welfare system go? Is the current system working? Here are some proposed changes to the welfare system:

1. The welfare system must be just and treat all people with respect and dignity. How do we explain compassion for the less fortunate when we have a welfare program that only allows a maximum of five years of assistance in a lifetime? Some people, no matter what we do, just won't be able to care for themselves. Why do we penalize an unborn baby by denying it welfare benefits because the mother was already on assistance. What kind of life are we promising that child? A comprehensive welfare system embraces people and their strengths. We should move away from a punitive system to one based on hope.

2. American welfare carries an enormous stigma. Every day politicians, radio talk show hosts and callers, and newspaper columnists, among others, rail against the poor. With this constant barrage, it would be a wonder if welfare clients didn't hide from the general public. Being poor and receiving public assistance is not the fulfillment of a lifelong ambition. We should work to remove the stigma associated with public aid.

3. The goal of the welfare system should be to help all people with adequate benefits and supports. If the system works, then people who are capable of doing so will move to sustainable work. The purpose of the welfare system's benefits and supports is simple: help clients to meet their daily needs in order to focus their energies on becoming self-sufficient. The welfare system should concentrate on meeting basic needs: food, shelter, and protection. The level of these benefits must be sufficient. A second tier of services, which includes high-quality health care and childcare, supports adults in their efforts to work. A third tier of programs focuses on developing knowledge and skills necessary to become self-sufficient in a technological society. Transportation and education and training programs are the two principal components of this tier. Reliable transportation is needed to ensure that people can get to the training programs; not everyone has a car and not all cities and towns have public transportation. The fourth and final tier of the welfare system includes access to permanent, good-paying jobs that offer upward mobility and self-sufficiency. Once employed, the client is able to receive workplace benefits and no longer needs public welfare support.

4. A comprehensive welfare system is expensive. But if we care for the poor and less fortunate, the price tag should not matter. Funding decisions for programs are made in a political context. The decision to fund roads and highways at one level and after-school childcare at a much lower level is a statement about our beliefs. Funds are available to support a comprehensive welfare system, either by changing governmental spending patterns or by raising taxes. Throughout the text we have referred directly and indirectly to the influence of the political system on social welfare, and in chapter 13 we outlined the role that social workers can assume in politics. As we consider the

role of politics in social welfare and questions related to funding, we must first answer two questions: What is the goal of our welfare system? What commitments are we willing to make to achieve that goal?

5. Social welfare and social work should do no harm to any person, group, or community. The "do no harm" philosophy is a fundamental value embraced by the medical community and its ideas should resonate throughout our helping systems. Do we want to create social policies that harm people? Of course not. Yet, through TANF we put in place a lifetime limit on the number of months a person can receive federal assistance. Why do we allow millions of our children not to be fully immunized? Under a "do no harm" philosophy, we would ensure that ALL children would be fully immunized. "Do no harm" is a core concept that serves as a pivotal girder in the foundation of a just, compassionate society.

SOCIAL WORK PRACTICE

In the new environment of cost containment and managed care social workers must either accept this challenge for change or lose the opportunity to be players in this era of competition for the provision of outcome-based services. Social workers must be able to show that what they do is necessary and effective while maintaining their own ethical and moral standards for the helping relationship.

All social workers must take a PROACTIVE stance regardless of their practice area. This book is designed to serve as a practical guide for understanding and applying this philosophy in our social work practice environment. Simply stated, all social workers need to embrace the following imperatives at all levels of practice:

P   PRESENT and POSITION themselves as competent professionals with POSITIVE attitudes in all service settings, whatever the type of practice.

R   RECEIVE adequate training and continuing education in the current and future practice area of social work
RESEARCH time-limited treatment approaches that can provide alternatives for social workers struggling to provide high-quality services while cutting costs

O   ORGANIZE individuals and communities to help themselves to access safe and affordable services
ORGANIZE other social workers to prepare for the changes that are occurring and develop strategies to continue to provide ethical, cost-effective service

A   ADDRESS policies and issues that are relevant to providing ethical, effective, efficient service

C   COLLABORATE with other helping professionals to address client concerns and needs utilizing an interdisciplinary team approach
COMPLEMENT orthodox practices by utilizing holistic practices and alternative strategies that can help clients achieve increased well-being

T   TEACH others about the value and the importance of including social work services and techniques

TAKE TIME to help ourselves holistically by preventing professional burnout thus remaining productive and receptive and serving as good role models for clients and other professionals

I   INVESTIGATE and apply INNOVATIVE approaches to client care problems and issues

INVOLVE all social workers in the change process that needs to occur in traditional social work

V   VISUALIZE and work toward positive outcomes for all clients and potential clients

VALUE the roles of all other helping professionals and support them as they face similar challenges and changes

E   EXPLORE supplemental therapies and strategies that clients can self-administer at little or no cost to preserve and enhance well-being

EMPOWER clients and ourselves by stressing the importance of EDUCATION for self-betterment as well as individual and societal change (adapted from Dziegielewski, 2004)

We will need to face the many changes that are in store for helping professionals, and we need to remember that in this area of budget cutting and cost containment we can be viable players. The NASW Code of Ethics directs us to charge reasonable fees and base our charges on ability to pay. This means that the fees social work professionals charge are very competitive with those of psychiatrists, psychologists, family therapists, psychiatric nurses, and mental health counselors, who provide similar services. This fact could entice managed care agencies to contract with social workers instead of other professionals to provide services that have traditionally fallen in the domain of social work practice. In this era of managed care, no aspect of taking a proactive stance can be underestimated.

SPECIAL TOPIC: REGULATION OF PROFESSIONAL SOCIAL WORK PRACTICE

The government regulates all professions throughout the United States. Regulation is important to ensure that the public is protected from harm caused by unqualified persons. Regulation includes "licensing, registration, and certification and confers credentials recognized by the public" (Biggerstaff, 1995, p. 1617). According to Biggerstaff, a credential is evidence that the practitioner meets minimum standards for providing specific services to the public.

Why do we regulate occupations? What does credentialing do for us in the long run? First, a regulated occupation's activities are such that the average citizen may be harmed physically, emotionally, or financially if he is exposed to the practice of an unqualified person. Second, credentialing suggests that a specific educational background is needed to make a person qualified to carry out the tasks in a regulated occupation. Third, the public is assured that all regulated persons meet minimum standards of competence as set forth by the state. Finally, the public is assured that mechanisms are available for the pursuit of grievances against regulated workers.

Activity...Contact your state's social work licensing board or regulatory body and ask for information about the regulation of social work practice. Are all levels of social work practice licensed? Does the board seem to reflect the social work profession's broad range of work, or is its membership restricted to one or two types of practice? Attend a licensing board meeting (they are open to the public), and determine how the board protects the public interest. Finally, how does the local social work community perceive licensing? (Check this out at a local NASW unit meeting.)

Think for a moment about the types of occupations that are regulated by the government. Decisions to regulate professions are left to state governments, so you'll find that some occupations are licensed in one state but not in another. Even when a profession is regulated by more than one state, the criteria that must be met for certification may differ. Types of educational degrees and years of experience required and the use of exams to test competence vary by state and occupation.

The list of occupations that states regulate seems endless. The state of Florida, for example, regulated 189 different occupations in 1998! Box 1 lists less than a quarter of the occupations regulated by the Florida state government. You'll note that the state oversees a wide array of occupations that can affect people's lives for good or bad.

The profession of social work is regulated in all fifty states. By that we mean that some form of social work practice is licensed or certified by each state government. For the most part, regulation does not have two levels that mirror the two levels of social work practice, the BSW (generalist practice) and the MSW (specialist practice). For example, some states license both BSW and MSW practitioners

---

Box 1: Partial List of Occupations Regulated by the State of Florida

Architect	Interior designer	Barber
Public Accountant	Pool contractor	Solar contractor
Building Contractor	Chiropractor	Nail specialist
Cosmetologist	Hair braiders	Dental hygienist
Dentist	Electrical contractor	Alarm system contractor
Embalmer	Talent agency	Physician
Optometrist	Podiatrist	Veterinarian
Nurse	Auctioneer	Athletic trainer
Respiratory therapist	Midwife	Nutrition counselor
Surveyor and mapper	Audiologist	School psychologist
Mental health counselor	Asbestos contractor	Physical therapist
Occupational therapist	Liquor salesperson	Building inspector

Current and Future Perspectives on Licensing and Credentialing

We must first recognize that social workers cannot be forced to subscribe to voluntary credentialing. In other words, a social worker does not have to join NASW to be held accountable to the association's Code of Ethics or thereby qualify for credentialing in the field. Credentialing needs to take place in the public domain, which through law would require that all social workers meet minimum educational and practice standards and be held accountable for their work. Then, and only then, will the public have an opportunity to be protected from incompetent and unethical practitioners. The differences that currently exist in licensure and certification requirements among the different states appears to mirror the ongoing ambivalence that continues to plague social work licensure and certification in the social work profession. Two inaccurate yet strong beliefs remain prominent and these beliefs continue to influence the social work profession. First is the erroneous belief that anyone can do social work and that the work doesn't require a professional education or specialized training. Second is the misconception that the tasks and functions that most social workers perform cannot place the public at-risk so therefore they can indeed be performed by non-social work professionals. As a profession, it is important to note that we are not above our own internal disagreements and conflicts. Yet, we must rise above them and continue to actively debate and struggle with answering such questions as "should we license all levels of social work practice?" For now, we certainly do not have professional consensus on that question and there are some social workers, particularly some MSW practitioners, that do not agree. Further, there are some MSWs and special interest organizations that believe that licensing should be restricted to only certain social work activities, such as the practice of clinical social work. Given that NASW continues to limit its credentialing and certification process to MSWs and no longer sponsors a voluntary BSW form of certification, this inadvertently supports the continued debate between practice levels within the profession.

The research shows that different types of social work practice are regulated. Some states regulate only clinical practice while other states do not specify a practice methodology but license based on the degree. Even so, indications are that more and more states are moving toward multi-level licensure.

Just as problematic is the fact that the practice of social work is so diverse that it has no specific domain. For the most part, there is no national label or title for our work. Given that states establish their own licensing laws, each state has also developed its own titles for social work practitioners. Given that there are 39 different titles nationwide for social workers, it is no wonder that people are confused about the profession!

There is a clear-cut need to adopt a national model licensing law. The American Association of State Social Work Boards proposes one. Prior to the AASSW 1997 proposal, NASW, in 1973, also put forth a model law (NASW, 1973). A model law adopted by all states will accomplish a number of important tasks and benefit the public and the profession alike.

1. All states will regulate the same types of social work practice.
2. All states will maintain similar education and continuing education standards.
3. All states will use similar titles for professionals.
4. There will be less confusion among the public concerning the function and activities of social workers.
5. All social workers will be held accountable for their activities.
6. The public, in particular the poor and clients of public social services, will be assured that their social workers meet minimal educational and practice competencies.
7. Mechanisms will be in place for clients to pursue incompetent and unethical social work practice.

Overall, regulation is a positive step for ensuring quality service provision for the public and the profession alike. It is not surprising that it remains difficult to achieve and maintain order to protect the public. Public regulation should be comprehensive and include all levels of social work practice. Finally, state licensing should be augmented and supported by membership associations' internal voluntary credentialing programs. Together, voluntary association credentialing and state licensing can put forth a strong shield of protection for the public.

together, while other states limit licensing to MSW practitioners who specialize in clinical social work. Most, but not all, states require passage of a written examination; and most, but not all, states require ongoing continuing education after being licensed.

The regulation of social work practice is subject to a number of complications. First, it is tied to the intricacies of the political process. As with any law passed by a state legislature, it reflects political interests. What seems to be a logical, straightforward piece of legislation may end up being defeated for any number of reasons. Some social workers are against formal licensure for the profession, but if we license and regulate hair braiders and surveyors (as listed in box 1), doesn't it make sense also to regulate a profession that is concerned with the emotional and psychological well-being of people?

Second, licensing requires social work professionals to overcome their own biases and act in the best interests of the profession. Unfortunately, this is easier said than done. Many social work special interest groups are most concerned with protecting their own members. Once a group feels its interests are enhanced and not compromised, it will support the legislation. You can imagine what happens to a licensing bill that must satisfy any number of social work interest groups, and what can result when ten or more interest groups are all actively lobbying at any given time.

Third, once the profession has pieced together a compromise proposal, it must then meet the demands of other human service professions and organizations.

Typically, these groups feel that their activities will be affected by the social work licensing act. As a result, these groups work to ensure that the final legislation will not interfere with their day-to-day activities or finances.

Finally, licensing BSW and MSW practice can become very cumbersome and confusing. While licensing protects the public from non-professional practice, state regulation also carves out specific practice areas or "turf" for professions. And "turf battles" can be hard fought. In Texas, for example, the state legislature in 2003 amended the licensing law to allow BSW degreed individuals to conduct "independent" practice. For some, this is very confusing—could one interpret "independent practice" as being similar to "private practice"? According to the Texas law, this is not the case. But will the public understand the "legal" definition—probably not, given that most social workers themselves are not able to differentiate the differences between independent and private practice.

FINAL THOUGHTS

You should be writing this chapter. As future social workers and members of the global community, you will ultimately be responsible for the social welfare system of the twenty-first century. The types of programs, levels of assistance, and the clients eligible for benefits will all be issues that you will address.

The social work profession will always be part of our community as long as complex human social problems remain. As social workers, our challenge is to remain relevant to our nation's goals and our clients' needs. We can do this by vigorously pursuing competence in practice, by discovering and validating innovative interventions, and by ensuring that our educational and training programs continue to excel.

As you tackle social welfare issues be passionate in your convictions, ethical in your actions, knowledgeable about your information, and, above all, committed to the view that social justice is due to all people. Our community will be a better place because of people like you.

References

Biggerstaff, M. (1995). Licensing, regulation, and certification. In R. L. Edwards et al. (Eds.), *Encyclopedia of social work* (19th ed., pp. 1616–1624). Washington, DC: NASW Press.

Bloom, M. (1990). *The drama of social work*. Itasca, IL: Peacock.

Dziegielewski, S. F. (2004). *The changing face of health care social work: Professional practice in the era of behaviorally based managed care*. New York: Springer.

Lubove, C. (1965). *The professional altruist*. Cambridge, MA: Harvard University Press.

Morales, A., & Sheafor, B. (1997). *Social work: A profession of many faces* (8th ed.). Boston: Allyn and Bacon.

NASW (1973). *Legal regulation of social work practice*. Washington, DC: Author.

Richan, W., & Mendelsohn, A. R. (1973). *Social work, the unloved profession*. New York: Franklin Watts.

Specht, H., & Courtney, M. (1994). *Unfaithful angels*. New York: Free Press.

Glossary

absolute poverty qualitative measure of poverty that compares a person's situation with a numerical standard that usually reflects bare subsistence; cf. relative poverty.

abuse improper behavior that can result in physical, psychological, or financial harm to an individual, family, group, or community. In social work the term is most often related to acts against children, the elderly, the mentally impaired, or spouses or used in relation to drug or other substance abuse.

accreditation professional recognition that a social work program meets explicit standards; voted on by the CSWE Commission on Accreditation after it reviews the program's self-study documents, the site visitors' written report, and the program's written response to the site visit.

advocacy professional activities aimed at educating, informing, or defending and representing the needs and wants of clients through direct intervention or empowerment.

agency organization that provides social services and is typically staffed by social service professionals, including social workers. Public, private, and not-for-profit agencies provide an array of services, usually to a target population. Policy is set by a board of directors and is implemented by administrators.

agency-based occurring in an agency. Agency-based practice can include a few specific practice methodologies or can span the continuum of social work practice, depending on the agency's size, mission, and purpose.

Aid to Families with Dependent Children (AFDC) a means-tested program that provided financial aid to children in need due to parental disability, absence, or death. It was administered nationally through the Administration for Children and Families division of the U.S. Department of Health and Human Services; state and county departments of public welfare provided local administration. AFDC ended in 1996 with the creation of Temporary Assistance for Needy Families.

almshouse (also know as poorhouse) place of refuge for the poor, medically ill, and mentally ill of all ages; considered the forerunner of the hospital.

assessment process of determining the nature, cause, progression, and prognosis of a problem and identifying the personalities and situations involved; process of reasoning from facts to tentative conclusions about their meaning.

at-risk populations (also known as vulnerable populations) groups with increased exposure to potential harm due to specific characteristics. Examples are infants born to drug-using mothers, who are at risk for birth defects; minorities, who are at risk for oppression; and poor children, who are at risk for malnutrition.

biopsychosocial approach   approach to social work practice, especially in health care and mental health, that assesses and places appropriate emphasis on the biological, psychological, and social or environmental aspects of the client's situation.

block grant   lump sum of funds given to a state by the federal government. The state has authority over expenditure of block grants and may supplement them with state funds.

BSW (baccalaureate in social work)   undergraduate degree in social work from a CSWE-accredited program; the entry-level social work qualification. BSSW and BA or BS in social work are equivalent degrees.

candidacy   preaccreditation status for a social work program, which generally lasts two years; signifies that an educational program meets general criteria to conduct a self-study for accreditation.

charity assistance   aid given to the poor in the 1600s; viewed as a mechanism that reinforced dependent lifestyles.

charity organization society (COS)   privately or philanthropically funded agency that delivered social services to the needy in the mid- to late nineteenth century; considered the forerunner of the nonprofit social service agency.

child welfare   series of human service and social welfare programs designed specifically to promote the protection, care, and health development of children; found at the national, state, and local levels.

client   individual, couple, family, group, or community that is the focus of intervention.

Commission on Accreditation   CSWE committee of twenty-five social work educators and practitioners who oversee the accreditation process. The commission establishes educational standards and reviews programs to ensure that they meet the standards.

continuing education   training acquired after the completion of a degree program. NASW and state licensure boards require specified hours of continuing education in order to maintain a license or certification.

Council on Social Work Education (CSWE)   sole national accreditation board for schools of social work; founded in 1952 from the merger of the American Association of Schools of Social Work (founded 1919) and the National Association of Schools of Social Administration (founded 1942).

diagnosis   process of identifying a problem—social, mental, or medical—and its underlying causes and formulating a solution.

disadvantaged   term used to describe individuals, groups, communities, and the like, that are unable to access the resources and services needed to maintain a minimal standard of living.

discharge planning   service provided by health care social workers to assist clients in, for example, securing placement and services to support a timely transition from a health care facility to home or to another less restrictive environment.

domestic violence   violent acts toward another person perpetrated in a domestic situation.

DSM-IV-TR (Diagnostic and Statistical Manual, 4th edition, Text Revision)   manual that presents a classification system designed to assist in reaching formal diagnoses. It uses five "axes": Axis I, the first level of coding, records such categories as major clinical syndromes, pervasive developmental disorders, learning disorders, motor skills disorders, communication disorders, and other disorders that may be the focus of clinical treatment. Axis II records personality disorders and mental retardation. Axis III records general medical conditions that can affect mental health. Axis IV records psychosocial and environmental problems/stressors. Axis V records level of functioning.

DSW (doctor of social welfare or social work)   highest social work degree; typically requires two years of full-time post-master's course work, passage of comprehensive examinations, and successful completion of a dissertation.

Educational Policy and Accreditation Standards (EPAS)   written document that outlines the purpose and framework of social work education programs. The CSWE Commission on Accreditation is responsible for oversight of the EPAS.

empirically based social work practice   type of intervention in which the professional social worker uses research as a practice and problem-solving tool. Data are collected systematically, and problems and outcomes are stated in measurable terms.

entitlement programs   these are governmental programs offered to all individuals that meet the predetermined criteria.

ethics   system of moral principles used in decision making to discern right from wrong or to choose between two or more seemingly equal alternatives.

field placement   work in an agency during the BSW or MSW educational experience, supervised by a social worker. Students are trained and monitored by the agency and the educational institution jointly.

Food Stamp Program   program that distributes to people in need "stamps" that can be used to purchase basic food items; implemented in 1964 and administered by the U.S. Department of Agriculture until 1996; now administered by states under the Personal Responsibility and Work Opportunity Reconciliation Act of 1996.

friendly visitor   volunteer from a charity organization society who visited poor families to offer aid and to serve a role model.

generalist practice   practice underpinned by knowledge and skills across a broad spectrum and by comprehensive assessment of problems and their solutions; includes coordination of activities of specialists.

Head Start   program intended to help preschool children of disadvantaged families to overcome or offset problems related to social deprivation; established in 1965 and administered by Child Youth and Families within the U.S. Department of Health and Human Services.

home care   in this type of health care, social work services are provided to individuals and families in their home or community and/or other home-like settings.

hospice care   this type of care involves providing services to individuals who are considered to be terminally ill and their family members. In this type of care there is open acknowledgment that no cure is expected for client's illness, and to support the process of dying in a dignified manner, physical, emotional, social, and spiritual care are provided.

hospital social worker   social worker who practices in hospitals and health care facilities; focuses on assessments, discharge planning, preventive services, interdisciplinary coordination, and individual and family counseling.

indoor relief   assistance provided during colonial times to the "unworthy" poor in poorhouses.

in kind   benefit in the form of food, clothing, education, and so forth, in place of, or in addition to, cash.

institutional social welfare   social programs available to all as a part of well-being in the modern state; cf. residual social welfare.

interdisciplinary team   variety of health care professionals brought together to provide a client with effective, better coordinated, and improved quality of services.

International Federation of Social Workers (IFSW)   international association of social workers comprising members through their national organizations; founded in 1928 in Paris; promotes social work, establishes standards, and provides a forum for exchange among associations throughout the world.

intervention   treatment, services, advocacy, mediation, or any other practice action, performed for or with clients, that is intended to ameliorate problems.

label   clinical diagnosis of a client that stays with the client indefinitely, possibly to the client's detriment.

macrosystem   community, administrative, and environmental forces that affect the human condition. Political action, community organizing, and administration of large public welfare agencies are examples of macropractice.

Meals on Wheels   delivery of meals to the homes of people unable to meet their own nutritional needs, usually due to physical or mental impairment. Service is usually provided by community agencies, such as senior citizen councils, local human service departments, and private agencies.

means-tested program: a means-tested program involves evaluating a potential program recipient's resources and whether the need is great enough for eligibility within a predetermined criteria set.

Medicaid   program established in 1965 that funds hospital and other medical services to people who meet means tests; administered by the federal Health Care Financing Administration.

Medicare   national health insurance program established in 1965. Eligibility is universal, with attainment of age 65 the criterion for most people; however, there are allied programs for the disabled among others. Medicare is funded through employee and employer contributions and administered by the Social Security Administration and the Health Care Financing Administration.

mezzosystem   system that connects micro- and macrosystems.

microsystem   individual, family, or small group. Direct intervention and casework are examples of micropractice.

MSW (master of social work)   degree requiring approximately sixty hours of postbaccalaureate education, including 900 hours of field placement, in a CSWE-accredited program. MSSW and MA or MS in social work are equivalent degrees.

multidisciplinary team   mix of health and social welfare professionals, with each discipline working, for the most part, on an independent or referral basis.

National Association of Social Workers (NASW)   world's largest social work membership association with approximately 160,000 members in 1999; established in 1955 through the merger of five special interest organizations; chapters exist in all fifty states and the District of Columbia, New York City, Puerto Rico, and the Virgin Islands, in addition to an international chapter.

New Deal   set of social welfare programs and legislation implemented during President Franklin D. Roosevelt's administration in response to the Great Depression. Examples include the Economic Security Act of 1935, Works Progress Administration, and Federal Emergency Relief Act.

outdoor relief   minimal assistance provided during the colonial period to the "worthy" poor in their own homes.

overseer of the poor   individual responsible during colonial times for identifying the poor, assessing their needs, and coordinating a community reponse by levying and collecting taxes; considered a colonial version of a social worker.

parens patriae   principle under which children can become wards of the state. The basic legal tool for carving out children's rights, this principle has allowed children's advocates to argue that children should be viewed differently from adults. It has been cited to support the creation of a range of juvenile services.

Person-in-Environment Classification System (PIE)   systematic approach to classifying social functioning. It employs four levels to aid in the systematic collection of data about clients and in planning interventions. Level I is social functioning problems. Level II is environmental problems. Level III is mental disorders—DSM-IV Axes I and II. Level IV is physical health problems.

person-in-situation (also called person-in-environment)   casework concept that focuses on the interrelation between problem, situation, and the interaction between them.

PhD (doctorate in philosophy)   highest social work degree, emphasizing research, knowledge expansion, and advanced clinical practice; similar, often identical to, DSW. See *DSW* for requirements.

policy   plan that an agency, organization, or governmental institution follows as a framework; includes formal written policies and unwritten (informal) policies.

political lens   political context—often candidates for public office and their campaigns—that influences how society defines a term, for example, "family."

poor laws   codified in 1601; redefined welfare as no longer a private affair but rather a public governmental responsibility.

poverty   general term used to describe a state of deprivation. See *absolute poverty* and *relative poverty*.

poverty threshold   level of income below which a person is living in poverty. This level is based on the cost of securing the basic necessities of living.

psychosocial history   systematic compilation of information about a client; encompasses family, health, education, spirituality, legal position, interpersonal relations, social supports, economic status, environment, sexual orientation, and culture.

reaffirmation   confirmation of CSWE accreditation, for which an accredited program must undergo the self-study and review process every seven years.

relative poverty subjective measure of poverty that compares a person's situation with a normative standard; cf. absolute poverty.

residual social welfare social programs activated only when normal structures of family and market are not sufficient; cf. institutional social welfare.

sanction 1) formal or informal authorization to perform services; 2) penalty imposed for noncompliance with policies and procedures. NASW sanctions members who have violated the Code of Ethics with membership suspension or removal of certification.

selective eligibility (also called means-tested eligibility) eligibility based on demonstrating need or inability to provide for one's needs; cf. universal eligibility.

site visit visit to a social work educational program by a site team composed of social work educators and, for graduate programs, an MSW practitioner. The site team makes a written report to the CSWE Commission on Accreditation that is considered during the commission's deliberations on the program's accreditation.

social justice a core social work value that involves efforts to confront discrimination, oppression, and other social inequities.

social welfare 1) society's specific system of programs to help people to meet basic health, economic, and social needs; 2) general state of well-being in society.

specialist practice practice focused in approach and knowledge on a specific problem or goal or underpinned by highly developed expertise in specific activities.

Strengths-based assessment this type of assessment relies on the social worker's ability to critically analyze the positive aspects, attributes, or strengths in a client or client system and utilize these strengths in every aspect of the problem-solving process.

stigma negative connotation attached to individuals, or groups of individuals, based on characteristics that may include economic status, health, appearance, education, sexual orientation, and mental health.

Temporary Assistance for Needy Families (TANF) program established in 1996 to replace AFDC; subject to strict eligibility requirements, which mandate employment, and to a lifetime limit on benefits of five years; funded through federal block grants to states, which administer the program.

universal eligibility availability to all people regardless of income or social support; cf. selective eligibility.

unworthy poor see *worthy poor*.

Violence Against Women Act (VAWA) passed in 1994; a comprehensive federal response to the problems of domestic violence that promotes preventive programs and victim's services.

worthy poor category of people "deserving" of public aid introduced by the 1601 poor laws; included the ill, the disabled, orphans, the elderly—people viewed as having no control over their life circumstances—as well as people who were involuntarily unemployed. The unworthy poor consisted of the vagrant or able-bodied who, while able to work, did not seek employment.

National Association of Social Workers, Code of Ethics

Approved by the 1996 NASW Delegate Assembly and revised by the 1999 NASW Delegate Assembly.

Preamble

The primary mission of the social work profession is to enhance human well-being and help meet the basic human needs of all people, with particular attention to the needs and empowerment of people who are vulnerable, oppressed, and living in poverty. A historic and defining feature of social work is the profession's focus on individual well-being in a social context and the well-being of society. Fundamental to social work is attention to the environmental forces that create, contribute to, and address problems in living.

Social workers promote social justice and social change with and on behalf of clients. "Clients" is used inclusively to refer to individuals, families, groups, organizations, and communities. Social workers are sensitive to cultural and ethnic diversity and strive to end discrimination, oppression, poverty, and other forms of social injustice. These activities may be in the form of direct practice, community organizing, supervision, consultation, administration, advocacy, social and political action, policy development and implementation, education, and research and evaluation. Social workers seek to enhance the capacity of people to address their own needs. Social workers also seek to promote the responsiveness of organizations, communities, and other social institutions to individuals' needs and social problems.

The mission of the social work profession is rooted in a set of core values. These core values, embraced by social workers throughout the profession's history, are the foundation of social work's unique purpose and perspective:

–service
–social justice
–dignity and worth of the person
–importance of human relationships
–integrity
–competence.

This constellation of core values reflects what is unique to the social work profession. Core values, and the principles that flow from them, must be balanced within the context and complexity of the human experience.

PURPOSE OF THE NASW CODE OF ETHICS

Professional ethics are at the core of social work. The profession has an obligation to articulate its basic values, ethical principles, and ethical standards. The NASW Code of Ethics sets forth these values, principles, and standards to guide social workers' conduct. The Code is relevant to all social workers and social work students, regardless of their professional functions, the settings in which they work, or the populations they serve.

The NASW Code of Ethics serves six purposes:

1. The Code identifies core values on which social work's mission is based.
2. The Code summarizes broad ethical principles that reflect the profession's core values and establishes a set of specific ethical standards that should be used to guide social work practice.
3. The Code is designed to help social workers identify relevant considerations when professional obligations conflict or ethical uncertainties arise.
4. The Code provides ethical standards to which the general public can hold the social work profession accountable.
5. The Code socializes practitioners new to the field to social work's mission, values, ethical principles, and ethical standards.
6. The Code articulates standards that the social work profession itself can use to assess whether social workers have engaged in unethical conduct. NASW has formal procedures to adjudicate ethics complaints filed against its members.[1] In subscribing to this Code, social workers are required to cooperate in its implementation, participate in NASW adjudication proceedings, and abide by any NASW disciplinary rulings or sanctions based on it.

The Code offers a set of values, principles, and standards to guide decision making and conduct when ethical issues arise. It does not provide a set of rules that prescribe how social workers should act in all situations. Specific applications of the Code must take into account the context in which it is being considered and the possibility of conflicts among the Code's values, principles, and standards. Ethical responsibilities flow from all human relationships, from the personal and familial to the social and professional.

Further, the NASW Code of Ethics does not specify which values, principles, and standards are most important and ought to outweigh others in instances when they conflict. Reasonable differences of opinion can and do exist among social workers with respect to the ways in which values, ethical principles, and ethical standards should be rank ordered when they conflict. Ethical decision making in a given situation must apply the informed judgment of the individual social worker and should also consider how the issues would be judged in a peer review process where the ethical standards of the profession would be applied.

Ethical decision making is a process. There are many instances in social work where simple answers are not available to resolve complex ethical issues. Social workers should take into consideration all the values, principles, and standards in this Code that are relevant to any situation in which ethical judgment is warranted. Social workers' decisions and actions should be consistent with the spirit as well as the letter of this Code.

In addition to this Code, there are many other sources of information about ethical thinking that may be useful. Social workers should consider ethical theory and principles generally, social work theory and research, laws, regulations, agency policies, and other relevant codes of ethics, recognizing that among codes of ethics social workers should consider the NASW Code of Ethics as their primary source. Social workers also should be aware of the impact on ethical decision making of their clients' and their own personal values and cultural and religious beliefs and practices. They should be aware of any conflicts between personal and professional values and deal with them

---

[1]For information on NASW adjudication procedures, see *NASW Procedures for the Adjudication of Grievances.*

responsibly. For additional guidance social workers should consult the relevant literature on professional ethics and ethical decision making and seek appropriate consultation when faced with ethical dilemmas. This may involve consultation with an agency-based or social work organization's ethics committee, a regulatory body, knowledgeable colleagues, supervisors, or legal counsel.

Instances may arise when social workers' ethical obligations conflict with agency policies or relevant laws or regulations. When such con-flicts occur, social workers must make a responsible effort to resolve the conflict in a manner that is consistent with the values, principles, and standards expressed in this Code. If a reasonable resolution of the conflict does not appear possible, social workers should seek proper consultation before making a decision.

The NASW Code of Ethics is to be used by NASW and by individuals, agencies, organizations, and bodies (such as licensing and regulatory boards, professional liability insurance providers, courts of law, agency boards of directors, government agencies, and other professional groups) that choose to adopt it or use it as a frame of reference. Violation of standards in this Code does not automatically imply legal liability or violation of the law. Such determination can only be made in the context of legal and judicial proceedings. Alleged violations of the Code would be subject to a peer review process. Such processes are generally separate from legal or administrative procedures and insulated from legal review or proceedings to allow the profession to counsel and discipline its own members.

A code of ethics cannot guarantee ethical behavior. Moreover, a code of ethics cannot resolve all ethical issues or disputes or capture the richness and complexity involved in striving to make responsible choices within a moral community. Rather, a code of ethics sets forth values, ethical principles, and ethical standards to which

professionals aspire and by which their actions can be judged. Social workers' ethical behavior should result from their personal commitment to engage in ethical practice. The NASW Code of Ethics reflects the commitment of all social workers to uphold the profession's values and to act ethically. Principles and standards must be applied by individuals of good char-acter who discern moral questions and, in good faith, seek to make reliable ethical judgments.

Ethical Principles

The following broad ethical principles are based on social work's core values of service, social justice, dignity and worth of the person, importance of human relationships, integrity, and competence. These principles set forth ideals to which all social workers should aspire.

Value: Service

Ethical Principle: Social workers' primary goal is to help people in need and to address social problems.

Social workers elevate service to others above self-interest. Social workers draw on their knowledge, values, and skills to help people in need and to address social problems. Social workers are encouraged to volunteer some portion of their professional skills with no expectation of significant financial return (pro bono service).

Value: Social Justice

Ethical Principle: Social workers challenge social injustice.

Social workers pursue social change, particularly with and on behalf of vulnerable and oppressed individuals and groups of people. Social workers' social change efforts are focused primarily on issues of poverty, unemployment, discrimination, and other forms of social injustice. These activities seek to promote sensitivity to and knowledge about oppression and cultural and ethnic diversity. Social workers strive to ensure access to needed information, services, and resources; equality of opportunity; and meaningful participation in decision making for all people.

Value: Dignity and Worth of the Person

Ethical Principle: Social workers respect the inherent dignity and worth of the person.

Social workers treat each person in a caring and respectful fashion, mindful of individual differences and cultural and ethnic diversity. Social workers promote clients' socially responsible self-determination. Social workers seek to enhance clients' capacity and opportunity to change and to address their own needs. Social workers are cognizant of their dual responsibility to clients and to the broader society. They seek to resolve conflicts between clients' interests and the broader society's interests in a socially responsible manner consistent with the values, ethical principles, and ethical standards of the profession.

Value: Importance of Human Relationships

Ethical Principle: Social workers recognize the central importance of human relationships.

Social workers understand that relationships between and among people are an important vehicle for change. Social workers engage people as partners in the helping process. Social workers seek to strengthen relationships among people in a purposeful effort to promote, restore, maintain, and enhance the well-being of individuals, families, social groups, organizations, and communities.

Value: Integrity

Ethical Principle: Social workers behave in a trustworthy manner.

Social workers are continually aware of the profession's mission, values, ethical principles, and ethical standards and practice in a manner consistent with them. Social workers act honestly and responsibly and pro-

mote ethical practices on the part of the organizations with which they are affiliated.

Value: Competence

Ethical Principle: Social workers practice within their areas of competence and develop and enhance their professional expertise.

Social workers continually strive to increase their professional knowledge and skills and to apply them in practice. Social workers should aspire to contribute to the knowledge base of the profession.

Ethical Standards

The following ethical standards are relevant to the professional activities of all social workers. These standards concern (1) social workers' ethical responsibilities to clients, (2) social workers' ethical responsibilitie to colleagues, (3) social workers' ethical responsibilities in practice settings, (4) social workers' ethical responsibilities as professionals, (5) social workers' ethical responsibilities to the social work profession, and (6) social workers' ethical responsibilities to the broader society.

Some of the standards that follow are enforceable guidelines for professional conduct, and some are aspirational. The extent to which each standard is enforceable is a matter of professional judgment to be exercised by those responsible for reviewing alleged violations of ethical standards.

1. Social Workers' Ethical Responsibilities to Clients

1.01 Commitment to Clients

Social workers' primary responsibility is to promote the well-being of clients. In general, clients' interests are primary. However, social workers' responsibility to the larger society or specific legal obli-gations may on limited occasions supersede the loyalty owed clients, and clients should be so advised. (Examples include when a social worker is required by law to report that a client has abused a child or has threatened to harm self or others.)

1.02   Self-Determination

Social workers respect and promote the right of clients to self-determination and assist clients in their efforts to identify and clarify their goals. Social workers may limit clients' right to self-determination when, in the social workers' professional judgment, clients' actions or potential actions pose a serious, foreseeable, and imminent risk to themselves or others.

1.03   Informed Consent

(a) Social workers should provide services to clients only in the context of a professional relationship based, when appropriate, on valid informed consent. Social workers should use clear and understandable language to inform clients of the purpose of the services, risks related to the services, limits to services because of the requirements of a third-party payer, relevant costs, reasonable alternatives, clients' right to refuse or withdraw consent, and the time frame covered by the consent. Social workers should provide clients with an opportunity to ask questions.

(b) In instances when clients are not literate or have difficulty understanding the primary language used in the practice setting, social workers should take steps to ensure clients' comprehension. This may include providing clients with a detailed verbal explanation or arranging for a qualified interpreter or translator whenever possible.

(c) In instances when clients lack the capacity to provide informed consent, social workers should protect clients' interests by seeking permission from an appropriate third party, informing clients consistent with the clients' level of understanding. In such instances social workers should seek to ensure that the third party acts in a manner consistent with clients' wishes and interests. Social workers should take reasonable steps to enhance such clients' ability to give informed consent.

(d) In instances when clients are receiving services involuntarily, social workers should provide information about the nature and extent of services and about the extent of clients' right to refuse service.

(e) Social workers who provide services via electronic media (such as computer, telephone, radio, and television) should inform recipients of the limitations and risks associated with such services.

(f) Social workers should obtain clients' informed consent before audiotaping or videotaping clients or permitting observation of services to clients by a third party.

1.04   Competence

(a) Social workers should provide services and represent themselves as competent only within the boundaries of their education, training, license, certification, consultation received, supervised experience, or other relevant professional experience.

(b) Social workers should provide services in substantive areas or use intervention techniques or approaches that are new to them only after engaging in appropriate study, training, consultation, and supervision from people who are competent in those interventions or techniques.

(c) When generally recognized standards do not exist with respect to an emerging area of practice, social workers should exercise careful judgment and take responsible steps (including appropriate education, research, training, consultation, and supervision) to ensure the competence of their work and to protect clients from harm.

1.05   Cultural Competence and Social Diversity

(a) Social workers should understand culture and its function in human behavior and society, recognizing the strengths that exist in all cultures.

(b) Social workers should have a knowledge base of their clients' cultures and be able to demonstrate competence in the provision of services that are sensitive to clients' cultures and to differences among people and cultural groups.

(c) Social workers should obtain education about and seek to understand the nature of social diversity and oppression with respect to race, ethnicity, national origin, color, sex, sexual orientation, age, marital status, political belief, religion, and mental or physical disability.

1.06   Conflicts of Interest

(a) Social workers should be alert to and avoid conflicts of interest that interfere with the exercise of professional discretion and impartial judgment. Social workers should inform clients when a real or potential conflict of interest arises and take reasonable steps to resolve the issue in a manner that makes the clients' interests primary and protects clients' interests to the greatest extent possible. In some cases, protecting clients' interests may require termination of the professional relationship with proper referral of the client.

(b) Social workers should not take unfair advantage of any professional relationship or exploit others to further their personal, religious, political, or business interests.

(c) Social workers should not engage in dual or multiple relationships with clients or former clients in which there is a risk of exploitation or potential harm to the client. In instances when dual or multiple relationships are unavoidable, social workers should take steps to protect clients and are responsible for setting clear, appropriate, and culturally sensitive boundaries. (Dual or multiple relationships occur when social workers relate to clients in more than one relationship, whether professional, social, or business. Dual or multiple relationships can occur simultaneously or consecutively.)

(d) When social workers provide services to two or more people who have a relationship with each other (for example, couples, family members), social workers should clarify with all parties which individuals will be considered clients and the nature of social workers' professional obligations to the various individuals who are receiving services. Social workers who anticipate a conflict of interest among the individuals receiving services or who anticipate having to perform in potentially conflicting roles (for example, when a social worker is asked to testify in a child custody dispute or divorce proceedings involving clients) should clarify their role with the parties involved and take appropriate action to minimize any conflict of interest.

1.07   Privacy and Confidentiality

(a) Social workers should respect clients' right to privacy. Social workers should not solicit private information from clients unless it is essential to providing services or conducting social work evaluation or research. Once private information is shared, standards of confidentiality apply.

(b) Social workers may disclose confidential information when appropriate with valid consent from a client or a person legally authorized to consent on behalf of a client.

(c) Social workers should protect the confidentiality of all information obtained in the course of professional service, except for compelling professional reasons. The general expectation that social workers will keep information confidential does not apply when disclosure is necessary to prevent serious, foreseeable, and imminent harm to a client or other identifiable person. In all instances, social workers should disclose the least amount of confidential information necessary to achieve the desired purpose; only information that is directly relevant to the purpose for which the disclosure is made should be revealed.

(d) Social workers should inform clients, to the extent possible, about the disclosure of confidential information and the potential consequences, when feasible before the disclosure is made. This applies whether social workers disclose confidential information on the basis of a legal requirement or client consent.

(e) Social workers should discuss with clients and other interested parties the nature of confidentiality and limitations of clients' right to confidentiality. Social workers should review with clients circumstances where confidential information may be requested and where disclosure of confidential information may be legally required. This discussion should occur as soon as possible in the social worker-client relationship and as needed throughout the course of the relationship.

(f) When social workers provide counseling services to families, couples, or groups, social workers should seek agreement among the parties involved concerning each individual's right to confidentiality and obligation to preserve the confidentiality of information shared by others. Social workers should inform participants in family, couples, or group counseling that social workers cannot guarantee that all participants will honor such agreements.

(g) Social workers should inform clients involved in family, couples, marital, or group counseling of the social worker's, employer's, and agency's policy concerning the social worker's disclosure of confidential information among the parties involved in the counseling.

(h) Social workers should not disclose confidential information to third-party payers unless clients have authorized such disclosure.

(i) Social workers should not discuss confidential information in any setting unless privacy can be ensured. Social workers should not discuss confidential information in public or semipublic areas such as hallways, waiting rooms, elevators, and restaurants.

(j) Social workers should protect the confidentiality of clients during legal proceedings to the extent permitted by law. When a court of law or other legally authorized body orders social workers to disclose confidential or privileged information without a client's consent and such disclosure could cause harm to the client, social workers should request that the court withdraw the order or limit the order as narrowly as possible or maintain the records under seal, unavailable for public inspection.

(k) Social workers should protect the confidentiality of clients when responding to requests from members of the media.

(l) Social workers should protect the confidentiality of clients' written and electronic records and other sensitive information. Social workers should take reasonable steps to ensure that clients' records are stored in a secure location and that clients' records are not available to others who are not authorized to have access.

(m) Social workers should take precautions to ensure and maintain the confidentiality of information transmitted to other parties through the use of computers, electronic mail, facsimile machines, telephones and telephone answering machines, and other electronic or computer technology. Disclosure of identifying information should be avoided whenever possible.

(n) Social workers should transfer or dispose of clients' records in a manner that protects clients' confidentiality and is consistent with state statutes governing records and social work licensure.

(o) Social workers should take reasonable precautions to protect client confidentiality in the event of the social worker's termination of practice, incapacitation, or death.

(p) Social workers should not disclose identifying information when discussing clients for teaching or training purposes unless the client has consented to disclosure of confidential information.

(q) Social workers should not disclose identifying information when discussing clients with consultants unless the client has consented to disclosure of confidential information or there is a compelling need for such disclosure.

(r) Social workers should protect the confidentiality of deceased clients consistent with the preceding standards.

1.08   Access to Records

(a) Social workers should provide clients with reasonable access to records concerning the clients. Social workers who are concerned that clients' access to their records could cause serious misunderstanding or harm to the client should provide assistance in interpreting the records and consultation with the client regarding the records. Social workers should limit clients' access to their records, or portions of their records, only in exceptional circumstances when there is compelling evidence that such access would cause serious harm to the client. Both clients' requests and the rationale for withholding some or all of the record should be documented in clients' files.

(b) When providing clients with access to their records, social workers should take steps to protect the confidentiality of other individuals identified or discussed in such records.

1.09   Sexual Relationships

(a) Social workers should under no circumstances engage in sexual activities or sexual contact with current clients, whether such contact is consensual or forced.

(b) Social workers should not engage in sexual activities or sexual contact with clients' relatives or other individuals with whom clients maintain a close personal relationship when there is a risk of exploitation or potential harm to the client. Sexual activity or sexual contact with clients' relatives or other individuals with whom clients maintain a personal relationship has the potential to be harmful to the client and may make it difficult for the social worker and client to maintain appropriate professional boundaries. Social workers—not their clients, their clients' relatives, or other individuals with whom the client maintains a personal relationship—assume the full burden for setting clear, appropriate, and culturally sensitive boundaries.

(c) Social workers should not engage in sexual activities or sexual contact with former clients because of the potential for harm to the client. If social workers engage in conduct contrary to this prohibition or claim that an exception to this prohibition is warranted because of extraordinary circumstances, it is social workers—not their clients—who assume the full burden of demonstrating that the former client has not been exploited, coerced, or manipulated, intentionally or unintentionally.

(d) Social workers should not provide clinical services to individuals with whom they have had a prior sexual relationship. Providing clinical services to a former sexual partner has the potential to be harmful to the individual and is likely to make it difficult for the social worker and individual to maintain appropriate professional boundaries.

1.10   Physical Contact

Social workers should not engage in physical contact with clients when there is a possibility of psychological harm to the client as a result of the contact (such as cradling or caressing clients). Social workers who engage in appropriate physical contact with clients are responsible for setting clear, appropriate, and culturally sensitive boundaries that govern such physical contact.

1.11   Sexual Harassment

Social workers should not sexually harass clients. Sexual harassment includes sexual advances, sexual solicitation, requests for sexual favors, and other verbal or physical conduct of a sexual nature.

1.12   Derogatory Language

Social workers should not use derogatory language in their written or verbal communications to or about clients. Social workers should use accurate and respectful language in all communications to and about clients.

1.13 Payment for Services

(a) When setting fees, social workers should ensure that the fees are fair, reasonable, and commensurate with the services performed. Consideration should be given to clients' ability to pay.

(b) Social workers should avoid accepting goods or services from clients as payment for professional services. Bartering arrangements, particularly involving services, create the potential for conflicts of interest, exploitation, and inappropriate boundaries in social workers' relationships with clients. Social workers should explore and may participate in bartering only in very limited circumstances when it can be demonstrated that such arrangements are an accepted practice among professionals in the local community, considered to be essential for the provision of services, negotiated without coercion, and entered into at the client's initiative and with the client's informed consent. Social workers who accept goods or services from clients as payment for professional services assume the full burden of demonstrating that this arrangement will not be detrimental to the client or the professional relationship.

(c) Social workers should not solicit a private fee or other remuneration for providing services to clients who are entitled to such available services through the social workers' employer or agency.

1.14 Clients Who Lack Decision-Making Capacity

When social workers act on behalf of clients who lack the capacity to make informed decisions, social workers should take reasonable steps to safeguard the interests and rights of those clients.

1.15 Interruption of Services

Social workers should make reasonable efforts to ensure continuity of services in the event that services are interrupted by factors such as unavailability, relocation, illness, disability, or death.

1.16 Termination of Services

(a) Social workers should terminate services to clients and professional relationships with them when such services and relationships are no longer required or no longer serve the clients' needs or interests.

(b) Social workers should take reasonable steps to avoid abandoning clients who are still in need of services. Social workers should withdraw services precipitously only under unusual circumstances, giving careful consideration to all factors in the situation and taking care to minimize possible adverse effects. Social workers should assist in making appropriate arrangements for continuation of services when necessary.

(c) Social workers in fee-for-service settings may terminate services to clients who are not paying an overdue balance if the financial contractual arrangements have been made clear to the client, if the client does not pose an imminent danger to self or others, and if the clinical and other consequences of the current nonpayment have been addressed and discussed with the client.

(d) Social workers should not terminate services to pursue a social, financial, or sexual relationship with a client.

(e) Social workers who anticipate the termination or interruption of services to clients should notify clients promptly and seek the transfer, referral, or continuation of services in relation to the clients' needs and preferences.

(f) Social workers who are leaving an employment setting should inform clients of appropriate options for the continuation of services and of the benefits and risks of the options.

2. Social Workers' Ethical Responsibilities to Colleagues

2.01 Respect

(a) Social workers should treat colleagues with respect and should represent accurately and fairly the qualifications, views, and obligations of colleagues.

(b) Social workers should avoid unwarranted negative criticism of colleagues in communications with clients or with other professionals. Unwarranted negative criticism may include demeaning comments that refer to colleagues' level of competence or to indi-viduals' attributes such as race, ethnicity, national origin, color, sex, sexual orientation, age, marital status, political belief, religion, and mental or physical disability.

(c) Social workers should cooperate with social work colleagues and with colleagues of other professions when such cooperation serves the well-being of clients.

2.02   Confidentiality

Social workers should respect confidential information shared by colleagues in the course of their professional relationships and transactions. Social workers should ensure that such colleagues understand social workers' obligation to respect confidentiality and any exceptions related to it.

2.03   Interdisciplinary Collaboration

(a) Social workers who are members of an interdisciplinary team should participate in and contribute to decisions that affect the well-being of clients by drawing on the perspectives, values, and experiences of the social work profession. Professional and ethical obligations of the interdisciplinary team as a whole and of its individual members should be clearly established.

(b) Social workers for whom a team decision raises ethical concerns should attempt to resolve the disagreement through appropriate channels. If the disagreement cannot be resolved, social workers should pursue other avenues to address their concerns consistent with client well-being.

2.04   Disputes Involving Colleagues

(a) Social workers should not take advantage of a dispute between a colleague and an employer to obtain a position or otherwise advance the social workers' own interests.

(b) Social workers should not exploit clients in disputes with colleagues or engage clients in any inappropriate discussion of conflicts between social workers and their colleagues.

2.05   Consultation

(a) Social workers should seek the advice and counsel of colleagues whenever such consultation is in the best interests of clients.

(b) Social workers should keep themselves informed about colleagues' areas of expertise and competencies. Social workers should seek consultation only from colleagues who have demonstrated knowledge, expertise, and competence related to the subject of the consultation.

(c) When consulting with colleagues about clients, social workers should disclose the least amount of information necessary to achieve the purposes of the consultation.

2.06   Referral for Services

(a) Social workers should refer clients to other professionals when the other professionals' specialized knowledge or expertise is needed to serve clients fully or when social workers believe that they are not being effective or making reasonable progress with clients and that additional service is required.

(b) Social workers who refer clients to other professionals should take appropriate steps to facilitate an orderly transfer of responsibility. Social workers who refer clients to other professionals should disclose, with clients' consent, all pertinent information to the new service providers.

(c) Social workers are prohibited from giving or receiving payment for a referral when no professional service is provided by the referring social worker.

2.07   Sexual Relationships

(a) Social workers who function as supervisors or educators should not engage in sexual activities or contact with supervisees, students, trainees, or other colleagues over whom they exercise professional authority.

(b) Social workers should avoid engaging in sexual relationships with colleagues when there is potential for a conflict of interest. Social workers who become involved in, or anticipate becoming involved in, a sexual relationship with a colleague have a duty to transfer professional responsibilities, when necessary, to avoid a conflict of interest.

2.08 Sexual Harassment

Social workers should not sexually harass supervisees, students, trainees, or colleagues. Sexual harassment includes sexual advances, sexual solicitation, requests for sexual favors, and other verbal or physical conduct of a sexual nature.

2.09 Impairment of Colleagues

(a) Social workers who have direct knowledge of a social work colleague's impairment that is due to personal problems, psychosocial distress, substance abuse, or mental health difficulties and that interferes with practice effectiveness should consult with that colleague when feasible and assist the colleague in taking remedial action.

(b) Social workers who believe that a social work colleague's impairment interferes with practice effectiveness and that the colleague has not taken adequate steps to address the impairment should take action through appropriate channels established by employers, agencies, NASW, licensing and regulatory bodies, and other professional organizations.

2.10 Incompetence of Colleagues

(a) Social workers who have direct knowledge of a social work colleague's incompetence should consult with that colleague when feasible and assist the colleague in taking remedial action.

(b) Social workers who believe that a social work colleague is incompetent and has not taken adequate steps to address the incompetence should take action through appropriate channels established by employers, agencies, NASW, licensing and regulatory bodies, and other professional organizations.

2.11 Unethical Conduct of Colleagues

(a) Social workers should take adequate measures to discourage, prevent, expose, and correct the unethical conduct of colleagues.

(b) Social workers should be knowledgeable about established policies and procedures for handling concerns about colleagues' unethical behavior. Social workers should be familiar with national, state, and local procedures for handling ethics complaints. These include policies and procedures created by NASW, licensing and regulatory bodies, employers, agencies, and other professional organizations.

(c) Social workers who believe that a colleague has acted unethically should seek resolution by discussing their concerns with the colleague when feasible and when such discussion is likely to be productive.

(d) When necessary, social workers who believe that a colleague has acted unethically should take action through appropriate formal channels (such as contacting a state licensing board or regulatory body, an NASW committee on inquiry, or other professional ethics committees).

(e) Social workers should defend and assist colleagues who are unjustly charged with unethical conduct.

3. Social Workers' Ethical Responsibilities in Practice Settings

3.01 Supervision and Consultation

(a) Social workers who provide supervision or consultation should have the necessary knowledge and skill to supervise or consult appropriately and should do so only within their areas of knowledge and competence.

(b) Social workers who provide supervision or consultation are responsible for setting clear, appropriate, and culturally sensitive boundaries.

(c) Social workers should not engage in any dual or multiple relationships with supervisees in which there is a risk of exploitation of or potential harm to the supervisee.

(d) Social workers who provide supervision should evaluate supervisees' performance in a manner that is fair and respectful.

3.02   Education and Training

(a) Social workers who function as educators, field instructors for students, or trainers should provide instruction only within their areas of knowledge and competence and should provide instruction based on the most current information and knowledge available in the profession.

(b) Social workers who function as educators or field instructors for students should evaluate students' performance in a manner that is fair and respectful.

(c) Social workers who function as educators or field instructors for students should take reasonable steps to ensure that clients are routinely informed when services are being provided by students.

(d) Social workers who function as educators or field instructors for students should not engage in any dual or multiple relationships with students in which there is a risk of exploitation or potential harm to the student. Social work educators and field instructors are responsible for setting clear, appropriate, and culturally sensitive boundaries.

3.03   Performance Evaluation

Social workers who have responsibility for evaluating the performance of others should fulfill such responsibility in a fair and considerate manner and on the basis of clearly stated criteria.

3.04   Client Records

(a) Social workers should take reasonable steps to ensure that documentation in records is accurate and reflects the services provided.

(b) Social workers should include sufficient and timely documentation in records to facilitate the delivery of services and to ensure continuity of services provided to clients in the future.

(c) Social workers' documentation should protect clients' privacy to the extent that is possible and appropriate and should include only information that is directly relevant to the delivery of services.

(d) Social workers should store records following the termination of services to ensure reasonable future access. Records should be maintained for the number of years required by state statutes or relevant contracts.

3.05   Billing

Social workers should establish and maintain billing practices that accurately reflect the nature and extent of services provided and that identify who provided the service in the practice setting.

3.06   Client Transfer

(a) When an individual who is receiving services from another agency or colleague contacts a social worker for services, the social worker should carefully consider the client's needs before agreeing to provide services. To minimize possible confusion and conflict, social workers should discuss with potential clients the nature of the clients' current relationship with other service providers and the implications, including possible benefits or risks, of entering into a relationship with a new service provider.

(b) If a new client has been served by another agency or colleague, social workers should discuss with the client whether consultation with the previous service provider is in the client's best interest.

3.07 Administration

(a) Social work administrators should advocate within and outside their agencies for adequate resources to meet clients' needs.

(b) Social workers should advocate for resource allocation procedures that are open and fair. When not all clients' needs can be met, an allocation procedure should be developed that is nondiscriminatory and based on appropriate and consistently applied principles.

(c) Social workers who are administrators should take reasonable steps to ensure that adequate agency or organizational resources are available to provide appropriate staff supervision.

(d) Social work administrators should take reasonable steps to ensure that the working environment for which they are responsible is consistent with and encourages compliance with the NASW Code of Ethics. Social work administrators should take reasonable steps to eliminate any conditions in their organizations that violate, interfere with, or discourage compliance with the Code.

3.08 Continuing Education and Staff Development

Social work administrators and supervisors should take reasonable steps to provide or arrange for continuing education and staff development for all staff for whom they are responsible. Continuing education and staff development should address current knowledge and emerging developments related to social work practice and ethics.

3.09 Commitments to Employers

(a) Social workers generally should adhere to commitments made to employers and employing organizations.

(b) Social workers should work to improve employing agencies' policies and procedures and the efficiency and effectiveness of their services.

(c) Social workers should take reasonable steps to ensure that employers are aware of social workers' ethical obligations as set forth in the NASW Code of Ethics and of the implications of those obligations for social work practice.

(d) Social workers should not allow an employing organization's policies, procedures, regulations, or administrative orders to interfere with their ethical practice of social work. Social workers should take reasonable steps to ensure that their employing organizations' practices are consistent with the NASW Code of Ethics.

(e) Social workers should act to prevent and eliminate discrimination in the employing organization's work assignments and in its employment policies and practices.

(f) Social workers should accept employment or arrange student field placements only in organizations that exercise fair personnel practices.

(g) Social workers should be diligent stewards of the resources of their employing organizations, wisely conserving funds where appropriate and never misappropriating funds or using them for unintended purposes.

3.10 Labor-Management Disputes

(a) Social workers may engage in organized action, including the formation of and participation in labor unions, to improve services to clients and working conditions.

(b) The actions of social workers who are involved in labor-management disputes, job actions, or labor strikes should be guided by the profession's values, ethical principles, and ethical standards. Reasonable differences of opinion exist among social workers concerning their primary obligation as professionals during an actual or threatened labor strike or job action. Social workers should carefully examine relevant issues and their possible impact on clients before deciding on a course of action.

4. Social Workers' Ethical Responsibilities as Professionals

4.01 Competence

(a) Social workers should accept responsibility or employment only on the basis of existing competence or the intention to acquire the necessary competence.

(b) Social workers should strive to become and remain proficient in professional practice and the performance of professional functions. Social workers should critically examine and keep current with emerging knowledge relevant to social work. Social workers should routinely review the professional literature and participate in continuing education relevant to social work practice and social work ethics.

(c) Social workers should base practice on recognized knowledge, including empirically based knowledge, relevant to social work and social work ethics.

4.02 Discrimination

Social workers should not practice, condone, facilitate, or collaborate with any form of discrimination on the basis of race, ethnicity, national origin, color, sex, sexual orientation, age, marital status, political belief, religion, or mental or physical disability.

4.03 Private Conduct

Social workers should not permit their private conduct to interfere with their ability to fulfill their professional responsibilities.

4.04 Dishonesty, Fraud, and Deception

Social workers should not participate in, condone, or be associated with dishonesty, fraud, or deception.

4.05 Impairment

(a) Social workers should not allow their own personal problems, psychosocial distress, legal problems, substance abuse, or mental health difficulties to interfere with their professional judgment and performance or to jeopardize the best interests of people for whom they have a professional responsibility.

(b) Social workers whose personal problems, psychosocial distress, legal problems, substance abuse, or mental health difficulties interfere with their professional judgment and performance should immediately seek consultation and take appropriate remedial action by seeking professional help, making adjustments in workload, terminating practice, or taking any other steps necessary to protect clients and others.

4.06 Misrepresentation

(a) Social workers should make clear distinctions between statements made and actions engaged in as a private individual and as a representative of the social work profession, a professional social work organization, or the social worker's employing agency.

(b) Social workers who speak on behalf of professional social work organizations should accurately represent the official and authorized positions of the organizations.

(c) Social workers should ensure that their representations to clients, agencies, and the public of professional qualifications, credentials, education, competence, affiliations, services provided, or results to be achieved are accurate. Social workers should claim only those relevant professional credentials they actually possess and take steps to correct any inaccuracies or misrepresentations of their credentials by others.

4.07 Solicitations

(a) Social workers should not engage in uninvited solicitation of potential clients who, because of their circumstances, are vulnerable to undue influence, manipulation, or coercion.

(b) Social workers should not engage in solicitation of testimonial endorsements (including solicitation of consent to use a client's prior statement as a testimonial endorsement) from current clients or from other people who, because of their particular circumstances, are vulnerable to undue influence.

4.08 Acknowledging Credit

(a) Social workers should take responsibility and credit, including authorship credit, only for work they have actually performed and to which they have contributed.

(b) Social workers should honestly acknowledge the work of and the contributions made by others.

5. Social Workers' Ethical Responsibilities to the Social Work Profession

5.01 Integrity of the Profession

(a) Social workers should work toward the maintenance and promotion of high standards of practice.

(b) Social workers should uphold and advance the values, ethics, knowledge, and mission of the profession. Social workers should protect, enhance, and improve the integrity of the profession through appropriate study and research, active discussion, and responsible criticism of the profession.

(c) Social workers should contribute time and professional expertise to activities that promote respect for the value, integrity, and competence of the social work profession. These activities may include teaching, research, consultation, service, legislative testimony, presentations in the community, and participation in their professional organizations.

(d) Social workers should contribute to the knowledge base of social work and share with colleagues their knowledge related to practice, research, and ethics. Social workers should seek to con-tribute to the profession's literature and to share their knowledge at professional meetings and conferences.

(e) Social workers should act to prevent the unauthorized and unqualified practice of social work.

5.02 Evaluation and Research

(a) Social workers should monitor and evaluate policies, the implementation of programs, and practice interventions.

(b) Social workers should promote and facilitate evaluation and research to contribute to the development of knowledge.

(c) Social workers should critically examine and keep current with emerging knowledge relevant to social work and fully use evaluation and research evidence in their professional practice.

(d) Social workers engaged in evaluation or research should carefully consider possible consequences and should follow guidelines developed for the protection of evaluation and research participants. Appropriate institutional review boards should be consulted.

(e) Social workers engaged in evaluation or research should obtain voluntary and written informed consent from participants, when appropriate, without any implied or actual deprivation or penalty for refusal to participate; without undue inducement to participate; and with due regard for participants' well-being, privacy, and dignity. Informed consent should include information about the nature, extent, and duration of the participation requested and disclosure of the risks and benefits of participation in the research.

(f) When evaluation or research participants are incapable of giving informed consent, social workers should provide an appropriate explanation to the participants, obtain the participants' assent to the extent they are able, and obtain written consent from an appropriate proxy.

(g) Social workers should never design or conduct evaluation or research that does not use consent procedures, such as certain forms of naturalistic observation and archival research, unless rigorous and responsible review of the research has found it to be justified because of its prospective scientific, educational, or applied value and unless equally effective alternative procedures that do not involve waiver of consent are not feasible.

(h) Social workers should inform participants of their right to withdraw from evaluation and research at any time without penalty.

(i) Social workers should take appropriate steps to ensure that participants in evaluation and research have access to appropriate supportive services.

(j) Social workers engaged in evaluation or research should protect participants from unwarranted physical or mental distress, harm, danger, or deprivation.

(k) Social workers engaged in the evaluation of services should discuss collected information only for professional purposes and only with people professionally concerned with this information.

(l) Social workers engaged in evaluation or research should ensure the anonymity or confidentiality of participants and of the data obtained from them. Social workers should inform participants of any limits of confidentiality, the measures that will be taken to ensure confidentiality, and when any records containing research data will be destroyed.

(m) Social workers who report evaluation and research results should protect participants' confidentiality by omitting identifying information unless proper consent has been obtained authorizing disclosure.

(n) Social workers should report evaluation and research findings accurately. They should not fabricate or falsify results and should take steps to correct any errors later found in published data using standard publication methods.

(o) Social workers engaged in evaluation or research should be alert to and avoid conflicts of interest and dual relationships with participants, should inform participants when a real or potential conflict of interest arises, and should take steps to resolve the issue in a manner that makes participants' interests primary.

(p) Social workers should educate themselves, their students, and their colleagues about responsible research practices.

6.   Social Workers' Ethical Responsibilities to the Broader Society

6.01   Social Welfare

Social workers should promote the general welfare of society, from local to global levels, and the development of people, their communities, and their environments. Social workers should advocate for living conditions conducive to the fulfillment of basic human needs and should promote social, economic, political, and cultural values and institutions that are compatible with the realization of social justice.

6.02   Public Participation

Social workers should facilitate informed participation by the public in shaping social policies and institutions.

6.03   Public Emergencies

Social workers should provide appropriate professional services in public emergencies to the greatest extent possible.

6.04   Social and Political Action

(a) Social workers should engage in social and political action that seeks to ensure that all people have equal access to the resources, employment, services, and opportunities they require to meet their basic human needs and to develop fully. Social workers should be aware of the impact of the political arena on practice and should advocate for changes in policy and legislation to improve social conditions in order to meet basic human needs and promote social justice.

(b) Social workers should act to expand choice and opportunity for all people, with special regard for vulnerable, disadvantaged, oppressed, and exploited people and groups.

(c) Social workers should promote conditions that encourage respect for cultural and social diversity within the United States and globally. Social workers should promote policies and practices that demonstrate respect for difference, support the expansion of cultural knowledge and resources, advocate for programs and institutions that demonstrate cultural competence, and promote policies that safeguard the rights of and confirm equity and social justice for all people.

(d) Social workers should act to prevent and eliminate domination of, exploitation of, and discrimination against any person, group, or class on the basis of race, ethnicity, national origin, color, sex, sexual orientation, age, marital status, political belief, religion, or mental or physical disability.

Appendix B

International Federation of Social Workers, The Ethics of Social Work: Principles and Standards

1 Background

Ethical awareness is a necessary part of the professional practice of any social worker. His or her ability to act ethically is an essential aspect of the quality of the service offered to clients.

The purpose of IFSW's work on ethics is to promote ethical debate and reflection in the member associations and among the providers of social work in member countries.

The basis for the further development of IFSW's work on ethics is to be found in *Ethics of Social Work: Principles and Standards* which consists of two documents, *International Declaration of Ethical Principles of Social Work* and *International Ethical Standards for Social Workers*. These documents present the basic ethical principles of the social work profession, recommend procedures when the work presents ethical dilemmas, and deal with the profession's and the individual social worker's relation to clients, colleagues, and others in the field. The documents are components in a continuing process of use, review and revision.

2 International Declaration of Ethical Principles of Social Work

2.1 Introduction

The IFSW recognises the need for a declaration of ethical principles for guidance in dealing with ethical problems in social work.

The purposes of the *International Declaration of Ethical Principles* are:

1. to formulate a set of basic principles for social work, which can be adapted to cultural and social settings,
2. to identify ethical problem areas in the practice of social work (below referred to as "problem areas"), and
3. to provide guidance as to the choice of methods for dealing with ethical issues/problems (below referred to as "methods for addressing ethical issues/problems").

Compliance

The *International Declaration of Ethical Principles* assumes that both member associations of the IFSW and their constituent members adhere to the principles formulated therein. The IFSW expects each

Published by International Federation of Social Workers, P.O. Box 4649, Sofienberg, N-0506 Oslo, Norway; October 1994. Adopted by the IFSW General Meeting, Colombo, Sri Lanka, July 6–8, 1994.

member association to assist its members in identifying and dealing with ethical issues/problems in the practice of their profession.

Member associations of the IFSW and individual members of these can report any member association to the Executive Committee of the IFSW should it neglect to adhere to these principles. National associations who experience difficulties adopting these principles should notify the Executive Committee of IFSW. The Executive Committee may impose the stipulations and intentions of the *Declaration of Ethical Principles* on an association which neglects to comply. Should this not be sufficient the Executive Committee can, as a following measure, suggest suspension or exclusion of the association.

The *International Declaration of Ethical Principles* should be made publicly known. This would enable clients, employers, professionals from other disciplines, and the general public to have expectations in accordance with the ethical foundations of social work.

We acknowledge that a detailed set of ethical standards for the member associations would be unrealistic due to legal, cultural and governmental differences among the member countries.

2.2 The Principles

Social workers serve the development of human beings through adherence to the following basic principles:

2.2.1. Every human being has a unique value, which justifies moral consideration for that person.

2.2.2. Each individual has the right to self-fulfilment to the extent that it does not encroach upon the same right of others, and has an obligation to contribute to the well-being of society.

2.2.3. Each society, regardless of its form, should function to provide the maximum benefits for all of its members.

2.2.4. Social workers have a commitment to principles of social justice.

2.2.5. Social workers have the responsibility to devote objective and disciplined knowledge and skill to aid individuals, groups, communities, and societies in their development and resolution of personal-societal conflicts and their consequences.

2.2.6. Social workers are expected to provide the best possible assistance to anybody seeking their help and advice, without unfair discrimination on the basis of gender, age, disability, colour, social class, race, religion, language, political beliefs, or sexual orientation.

2.2.7. Social workers respect the basic human rights of individuals and groups as expressed in the *United Nations Universal Declaration of Human Rights* and other international conventions derived from that Declaration.

2.2.8. Social workers pay regard to the principles of privacy, confidentiality, and responsible use of information in their professional work. Social workers respect justified confidentiality even when their country's legislation is in conflict with this demand.

2.2.9. Social workers are expected to work in full collaboration with their clients, working for the best interests of the clients but paying due regard to the interests of others involved. Clients are encouraged to participate as much as possible, and should be informed of the risks and likely benefits of proposed courses of action.

2.2.10. Social workers generally expect clients to take responsibility, in collaboration with them, for determining courses of action affecting their lives. Compulsion which might be necessary to solve one party's problems at the expense of the interests of others involved should only take place after careful explicit evaluation of the claims of the conflicting parties. Social workers should minimise the use of legal compulsion.

2.2.11. Social work is inconsistent with direct or indirect support of individuals, groups, political forces or power structures suppressing their fellow human beings by employing terrorism, torture or similar brutal means.

2.2.12. Social workers make ethically justified decisions, and stand by them, paying due regard to the *IFSW International Declaration of Ethical Principles* and to the *International Ethical Standards for Social Workers* adopted by their national professional association.

2.3 Problem Areas

2.3.1. The problem areas raising ethical issues directly are not necessarily universal due to cultural and governmental differences. Each national association is encouraged to promote discussion and clarification of important issues and problems particularly relevant to its country. The following problem areas are, however, widely recognized:

1. *When the loyalty of the social worker is in the middle of conflicting interests*
   - between those of the social workers own and the clients
   - between conflicting interests of individual clients and other individuals
   - between the conflicting interests of groups of clients
   - between groups of clients and the rest of the population
   - between systems/institution and groups of clients
   - between system/institution/employer and social workers
   - between different groups of professionals
2. *The fact that the social worker functions both as a helper and controller*
   The relation between these two opposite aspects of social work demands a clarification based on an explicit choice of values

in order to avoid a mixing-up of motives or the lack of clarity in motives, actions and consequences of actions. When social workers are expected to play a role in the state control of citizens they are obliged to clarify the ethical implications of this role and to what extent this role is acceptable in relation to the basic ethical principles of social work.

3. *The duty of the social worker to protect the interests of the client will easily come into conflict with demands for efficiency and utility*
   This problem is becoming important with the introduction and use of information technology within the fields of social work.

2.3.2. The principles declared in section 2.2 should always be at the base of any consideration given or choice made by social workers in dealing with issues/problems within these areas.

2.4 Methods For The Solution of Issues/Problems

2.4.1. The various national associations of social workers are obliged to treat matters in such a way that ethical issues/problems may be considered and tried to be solved in collective forums within the organization. Such forums should enable the individual social worker to discuss, analyse and consider ethical issues/problems in collaboration with colleagues, other expert groups and/parties affected by the matter under discussion. In addition such forums should give the social worker opportunity to receive advice from colleagues and others. Ethical analysis and discussion should always seek to create possibilities and options.

2.4.2. The member associations are required to produce and/or adapt ethical standards for the different fields of work, especially for those fields where there are complicated ethical issues/problems as well as areas where the ethical principles of social work may come into conflict with the respective country's legal system or the policy of the authorities.

2.4.3. When ethical foundations are laid down as guidelines for actions within the practice of social work, it is the duty of the associations to aid the individual social worker in analysing and considering ethical issues/problems on the basis of:

1. The basic *principles* of the Declaration (section 2.2)
2. The ethical/moral and political *context* of the actions, i.e. an analysis of the values and forces constituting the framing conditions of the action
3. The *motives* of the action, i.e. to advocate a higher level of consciousness of the aims and intentions the individual social worker might have regarding a course of action
4. The *nature* of the action, i.e. help in providing an analysis of the moral content of the action, e.g. the use of compulsion as opposed to voluntary co-operation, guardianship vs participation, etc.
5. The *consequences* the action might have for different groups, i.e. an analysis of the consequences of different ways of action for all involved parties in both the short and long term.

2.4.4. The member associations are responsible for promoting debate, education and research regarding ethical questions.

3 International Ethical Standards for Social Workers

(This section is based on the *International Code of Ethics for the Professional Social Worker* adopted by the IFSW in 1976, but does not include ethical principles since these are now contained in the new separate International Declaration of Ethical Principles of Social Work in section 2.2 of the present document.)

3.1 Preamble

Social work originates variously from humanitarian, religious and democratic ideals and philosophies and has universal application to meet human needs arising from personal-societal interactions and to develop human potential. Professional social workers are dedicated to service for the welfare and self-fulfilment of human beings; to the development and disciplined use of validated knowledge regarding human and societal behaviour; to the development of resources to meet individual, group, national and international needs and aspirations; and to the achievement of social justice. On the basis of the *International Declaration of Ethical Principles of Social Work,* the social worker is obliged to recognise these standards of ethical conduct.

3.2 General Standards of Ethical Conduct

3.2.1. Seek to understand each individual client and the client system, and the elements which affect behaviour and the service required.

3.2.2. Uphold and advance the values, knowledge and methodology of the profession, refraining from any behaviour which damages the functioning of the profession.

3.2.3. Recognise professional and personal limitations.

3.2.4. Encourage the utilisation of all relevant knowledge and skills.

3.2.5. Apply relevant methods in the development and validation of knowledge.

3.2.6. Contribute professional expertise to the development of policies and programs which improve the quality of life in society.

3.2.7. Identify and interpret social needs.

3.2.8. Identify and interpret the basis and nature of individual, group, community, national, and international social problems.

3.2.9. Identify and interpret the work of the social work profession.

3.2.10. Clarify whether public statements are made or actions performed on an individual basis or as representative of a professional association, agency or organisation, or other group.

3.3 Social Work Standards Relative to Clients

3.3.1. Accept primary responsibility to identified clients, but within limitations set by the ethical claims of others.

3.3.2. Maintain the client's right to a relationship of trust, to privacy and confidentiality, and to responsible use of information. The collection and sharing of information or data is related to the professional service function with the client informed as to its necessity and use. No information is released without prior knowledge and informed consent of the client, except where the client cannot be responsible or others may be seriously jeopardized. A client has access to social work records concerning them.

3.3.3. Recognise and respect the individual goals, responsibilities, and differences of clients. Within the scope of the agency and the client's social milieu, the professional service shall assist clients to take responsibility for personal actions and help all clients with equal willingness. Where the professional service cannot be provided under such conditions the clients shall be so informed in such a way as to leave the clients free to act.

3.3.4. Help the client—individual, group, community, or society—to achieve self-fulfilment and maximum potential within the limits of the respective rights of others. The service shall be based upon helping the client to understand and use the professional relationship, in furtherance of the clients legitimate desires and interests.

3.4 Social Work Standards Relative to Agencies and Organizations

3.4.1. Work and/or cooperate with those agencies and organizations whose policies, procedures, and operations are directed toward adequate service delivery and encouragement of professional practice consistent with the ethical principles of the IFSW.

3.4.2. Responsibly execute the stated aims and functions of the agency or organizations, contributing to the development of sound policies, procedures, and practice in order to obtain the best possible standards or practice.

3.4.3. Sustain ultimate responsibility to the client, initiating desirable alterations of policies, procedures, and practice, through appropriate agency and organization channels. If necessary remedies are not achieved after channels have been exhausted, initiate appropriate appeals to higher authorities or the wider community of interest.

3.4.4. Ensure professional accountability to client and community for efficiency and effectiveness through periodic review of the process of service provision.

3.4.5. Use all possible ethical means to bring unethical practice to an end when policies, procedures and practices are in direct conflict with the ethical principles of social work.

3.5 Social Work Standards Relative to Colleagues

3.5.1. Acknowledge the education, training and performance of social work colleagues and professionals from other disciplines, extending all necessary cooperation that will enhance effective services.

3.5.2. Recognise differences of opinion and practice of social work colleagues and other professionals, expressing criticism through channels in a responsible manner.

3.5.3. Promote and share opportunities for knowledge, experience, and ideas with all social work colleagues, professionals from other disciplines and volunteers for the purpose of mutual improvement.

3.5.4. Bring any violations of professional ethics and standards to the attention of the appropriate bodies inside and outside the profession, and ensure that relevant clients are properly involved.

3.5.5. Defend colleagues against unjust actions.

3.6 Standards Relative to the Profession

3.6.1. Maintain the values, ethical principles, knowledge and methodology of the profession and contribute to their clarification and improvement.

3.6.2. Uphold the professional standards of practice and work for their advancement.

3.6.3. Defend the profession against unjust criticism and work to increase confidence in the necessity for professional practice.

3.6.4. Present constructive criticism of the profession, its theories, methods and practices

3.6.5. Encourage new approaches and methodologies needed to meet new and existing needs.

IFSW Homepage General Directory Activities Publications Partnerships information
Contact IFSW: secr.gen@ifsw.org
Last updated 13 September 2000
Designed and produced by X Kommunikation

Appendix C

Council on Social Work Education Educational Policy and Accreditation Standards

PREAMBLE

Social work practice promotes human well-being by strengthening opportunities, resources, and capacities of people in their environments and by creating policies and services to correct conditions that limit human rights and the quality of life. The social work profession works to eliminate poverty, discrimination, and oppression. Guided by a person-in-environment perspective and respect for human diversity, the profession works to effect social and economic justice worldwide.

Social work education combines scientific inquiry with the teaching of professional skills to provide effective and ethical social work services. Social work educators reflect their identification with the profession through their teaching, scholarship, and service. Social work education, from baccalaureate to doctoral levels, employs educational, practice, scholarly, interprofessional, and service delivery models to orient and shape the profession's future in the context of expanding knowledge, changing technologies, and complex human and social concerns.

The Council on Social Work Education (CSWE) Educational Policy and Accreditation Standards (EPAS) promotes academic excellence in baccalaureate and master's social work education. The EPAS specifies the curricular content and educational context to prepare students for professional social work practice. The EPAS sets forth basic requirements for these purposes. Beyond these basic requirements of EPAS, individual programs focus on areas relevant to their institutional and program mission, goals, and objectives.

The EPAS permits programs to use time-tested and new models of program design, implementation, and evaluation. It does so by balancing requirements that promote comparability across programs with a level of flexibility that encourages programs to respond to changing human, professional, and institutional needs.

The EPAS focuses on assessing the results of a program's development and its continuous improvement. While accreditation is ultimately evaluative, in social work education it is based on a consultative and collaborative process that determines whether a program meets the requirements of the EPAS.

FUNCTIONS OF EDUCATIONAL POLICY AND ACCREDITATION

Educational Policy

The Educational Policy promotes excellence, creativity, and innovation in social work education and practice. It sets forth required content areas that relate to each other and to the purposes, knowledge, and values of the profession. Programs of social work education are offered at the baccalaureate, master's, and doctoral levels. Baccalaureate and master's programs are accredited by CSWE. This document supersedes all prior statements of curriculum policy for baccalaureate and master's program levels.

Accreditation

Accreditation ensures that the quality of professional programs merits public confidence. The Accreditation Standards establish basic requirements for baccalaureate and master's levels.

Accreditation Standards pertain to the following program elements:

- Mission, goals, and objectives
- Curriculum
- Governance, structure, and resources
- Faculty
- Student professional development
- Nondiscrimination and human diversity
- Program renewal
- Program assessment and continuous improvement

Relationship of Educational Policy to Accreditation

CSWE uses the EPAS for the accreditation of social work programs. The Educational Policy and the Accreditation Standards are conceptually integrated. Programs use Educational Policy, Section 1 as one important basis for developing program mission, goals, and objectives. Programs use Educational Policy, Section 3 to develop program objectives and Educational Policy, Sections 4 and 5 to develop content for demonstrating attainment of the objectives. The accreditation process reviews the program's self-study document, site team report, and program response to determine compliance

with the Educational Policy and Accreditation Standards. Accredited programs meet all standards.

EDUCATIONAL POLICY

1. PURPOSES

1.0   Purposes of the Social Work Profession

The social work profession receives its sanction from public and private auspices and is the primary profession in the development, provision, and evaluation of social services.

Professional social workers are leaders in a variety of organizational settings and service delivery systems within a global context.

The profession of social work is based on the values of service, social and economic justice, dignity and worth of the person, importance of human relationships, and integrity and competence in practice. With these values as defining principles, the purposes of social work are:

- To enhance human well-being and alleviate poverty, oppression, and other forms of social injustice.
- To enhance the social functioning and interactions of individuals, families, groups, organizations, and communities by involving them in accomplishing goals, developing resources, and preventing and alleviating distress.
- To formulate and implement social policies, services, and programs that meet basic human needs and support the development of human capacities.
- To pursue policies, services, and resources through advocacy and social or political actions that promote social and economic justice.
- To develop and use research, knowledge, and skills that advance social work practice.
- To develop and apply practice in the context of diverse cultures.

1.1 Purposes of Social Work Education

The purposes of social work education are to prepare competent and effective professionals, to develop social work knowledge, and to provide leadership in the development of service delivery systems. Social work education is grounded in the profession's history, purposes, and philosophy and is based on a body of knowledge, values, and skills. Social work education enables students to integrate the knowledge, values, and skills of the social work profession for competent practice.

1.2   Achievement of Purposes

Among its programs, which vary in design, structure, and objectives, social work education achieves these purposes through such means as:

- Providing curricula and teaching practices at the forefront of the new and changing knowledge base of social work and related disciplines.
- Providing curricula that build on a liberal arts perspective to promote breadth of knowledge, critical thinking, and communication skills.
- Developing knowledge.
- Developing and applying instructional and practice-relevant technology.
- Maintaining reciprocal relationships with social work practitioners, groups, organizations, and communities.
- Promoting continual professional development of students, faculty, and practitioners.
- Promoting interprofessional and interdisciplinary collaboration.
- Preparing social workers to engage in prevention activities that promote well-being.
- Preparing social workers to practice with individuals, families, groups, organizations, and communities.

- Preparing social workers to evaluate the processes and effectiveness of practice.
- Preparing social workers to practice without discrimination, with respect, and with knowledge and skills related to clients' age, class, color, culture, disability, ethnicity, family structure, gender, marital status, national origin, race, religion, sex, and sexual orientation.
- Preparing social workers to alleviate poverty, oppression, and other forms of social injustice.
- Preparing social workers to recognize the global context of social work practice.
- Preparing social workers to formulate and influence social policies and social work services in diverse political contexts.

2. STRUCTURE OF SOCIAL WORK EDUCATION

2.0   Structure

Baccalaureate and graduate social work education programs operate under the auspices of accredited colleges and universities. These educational institutions vary by auspices, emphasis, and size. With diverse strengths, missions, and resources, social work education programs share a common commitment to educate competent, ethical social workers.

The baccalaureate and master's levels of social work education are anchored in the purposes of the social work profession and promote the knowledge, values, and skills of the profession. Baccalaureate social work education programs prepare graduates for generalist professional practice. Master's social work education programs prepare graduates for advanced professional practice in an area of concentration. The baccalaureate and master's levels of educational preparation are differentiated according to (a) conceptualization and design, (b) content, (c) program objectives, and (d) depth, breadth, and specificity of knowledge and skills. Frameworks and perspectives for concentration include fields of practice, problem areas, intervention methods, and practice contexts and perspectives.

Programs develop their mission and goals within the purposes of the profession, the purposes of social work education, and their institutional context. Programs also recognize academic content and professional experiences that students bring to the educational program. A conceptual framework, built upon relevant theories and knowledge, shapes the breadth and depth of knowledge and practice skills to be acquired.

2.1   Program Renewal

Social work education remains vital, relevant, and progressive by pursuing exchanges with the practice community and program stakeholders and by developing and assessing new knowledge and technology.

3. PROGRAM OBJECTIVES

Social work education is grounded in the liberal arts and contains a coherent, integrated professional foundation in social work. The graduate advanced curriculum is built from the professional foundation. Graduates of baccalaureate and master's social work programs demonstrate the capacity to meet the foundation objectives and objectives unique to the program. Graduates of master's social work programs also demonstrate the capacity to meet advanced program objectives.

3.0   Foundation Program Objectives

The professional foundation, which is essential to the practice of any social worker, . . . includes, but is not limited to, the following

program objectives. Graduates demonstrate the ability to:

1. Apply critical thinking skills within the context of professional social work practice.
2. Understand the value base of the profession and its ethical standards and principles, and practice accordingly.
3. Practice without discrimination and with respect, knowledge, and skills related to clients' age, class, color, culture, disability, ethnicity, family structure, gender, marital status, national origin, race, religion, sex, and sexual orientation.
4. Understand the forms and mechanisms of oppression and discrimination and apply strategies of advocacy and social change that advance social and economic justice.
5. Understand and interpret the history of the social work profession and its contemporary structures and issues.
B6. Apply the knowledge and skills of generalist social work practice with systems of all sizes.[1]
M6. Apply the knowledge and skills of a generalist social work perspective to practice with systems of all sizes.
7. Use theoretical frameworks supported by empirical evidence to understand individual development and behavior across the life span and the interactions among individuals and between individuals and families, groups, organizations, and communities.
8. Analyze, formulate, and influence social policies.
9. Evaluate research studies, apply research findings to practice, and evaluate their own practice interventions.
10. Use communication skills differentially across client populations, colleagues, and communities.

[1] Items preceded by a B or M apply only to baccalaureate or master's programs, respectively.

11. Use supervision and consultation appropriate to social work practice.
12. Function within the structure of organizations and service delivery systems and seek necessary organizational change.

3.1 Concentration Objectives

Graduates of a master's social work program are advanced practitioners who apply the knowledge and skills of advanced social work practice in an area of concentration. They analyze, intervene, and evaluate in ways that are highly differentiated, discriminating, and self-critical. Graduates synthesize and apply a broad range of knowledge and skills with a high degree of autonomy and proficiency. They refine and advance the quality of their practice and that of the larger social work profession.

3.2 Additional Program Objectives

A program may develop additional objectives to cover the required content in relation to its particular mission, goals, and educational level.

4. FOUNDATION CURRICULUM CONTENT

All social work programs provide foundation content in the areas specified below. Content areas may be combined and delivered with a variety of instructional technologies. Content is relevant to the mission, goals, and objectives of the program and to the purposes, values, and ethics of the social work profession.

4.0 Values and Ethics

Social work education programs integrate content about values and principles of ethical decision making as presented in the National Association of Social Workers Code of Ethics. The educational experience provides students with the opportunity to be aware of personal values; develop, demonstrate, and promote the values of the profession; and analyze ethical dilemmas and the ways in which these affect practice, services, and clients.

4.1 Diversity

Social work programs integrate content that promotes understanding, affirmation, and respect for people from diverse backgrounds. The content emphasizes the interlocking and complex nature of culture and personal identity. It ensures that social services meet the needs of groups served and are culturally relevant. Programs educate students to recognize diversity within and between groups that may influence assessment, planning, intervention, and research. Students learn how to define, design, and implement strategies for effective practice with persons from diverse backgrounds.

4.2 Populations-at-Risk and Social and Economic Justice

Social work education programs integrate content on populations-at-risk, examining the factors that contribute to and constitute being at risk. Programs educate students to identify how group membership influences access to resources, and present content on the dynamics of such risk factors and responsive and productive strategies to redress them.

Programs integrate social and economic justice content grounded in an understanding of distributive justice, human and civil rights, and the global interconnections of oppression.

Programs provide content related to implementing strategies to combat discrimination, oppression, and economic deprivation and to promote social and economic justice.

Programs prepare students to advocate for nondiscriminatory social and economic systems.

4.3 Human Behavior and the Social Environment

Social work education programs provide content on the reciprocal relationships between human behavior and social environments. Content includes empirically based theories and knowledge that focus on the interactions between and among individuals, groups, societies, and economic systems. It includes theories and knowledge of biological, sociological, cultural, psychological, and spiritual development across the life span; the range of social systems in which people live (individual, family, group, organizational, and community); and the ways social systems promote or deter people in maintaining or achieving health and well-being.

4.4   Social Welfare Policy and Services

Programs provide content about the history of social work, the history and current structures of social welfare services, and the role of policy in service delivery, social work practice, and attainment of individual and social well-being. Course content provides students with knowledge and skills to understand major policies that form the foundation of social welfare; analyze organizational, local, state, national, and international issues in social welfare policy and social service delivery; analyze and apply the results of policy research relevant to social service delivery; understand and demonstrate policy practice skills in regard to economic, political, and organizational systems, and use them to influence, formulate, and advocate for policy consistent with social work values; and identify financial, organizational, administrative, and planning processes required to deliver social services.

4.5   Social Work Practice

Social work practice content is anchored in the purposes of the social work profession and focuses on strengths, capacities, and resources of client systems in relation to their broader environments. Students learn practice content that encompasses knowledge and skills to work with individuals, families, groups, organizations, and communities. This content includes engaging clients in an appropriate working relationship; identifying issues, problems, needs, resources, and assets; collecting and assessing information; and planning for service delivery. It includes using communication skills, supervision, and consultation. Practice content also includes identifying, analyzing, and implementing empirically based interventions designed to achieve client goals; applying empirical knowledge and technological advances; evaluating program outcomes and practice effectiveness; developing, analyzing, advocating, and providing leadership for policies and services; and promoting social and economic justice.

4.6   Research

Qualitative and quantitative research content provides understanding of a scientific, analytic, and ethical approach to building knowledge for practice. The content prepares students to develop, use, and effectively communicate empirically based knowledge, including evidence-based interventions. Research knowledge is used by students to provide high-quality services; to initiate change; to improve practice, policy, and social service delivery; and to evaluate their own practice.

4.7   Field Education

Field education is an integral component of social work education anchored in the mission, goals, and educational level of the program. It occurs in settings that reinforce students' identification with the purposes, values, and ethics of the profession; fosters the integration of empirical and practice-based knowledge; and promotes the development of professional competence. Field education is systematically designed, supervised, coordinated, and evaluated on the basis of criteria by which students demonstrate the achievement of program objectives.

5. ADVANCED CURRICULUM CONTENT

The master's curriculum prepares graduates for advanced social work practice in an area of concentration. Using a conceptual framework to identify advanced knowledge and skills, programs build an advanced curriculum from the foundation content. In the advanced curriculum, the foundation content areas (Section 4, 4.0–4.7) are addressed in greater depth, breadth, and specificity and support the program's conception of advanced practice.

ACCREDITATION STANDARDS

1. Program Mission, Goals, and Objectives

1.0   The social work program has a mission appropriate to professional social work education as defined in Educational Policy, Section 1.1. The program's mission is appropriate to the level or levels for which it is preparing students for practice and is consistent with the institution's mission.

1.1   The program has goals derived from its mission. These goals reflect the purposes of the Educational Policy, Section 1.1. Program goals are not limited to these purposes.

1.2   The program has objectives that are derived from the program goals. These objectives are consistent with Educational Policy, Section 3. Program objectives are reflected in program implementation and continuous assessment (see Accreditation Standard 8).

1.3   The program makes its constituencies aware of its mission, goals, and objectives.

2. Curriculum

2.0   The curriculum is developed and organized as a coherent and integrated whole consistent with program goals and objectives. Social work education is grounded in the liberal arts and contains a coherent, integrated professional foundation in social work practice from which an advanced practice curriculum is built at the graduate level.

B2.0.1   The program defines its conception of generalist social work practice, describes its coverage of the professional foundation curriculum identified in Educational Policy, Section 4, and demonstrates how its conception of generalist practice is implemented in all components of the professional curriculum.

M2.0.1   The program describes its coverage of the foundation and advanced curriculum content, identified in Educational Policy, Sections 4 and 5. The program defines its conception of advanced practice and explains how the advanced curriculum is built from the professional foundation. The master's program has a concentration curriculum that includes (a) concentration objectives, (b) a conceptual framework built on relevant theories, (c) curriculum design and content, and (d) field education that supports the advanced curriculum. The program demonstrates how the depth, breadth, and specificity of the advanced curriculum are addressed in relation to the professional foundation.

2.1   The social work program administers field education (Educational Policy, Section 4.7 Section 5) consistent with program goals and objectives that:

2.1.1   Provides for a minimum of 400 hours of field education for baccalaureate programs and 900 hours for master's programs.

2.1.2   Admits only those students who have met the program s specified criteria for field education.

2.1.3   Specifies policies, criteria, and procedures for selecting agencies and field instructors; placing and monitoring students; maintaining field liaison contacts with agencies; and evaluating student learning and agency effectiveness in providing field instruction.

2.1.4 Specifies that field instructors for baccalaureate students hold a CSWE-accredited baccalaureate or master's social work degree.[2] Field instructors for master's students hold a CSWE-accredited master's social work degree. In programs where a field instructor does not hold a CSWE-accredited baccalaureate or master's social work degree, the program assumes responsibility for reinforcing a social work perspective.

2.1.5 Provides orientation, field instruction training, and continuing dialog with agencies and field instructors.

2.1.6 Develops policies regarding field placements in an agency in which the student is also employed. Student assignments and field education supervision differ from those associated with the student's employment.

3. Program Governance, Administrative Structure, and Resources

3.0 The social work program has the necessary autonomy and administrative structure to achieve its goals and objectives (Educational Policy, Section 2.0).

3.0.1 The social work faculty defines program curriculum consistent with the Educational Policy and Accreditation Standards and the institution's policies.

3.0.2 The administration and faculty of the social work program participate in formulating and implementing policies related to the recruitment, hiring, retention, promotion, and tenure of program personnel.

3.0.3 The chief administrator of the social work program has either a CSWE-accredited master's social work degree, with a doctoral degree preferred, or a professional degree in social work from a CSWE-accredited program and a doctoral degree. The chief administrator also has demonstrated leadership ability through teaching, scholarship, curriculum development, administrative experience, and other academic and professional activities in the field of social work.

3.0.4 The chief administrator of the social work program has a full-time appointment to the program and sufficient assigned time (at least 25% for baccalaureate programs and 50% for master's programs) to provide educational and administrative leadership. Combined programs designate a social work faculty member and assign this person sufficient time to administer the baccalaureate social work program.

3.0.5 The field education director has a master's degree in social work from a CSWE-accredited program and at least two years post–baccalaureate or post–master's social work degree practice experience.

3.0.6 The field education director has a full-time appointment to the program and sufficient assigned time (at least 25% for baccalaureate programs and 50% for master's programs) to provide educational and administrative leadership for field education.

3.1 The social work program has sufficient resources to achieve program goals and objectives.

3.1.1 The program has sufficient support staff, other personnel, and technological resources to support program functioning.

[2] This and all future references to "CSWE-accredited baccalaureate or master's social work degree" include degrees from CSWE-accredited programs or programs approved by its Foreign Equivalency Determination Service.

3.1.2 The program has sufficient and stable financial supports that permit program planning and achievement of program goals and objectives. These include a budgetary allocation and procedures for budget development and administration.

3.1.3 The program has comprehensive library holdings and electronic access, as well as other informational and educational resources necessary for achieving the program's goals and objectives.

3.1.4 The program has sufficient office and classroom space, computer-mediated access, or both to achieve the program's goals and objectives.

3.1.5 The program has access to assistive technology, including materials in alternative formats (such as Braille, large print, books on tape, assistive learning systems).

4. Faculty

4.0 The program has full-time faculty, which may be augmented by part-time faculty, with the qualifications, competence, and range of expertise in social work education and practice to achieve its goals and objectives. The program has a sufficient full-time equivalent faculty-to-student ratio (usually 1:25 for baccalaureate programs and 1:12 for master's programs) to carry out ongoing functions of the program.

4.1 The program demonstrates how the use of part-time faculty assists in the achievement of the program's goals and objectives.

4.2 Faculty size is commensurate with the number and type of curricular offerings in class and field; class size; number of students; and the faculty's teaching, scholarly, and service responsibilities.

B4.2.1 The baccalaureate social work program has a minimum of two full-time faculty with master's social work degrees from a CSWE-accredited program, with full-time appointment in social work, and whose principal assignment is to the baccalaureate program. It is preferred that faculty have a doctoral degree.

M4.2.1 The master's social work program has a minimum of six full-time faculty with master's social work degrees from a CSWE-accredited program and whose principal assignment is to the master's program. The majority of the full-time master's social work program faculty have a master's degree in social work and a doctoral degree.

4.3 Faculty who teach required practice courses have a master's social work degree from a CSWE-accredited program and at least two years post–baccalaureate or post–master's social work degree practice experience.

4.4 The program has a faculty workload policy that supports the achievement of institutional priorities and the program's goals and objectives.

5. Student Professional Development

5.0 The program has admissions criteria and procedures that reflect the program's goals and Objectives.

M5.1 Only candidates who have earned a bachelor's degree are admitted to the master's social work degree program.

5.2 The program has a written policy indicating that it does not grant social work course credit for life experience or previous work experience.

5.3 In those foundation curriculum areas where students demonstrate required knowledge and skills, the program describes how it ensures that students do not repeat that content.

5.3.1 The program has written policies and procedures concerning the transfer of credits.

M5.3.2 Advanced standing status is only awarded to graduates of baccalaureate social work programs accredited by CSWE.

5.4 The program has academic and professional advising policies and procedures that are consistent with the program's goals and objectives. Professional advising is provided by social work program faculty, staff, or both.

5.5 The program has policies and procedures specifying students' rights and responsibilities to participate in formulating and modifying policies affecting academic and student affairs. It provides opportunities and encourages students to organize in their interests.

5.6 The program informs students of its criteria for evaluating their academic and professional performance.

5.7 The program has policies and procedures for terminating a student's enrollment in the social work program for reasons of academic and professional performance.

6. Nondiscrimination and Human Diversity

6.0 The program makes specific and continuous efforts to provide a learning context in which respect for all persons and understanding of diversity (including age, class, color, disability, ethnicity, family structure, gender, marital status, national origin, race, religion, sex, and sexual orientation) are practiced. Social work education builds upon professional purposes and values; therefore, the program provides a learning context that is nondiscriminatory and reflects the profession's fundamental tenets. The program describes how its learning context and educational program (including faculty, staff, and student composition; selection of agencies and their clientele as field education settings; composition of program advisory or field committees; resource allocation; program leadership; speakers series, seminars, and special programs; research and other initiatives) and its curriculum model understanding of and respect for diversity.

7. Program Renewal

7.0 The program has ongoing exchanges with external constituencies that may include social work practitioners, social service recipients, advocacy groups, social service agencies, professional associations, regulatory agencies, the academic community, and the community at large.

7.1 The program's faculty engage in the development and dissemination of research, scholarship, or other creative activities relevant to the profession.

7.2 The program seeks opportunities for innovation and provides leadership within the profession and the academic community.

8. Program Assessment and Continuous Improvement

8.0 The program has an assessment plan and procedures for evaluating the outcome of each program objective. The plan specifies the measurement procedures and methods used to evaluate the outcome of each program objective.

8.1 The program implements its plan to evaluate the outcome of each program objective and shows evidence that the analysis is used continuously to affirm and improve the educational program.

PROGRAM CHANGES

The EPAS supports change necessary to improve the educational quality of a program in relation to its goals and objectives. The EPAS recognizes that such change is ongoing. When a program is granted initial accreditation or its accreditation is reaffirmed, the program is, by that action, accredited only at the level or levels and for the components that existed and were reviewed at the time of that action. Prior to the next scheduled accreditation review, changes may take place within the program. Although it is not necessary to report minor changes, programs notify the Commission on Accreditation (COA) of such changes as new leadership, governance, structure, off-campus programs, etc. Depending on the nature of the change, the COA may request additional information. Prior to the implementation of a substantive change the program submits a proposal and receives approval. Substantive changes are defined as those that require a waiver of one or more aspects of EPAS.

Appendix D

Accredited MSW Programs in the United States, Fall 2003

MSW Programs

Alabama A & M University, Graduate Social Work Department, P.O. Box 302, Normal, AL 35762

University of Alabama, School of Social Work, Box 870314, Tuscaloosa, AL 35487-0314

University of Alaska Anchorage, School of Social Work CHESW, 3211 Providence Drive, Anchorage, AK 99508-8230

Arizona State University, School of Social Work, Box 871802, Tempe, AZ 85287-1802

University of Arkansas at Little Rock, School of Social Work, 2801 S. University, Little Rock, AR 72204

California State University, Fresno, Department of Social Work Education, 5310 Campus Drive, PH 102, Fresno, CA 93740-8019

California State University, Long Beach, Department of Social Work, 1250 Bellflower Boulevard, Long Beach, CA 90840-0902

California State University, Los Angeles, Department of Social Work, 5151 State University Drive, Los Angeles, CA 90008

California State Univer., San Bernardino, Department of Social Work, 5500 University Parkway, San Bernardino, CA 92407-2397

California State University, Sacramento, Division of Social Work, 6000 J Street, Sacramento, CA 95819-6090

California State University, Stanislaus, Social Work Department, 801 W. Monte Vista Avenue, Turlock, CA 95382

Loma Linda University, Department of Social work, Griggs Hall, Loma Linda, CA 92350

San Diego State University, School of Social Work, 5500 Campanile Drive, San Diego, CA 92182-4119

San Francisco State University, School of Social Work, 1600 Holloway Avenue, San Francisco, CA 94132

San Jose State University, College of Social Work, One Washington Square, Suite 215, San Jose, CA 95192-0124

University of California at Berkeley, School of Social Welfare, 120 Haviland Hall, Berkeley, CA 94720-7400

University of California at Los Angeles, Department of Social Welfare, PPSR, 3250 Public Policy Building, Box 951656, Los Angeles, CA 90095-1656

University of Southern California, School of Social Work, MRF Building, Room 214, 699 W. 34th Street, Los Angeles, CA 90089-0411

Colorado State University, School of Social Work, 127 Education Building, Fort Collins, CO 80523-1586

University of Denver, Graduate School of Social Work, 2148 S. High Street, Denver, CO 80208-2886

Southern Connecticut State University, Graduate Social Work Program, Department of Social Work, 101 Farnham Avenue, New Haven, CT 06515

University of Connecticut, School of Social Work, 1798 Asylum Avenue, West Hartford, CT 06117

Delaware State University, Master of Social Work Program, Department of Social Work, 1200 N. Dupont Highway, Dover, DE 19901

Catholic University of America, National Catholic School of Social Svc., Shahan Hall-Cardinal Station, Washington, DC 20064

Gallaudet University, Department of Social Work, 800 Florida Avenue N.E., Washington, DC 20002-3695

Howard University, School of Social Work, 601 Howard Place N.W., Washington, DC 20059

Barry University, School of Social Work, 11300 N.E. 2nd Avenue, Miami Shores, FL 33161

Florida International University, School of Social Work, 11200 S.W. 8th Street ECS 460, Miami, FL 33199

Florida State University, School of Social Work, UCC 2505, Tallahassee, FL 32306-2570

University of Central Florida, School of Social work, P.O. Box 163358, Orlando, FL 32828

University of South Florida, School of Social Work–MGY 132, 4202 E. Fowler Avenue, Tampa, FL 33620-8100

Clark Atlanta University, School of Social Work, James P. Brawley Dr at Fair Street S.W., Atlanta, GA 30314-4391

Savannah State University, Master's Department of Social Work, College of Liberal Arts and Social Sciences, P.O. Box 20553, Savannah, GA 31404

University of Georgia, School of Social Work, Tucker Hall, Athens, GA 30602-7016

Valdosta State University, Division of Social Work, 1500 Patterson Street, Valdosta, GA 31698

University of Hawaii at Manoe, School of Social Work, 1800 East-West Road, Honolulu, HI 96822

Boise State University, School of Social Work, 1910 University Drive, Boise, ID 83725

Aurora University, George Williams College, School of Social Work, 347 S. Gladstone Avenue, Aurora, IL 60506-4892

Loyola University of Chicago, School of Social Work, 820 N. Michigan Avenue, Chicago, IL 60611

Southern Illinois University Carbondale, School of Social Work, Quigley Hall, Room 6, Carbondale, IL 62901-4329

University of Chicago, School of Social Service Administration, 969 E. 60th Street, Chicago, IL 60637

University of Illinois at Chicago, Jane Addams College of Social Work, 1040 W. Harrison Street, Chicago, IL 60607-7134

University of Illinois at Urbana-Champaign, School of Social Work, 1207 W. Oregon Street, Urbana, IL 61801

Indiana University, School of Social Work, 902 W. New York Street, Indianapolis, IN 46202-5156

Indiana University: Northwest Campus, Raintree Hall Room 213, 3400 Broadway, Gary, IN 46408

University of Southern Indiana, Social Work Department, 8600 University Boulevard, Evansville, IN 47712

St. Ambrose University, School of Social Work, 518 W. Locust Street, Davenport, IA 52803

University of Iowa, School of Social Work, 308 North Hall, Iowa City, IA 52242-1223

University of Kansas, School of Social Welfare, 1545 Lilac Lane, Lawrence, KS 66055-3184

Washburn University, Department of Social Work, 1700 College Avenue, Topeka, KS 66621

Spalding University, School of Social Work, 857 S. Fourth Street, Louisville, KY 40203-2115

University of Kentucky, College of Social Work, 619 Patterson Office Tower, Lexington, KY 40506-0027

University of Louisville, Raymond A. Kent School of Social Work, Oppenheimer Hall, Louisville, KY 40292

Grambling State University, School of Social Work, P.O. Box 907, Grambling, LA 71245

Louisiana State University, School of Social Work, Huey P. Long Field House, Baton Rouge, LA 70803

Southern University at New Orleans, School of Social Work, 6400 Press Drive, New Orleans, LA 70126

Tulane University, School of Social Work, 6823 St. Charles Avenue, New Orleans, LA 70118-5672

University of Maine, School of Social Work, 5770 Social Work Building, Orono, ME 04469

University of New England, School of Social Work, 716 Stevens Avenue, Portland, ME 04103

University of Maryland-Baltimore, School of Social Work, Louis L. Kaplan Hall, 525 W. Redwood Street, Baltimore, MD 21201-1777

Boston College, Graduate School of Social Work, MaGuinn Hall, 140 Commonwealth Avenue, Chestnut Hill, MA 02467-3807

Boston University, School of Social Work, 264 Bay State Road, Boston, MA 02215

Salem State College, School of Social Work, 352 Lafayette Street, Salem, MA 01970

Simmons College, Graduate School of Social Work, 300 The Fenway, Boston, MA 02115-5898

Smith College, School for Social Work, Lilly Hall, Northampton, MA 01063

Springfield College, School of Social Work, 263 Alden Street, Springfield, MA 01109-3797

Andrews University, Department of Social work, Nethery Hall, Berrien Springs, MI 49104

Eastern Michigan University, MSW Program Office, 317 Marshall Building, Ypsilanti, MI 48197

Grand Valley State University, School of Social Work, 3rd Floor, De Vos Center, 401 W. Fulton, Grand Rapids, MI 49504

Michigan State University, School of Social Work, 254 Baker Hall, East Lansing, MI 48824

University of Michigan, School of social work, 1080 S. University, Ann Arbor, MI 48109-1106

Wayne State University, School of Social work, 4756 Cass Avenue, 201 Thompson Home, Detroit, MI 48202

Western Michigan University, School of Social Work, 1903 Western Avenue, Kalamazoo, MI 49008-5034

Augsburg College, Department of Social Work, 2211 Riverside Avenue, Minneapolis, MN 55454

University of Saint Thomas, School of Social Work, LOR 406, 2115 Summit Avenue, St. Paul, MN 55105

University of Minnesota-Duluth, Department of Social Work, 220 Bihannon Hall, Duluth, MN 55812-2496

University of Minnesota-Twin Cities, School of Social Work, 105 Peters Hall, 1404 Gortner Avenue, St. Paul, MN 55108

Jackson State University, School of Social Work, 3825 Ridgewood Road , Suite 9, Jackson, MS 39211

University of Southern Mississippi, School of Social Work, Box 5114, Hattiesburg, MS 39406

Saint Louis University, School of Social Service, 3550 Lindell Boulevard, St. Louis, MO 63103

Southwest Missouri State University, School of Social Work, Professional Building, Suite 200, 901 S. National Avenue, Springfield, MO 65804

University of Missouri-Columbia, School of Social Work, 729 Clark Hall, Columbia, MO 65211-4470

Washington University, George Warren Brown School of Social Work, One Brookings Drive, St. Louis, MO 63130-4899

University of Nebraska at Omaha, School of Social work, 60th and Dodge Streets, Omaha, NE 68182-0293

University of Nevada, Las Vegas, School of Social Work, 4505 Maryland Parkway, Box 455032, Las Vegas, NV 89154-5032

University of Nevada, Reno, School of Social Work, Business Building, Room 523, Mail Stop 090, Reno, NV 89557-0068

University of New Hampshire, Department of Social Work, Pettee Hall, 50 College Road, Durham, NH 03824-3596

Kean University, Master of Social Work Program, 1000 Morris Avenue, Hutchinson Hall, Room 305, Union, NJ 0783-7131

Monmouth University, Social Work Department, Norwood and Cedar Avenue, West Long Branch, NJ 07764-1898

Rutgers, The State University of New Jersey, School of Social work, 536 George Street, New Brunswick, NJ 08901-1167

University of Toronto, 27 King's College Circle, Toronto, Ontario M5S 1A1, Canada

New Mexico Highlands University, School of Social Work, Las Vegas, NM 87701

New Mexico State University, School of Social Work, P.O Box 3001, MSC 3SW, Las Cruces, NM 88003-8001

Adelphi University, School of Social Work, South Avenue, Garden City, NY 11530

Columbia University, School of Social Work, 622 W. 113th Street, New York, NY 10025

Fordham University, Graduate School of Social Service, 113 W. 60th Street, Lincoln Center Campus, New York, NY 10023-7479

Hunter College of the City University, of New York, School of Social Work, 129 E. 79th Street, New York, NY 10021

New York University, Shirley M. Ehrenkranz School of Social Work, One Washington Square North, New York, NY 10003

Roberts Wesleyan College, Master of Social work Program, 2301 Westside Drive, Rochester, NY 14624-1997

State University of New York at Stony Brook, School of Social Welfare, Health Science Center, Level 2, Room 093, Stony Brook, NY 11794-8231

State University of New York, University at Albany, School of Social Welfare, 135 Western Avenue, Albany, NY 12222

State University of New York at Buffalo, School of Social Work, 685 Baldy Hall, Box 601050, Buffalo, NY 14260-1050

Syracuse University, School of Social Work, Sims Hall, Syracuse, NY 13244-1230

Yeshiva University, Wurzweiler School of Social Work, Belfer Hall, 2495 Amsterdam Avenue, New York, NY 10033

East Carolina University, School of Social Work and Criminal, Justice Studies, Ragsdale Building, Room 134, Greenville, NC 27858-4353

University of Calgary, 2500 University Drive North West, Calgary, Alberta T2N 1N4, Canada

University of North Carolina at Chapel Hill, School of Social Work, Tate-Turner-Kuralt Building, CB 3550, 301 Pittsboro Street, Chapel Hill, NC 27599-3550

University of Arkansas, School of Social Work, 105 Old Main, Fayetteville, AR 72701

University of North Dakota, Department of Social Work, Gillette Hall–Box 7135, Grand Forks, ND 58202-7135

Case Western Reserve University, Mandel School of Applied Social Sciences, 10900 Euclid Avenue, Cleveland, OH 44106-7164

McGill University, 845 Sherbrooke Street West, Montreal, Quebec H3A 2T5, Canada

Ohio State University, College of Social Work, 300 Stillman Hall, Columbus, OH 43210-1162

University of Akron, School of Social Work, Polsky Building, Room 411, Akron, OH 44325-8001

University of Cincinnati, School of Social Work, P.O. Box 210108, Cincinnati, OH 45220

University of Oklahoma, School of Social Work, 1005 Jenkins Avenue, Norman, OK 73019

Portland State University, Graduate School of Social Work, P.O. Box 751, Portland, OR 97207-0751

Bryn Mawr College, Graduate School of Social Work, 300 Airdale Road, Bryn Mawr, PA 19010-1697

Marywood University, School of Social Work, 2300 Adams Avenue, Scraton, PA 18509-1598

Temple University, School of Social Administration, 1301 Cecil B. Moore Avenue, Philadelphia, PA 19122

University of Pennsylvania, School of Social Work, 3701 Locust Walk, Philadelphia, PA 19104-6214

University of Pittsburgh, School of Social Work, 2117 Cathedral of Learning, Pittsburgh, PA 15260

Widener University, Center for Social Work Education, One University Place, Chester, PA 19013

Universidad Interamricana de Puerto Rico, Recinto Metropolitano, Graduate Social Work Program, P.O. Box 191293, San Juan, PR 00919-1293

University of Puerto Rico, Rio Piedras Campus, Beatriz Lassalle Graduate School of Social Work, P.O. Box 23345, San Juan, PR 00931-3345

Rhode Island College, School of Social Work, Providence, RI 02908

University of South Carolina, College of Social Work, Columbia, SC 29208

University of Tennessee, College of Social Work, 109 Henson Hall, Knoxville, TN 37996-3333

University of Houston, Graduate School of Social Work, 237 Social Work Building, Houston, TX 77204-4013

Governors State University, Bachelor of Social Work Program, University Park, IL 60466

Baylor University, School of Social Work, P.O. Box 97320, Waco, TX 76798-7320

Our Lady of the Lake University, Worden School of Social Work, 411 S. W. 24th Street, San Antonio, TX 78207-4689

Southwest Texas State University, School of Social Work, 601 University Drive, San Marcos, TX 7866-4616

Stephen F. Austin State University, Master of Social Work Program, School of Social Work, P.O. Box 6104–SFA Station, Nacogdoches, TX 75962-6104

West Chester University, Department of Graduate Social Work, Reynolds Hall, West Chester, PA 19383

University of Texas at Arlington, School of Social work, Box 19129, Arlington, TX 76019

University of Texas at Austin, School of Social Work, 1925 San Jacinto Boulevard, Austin, TX 78712

Brigham Young University, School of Social Work, 221 Knight Mangum Building, P. O. Box 24476, Provo, UT 84602-4476

University of Utah, Graduate School of Social work, 395 S. 1500 E.–Room 111, Salt Lake City, UT 84112-0260

University of Vermont, Department of Social Work, 228 Waterman Building, Burlington, VT 05405

Norfolk State University, Ethelyn R. Strong School of Social Work, 700 Park Avenue, Norfold, VA 23504

Radford University, School of Social Work, Box 6958, Radford, VA 24142

Virginia Commonwealth University, School of Social Work, 1001 W. Franklin Street, P.O. Box 842027, Richmond, VA 23284-2027

Eastern Washington University, School of Social Work and Human Services, 203 SNR, Cheney, WA 99004-2441

University of Washington, School of Social Work, 4101 15th Avenue N. E., Seattle, WA 98105-6299

Walla Walla College, Graduate School of Social Work, 204 S. College Avenue, College Place, WA 99324-1198

West Virginia University, School of Applied Social Sciences, Division of Social Work, P.O. Box 6830, Morgantown, WV 26506-6830

University of Wisconsin-Madison, School of Social Work, 1350 University Avenue, Madison, WI 53706-1510

University of Wisconsin-Milwaukee, School of Social Welfare, P.O. Box 786, Milwaukee, WI 53201

University of Wyoming, Division of Social Work, Box 3632, Laramie, WY 82071

Appendix E

Selected National and International Social Work Associations and Related Web pages

Authors Note: Web site addresses often change over time. As a result, you may find that some of the following web sites may have changed; some of the listed organizations did not have a web site at the time this edition was printed, but we want you to at least know the organization exists. Web addresses can be found through a variety of ways. The most common way to find an organization (or, for that matter, information on any subject) is to use a "search engine" such as "Google" (www.google.com) ; type in the name of the organization and you will be directed to a number of possible web sources. A alternative and common vehicle to find organizations is to go to exisiting "links" that are found on many organizations' web pages. For example, go to CSWE's web page (www.cswe.org) and look for the "links & announcements" bar; http://www.nyu.edu/socialwork/wwwrsw/ or http://www.sc.edu/swan/ are two examples of social work specific search engines and sites.

American Association of Spinal Cord Injury Psychologists and Social Workers (AASCIPSW)
http://www.aascipsw.org/

American Board of Examiners in Clinical Social Work (ABE)
http://www.abecsw.org

American Case Management Association (ACMA)
http://www.acmaweb.org/

American Network of Home Health Care Social Workers (ANHHCSW)
http://homehealthsocialwork.org/

Action Network for Social Work Education and Research Coalition (ANSWER)
http://www.socialworkers.org/advocacy/answer/default.asp

American Public Health Association-Social Work Section (APHA-SWS)
http://www.apha.org/sections/sectioninfo/swinfo.html

Association for Community Organization and Social Administration (ACOSA)
http://www.acosa.org/

Association for Gerontology Education in Social Work (AGE-SW)
http://www.agesocialwork.org

Association for the Advancement of Social Work with Groups, Inc. (AASWG)
http://www.aaswg.org/

Association for Women in Social Work (AWSW)
(No Web Address)

Association of Australian Social Work
http://www.aasw.asn.au/

Association of Baccalaureate Social Work Program Directors (BPD)
www.bpdonline.org

Association of Oncology Social Work (AOSW)
http://www.aosw.org/

Association of Social Work Boards (ASWB)
http://www.aswb.org/

Association of State and Territorial Health Officials (ASTHO)
http://www.astho.org

British Association of Social Workers
http://www.basw.co.uk/

Canadian Association of Schools of Social Work
http://www.cassw-acess.ca/

Clinical Social Work Federation (CSWF)
http://www.cswf.org/

Council on Social Work Education (CSWE)
http://www.cswe.org

General Social Care Council-United Kingdom
http://www.gscc.org.uk/

Department of Veterans Affairs (VA)
www.va.gov/socialwork/

German Social Work Web Index
http://www.sozpaed.de/

Group for the Advancement of Doctoral Education (GADE)
http://www.socwk.utah.edu/gade

Influencing State Policy (ISP)
www.statepolicy.org

Information for Practice from NYU
http://www.nyu.edu/socialwork/wwwrsw/ip/

Institute for the Advancement of Social Work Research (IASWR)
http://www.cosw.sc.edu/iaswr/

International Association of Schools of Social Work
http://www.iassw.soton.ac.uk/Generic/default.asp?lang=en

International Federation of Social Workers
http://www.ifsw.org/

International Society for the Prevention of Child Abuse and Neglect
http://www.ispcan.org/

Inter-University Consortium for International Social Development
http://www.iucisd.org/

Latino Social Workers Organization (LSWO)
http://www.lswo.org

National Association of Black Social Workers
http://www.nabsw.org/

National Association of Deans and Directors of Schools of Social Work (NADD)
http://www.cosw.sc.edu/nadd/

National Association of Puerto Ricans/ Hispanic Social Workers (NAPRHSW)
http://www.naprhsw.org

National Association of Social Workers (NASW)
www.socialworkers.org

National Membership Committee on Psychoanalysis in Clinical Social Work, Inc.
http://www.nmcop.org/

National Social Work Qualifications Board of Ireland
http://www.nswqb.ie/

National Hospice and Palliative Care Organization, Social Work Section, National Council of Hospice and Palliative Professionals (NHPCO)
http://www.nhpco.org/

National Kidney Foundation Council of Nephrology Social Workers (NKFC-NSW)
www.kidney.org/professionals/cnsw/index.cfm

National Membership Committee on Psychoanalysis in Clinical Social Work (NMCOP)
http://www.nmcop.org/

National Network for Social Work Managers (NNSWM)
www.socialworkmanager.org

National Organization of Forensic Social Workers (NOFSW)
http://www.nofsw.org

North American Association of Christians in Social Work (NACSW)
http://www.nacsw.org/

Newfoundland and Labrador Association of Social Workers
http://www.nlasw.ca/

Ontario Association of Social Workers
http://oasw.org/

Rural Social Work Caucus (RSWC)
http://www.uncp.edu/sw/rural/

Salvation Army National Headquarters (SA)
http://www.salvationarmyusa.org/www_usn.nsf

School Social Work Association of America (SSWAA)
http://www.sswaa.org/

Social Welfare Action Alliance (SWAA)
(No web address)

Social Work World
http://pages.prodigy.net/lizmitchell/volksware/socialwork.htm

Social Work PRN
http://socialworkprn.com/

Social Work Image Campaign
http://www.socialworkimage.org/

Social Workers HELPING Social Workers (SWHSW)
http://www.socialworkershelping.org

Society for Leadership in Health Care
http://www.sswlhc.org/

Society for Social Work and Research (SSWR)
http://www.sswr.org/

Society for Social Work Leadership in Health Care (SSWLHC)
http://www.sswlhc.org/

Uniformed Services Social Workers (USSW)
(No web address)

U.S. Public Health Service Social Work Professional Advisory Group (UPHS-SWPAG)
(No web address)

Index

Note: Page numbers in **boldface** refer to glossary terms.